Furrows

////

Compiled and edited, with an introduction, by **Helen F. Siu**

FURROWS

Peasants, Intellectuals, and the State

Stories and Histories from Modern China

Stanford University Press, Stanford, California, 1990

Stanford University Press, Stanford, California
© 1990 by the Board of Trustees of the Leland Stanford Junior University
Printed in the United States of America

CIP data appear at the end of the book

I am pain.
I hear the severed grassroots moan.
My heart turns over,
Quivers
With the black ripples.
—Yang Lian, excerpt from "Plowing"

Preface

//// The interaction between literary imagination and political culture in twentieth-century China is not an unfamiliar theme, but the subject of this work may be. This anthology focuses on the changing images of peasants created by writers from the 1930's to the 1980's, writers who consciously used the peasantry to condemn or support the political authorities. It is interesting that urban Chinese intellectuals have concentrated on portraying a social world they seldom grasp. Whether objects of abuse in traditional society or objects of transformation in the decades of socialism, the peasants have been, in the eyes of these writers, as much a political and moral metaphor as living, suffering, and functioning human beings. However unreal these literary images of peasants may be, they reveal the evolution of the writers' fitful, ambivalent, but compelling relationships with the peasantry on the one hand and with state-building efforts on the other hand. In a sense, this anthology uses literature on the peasants to describe the odyssey of modern Chinese intellectuals, an odyssey that illustrates the larger processes of cultural, historical, and political changes to whose creation intellectuals and peasants have contributed with a desperate energy.

The short stories and essays translated here are presented chronologically. Part I contains short stories written in the 1930's, when many authors were moved by intense patriotism. Part II consists of stories written from the early 1950's to the early 1970's. During this period, the authors, who were committed Marxists, were confronted by the growing power of the Communist party bureaucracy. Part III covers the period of blooming and contention in the 1980's, when there seemed to be room for ambivalence and critical reflection. Part IV presents authors' thoughts on their own writing. This part begins with a piece by Lu Xun written in 1932 and ends with three essays from the short period of relative liberalism during the 1980's, before the brutal suppression of the pro-democracy forces in 1989. The selections in this part sum up the compelling journey of modern Chinese writers in their own voices.

I started this project as a Mellon Fellow at the Whitney Humanities Center of Yale University. I thank the members of the center for providing a stimulating intellectual environment. Thanks also to my colleagues in the Anthropology department at Yale, who have treated my literary interests with a sense of humor. Many others have been helpful at various stages of preparing the manuscript: Cheng Wentao, Chou Ying-hsiung, Margaret Decker, Susanne Jorn, Jerry Dennerline, Karl Gao, Gao Xiaosheng, Leo Lee, Qian Nanxiu, Michael Smith, Jonathan Spence, Allan Trachtenberg, Carolyn Wakeman, Ye Weili, and Susanne Wofford. I would like to thank in particular Marston Anderson, Howard Goldblatt, Lee Yee, and William Tay for offering valuable advice on the choice of stories and analytical themes and on the translations and bibliographical details. Jack Goody kindly made meticulous comments on the manuscript's content and language. Al Essa and Elizabeth Kyburg graciously helped me put words on disks and made them come out on paper. Helen Tartar, the Humanities Editor at Stanford University Press, has been most supportive. The thoroughness of John Ziemer as production editor is much appreciated. Finally, many thanks to the authors and translators, whose enthusiasm for the project has made the work all the more worthwhile.

H.F.S.

Contents

Part IV Furrows

Reference Matter

Translators

//// MARSTON ANDERSON received a Ph.D. in Comparative
Literature from the University of California at Berkeley in 1985. He
is an Assistant Professor in the East Asian Languages and Literatures
Department at Yale University. He is the author of *The Limits of Realism:
Chinese Fiction in the Revolutionary Period*.

JOHN BALCOM received an M.A. in Chinese from San
Francisco State University. He is currently working on a Ph.D. in Chinese and Comparative Literature at Washington University, St. Louis.

MARGARET H. DECKER is Assistant Professor of Chi-
nese at the University of Minnesota. She received a doctorate from
Stanford University, and her interest is contemporary Chinese literature. During 1979–82, she taught English at Nankai University in
Tianjin, China.

HOWARD GOLDBLATT teaches Chinese literature at the
University of Colorado at Boulder, where he also edits the journal
Modern Chinese Literature. His latest translations are Zhang Jie's *Heavy
Wings* and Pai Hsien-yung's *Outcasts: The Boys of New York*. He has
edited and contributed to *Worlds Apart: Recent Chinese Writing and Its
Audiences*.

TED HUTERS is Professor of Chinese in the Department
of East Asian Languages and Literatures at the University of California at Irvine. He is the author of *Qian Zhongshu* as well as a number of
articles on modern Chinese literature and literary theory.

RICHARD KING teaches Chinese language and literature
at the University of Victoria, British Columbia. He studied Chinese
at Cambridge and at Fudan University in Shanghai. Since completing
his doctoral dissertation (University of British Columbia) on literature
during the Cultural Revolution, he has concentrated on fiction in the
post-Mao era.

JEFFREY C. KINKLEY is an Associate Professor of History at St. Johns University, New York. Author of *The Odyssey of Shen Congwen* and editor of *After Mao: Chinese Literature and Society, 1978–81*, he has translated many works of modern Chinese fiction and non-fiction, most recently the memoirs of Xian Qian.

WENDY LOCKS received a B.A. in French Literature from the University of California at Los Angeles and an M.A. in Chinese from the University of California at Berkeley. From 1981 to 1983, she studied at the Beijing University. Her M.A. thesis concerned the early works of Jiang Zilong.

NG MAU-SANG teaches Chinese at the University of California at Davis. He is the author of *The Russian Hero in Modern Chinese Fiction*. He is currently researching popular fiction.

REN XIAOPING is Associate Professor of English and American Studies at Beijing Foreign Affairs College. She is a graduate of Beijing International Studies University (Beijing Foreign Languages Institute) and spent several years in British universities. She also hosted an English-instruction program on China's Central Television. She has translated Ah Cheng's *King of Children* (with Bonnie McDougall), among other works.

KATE SEARS studied Chinese in Taiwan in 1975–76 and conducted research in Shanghai and Hong Kong in 1981–82. She received a Ph.D. degree in comparative politics from the University of Michigan in 1985 and a law degree from Harvard University in 1989. She is presently an associate in the Washington D.C., office of Gibson, Dunn & Crutcher.

HELEN F. SIU received an M.A. (East Asian Studies) and a Ph.D. (Anthropology) from Stanford University. She is Associate Professor of Anthropology at Yale University. She is the co-editor and co-translator of *Mao's Harvest: Voices from China's New Generation* and author of *Agents and Victims in South China: Accomplices in Rural Revolution*.

TAM KING-FAI graduated from the Chinese University of Hong Kong with a B.A. in English and an M.Phil. in Comparative Literature. He completed his Ph.D. thesis (Princeton, 1990) on the writer of popular fiction Zhang Henshui. He teaches in the Department of Modern Languages at Trinity College, Connecticut.

ELLEN LAI-SHAN YEUNG received a B.A. (English) and an M.A. (Chinese) from San Francisco State University. She was a part-time lecturer in Chinese language and literature at SFSU (1981–83) and a teaching fellow in the Department of East Asian Languages at Stanford University (1984–88). She is the co-translator of *Field of Life and Death* and *Tales of Hulan River* by Xiao Hong and *The Butcher's Wife* by Li Ang.

"A Searcher in the Capital," 1976. Photograph by Li Xiao Bin. Printed in *Dazhong sheying*, August 1986. Reproduced by permission of Li Xiao Bin.

Furrows

Introduction

////

Social Responsibility and Self-expression

To the world
I will always be a stranger.
I do not know its language,
It does not know my silence.
We exchange
Only a touch of nonchalance.
As if we meet in a mirror.

To myself
I will always be a stranger.
I fear darkness.
But I let the body block
The single light.
My shadow is my lover.
The heart is the enemy.
—Bei Dao, Untitled poem

The literary scene in China during the 1980's was, at least until June 1989, lively, and puzzling. The official concern about "spiritual pollution" and "bourgeois liberalism" revealed the prevailing lack of faith among intellectuals (of which writers are a subset) in Marxism and in the party.[1] Although party leaders have tolerated more divergent political views since the early 1980's, they continue to expect unquestioning commitment to the country. But the reluctance of writers to engage in this dialogue, as expressed in Bei Dao's poem, poses a unique problem for the party. Ideological engineers find it difficult to mold opinion when the subject refuses to think or speak in the required language. Even more interesting has been the rumbling among the writers themselves. "Obscure poetry" (*menglong shi*), a style represented by the poem by Bei Dao quoted as the epigraph to this introduction, is attacked by established poets as unintelligible and an unjustified deviation from the rhetorical conventions of Chinese poetry.[2]

Moreover, its poignant sentiments are said to show a lack of appreciation for the larger cultural forces that permeate poetic sensitivities. The moral message in the artistic squabble is clear to all: the new-style poets are indulging in a subjectivity that cannot transcend personal experiences, and hence their poetry is devoid of social commitment and effectiveness.

Writers of fiction feel similar tensions. Experiments in new techniques and emerging themes that dwell on individual psychology and feelings of estrangement have become intensely controversial.[3] As with the new poetry, complaints about the new style and content of fiction are morally charged. To many modern Chinese writers, the May Fourth Movement of 1919 symbolizes Chinese intellectuals' intense involvement in cultural criticism and political regeneration. That awakening in thought brought with it a strong sense of mission (shi-ming gan), a deep commitment to society. To turn one's back on the world is seen as an affront to an enduring intellectual tradition.

Liu Binyan, a forthright writer-journalist and a severe critic of the Chinese Communist Party, believes that writers should assume responsibility for society's troubles. Social responsibility sustains a writer's identity and inspires artistic creativity. Liu asserts that because contemporary politics has stamped its presence on social life, the urgent task facing writers today is to expose political contradictions as a means of working toward their solution. Divorcing politics from literature is unrealistic because it alienates writers further from the true nature of their subject matter.[4] Moreover, many Chinese intellectuals have suffered because of their convictions, and indulgence in individualism today is seen as a moral betrayal. It demeans what they have fought for; it demeans what they have preserved in the face of terrible political persecutions.[5] Many who look back on their part in the tortured path of the Chinese revolution wonder if, in their eagerness to destroy tradition by political means, they may have inadvertently damaged a deeper cultural ethos. They also ask whether the subsequent cultural estrangement and the political alienation of a younger generation of writers are precipitating further errors.[6]

A revealing series of articles in 1988 in the overseas edition of the People's Daily mixed patronizing attitudes with bruised feelings.[7] One essay was written by Liu Xinwu, a writer in his forties noted for his concern for the younger generation.[8] Another is a dialogue between Li Zehou, a liberal-minded philosopher, and Liu Zaifu, a daring literary critic. The tone is mild; the authors insist that they understand and respect what the young writers have gone through. But the message is clear: the young writers are unwilling to face the test of their times and are shirking their responsibilities. Liu Xinwu's comments are typical.

In the past things were too closed off, too calcified. Once a window is open and lively exploration possible, one is shocked and saddened; it is because the world outside seems to have become unreachable; even if one surges forward at full speed, it is impossible to narrow the distance. Anxiety, restlessness, and impatience prevail. This mood naturally makes one eager to find an easy way out.

What is surprising in view of these critics' attitude is that they are young by Chinese standards. Moreover, they are hardly party hacks. They have opposed the party line on literature, they are not identified with the party's cultural czars, and in the recent decade of reforms they broadened their horizons by foreign travel. In February 1989, Li Zehou joined 32 other top Chinese intellectuals in signing a letter to the central authorities urging amnesty for those who were imprisoned for their involvement in the democracy movement of the late 1970's (subsequently another 42 scientists and 43 young and middle-aged intellectuals put their names on similar petitions).[9] Ironically, given their criticism of younger writers, the letter signers' focus on the well-known dissident Wei Jingsheng was triggered by the sympathies of the poet Bei Dao. If these critics' disagreements with the younger writers are not entirely ideological, what is at issue?

The critics seem unable to accept an art that has become cynical and detached, and they are reasserting a sense of involvement that they expect the younger writers to be proud of.[10] The dispute arises from differing views of the cultural identity of modern Chinese intellectuals and the political activism proper to them. It forces the protagonists to rethink how they relate their art to society and the state in an era of revolutionary change, and to consider where they should direct their critical energies under a party-state that firmly and often mercilessly asserts its power. In fact, the new-style writers range widely in their degree of detachment from political reality. Bei Dao's part in the amnesty campaign brought him closer to the position of the politically committed writers than may be apparent in his art. His preference is detachment, but at times he finds this difficult. After the government tried to discredit the amnesty campaign he initiated, he wrote, "I am a poet. Politics does not interest me very much. I am tired of being a celebrity. I originally intended to retire to my desk and to the world of my imagination after the publication of the petition. But if China, vast as it is, cannot accommodate a desk, I certainly cannot choose to be silent."[11]

The ambivalence of the new-style writers toward their culturally expected roles is complex. Most of them came of age during the Cultural Revolution in the late 1960's and are painfully aware of their own political baptism. They witnessed the upheavals of the late 1960's and spent years of soul-searching in the countryside as educated youths who were "sent down." [12] Xie Mian, editor of the poetry journal *Shikan*, puts their anguish in context: in the past five decades, the literary scene experienced little flourishing of thought and emotions; the young writers matured under this stifling reality. [13] It has become clear to them that political criticism is not a right and that commitment to society has been twisted to serve dehumanizing political ends. [14] They see how a sense of mission has compelled generations of intellectuals to mold themselves to ideologies that "devour" them just as the traditional morality about which the early twentieth-century novelist Lu Xun wrote devoured the Chinese people. [15] That it is a crime to work with the mind instead of with the hands was made explicit in the Maoist era. During that time, intellectuals were assigned to labor in the fields. In confronting the state, they were as helpless as the peasants for whom they had intended to speak. The young writers may appreciate that some of their elders faced their plight with the quiet sense of dignity revealed in Yang Jiang's *Six Chapters of My Life "Downunder" (Ganxiao liuji)*. Yet the complicity involved in victimization has made them cynical about the culture and society in which they find themselves. The poet Gu Cheng, for example, treats the Jialing river, traditionally portrayed as a source of sustenance, as malevolent: [16]

> The landslide has stopped.
> High up on the bank rear giant heads.
> Boats in mourning sail by,
> unfolding drab yellow shrouds.

His anguish is clear:

> My shadow
> is twisted.
> I am trapped in a landmass.
> My voice is covered with
> glacial scars.
> Only the line of my gaze
> is free to stretch.

Some young writers have embarked on superficial and self-serving experiments in order to gain quick recognition in a rapidly commercializing world. [17] Others have plunged into "pure art" to defy a political ideology distasteful to them. But many are ambivalent about a socially involved art because they personally understand the tragedy of their parents' generation. This feeling was expressed, solemnly but compassionately, by the writer Ah Cheng when his father, a film critic condemned as a "rightist" for twenty years, received notification on a night in 1979 of his rehabilitation. From the standpoint of a friend, Ah Cheng spoke the words of a son.

If I were overjoyed tonight, my past thirty years would be reduced to nothing. As a person, you have already affirmed yourself. There is no need for others to judge you. If the power of such judgment is in the hands of others, they may well support you today and deny you tomorrow. Therefore, in my view, your rehabilitation has no real significance outside of mere technical convenience. Moreover, the political vicissitudes that have afflicted you are not without blessings. They have forced me to rely on my own efforts to acquire confidence in life, although for you these twenty years must have been brutal. [18]

Seventy years ago, Lu Xun portrayed the human condition of his time as mired in tradition: "an iron house having not a single window, and virtually indestructible, with all its inmates sound asleep and about to die of suffocation." Although he wondered whether it was fair to wake up the few light sleepers, only for them "to suffer the agony of irrevocable death," he did pick up his pen and face up to his predicament. [19] As the contributors to the book *Lu Xun and His Legacy* convincingly argue, the fearless originality of his art is based on his uncompromising conviction that he must not only unveil the irrational powers that enforce social life but also ruthlessly scrutinize his own compulsions. The sardonic wit that permeates his prose reveals an introspective spirit as full of anguish over external enemies as over his own inner ghosts, an anguish rooted in a culture and history of which he felt himself an integral part. In this way, "he gave artistic form to the experience of being a modern Chinese intellectual." [20]

On the issue of the "agony of wisdom," Ah Cheng and his father were probably in agreement. [21] The difference is that whereas some older writers continue to feel committed to working toward a better world, some younger writers wonder if they have not constructed a new iron house through their very attempts at emancipation. They question the revolutionary movement and dispute its sense of mission. Is the latter part of an "eternal" cultural repertoire, or does it bear the unique imprint of the political contingencies of the twentieth century? Are the defenders of this sense of mission so preoccupied with fighting the external powers of the world that they are unaware of their own inner compulsions and the political consequences of their acts? Some among the younger generation drawn into the eventful journey have come to appreciate it as a point of awakening and departure. In consciously disengaging themselves from what is politically expected of intellectuals, are they examining their cultural baggage more intro-spectively? If they refuse to be captive spirits now, how will they break new ground? According to Ah Cheng, the way lies through critical cultural reflection. To him, it is tempting to forget one's past, but in fact the past is hard to dismiss.

If we acknowledge that the prerequisite for freedom of creativity is the free-dom to explore our own consciousness, just imagine how little freedom we would have if we were not aware of the forces of our culture or world cul-ture. . . . The older generation of writers has often assumed a negative stance when they represent the national tradition. The younger writers have started to assume a positive stance . . . in order to illustrate the new direction of a Chinese literature built on a critical [approach to] cultural inheritance and development. [22]

Political Authority and Cultural Critique

Disengagement as a means of cultural reflection, the proposal of the new-style writers, is disorienting both for party officials and for their fellow artists. The controversy speaks to the delicate yet entrenched position of intellectuals in the system of authority in twentieth-century China.[23] Traditionally, to be Chinese has meant a commitment to and an identification with the evolution of Chinese culture, society, and polity, a historical process heavily informed by the interpenetration of moral and political authority and anchored in the power of the written word.

To understand why scholars have felt compelled to attach them-selves to moral and political authority, and to appreciate the profound effect of their writing on society, some knowledge of the historical sources of literacy in China and the vitality it has generated is neces-sary. "The Chinese" have diverse racial, linguistic, and cultural origins; their identity as Chinese has rested on the written language, which dates to around 2000 to 1500 B.C.[24] The state culture was recorded first by shamans and scribes in the early dynasties and then by court historians and literati during the institutionalization of the imperial bureaucracy in subsequent dynasties. The ethical and intellectual prin-ciples of the written tradition were created by generations of scholars, who shared as well as contested its substance. Through the written record, the debates among the ancient sages left an enduring imprint on the culture.[25]

Until this century, to be Chinese meant sharing a cosmos and participating in a way of life that bound an individual to kin, community, and state. Everyone had a place in an ordered universe. The confirmation of this way of life was intricately tied to manipulations of the symbols of power. The virtual monopoly of scholarly writing by a group of administrative specialists constituted the core of this symbolic complex, which had become firmly diffused in everyday life by the eleventh and twelfth centuries.[26] What was at stake when control of the written tradition was contested in the political arena was not only the fate of the ruler but also the object of the government's ever-expanding "civilizing" process—the land, the people, the historical memories, the very moral and cultural dialogue.[27]

The process of a written state culture percolating downward was not limited to official writings. In each dynasty a distinctive repertoire of popular artistic cultures interacted with the official culture. For example, during the last two dynasties,

Chinese stories and novels no doubt belonged to a minor tradition rather than to the central elite culture of historiography, philosophical prose, and lyric verse. But the divergence can easily be exaggerated. The long early cycles that seem to have grown like coral reefs by processes of accretion ended by enshrining the moral values and philosophical bases of an entire civilization. . . . Read by the children of the semi-educated, orally presented by storytellers or transferred to the dramatic stage, the great masterpieces of fiction confirmed cultural identity just as surely as the dazzling beauty of the cathedral told the European peasant he was a Christian.[28]

The written tradition as civilizer of the polity readily became part of popular consciousness, and scholars saw themselves as agents indispensable to this process.

Precisely because political authority was so directly involved in the construction of society and its ethics, China lacked the trappings of a modern nation-state until the twentieth century. The term *tianxia* (all under heaven) was replaced by *guojia* (nation-state) only in the modern era. The realization that the vast empire was held together more by a shared cultural heritage and less by military might or legalistic-political administration led the philosopher Bertrand Russell and the sociologist Robert Park, both visitors to China in the Republican period, to comment that "the Chinese polity is a cultural phenomenon."[29]

China, however, has never lacked for despots who obtain compliance by force. To deny their power is unrealistic, but the issue here is the nature and the bases of that power and the means by which they exercise it. The ancient philosophies, revised through the centuries, have become a state culture that consumes rulers and ruled alike. At the core of this culture is a set of rites and mutual obligations within the cardinal social relationships (ruler-ruled, parent-child, husband-wife, older sibling–younger sibling, friend-friend). Human fulfillment comes with the realization of these relationships through moral self-cultivation and social practice. Cultural vitality emerges from this inner force and extends outward to order family, society, and universe. Heaven bestows the mandate to rule on a political leader who has proved himself worthy by behaving morally (in Confucian terminology, *neisheng waiwang*). In imperial times, benevolent government was expected, and the failings of the ruler were chastised by the literati, who represented this system of values. More seriously, the ruler's shortcomings justified peasant rebellions, whose leaders claimed that the ruler had violated Heaven's mandate. Although the opposite was more often true—military rulers claimed their dominant position was an indication of their mandate to rule, and they forced court philosophers and historians to affirm their de facto status in the value system —the significant fact is that they felt obliged to do so.

Whereas peasants rebelled against imperial excesses in order to force a restoration of the moral and political order, their leaders, often displaced gentry and militarists, claimed to act according to the Way of Heaven (*titian xingdao*). The literati, on the other hand, could choose between two different but related courses of action. They could actively intervene on behalf of society (*weimin qingming*) by castigating the ruler (*jian*). Or they could retreat from the political whirlpool, live the life of a hermit (*yin*), and refuse to serve an illegitimate power until order was reinstated. Both acts appealed to a moral paradigm to which the literati remained committed. Such acts may have been infrequent, but they were imprinted on the historical consciousness that was a major part of the symbolic repertoire in the literati culture and the popular mind.[30]

Given the cultural expectations, the position of the literati was never very easy. They occupied the highest places in the societal complex and were privileged in terms of education and access to political office and wealth. They used their writings to propagate a system of morality (*wen yi zai dao*) that legitimized the political order as well as their place in it. "Those who excel in scholarship serve the state" (*xue er you ze shi*) was a motto for scholars, and this attitude bound some of the best minds to the imperial court. But another principle made them answerable to society. Criticism of political excesses was a moral privilege and a social responsibility. If few scholar-officials exercised this principle of action against imperial power, their acts nevertheless gained significance in the historical consciousness as exemplary behavior. They were thus a necessary thorn in the side of the powerholders, whose legitimacy depended on the system of values they represented. Despite drastic transformations in substance and meaning through the centuries, this precarious marriage between scholarship and power continues to be taken for granted.[31]

In the early twentieth century, the educated elites were heavily influenced by Western thought, especially by the ideals of progress, scientific rationalism, and democracy in a modern nation-state led by a dynamic, autonomous, urban-based cultural elite. Both Chinese and Western scholars have regarded the Chinese enlightenment, as the May Fourth Movement has been termed,[32] as the epitome of a passionate attempt to criticize the primordial sentiments of an agrarian state. The success of these efforts is subject to debate, but the urban intellectuals did sever kin and communal loyalties to the countryside, the same loyalties that had once supported imperial and bureaucratic power. In so doing, they redefined their position in the system of government. Instead of using tradition to serve political ends, they claimed the authority to create a new political and moral order.

Modern intellectuals were sincere in examining their own roles and assumptions. In the preface to *The Gate of Heavenly Peace*, Jonathan Spence eloquently sums up their painful involvement in society.

The Chinese whose thoughts, words, and actions constitute the heart of this book were all intellectuals in some form or other, yet though they could not speak at first hand for workers or peasants, they were far from being mere spectators. At their more strident or ineffective moments, certainly, one can see them as being in some senses parallel to the members of the chorus in a Greek play, watching in horror and fascination the tragic working out on center stage of a conflict between mortals and gods, the end of which has been long foretold. Yet though the cultured voices of these Chinese may seem at times too piercing, and their gestures too ritualized, they still possess the essential power—denied to the traditional chorus—of leaving their apparently allotted space and marching to the center of the stage. It is often true that those who do this die earlier than the others—"before their time," to use a simple phrase—but one cannot deny that they often show a startling wisdom, the wisdom of those who have seen the hidden directions of this particular play, who have understood that this is not the kind of drama in which those who stay on the periphery will be left in peace.[33]

Paradoxically, the fateful drama of revolution, cultural pride, and human dignity, which the protagonists in the historical narrative unveiled in their lives, illuminates the stubborn vitality of a structure of values that continued to bind writers to a polity and its changing bases of authority. Certain forward-looking attempts to build a modern nation-state were heavily informed by what remained of the literati tradition. Tu Wei-Ming maintains that although anti-traditional in content, the intellectual culture followed tradition in being episte-mologically authoritarian (*quanwei xing*). Leo Lee stresses that "mod-ernism" in China differs considerably from the anti-establishment ori-entations of European modernism. During the May Fourth period, the belief prevailed that an urban, "bourgeois," intellectual elite would lead China in building a new establishment, a strong nation-state.[34] Moreover, not unlike their predecessors, intellectuals struggled to rep-resent an autonomous ethical system with the intent of chastising powerholders for their failings. They expected to be the leading agents in the creation of a new political culture.

The partnership between cultural iconoclasm and an emotional commitment to building a nation-state was tense.[35] The first aimed at critical self-reflection; the second threatened that spirit. How did the patriotic momentum unintentionally prevent a deeper examination of the authoritarian assumptions of the state as well as the participants' own motives and roles? Such "external" factors as political constraints obviously tied people's hands, but "internal" factors, embedded in cul-tural expectations, permeated the heart and rigidified the mind.

In their eagerness to deliver the country from an unprecedented crisis, modern Chinese intellectuals immersed themselves in state-building, which, initially at least, seemed to offer solutions. This pre-vented them from attaining a crucial level of cultural reflection—not on the material or institutional changes themselves, but on the epistemological values that informed them. This lack of self-scrutiny distorted evaluations of the Chinese cultural tradition in the face of pressures to modernize and led to a moral and an analytical impasse.[36] The protagonists mechanically opposed either tradition or modern-ization and did not question their own positions and commitments. Consequently, they could not fully appreciate the changing nature of their role. They were wedged uncomfortably between the moral and the political authorities, whose positions were themselves increasingly undermined by war and revolution. This powerful but unfinished pro-cess of reflection shaped their predicament, especially their relations to the Communist movement (and after 1949 to the Marxist-Leninist state) and to the laboring population, the vast majority of whom were peasants.[37]

The tension between morality and power intensified during the twentieth century. The efforts at a thoroughgoing critique of tradition were an acute reaction to a pervasive political crisis. When the Qing empire faltered under the aggressive expansion of the Western powers and Japan, economic and political paralysis led to a crisis of confidence in the moral foundations of the culture. The May Fourth Movement and the decades of intellectual activity that followed attest to the depth of the problem and the intense commitment to find solutions. Throughout this process, the relationship between moral authority and political power has been redefined through the participation of intellectuals with a heightened sense of mission.

The dilemmas the intellectuals faced were obvious. Confronted by the challenge from the West and by the impoverishment of the peasantry, many concluded—after nearly a century of soul-searching—that China needed the apparatus of a modern nation-state. In the mid-nineteenth century, some high-ranking Qing administrators advocated the adoption of Western technology for the practical purpose of defending the empire against foreign aggression.[38] When the empire suffered humiliating defeats in the 1890's, the constitutional monarchists suggested reforms in political institutions to solve the country's problems. Both movements were attempts to preserve the imperial order by a limited adoption of Western technology and institutions. But the failure of the movement known as the Hundred Days Reform (1898) and the persecution of its advocates by conservative forces at court finally led some literati to join the movement to overthrow the monarchy. In 1912 a republic was set up, but the ambitions of regional warlords shattered liberal hopes for a democratic and unified polity. Instead of providing a means to improve national livelihood, the military adventurers, backed by competing foreign interests, became the major source of disorder. For those who participated in the antigovernment demonstrations in Beijing on May 4, 1919, all of Chinese civilization, material and spiritual, was at stake. Whether nationalism rallied energies to fight for survival or to console a badly bruised cultural pride, it became almost an obsession. But the nature of the proposed new polity, *guojia*, which attracted the educated elite's commitment and nurtured their hopes, had only begun to be explored. A dazzling array of ideologies for nation-building was adopted by the warlord regimes, by the Nationalists, and by the Communists, but the ill-defined relationship between moral authority and political power made the position of the educated elite increasingly precarious.

On the one hand, the semiliterate militarists who arose after the fall of the Qing dynasty were too preoccupied with struggling for spoils to seriously seek legitimacy from traditional morality. New bases of authority were invented, but their blatant violations revealed the superficiality of the effort.[39] After 1927 the delicate facade of national unity under the Nationalists generated some enthusiasm among the liberal-minded, but survivors of the "White terror" conducted by Chiang Kai-shek against leftists were fearful of his moves. The ineffectiveness of the Nationalists in blocking the advances of the Japanese in the 1930's disappointed many patriots. Their lingering hopes were dashed when they witnessed the Nationalist government's acts of terror against dissidents in the cities and its army's mistreatment of peasants in the villages.

The peasantry has often been a symbol of the life force of Chinese culture and polity. Their well-being justifies the powerholder's Mandate of Heaven; their abuse discredits it. In the early twentieth century, writers were divorced from peasant life, but enraged and horrified, they produced a literature obsessed with images of brute force exercised on an innocent peasantry—war, rape, indiscriminate killing —the way of the beast in which morality and authority were no longer respected. Images of peasants being ruthlessly abused, however unrealistic, were used as symbols to condemn the various regimes.

Mao Dun, whose work "Mud" ("Nining") begins this volume, and a few others such as Ye Shengtao, Xu Dishan, Ba Jin, and Ding Ling whose works were published by the Shanghai literary journal *Xiaoshuo yuebao* (Short story monthly; 1921–31) remained true to the realism popularized in the 1920's. Their humanist concern and their eagerness to absorb Western thought gave their works a cosmopolitan outlook. Wu Zuxiang, whose short story "A Certain Day" ("Mouri") is included here and who is recognized as one of the best left-wing writers on rural themes of the 1930's, skillfully combined humanism with the techniques of realism. But this urbane focus became less evident among writers later drawn to revolutionary romanticism.[40]

Many fell early in their journey. The Five Martyrs, as Lu Xun sadly remembered the young writers killed for their Marxist sympathies, were probably noted more for their political convictions than for their literary abilities. Yet behind the martyrdoms were often moments of painful self-scrutiny, as revealed in Qu Qiubai's "Superfluous Words" ("Duoyu de hua"), written in jail shortly before he was executed in 1935. At the age of 36, he was an established Marxist literary critic and theoretician, and for a brief period in 1927–28, he had been general secretary of the Chinese Communist Party. In 1934, when the majority of party leaders headed for Yan'an in northwestern China, he remained behind and was captured by Nationalist troops. Knowing his end was near (he was also dying of tuberculosis), he dissected the layers of romantic optimism that he had wrapped around himself for the preceding fifteen years and concluded that his political life had been untruthful, that he was nothing but a "petty bourgeois," superfluous to the very movement he had helped to build. The essay was a

controversial one. His comrades largely denied its authenticity, claim-
ing that the Nationalists had fabricated it to show the futility of urban
intellectuals' serving the Communist cause. Pragmatists concluded that
it was Qu's effort to make a confession in order to save his neck. His
motive for writing it, if he did write it, was probably a complex one.
To insist on one or another reason would deny the anguish shared by
many modern Chinese intellectuals. [41]

The disenchanted who joined the Communists in Yan'an also under-
took a long ideological scrutiny, a process that was exhilarating at
times, painful at others, but in the end compelling. Those who had
entertained the idea that the Communists represented the vanguard
of an urban proletariat must have been disappointed. The Chinese
Communists had made major adjustments in Marxism as early as the
1920's. Li Dazhao, a founder of the Communist party and a professor
at Beijing University, argued for a revolution in China that involved
the peasantry. In Li's conceptual scheme, China was "a proletarian
nation" exploited by foreign imperialism. His revolutionary strategy
called for a broad united front of workers, national bourgeoisie, and
peasants, whom he believed to have an innate spirit of nationalism. [42]
Although Li was captured by the Beijing warlord government and shot
in 1926, his ideas on the Chinese peasantry were adopted by Mao Zedong. After the Communists were driven to rural areas by the armies
of Chiang Kai-shek, Mao, who assumed leadership of the party in the
mid-1930's, directed its energies toward the peasantry. [43] Hampered
by both the Nationalists and the Japanese, the Communist movement
turned increasingly rural and patriotic. Communist documents and
leftist literature identified the Japanese as a direct foreign aggressor
and disparaged the Nationalists under Chiang Kai-shek as ineffectual
in defending China against foreign aggression. The emerging political language referred to collaborators (*hanjian*), together with military
officers, petty government functionaries, the landlords, and the com-
prador bourgeoisie, as enemies of the revolution.

National salvation colored literary language in the mid-1930's. Increasingly fiction was couched in sinicized terms. [44] In the cultural
arena, writers debated the application of Marxist philosophy to literary criticism, discussed the development of a more rustic style and a
literature for national defense, and raised the questions of the nature
of the new Chinese polity, the identity of its allies and enemies, and the
conduct proper to participants in the movement. One decisive debate
among the leftist writers centered on the direction of literature during the War of Resistance against the Japanese. Those who joined Lu
Xun argued for an uncompromising critique of Chinese tradition and

politics. Those who had chosen the political pragmatism of the Communists and were grouped around the literary theorist Zhou Yang promoted a literature for national defense (*guofang wenxue*). They rejected Western rationalism and literary techniques in favor of Chinese roots, with the intention of tapping energies across a broad united front.[45]

The writers who congregated in Yan'an had different motives and assumptions, but they were basically concerned with national salvation, a goal to which the Communists seemed committed at the time. The historian of modern Chinese literature C. T. Hsia points particularly to "its obsession with China," its patriotic passion, which arose from "a burden of moral contemplation." Coupled with this was a vague sense of class justice.[46] The two dovetailed with the traditional belief that educated elites should show a social commitment by rejuvenating the political and moral order—a belief shared by the leaders and the led. To some extent, the Communists subscribed to the belief that the vast scope of state power rested on a shared moral consensus, but the party was to be the leading agent and vanguard in defining and fighting for that morality.

Influenced by Stalin, Communist leaders in the 1930's had additional items on their political agenda, and they demanded a commitment to that agenda from all those within their grasp, peasants and intellectuals alike. Ideological unity in the revolutionary struggle meant embracing the Leninist and Stalinist strategies of party-building. Mao in particular warned fellow revolutionaries against the "feudal" beliefs of the Chinese peasantry and the "petty-bourgeois" tendencies of the Westernized intellectuals, both of which rested on value systems different from that of the party. Although Mao believed in the ultimate revolutionary potential of the peasantry, he had less sympathy for the articulate, urbane, and independent-minded intellectuals. To generate revolutionary changes, Mao required of his comrades a worldview that served the party's political ends, not one that stood independent of them. Criticism was possible only after the language of discourse had been thus defined.

In a speech at the 1942 Yan'an Forum on Arts and Literature, Mao held writers responsible for ideological engineering, thus making the political straitjacket explicit.[47] The speech inaugurated a three-year party rectification movement during which Mao's ideological authority was imposed. It also put an end to a year of grumbling and confusion among the artists themselves. Four years into the war, the patriotism the urban intellectuals had brought with them had been worn down by the harshness of life in the caves of Shaanxi that housed the party in exile. More important, the political realities of a growing party bureaucracy gnawed into their revolutionary romanticism. They accepted their circumstances only after a struggle. Luo Feng, for example, insisted that the satirical tradition of Lu Xun be continued. In an article entitled "Thoughts on March 8" ("Sanbajie yougan"), Ding Ling poignantly revealed the difficulties of women in Yan'an, where the traditional hierarchy and male authority continued to be taken for granted. Xiao Jun lamented that the pragmatism of cadre work killed moral vigor. However, Mao demanded that realism recognize the progress made under Communist leadership and that sympathy be offered only to class allies and satire be directed only against class enemies. Ding Ling and a host of others who voiced their discontent were persuaded to change their petty-bourgeois views after a severe public attack from Mao.[48]

A more serious confrontation occurred between the party hardliners (such as Chen Boda, Mao's secretary) and Wang Shiwei, a radical urban intellectual. Born in 1907 to a literati family whose fortunes had declined, Wang enrolled in the English department of Beijing University in 1925 and joined the party in 1926. He was a gifted translator. His interest in Marxist theory led him to translate major works of Lenin and Trotsky. He left his family in Hunan and made his way to Yan'an in late 1937. But in April 1943, a year after his essay "Wild Lilies" ("Ye baihehua"), attacking the corruption and privileges of party cadres in Yan'an, appeared in *Jiefang ribao* (March 13 and 23, 1942), he was jailed. In his defense against those who accused him of promoting absolute egalitarianism, he justified his complaints by warning against a mechanical view of historical progress that ignored the errors of the revolutionary vanguard itself.[49] The tense public debates over his behavior and the harsh disciplinary action taken later came to be known as the Wang Shiwei Incident. His sympathies for Trotsky were branded as counterrevolutionary. A chilling account of his last years in Yan'an and of his execution in 1947 highlights the tensions between the emerging Stalinists in the party and their military commanders on the one hand, and the independent-minded urban intellectuals on the other hand.[50]

Spring 1947, Shaanxi.

The wind swept over the rolling hills, blowing dust through every gap in the tightly sewn clothes. The Qingming Festival had passed, yet there was not a touch of green.

Xing Xian: a small and dilapidated town. It was the capital of the Jinsui Base Area; but the only signs were the little flags hanging from the windows of a few cave-like houses.

There was fighting at the western bank of the river hundreds of *li* away. The dusk here was tranquil.

Caijia Cave, the headquarters of the public security office of the Jinsui Base Area Administration.

A young man with a heavy sword in his hand, who appeared to be a cadre, went into a cave. He dragged out another, middle-aged man of similar appearance and took him to a remote hillside.

The heavy sword was raised . . .

Bright red blood spilled over the hardened yellow earth.

The executed: Wang Shiwei. Crime: Trotskyist, Nationalist agent, member of a counterrevolutionary group. There was no verdict, no appeal, no denial. The only basis for the execution was a report approved by some authorities.[51]

This account of Wang's execution forms an ironic contrast to that of Qu Qiubai. Despite Qu's doubts about his own role in the revolution, his execution, brutal as it was, was debated among the highest echelons of the Nationalist leadership. His martyrdom was witnessed and given a degree of respect. The order for Wang's execution came secretly from someone higher up in the party who felt challenged by Wang's revolutionary enthusiasm.[52] In retrospect, however bleak his end, it was but a rehearsal for worse to come.

The confrontations between the leftist writers and the party in the 1930's and 1940's illustrate an important fact—that the intellectuals in Yan'an put up a struggle for autonomy of thought, and that party leaders were not yet established enough to monopolize opinion. It is also clear that the Chinese writers acted from the apex of a cultural nexus of authority, only to condemn the very social and political codes that gave them the position to voice such opinions. The leftists who joined the Communists found themselves compelled to promote the cause of a political power that increasingly negated their right to speak their mind. In the years to come, the mission and conscience of the scholar changed. Instead of challenging a power that had deviated from truthful and moral behavior, it became a struggle against a power that claimed to dictate truth. A gnawing question remains: Why did these intellectuals stay with the Communists? Conditions in the war-torn cities were no less harsh than those in Shaanxi. Furthermore, at the time the party could not have prevented those who were disenchanted from leaving. What was behind their conclusion that there was no turning back?

By the time the Communists firmly established their power in the 1950's, the ideological impositions on writers had come down with full force. The issues involved in the struggle were complex. Although dissident voices had become muted since the days of Yan'an, party ideologues were concerned with curbing the "bourgeois liberalism" of leftist intellectuals who remained unconvinced. More important, party leaders confronted mounting challenges from a younger generation of committed Marxists, many of them party members, who questioned the political orthodoxy of the leaders. The tradition of the intellectual's mission and conscience continued to be invoked, but it was reconstituted on a new political stage where the power relationships between the protagonists and their ideological assumptions had changed considerably. The battles were fought within a Marxist-Leninist paradigm that was increasingly taken for granted. The legitimacy of the party was not questioned, although the definition of party orthodoxy was fiercely debated.

Such tensions were revealed in the mid-1950's persecution of a leading Marxist literary critic, Hu Feng, who had staunchly opposed party dogma since the 1930's.[53] Hu Feng continued his stubborn independence in the early 1950's by contradicting Maoist orthodoxy. In a long article entitled "The Five Blades" ("Wuba daozi"), he charged that party dogma had strangled artistic sensitivities. His views were subsequently branded "petty-bourgeois liberalism" and, more seriously, "counterrevolutionary," a crime that led to his long imprisonment. Many of his friends were made to criticize him, including Lu Xun's widow, Xu Guangping, who wrote that Hu had "betrayed" them. The novelist Ba Jin later recalled the rudeness of the party cadres who asked him to denounce Hu Feng.[54]

The liberal Hundred Flowers Campaign of 1956–57 and the subsequent Anti-rightist Campaign revealed the uncomfortable marriage between the sincere belief of these intellectuals in an independent authority based on enlightened critical thought and their faith in a revolution based on patriotism and Marxism. The end result seemed like total capitulation. In 1957 those who had been bold enough to speak out against the party bore the brunt of persecution. The new political classification given their "crime" is important. Huang Qiuyun, Gao Xiaosheng, and Fang Zhi, among many others whose works are included in this volume, were labeled "rightists" of various degrees. They became enemies of the party to be banished to labor camps for "re-education."

Ru Zhijuan, whose 1958 short story "Lilies on a Comforter" ("Baihehua") brought a breath of freshness to the literary world, looked back in 1980 and admitted that if it hadn't been for a moment of "numbness" toward the political currents at the time, when she gained some space and distance, she would not have produced the story. One wonders whether the young Marxist writers were too committed and too naïve to reckon the political price of their acts. In fact, that was very much in the mind of Ba Jin when the 26-year-old Fang Zhi came to him with his plans to form the "Explorers" (Tanqiuzhe).

> I met Comrade Fang Zhi once at the beginning of the Anti-rightist Campaign. I can no longer recall his face. I only remember that he and Comrade Lu Wenfu came to discuss their plans for organizing the Explorers. . . . They said that they had already discussed the matter with a comrade and were encouraged. I understood them. We had given much thought to similar attempts in the 1930's. The two young men were trying to pursue some creative ends. They had ideals and convictions. I sympathized with them, but I was also concerned. Feeling the changing climate, I thought they were too naïve. I tried to persuade them not to organize the Explorers or the *Tongren zazhi* [Colleagues' journal], and to give up their plans for "exploration." I cannot now remember whether they had already issued the manifesto of the Explorers or whether they did it afterward. But I am certain on one point: they had not understood my concern; nor had I made myself clear. They certainly did not follow what I wished.[55]

If there was room for reflection and debate in the 1950's and for critical reassessment in the early 1960's, the nationwide witch-hunt of the Cultural Revolution spared no one. In an atmosphere of feverish ideological confrontations, silence and retreat were no longer viable options. Old "rightists" were dragged out and humbled and humiliated alongside party patrons accused of having followed the wrong political line. To stay in the middle of the road required a precarious balancing act. In the eyes of the competing political factions, it was a life and death struggle. The intense factionalism forcibly polarized the already fragmented intellectual circles. During moments of ideological extremes, even the writer Hao Ran, who followed the Maoist line closely and who rose high in the decade of radical politics, was criticized for not having expressed enough faith in the party. The definition of artistic positions and orientation had become the monopoly of party officials.

In retrospect, in the 1980's survivors insist that they had no choice but to drone on.[56] Their reasons are unclear. One can understand that peasants, who had no livelihood outside the collectives controlled by local party cadres, had to comply with the dictates of the party. One might even argue that by the mid-1960's, the Chinese Communist Party's successful monopoly of the representation of moral and political authority left intellectuals little ground for independent judgment. The only viable course of action left, if they were to survive, was to transform themselves under the party's ideological dictates and to continue to believe in the possibility of reducing its excesses. But was it entirely a matter of survival? Why did many writers who prided themselves on belonging to an intellectual tradition of protesting illegitimate power, and who had courageously faced the deadly consequences of doing so decades before, feel a lack of choice in the post-revolutionary era?

This is the central issue disputed among writers today. To what extent was the lack of choice self-imposed? Many leftist writers of the 1930's retreated to the background after the Communist revolution, but did Marxist writers from the 1950's to the 1970's reconstitute the legacy of modern Chinese intellectuals and make it into their own "iron house"? Ba Jin, in his memoirs, boldly admitted that at the beginning of the Cultural Revolution, he remained faithful to the need for ideological transformation as dictated by the party.[57] Moreover, what was the basis of the commitment of Liu Binyan, who remained loyal to the party despite being condemned for 22 years and expelled in 1987? When he portrays the attempt of the protagonist in "A Second Kind of Loyalty" ("Dierzhong zhongcheng") to right a wrong committed by a party cadre years ago, is he speaking about himself?

Today many writers claim the humanist ideal and a renewed sense of mission as their sources of strength against an engulfing political power, but the issues behind their spirit of resistance assume new meanings because of the much-transformed nature of the polity. For some, "social responsibility" is a disguised effort on the part of writers to achieve self-expression at a time when the brutal denial of the intellectuals' right to define and represent moral authority is still vividly remembered. For those who remain faithful to Marxist-Leninist ideals and to the party's basic assumptions, it is time for a revival of protest against political excesses. The call in early 1989 for amnesty of political prisoners is one example of courage and faith.[58] But the question remains Why, despite their unhappy experiences, do intellectuals remain committed to the national state? What is behind their agitation at the new-style writers' decision to abandon the accepted vocabulary in order to begin a new dialogue?

The literary works of the 1980's display a quiet empathy with the peasants. Together with the Yellow River, the peasantry has always symbolized the life force of Chinese culture and society, with which the literate elites have historically claimed affiliation. Today, there is an added dimension of compassion, perhaps because the years of exile in the countryside have given writers a more realistic understanding of the peasants. Also, both have been subjected to the abusive power of a state determined to transform them. Out of these experiences arose a bridge between the social and cultural distance separating writer and peasant, as expressed in the postscript to Li Zhun's two-volume *The Yellow River Rushes On* (*Huang he dongliu qu*). Critical realism again flourished, as illustrated by the writings of Gao Xiaosheng, Gu Hua, and Li Rui presented in this volume.

But this is not enough for the new generation of writers. Today, many of them have decided that as long as the party-state dictates moral authority, they will disengage themselves from ideological dialogue altogether. They turn to the private sentiments of peasants, which parallel their own, as painfully described by Ah Cheng's story "Chimney Smoke" ("Chui yan") in this anthology.[59] The peasant's burden arises from the insensitive, entrenched structure of the state; the writers' baggage, however, comes partly from the system of values on which their social mission is based. What they would like to explore is the motive force underlying their sentiments as well as those of the peasants. They believe that it is buried deep in the national culture, uncontaminated by ideology. Chen Cun, a literary critic, sees a parallel between the concerns of these writers and those of Gabriel García Márquez: they focus on a life force that extends beyond the struggle between good and evil, illusion and reality, joy and anger, but creates a world filled with these sentiments.[60] In view of their effort to free themselves from contemporary politics in order to excavate the culture that has shaped their lives and thoughts, can one justifiably dismiss these writers as indulgent individuals with no sense of social responsibility?

In April 1989, tens of thousands of students in Beijing marched to Tiananmen Square to criticize the government. In response to an official condemnation, they returned to the streets to insist on the patriotism of their behavior. Moreover, the citizens of Beijing turned out en masse to support the students' claim. The atmosphere was peculiarly familiar. There was a heightened sense of mission and self-sacrifice, euphoria over the power of idealism and goodwill, all in the name of cleaning up a morally bankrupt government and getting the country back to an honorable course. The students were naïve, but their intentions were considered noble and their sentiments were shared: this was what a Chinese of good conscience would do. For its part, the regime insisted that the democracy movement was nothing but a counterrevolutionary disturbance instigated by subversive foreign elements. It could not be equated with the patriotism of the May Fourth Movement of seventy years before. In its eyes, the students were un-Chinese.

Once again, "Chineseness" was being renegotiated. Implicated in the process were the moral choices, the social discipline, the economic initiative, and political compulsions of an educated sector increasingly drawn into a diverse and volatile modern world. Even those young enough to have escaped the vicissitudes of the Cultural Revolution realized that they too were not being spared. In the wake of the brutal repression of the student movement, can there be lingering hopes of merely removing the excesses of the party-state? Writers on both sides of the literary dispute were relatively silent as the events unfolded.[61] What do those who deeply mourn the thousands gunned down by the very government the victims believed in think now of the authoritarianism their own commitment unintentionally created only a few decades earlier?

To be human is neither to be entirely programmed by cultural principles nor yet to be simply driven by economic necessities. It is precisely the human involvement in the creation of a compelling political process that heightens the sense of tragedy. Scholarly works on modern Chinese intellectuals have often emphasized the involuntary nature of their involvement in contemporary political currents, but this view ignores their active role in the making of a political culture centered on a heightened sense of social responsibility. Deprived of an institutional base by the abolition of the imperial examinations in 1905 and especially by the fall of the Qing in 1911, the educated elites made their transition to the twentieth century by adhering to an intensified sense of mission. Whether this was a desperate attempt to retain their right to self-expression under the new moral order or a shrewd move to assert a self-assumed importance as new institutions were making them superfluous,[62] the traditional assumptions of responsibility to the state and to society were recycled to fit new political realities. This assertion of responsibility allowed a displaced educated elite to redefine a social identity and to acquire a unifying symbol of community and a political platform, both of which are ultimate forms of self-expression.[63] Social and political criticism based on a commitment to an entire civilization remains, even today, a cultural given in the eyes of the general public and a special calling for many intellectuals.* But it also dovetails with the interests of the powerholders. The Chinese Communist Party, for example, has seldom challenged the sense of mission that engages the intellectuals in a dialogue with the polity. The party is concerned, however, with controlling the power to define the terms of the dialogue. The question is Once the Communist party succeeded in doing so by disregarding the human costs, did the intellectuals and their cultural roles become even more superfluous?

---

*Many workers and other citizens supported the demonstrations, not only because they had their own frustrations to air but also because many believed that these students, the future leaders of society, were patriotically trying to bring about a better state and nation. Might this be a sign that traditional attitudes of looking to the educated elite for moral leadership are still alive?

Ten years into the post-Mao reforms, "cultural tradition" is a term no longer tabooed; it is now in vogue. A revived interest in neo-Confucianism has led to international conferences, and writers have traveled far into the rural fringes in the hope of understanding those cultural roots, untouched by revolutionary politics, that continue to inform contemporary consciousness. Others have begun to explore how China's particular national culture nurtured Maoist extremes. After the long interlude since Lu Xun scrutinized tradition in his "Diary of a Madman" in 1918, tradition is being examined instead of being categorically dismissed.[64] The question of complicity in the reproduction of cultural hegemony, a concern that fueled the self-scrutiny of Lu Xun, underlies discussions of the sense of mission today. The debate forces protagonists to examine their assumptions about the privileging power of the written word, the philosophical bases of their commitment to a state with humanist concerns for its subjects, and consequently their ambiguous relationships with those in power. When young writers dwell on artistic issues, for example, and claim that creativity can blossom only when both authors and the subject of their art are not tied together by political and moral obligations, are they redefining the self-image of the educated elite in modern China, an image embedded on the one hand in a structure of values originating deep in Chinese culture and on the other hand in a "recycling" of that tradition to cope with the political realities of the twentieth century?[65] The controversy over the nature of artistic expression and writers' pursuits seems to have initiated a long-overdue cultural criticism.[66]

In fact, the need for a critical self-reflection has also been made explicit by China's seniormost writer, Ba Jin, after a lifelong devotion to the revolution. In a postscript to five volumes of collected essays published in the 1980's, he writes:

With so much to say, I do not know where to begin. There are 150 essays about the joy, anger, and sorrow of ordinary characters. I call them "whimpers." In fact they are mostly bloody pus that oozes out of unhealed wounds. I squeeze them out not to kill time, but to lighten my own pain. When I began with *Random Thoughts* [*Suixiang lu*], my pen was not weighty. In the process of writing, I continued to explore and to know myself. In order to know myself, I cannot but dissect myself. With the aim of lightening pain, I thought the dissecting would be an easy task. But when I used the pen as a surgical knife to cut into my heart, I appeared clumsy. I could not press it in because I felt violent pain. I always reminded myself that I should demand a lot of myself. Yet I weakened when I needed to use a knife to gouge at my heart. I dared not dig deeply. Every page of the five volumes is stained with bloody pus. But there is more of it in a ten-year wound. I know that if I do not clean it out, it will poison the body. I also know: the wounds of many people, like mine, are oozing out bloody pus. We have shared experiences and a similar fate. I do not worry. Whatever I do not accomplish, others will. If I have not dug deep enough, there will be another who overtakes me and, without fearing pain, mercilessly gouges out his own heart. . . . To clean up the garbage, and to purify the air, it is not enough to demand only of myself. We are all responsible. We must find out the source of the problem, in myself, in others. . . . Gouge then.[67]

This anthology does not pretend to answer the questions it poses. It serves more to illustrate issues for contemplation than to explain. By tracing the intellectuals' deliberate rupture with tradition at one level and their reconstitution of it at another, I hope to reveal the tension underlying their artistic work and to capture the vitality of a conviction that lies behind the tragic and puzzling predicament of the modern Chinese intellectual.

Furrows

Both intellectuals and peasants have played vital roles in the political arena of twentieth-century China. The short stories that follow focus on peasant life and were written by leading literary figures from the 1930's to the 1980's. In my introduction to each part, I try to point to the structure of values that guided intellectual thought and actions and to demonstrate the cultural mechanisms that tied writer to subject in a political order rapidly being transformed by their often unintended efforts.

A major issue in the literature on peasants is that a literate elite is writing about an inarticulate peasantry whose world is far from their own but whose lives are interlocked with theirs in multiple ways. In the wake of the May Fourth period, writers indicted the old cultural tradition and the political order by describing what it had meant for the peasants to be victimized. But in treating the unawakened populace as objects of social engineering and themselves as the providers of that engineering, the intellectuals failed to bridge the distance between themselves and the peasants. By reifying tradition as an object of attack, they prevented themselves from reflecting on the roots of their claims to authority. I have selected works by those who chose to write about peasants as a way of exposing the frailty of power, peasants as objects of abuse. Most of these images of peasants should not be treated as "real." Rather, they disclose the authors' naïveté about village life and popular culture and their distance from rural reality. But they do reveal the authors' sense of outrage toward an entire social order. The works illumine how the underlying political assumptions of these writers guided their efforts to participate in a new political culture, a significant historical narrative in its own right.

Critical realism, a literary form popularized during the 1920's, depicted the soul-searching of the writers and their peasant subjects. Mao Dun, Wu Zuxiang, and Xiao Hong, whose works are included in this anthology, are among the best-known realist writers. I have juxtaposed these works with those by authors who, having joined the Communist party, devoted most of their efforts to writing about peasants.[68] Driven by the force of dogma effectively imposed by a political movement that later became a highly organized party-state, the act of writing came to assume very different meanings; so too did perceptions of political failings and the nature of abuse. The writers continued to fill their culturally prescribed roles, but Marxism-Leninism allowed them less room for maneuver. They were assigned the task of promoting the peasants' cause both as masters of the revolution and as objects of socialist engineering, a theme clearly shown in the works of Zhao Shuli, Kang Zhuo, and Zhou Libo. But both the legacy of their elitist assumptions and the primordial loyalties of the peasants were politically suspect.

The struggle against dogma, which became the overriding concern of many writers in the 1950's, revealed their uncomfortable position between the party's growing monopoly of ideological power and their perceptions of the bitter fruits tasted by the vast majority of peasants and produced by a revolution conducted in their name. Such tension is apparent in this collection in the stories by Kang Zhuo and Fang Zhi and in the essay by Huang Qiuyun. Some spoke out and paid the price, expecting that, as in the past, their banishment would affirm the importance of their voice. Others stopped writing altogether; for example, Mao Dun was given high positions in the administration of the arts but never joined the party. But the rigid language of class promoted by the Maoists meant that the intellectuals were faulted not only for what they wrote but also for what they were. Just as the peasants have complied with the Communist party, and at times conspired with it, the writers strained to follow the party's dictates and often confessed to more sins than they had committed.[69] The political straitjacket has prevented writers from getting close to their subject matter. The positive, forward-looking heroes of socialist realism reveal the forceful suppression of sensitivity to the peasants' plight. Eventually many writers came to appreciate what it means to be a victim. Yet many have hung onto a losing dialogue with a political machine in which they have placed so much faith. This is the unrequited love that Bai Hua poignantly alluded to in his play of that title.[70]

The fact that scholars of modern Chinese literature have paid over-whelming attention to the leftist literary movement speaks to the cap-tivating energies of its participants, which have dominated the artistic consciousness of this century. C. T. Hsia and Tsi-an Hsia have por-trayed these writers as unwittingly prostituting themselves to a politi-cal movement that ultimately engulfed them.[71] Leo Lee, on the other hand, argues that apart from using their pens to promote revolution-ary change, truly self-critical intellectuals like Lu Xun continued to search for a sense of values in a world where values were in flux. From the large corpus of leftist literature from the 1920's on, it is not dif-ficult to find works that examine the cultural repertoire and idealize the future. In a period of depression and contemplation in the 1920's, Lu Xun termed his retreat into the poetry of the Wei-Jin period (A.D. 220–316) as the "sound of silence on a written page."[72] On looking back, survivors of the Cultural Revolution agonize over the fact that they were not allowed to remain silent. Yet in the 1980's, the young poet Bei Dao cherishes his silence after his faith was shattered through his own political fervor. The changing meanings behind silence and protest, retreat and involvement, is what this anthology intends to explore. The process reveals how generations of writers, with their cultural assumptions and political commitments, have come to terms with a process of political transformation to which they subscribe with a desperate sincerity.

The works selected in this anthology are not entirely representa-tive. I am well aware that human responses to even the most engulfing of circumstances are infinitely diverse. It is nevertheless possible to see how the efforts presented here disclose the ethos that shapes the predicaments of both authors and subjects. The stories in each part share some underlying characteristics, but my ordering of them aims to capture their contribution to the central plot of each era, as cul-ture, art, and politics intertwine to form a meaningful narrative about cumulative human efforts as well as selective memories.

The notion of "furrows" contains several dimensions. It represents what several generations of Chinese writers have perceived as the lines that successive regimes have plowed on the backs of the peasants. Based on their sense of social responsibility, writers have voiced their opinions and created contours on the literary fields. These furrows crisscrossed numerous times over the decades. Together, they have provided the spiritual essence of a political landscape that has formed the consciousness of successive generations.

In the way modern Chinese writers have come to terms with the politics of nation-building and the dictates of a Marxist-Leninist party-state, they have something in common with writers elsewhere.[73] However, differences in cultural assumptions and politics create different tensions. In China, revolutionary goals contribute to literary vigor precisely because the intellectuals can draw inspiration from literati tradition dating back over two millennia as well as from a forward-looking desire for a modern state.[74] The heightened sense of social mission among the post–May Fourth intellectuals, however subversive in intent, continues to reinforce their complicity in an authoritarian state culture. Those who joined the Communist movement, however, found their voices smothered by the very language of the revolution they promoted. The peculiar turns of the movement have set urban intellectuals against the rural orientations of the party, though the two are linked by nationalism.

The political environment compels modern writers to fashion their works on terms dictated by party leaders, but they do this with increasing ambivalence. Ironically, compliance with the party-state has led to a profound loss of faith that in the end is subversive both of the new order and of the intellectuals' sense of mission. The process is an agonizing one. Because ambivalence challenges not only political commitment but also cultural identity and historical consciousness, debates about it are intense. The intensity reveals a collective human spirit captivated by its own sense of value. How this tension has informed artistic sensitivities in modern China is the focus of this anthology.

Part I The Frailty of Power

Introduction

////   This part begins with the short story "Mud" ("Nining"), written in 1929 by Mao Dun (pen name of Shen Yanbing). Born in Zhejiang in 1896, Mao Dun grew up under pro-reform parents. Influenced by Western literature, he was a founding member of the literary club Wenxue Yanjiuhui in 1921 and a regular contributor to *Xiaoshuo yuebao* (Short-story monthly). He was a prolific writer in the realist tradition, and his subject matter ranged from the mentality of the petty bourgeoisie to the plight of the peasants. He joined the Communist party but left it in 1927. He became a member of the League of Left-wing Writers in the 1930's and joined Lu Xun in opposing the "literature for national defense" promoted by party pragmatists such as Zhou Yang. During the war, he stayed in Guilin, Chongqing, and Hong Kong. After the revolution, he was appointed minister of culture and chairman of the Chinese Writers Association. Until his death in 1981, he wrote essays and made speeches but stopped writing artistic works.[1]

Although the critical, self-reflective spirit of Lu Xun was increasingly overshadowed by patriotic and political fervor in the 1930's, some writers still retained a broader humanism in their works. Among them was Wu Zuxiang, who emerged as a short-story writer in the mid-1930's. He was born to a landlord family in Anhui in 1908 and studied Chinese at Qinghua University in Beijing. He wrote skillfully about groups he was most familiar with—local gentry and peasants. "Eighteen hundred *dan* of rice" ("Yi qian ba bai dan"), a story in the well-known volume *Western Willow Collection* (*Xiliu ji*), is a meticulous and biting portrayal of the power and corruption of the gentry. "A Certain Day" ("Mouri"), published in 1936, singles out local bullies who live on the peasants as a "parasitic class." During this period,

Wu combined his critique of traditional rural society with realism and avoided romantic revolutionary themes.[2] In 1942, he wrote *Flash Flood* (*Shanhong*), which was praised as an outstanding patriotic novel. After the revolution, he devoted most of his time to classical studies. He is now a professor of Chinese literature at Beijing University.[3]

Born to a landlord family in Heilongjiang in 1911, Xiao Hong (pen name of Zhang Naiying) was educated at Harbin. At the age of 20, she fled from an arranged marriage and joined a group of young writers. Among them was Xiao Jun, with whom she lived. They went to Shanghai and became friends with Lu Xun. With his support, she published the famous novel *The Field of Life and Death* (*Sheng si chang*) in 1935. Her powerful portrayal of life in the Japanese-occupied northeast was among the earliest to appear. From then until her death in 1942 in Hong Kong, she was constantly fleeing the war. Poor, sick, and frequently abandoned by her male companions, she dwelt on the irreconcilable tragedy of the female in a male-dominated society. When she died at the age of 32, she left an impressive list of works, among which was the story "On the Oxcart" ("Niuche shang"), published in 1936.[4]

Sha Ting (pen name of Yang Chaoxi) grew up in a landlord family whose fortunes rose and fell with the instabilities of the Republican period. As a youth, he was put under the care of his mother's brother, a leading member of a quasi-military brotherhood in Sichuan. Sha later went to school in Chengdu and was caught up in the intellectual fervor of the May Fourth era. When militarists persecuted the progressives there, he fled to Shanghai. Early in his writing career, he and his schoolmate Ai Wu wrote to Lu Xun and Mao Dun. At one point Sha was secretary to the executive committee of the League of Left-wing Writers.[5] In 1936 he joined the Communists and worked in the base areas until the Liberation. He held the posts of chair of the Sichuan Artists League and of the Sichuan Writers Association and was a delegate to the National People's Congress. Purged during the Cultural Revolution, he was rehabilitated in the late 1970's. His early short stories focus on the interlocking fates of characters that resemble the types of people he knew as a youth—local bosses, members of secret brotherhoods, the semiliterate, and the poor of market towns and villages. His portrayal of deteriorating social conditions under the Nationalists is particularly vivid. "The Way of the Beast" ("Shou dao"), which I use here, was written in 1936.

The son of a village teacher in Sichuan, Ai Wu (pen name of Tang Daogeng) left home in his youth to wander in Kunming, Burma, and Singapore. He worked as a helper in the Red Cross, as a cook for an old monk in Rangoon, as a village teacher, and as a newspaper editor. He was arrested by the British in Burma for participating in movements of progressive workers and sent back to China via Hong Kong. He joined the League of Left-wing Writers in 1932 and fled to Guilin and Chongqing during the war. He became a prominent figure in artistic circles in Sichuan after the revolution but was jailed from 1968 to 1972. He was rehabilitated in the late 1970's.[6] He has written extensively on rural conditions under the Nationalists. "Autumn Harvest" ("Qiu shou"), for example, is a fine portrayal of the delicate relationships between peasant women and Nationalist soldiers caught in the larger web of war and revolution. Most of his works were published between 1938 and 1949. "Rumblings in Xu Family Village" ("Paoxiao de Xujiatun") was written in 1931.[7]

These authors have different backgrounds and political convictions, but certain themes run through their works. There is a sense of outrage over abusive acts against the innocent and the powerless. Wanton killing, rape, and plunder by soldiers and local bosses are vivid symbols of brute force. In spite of the misery, however, the authors see both resistance and hope. The peasant rebel in "Mud" is a pawn in the political games of military adventurers. When he is left dying of his wounds, he finally realizes the hidden agendas of those in power. For Xiao Hong, soldiers are at the same time abusers and victims. By pointing to the quiet sympathy that emerges between the young widow of an executed deserter and a former soldier whose family has probably perished in his absence, Xiao Hong rests her hope in the human bond itself. In Wu Zuxiang's story, the opium addiction of a local scoundrel foils his greedy attempt to extort money from his son-in-law. With the support of neighbors and friends, all poor and honest peasants, the young man chases off the old bully. The way of the beast heightens the sense of outrage in Sha Ting's young protagonist, who helplessly watches his family's helper, a compassionate old peasant woman, driven mad by the rape and suicide of her daughter-in-law and by the blame others unfairly put on her. Although in Ai Wu's story marauding soldiers once again force their way into the lives of innocent people, the victims take up arms and seek revenge. The message in these works is explicit: domination by brute force, however overwhelming, is in the end challenged.

If illegitimate power brings its own demise, what is morally acceptable to the authors is left implicit. The basis of authority is not explored. Are they challenging the excesses, or are they critically examining the sources of the excesses? If the latter, is a political solution enough? Moreover, what are the traditional cultural values that continue to inform the writers' vision of a just order? Rape is a central theme in several of the stories in this part. It is intriguing that all the victims of rape have to die. What would be threatened by the continued existence of their "contaminated" bodies? Could it be the patriarchal assumptions that permeate family and kin relationships and on which political legitimacy is based? By describing violation at one level (that is, the female body), has the underlying symbolism ironically preserved traditional male authority at another? In failing to question assumed values in their works, have these writers fallen short of the goals of the self-reflective cultural critique that makes the art of Lu Xun so inspiring?

Except for Xiao Hong, who died in destitution in Hong Kong during the war, the others joined the Communist revolution. Although their post-1949 careers mirrored the vicissitudes of party politics, their works in the 1930's revealed relatively independent outlooks energized by their own political convictions and humanitarian concerns. At the time, their sense of mission was not unlike that of the traditional literati: to rejuvenate a moral order, whose representatives they were, by chastizing powerholders for their failings. If a new order were to be built, they claimed a part in its construction.

Mao Dun # Mud

//// The machine guns howled like wolves all night long. Just before first light three cars mounted with iron armor plating arrived in front of whatever headquarters it was that was located in the village's earth-god temple. Several uniformed men tumbled out and scuttled into the temple. Soon a dozen-odd men swarmed out again, hoisted two heavy wooden crates into the cars and squeezed themselves in after; the cars creaked away. After that a group of gray-uniformed soldiers passed through the village like a receding tide. The pop-pop of intermittent gunfire, flame. By about 7:00 A.M. everything had become still: there were two or three bodies lying on the main road, and white smoke still rose from the thatched roof of the small general store, to one side of which lay a naked female corpse, her face the color of pig's liver and one of her small, bound feet cut off.

After a half-hour more, another group of gray-uniformed soldiers poured into the village on its three access roads. They appeared more dirty and tired than the soldiers that had just withdrawn, and a good deal smaller. They swept through the village like a wind, leaving only a small troop to hold the exit road. Some men on horseback found the temple, tore off the paper strips pasted at the door, and replaced them with new white strips written with red characters. Four riflemen then stood at the temple doorway.*

Then something new happened. Some unarmed ones in gray uniforms began to hand out leaflets; they pasted up slogans, and went from house to house knocking on doors to get the villagers to come out. A pale youth with round eyes, also wearing a gray uniform, stood

---

This story was written in 1929 and first published in *Xiaoshuo yuebao* in 1929. Translation by Ted Huters.

    *In rural China before the revolution, village temples were centers of social, cultural, and political activities.

in the middle of the road and barked through a metal bullhorn. Eventually, several pinched, sallow faces still wearing queues* poked out through the wooden windows of the thatched huts and stared with wide eyes. They saw that although the men knocking on the doors were wearing "tiger skins,"† they acted gentle enough and did not carry guns. So the people with the sallow faces began to come out and cautiously circled around the youth with the bullhorn, as if expecting a performance.

The bullhorn blurted out sounds which were like fantasy language; the people with the sallow faces did not understand. But one thing was clear: there was no need to fear. Colored printed papers were stuffed into their hands. They held them. The bullhorn soon went silent, and the men in the gray uniforms dispersed; the people of the village with their sallow faces returned to their thatched huts puzzling.

Old Man Huang and his two sons squatted by the side of their mud stove whispering. Half to himself, Old Man Huang said "What is this Republic stuff? The emperor was better! Sixteen years of the Republic and there has been fighting every year.‡ This year, too, of course! In the spring it was Marshal Wu's troops, then it was the Fengtian army, and now . . . ."§ He had a curse he wanted to spit out, but he held it in and cast his eyes all about the room. The two pieces of printed paper that he had taken had already been pasted on the mud wall. Old Man Huang glanced at the characters on the paper; forty years before he had in fact sat for a preliminary examination. He had later taught all the characters that he saw. He knew them all, but he could not figure out their meanings here.‖ Lao San imitated his father and looked at the flyers; he recognized the character for "farmer" and the one for "union," as well as the one for "united," since that same character had appeared in the name of the United Prosperity general store, which had been burned down that morning. Lao Qi had lived as a cowherd

*The Qing dynasty (1644–1911) required all Han Chinese males to wear their hair in queues as a sign of submission. In the context of this story, wearing a queue signifies the period after the fall of the Qing when political changes were just reaching the villages.

† Military uniforms.

‡ The story describes the turbulent time in 1927 when competing warlords and local military commanders were carving out territories. Since the Qing dynasty fell in 1911, there had hardly been a central government.

§ Before the completion (in 1927) of the Northern Expedition led by the Nationalists, North China was dominated by different warlords contending for power. Marshall Wu is Wu Peifu, who controlled Beijing and much of North China in the 1920's.

‖ The man must have been educated in village schools and had taken the lowest level of the civil service examinations used by the Qing to recruit aspiring scholars into the imperial bureaucracy. In 1905, the examinations were abolished, and new-style schools were established.

and farmhand all his life,* but all he cared to look at was the girl pictured on the flyer, with her slim waist and short sleeves, raising both arms in the air.

"Goddam! This means sharing wives for sure." Old Man Huang forgot himself and blurted out the curse. He had also seen the bare-armed girl, laughing in the midst of four or five men, and holding onto the arms of one to each side. Lao San blanched, cherishing the fact that his own wife had died the previous spring.

"Dad! Speak more softly so they won't hear!"

"Huh, communizing isn't so bad; after all, we don't have any women in our household."

Old Man Huang shot Lao Qi a severe stare and thought of what Confucius would have said. Father and sons could converse no more and instead immersed themselves in hard contemplation. Ping, Ping! The three immediately went into a panic. Should they hide in the dirt cellar? Old Man Huang was just thinking about this when someone began to knock on the door. Lao Qi went over. After quickly peering out, he pulled back the bolt. A man in gray uniform entered, accompanied by Pockmarked Li from their own village. There was the trace of a smile on the pale face of the uniformed man.

"This is Old Man Huang, he's the only one who can read and write."

"All right, come along with us then."

Old Man Huang's trembling lips could not utter a word. Pockmarked Li added an explanation: this commissioner wants the villagers to set up an organization to deal with village affairs; this requires someone who can read and write. He patted a big parcel of paper under his arm, saying that someone is to read the villagers these written "notices."

"Oh no, I am far too old. The eyes are blurred. I really cannot manage."

Old Man Huang fearfully declined and thought to himself that something was not right, that this could be a trap. But it was no use. He was finally borne away. Lao San squatted by the door, stupefied, but Lao Qi wanted to see the action and so followed along.

The Peasants' Association was established.† Old Man Huang worked every day with his heart in his mouth. His job was to write out

---

*It is common for sons to be addressed according to sibling order. Lao San is the third son. Lao Qi is the seventh.

† The Communists organized many peasant associations in the 1920's, and Mao Zedong himself wrote a piece in 1926 on the strength of the peasant movement in Hunan. Students from the cities were recruited to help with the movement and mobilized peasants to force landlords to reduce rents and to punish local bosses.

the "name roll." Working with him was a young man of seventeen or eighteen, who also wore a gray uniform. Old Man Huang treated him as his superior, and all the new tricks came from this "superior." The young fellows in the village rushed about looking for "local bullies"; they dragged out people who cowered in their houses and pressed them to join the association. Lao Qi found the whole thing amusing, but he was a trifle unhappy that they had not "shared out the wives." Nobody was ever serious about sharing wives—dammit, he thought.

The sound of machine-gun and cannon fire was now even farther away, and the small troop that had guarded the road into the village had long since moved forward; only the four soldiers were left in front of the temple and maybe a dozen-odd inside. There appeared to be fewer of the unarmed men in gray uniforms. Everything was to be more peaceful, except that the village reverberated with calls to "join the association!" Old and young women once again dared to venture outdoors.

One day another unarmed group of people in uniform arrived in the village. There were five or six of them. This was sure to be the "child soldiers," as their voices had yet to break. But as soon as the "child soldiers" arrived, they barged straight into the humble village houses, attempting to strike up conversations with the womenfolk. Cries of horror shook the whole village. Only later was it learned that the "child soldiers" were in fact "woman soldiers." The womenfolk in the village also had to organize an association, and the "woman soldiers" had been specifically charged with bringing this about.

As soon as Old Man Huang returned home, he complained to Lao San and Lao Qi.

"It's all because of that bastard Pockmarked Li's fanciful idea; and the same with the two of you, making your old man plod along. This is just terrific! Now the women are to have an association too. If that's not sharing wives, I don't know what is; sooner or later they're going to be shared, and whoever did something he shouldn't is going to be struck by lightning. So I find myself in the muck up to my waist! Even if the gods forgive me, who in the village will?"

Lao San opened his mouth unable to say half a word. Lao Qi, on the other hand, cocked his head and stared at the bare-armed girl on the wall. What he was wondering was How were they going to share? That night he had many dreams.

The atmosphere in the village became tense. The young fellows rushed about on some new business. Lao Qi spent the whole day tailing the "woman soldiers," greedily anticipating new tricks to happen.

Seven or eight ruffians crowded into Pockmarked Li's house and cursed through clenched teeth: Bastard! All right! You say no sharing? You are going to brownnose your way into something good? Where is your woman? We'll take her first! Pockmarked Li indeed had a wife, who was not pockmarked. She hid in the pigsty trembling.

By afternoon, Old Man Huang's "superior" knew about this and immediately summoned the entire village to a meeting. For half an hour, he stretched forth his neck and vociferously exhorted everyone not to be so suspicious. One of the "woman soldiers" also came out to give a speech. The villagers said nothing, but remained unconvinced. They went home and shut their doors tightly. The womenfolk hid themselves away yet again.

A dozen or so village toughs gathered in the woods beyond the village. The ground was heated red hot by the sun, and the yellow dust piles gathered by the wind crouched round like mangy dogs. One of the fellows with a long, narrow face was called "No Predicting."* He sat on the root of a big tree, rolled his eyes and growled: "It all sounds nice, but it's really a swindle! I haven't yet seen a chunk of mud, much less land. Those sons-of-bitches! It's the same old stuff with just a few new tricks—Meetings! Fuck! Summoning me to idle under the red-hot sun and sweat! Ha! This is our so-called benefits!"

"Inhuman sons-of-bitches! They are merrymaking in the temple. Lao Qi saw it with his own eyes, right? Then they cheat us by denying it. Who believes them?" A younger one spoke, blinking his eyes.

"They should let us have some fun! We want to have some fun too." Another one spoke.

"They say they're not sharing out wives! Hey! The five or six new ones, what are they there for? So they only share among themselves? Let us gents share theirs! Only sons of bitches would not come along. Fuck!"

"As if you have to tell us! That one with the long legs, whose ass wiggles when she walks, she makes me drool."

Everyone burst out laughing, swallowing a thick mouthful.

"Let's do it! Penting up the heat all our lives, we've had enough. This is a chance hard to come by. Whoever hesitates is a lousy son-of-a-bitch!"

No Predicting jumped up to make the declaration. A sudden burst of wind obliterated the last part of what he was saying. The yellow dirt blew up from the ground and rolled itself into a curtain of dust, enveloping them all.

---

*In the popular culture, Wuchang (No Predicting) is one of the runners of the lord of the underworld who takes life away. He supposedly has a long face. The Chinese term used here, *huo Wuchang*, means a living Wuchang.

It was probably Lao Qi who let the cat out of the bag. The "woman soldiers" disappeared from the village streets. Old Man Huang did not see his "superior" for several days, and the atmosphere relaxed somewhat. But No Predicting and his gang suddenly became active. First Pockmarked Li was beaten up. For that there were a few guesses: some said it was because he "was not careful" in what he said; others said it was a misfortune invited by his non-pockmarked wife. In addition, several *dan* of wheat hidden underground by the Zhang family were stolen. Who did it? The old man of the Zhang family would not dare to say. When Old Man Huang went outdoors, all gave him a wide berth and greeted him with their face half–turned away.

Suddenly one day the people discovered that the four soldiers in front of the temple were gone, a matter of great importance. A good many rumors followed, and a good many actions followed the rumors. There were several vicious fights within a day. It was unclear who was fighting with whom and for what reason. No Predicting was wounded and disappeared. The other side also sustained a few injuries. At night a fire erupted. Some people ran outdoors to gaze in the direction of the fire. They smiled in satisfaction and retreated into the houses. The temple of the earth god was burning.

The next morning a troop of soldiers arrived at the northern entrance to the village. They sent someone into the village, saying that they needed to have a word with the village head. There was no village head. When the gray-uniformed men who distributed flyers arrived the previous time, the village head and guarantor* had both fled. So they went to Old Man Huang, but he was lying sick on his broken old bed. Finally, Old Man Zhang was made to go. The villagers waited with trepidation.

The troops later marched into the village and set up their tents in the open air. They also wore gray uniforms, but they were taller and spoke with a northern accent. They were also carrying flyers and printed papers, but they did not distribute them.

Old Man Huang, who was said to be lying sick on his broken old bed, was dragged up. Lao San was also found. They were both escorted into one of the tents for interrogation. Old Man Huang was trembling all over, sensing that the situation was bad. But as soon as he got to the tent he saw the large flag stuck into the mud, and he felt somewhat relieved. He recognized the flag and understood that the characters written on its edge were the same as those of the troops of his "superior." Only the number was different.

*Informal local officials who mediated between village and government and who were active in community affairs.

"What have you done?" Two mustachioed men who looked to be officers asked him.

Old Man Huang told them everything as truthfully as he could.

"Is this your son? Don't you have a younger one?"

"Lao Qi hasn't returned home since last night."

The two officers smiled and nodded their heads. They gave a glance to the pistoleers who were standing off to one side, whereupon two soldiers led Old Man Huang and Lao San out and shot them right outside the tent. In the afternoon, the men in the tents came out to make their requisitions from the villagers. Pockmarked Li had a pig; the Zhang family still had some grain buried underground; some other family had something else; it was all requisitioned. The villagers thought that this was the sort of thing they had always been used to and there were to be no more new and incomprehensible terrors in store. They all breathed sighs of relief—everything had returned to normal.

Lao Qi squatted in the woods outside the village, his clothes stained with blood. His head was heavy. His body felt as if it were floating. His mouth tasted dry and bitter. From time to time an image flickered in front of his eyes—it was the beautiful girl on the flyer with her bare arms extended. In his delirium, his lips quivered, as if to say:

"It was a swindle all along! Fuck!"

Wu Zuxiang　　　　　　　　　　　　　　A Certain Day

////　　It was the beginning of the ninth lunar month, and the noon sun shining on one's back no longer felt hot. The dark blue sky was roofed overhead with thin white clouds layered like fish scales. A few unidentifiable birds circled through the clouds, flying higher and higher until they looked like so many tiny black spots. When a wind blew up from the distance, the grasses on the paths and the near-withered lentil vines bristled and swayed in a line, frightening the crickets and other singing insects into silence. A few fearless ones, however, kept crying sporadically, their voices weak and trembling.

The rice had long ago been harvested. On a few mounds dirty yellow stalks still soaked in the shallow mud, but most of the fields had been plowed, the earth turned over loosely in preparation for the planting of turnips and cabbage. As one approached the village, the paths between the paddies were neatly lined with mulberry and tallow trees. The tallows, many times more numerous than the mulberry, were loaded with clusters of seeds dangling under tiny heart-shaped leaves. When the wind blew, the seeds, their oily white contents bursting from black husks, would dance on the twigs as though impatiently calling the farmer to come pluck them. They were eager for the oil mill.

The proprietor of the farm, Da Mao, was perched in one of the larger tallows, where he was attentively prodding the fruit-laden branches with a bamboo pole to which a crescent-shaped blade had been tied. His back rested against the trunk of the tree, and his two feet were planted securely in the forks of its branches. Exhausted, his

This story was written in April 1936 and published in *Shinian* (Shanghai) in 1938. Translation by Marston Anderson.

body soaked with sweat, he squinted his eyes tightly against the sunlight that shone down on his face through the sparse leaves. He was only thirty years old, with a rectangular face and high nose and cheekbones, but his despondent expression, sluggish movements, and the earnest, lonely atmosphere that enveloped him seemed unsuited to his youth and the bright weather.

Close to the edge of the field crouched a squat, shabby hut of three rooms. Some of the tiles on its roof had been cracked by the wind and hail, and these had been haphazardly covered with reed mats held down by rocks. The walls were badly eroded, streaked with black traces from water seeping through the eaves and overgrown with dark green moss. In places the wall arched outward as though it were on the verge of collapse. On the threshing ground in front of the door, soybean bushes and sorghum straw were piled high as the cottage's roof. Several lofty mulberry trees, their entire forms powdered with straw, stood by like so many fat old gentlemen, too swollen to move.

Da Mao's aunt, a tall, robust old woman, sat on a rough stone near a bamboo fence and bent her head over the ingots she was folding out of tinfoil.* A four- or five-year-old child, dressed in dirty, frayed white mourning clothes, crouched by her side. His white cloth shoes were smudged grayish black. He watched the old lady's fingers with bulging, fascinated eyes.

"Be good, baby!" The old woman lovingly chided the child as she folded the ingots with a practiced hand. "You mustn't touch these. Day after tomorrow is your mother's *manqi*,† when your father will take you to her grave. Baby will pray, and Daddy will burn the ingots. Daddy will take off Baby's white clothes, and then Mama will protect you from underground as you grow up. When you're big, you'll take a wife, and be a great hero, plowing the fields without an ox, and carrying 800 *jin* on your back!"

Baby crooked his head and listened as though half understanding. Snot flowed down two well-traveled paths toward the sides of his mouth. He lifted his sleeve and wiped his face, leaving a black mark on his fierce-looking cheeks.

"I want one!" he said savagely, staring with dull, colorless eyes. "Give one to Baby, to play!"

"Be good now. Listen to your Auntie. Auntie loves Baby. Don't be bad-tempered like your mother. That won't do! Your mother's temper

---

*Paper money (commonly four-inch squares to which are affixed tinfoil or gold leaf) is burned at the grave as a way of remitting money to the departed in the afterworld.

† *Manqi* refers to the end of the seven-week period after a person's death, at which time the final funeral rites are observed.

gave your father half a lifetime of trouble. But Baby's good now and doesn't copy Mama. He's obedient. Baby's good now; Baby doesn't play with the ingots."

She deftly snatched the basket of ingots from her side and placed it behind her, then took Baby between her knees, blew his nose for him, and patted his head. The child, pacified, raised his head and looked at the black spots circling in the sky. After watching a while, he said, "Mama's, *hiccup, hiccup*—stomach got big and she died!"

"Yes, that's right! Ma was going to give you a little brother, but she died first. Is Baby sorry his mother died? Does Baby miss her?"

He shook his head.

"You don't miss her? Didn't Mama love Baby?"

"Mama hit me. Mama, *hiccup*, ate peanuts in bed. She cried and pulled Daddy's hair. She cried and swore. She was mean! *Hiccup, hiccup* —cried, lay in bed, never got up."

"Yes, Mother was bad. It's true! She lay in bed all day eating peanuts, didn't she? Wouldn't give any to Baby, would she? Fought with Daddy every day, and gave no one a day of peace. A strange kind of mother! A lazy baggage who did nothing but eat, hardly the daughter of a good home! . . . Baby should be good-tempered and obedient and not like his mother. Do you understand?"

The child didn't answer, but turned and watched his father, who was carefully severing the tallow seeds. The tree kept shaking as the clustered seeds fell to the ground bunch by bunch. He could see in profile the lean, squinting features of his father's face and, emerging from a rolled-up trouser leg, one of his dark thighs.

The wind swept through the fields, diffusing everywhere a faint odor of wildflowers, soil, and straw slightly mixed with the stench of manure. In front of the barn, facing the road, stood a heap of pig and cow dung mixed with refuse. A pig with lazy, drooping eyes lay beside the manure pile, jerking its nose forward occasionally. Four or five chickens poked through the refuse looking for something edible.

Suddenly the chickens started, and from the road behind the barn a man came sauntering up, carrying a shoulder pole with empty baskets dangling from it.

"Brother Flatfoot," Auntie said, "you move fast! In the time it took you to go the four or five *li* there and back, I've folded only eight ingots."

Flatfoot laughed, his broad brown face etched with deep wrinkles and his gums showing from behind his lips. He set the empty baskets on the ground, wiped his forehead with his blue cloak, and called toward the field: "Master Da Mao, this last load was 67 *jin*. With yesterday's load that comes to 172 *jin*. You remember it. I've a head like a rock; I'm sure to forget. Auntie, you try to remember too."

"Who was doing the weighing at the oil mill today?" Da Mao asked lazily from the tree.

"It was Mr. Hoardcash in charge. I have some other news: that gem of a father-in-law of yours is back. The millkeeper saw him in town yesterday."

Da Mao, his heart twisting in knots, brought the knife in his hand to a standstill. His rough eyebrows quivered, then locked together tightly. Looking out into space, he sighed and said with icy disgust: "Tell him he's not welcome here!"

He quickly lowered his head and continued to jab at the fruits.

The unexpected news threw Auntie into a fluster. She stood up and asked gravely, as though considering a problem of great magnitude: "Is it true? Is it true? What's he made of himself away from home all this time? Does he still smoke opium? Does he know his daughter's dead?"

"What's he made of himself? That good-for-nothing!" Flatfoot crouched down and puffed on his pipe. "Given up opium? Not likely! It was at one of those dens that the millkeeper ran into him. All along he's been sponging off his uncle's shop, but for Lord knows what wickedness, Uncle finally sent the old fart packing."

"Maotou," Auntie cried out in a raspy voice after a moment's meditation, "I say you should go see him today. Good or bad, he's still your father-in-law. That way you could say you'd notified him. Let him err, but don't you do so! Brother Flatfoot, am I right?"

"Auntie's right there. A pustule like that is better not irritated."

"That's the truth! When his daughter died, Maotou had nowhere to report it. I told him to inform Mr. Fang San. He's a member of the family, and as the go-between was responsible for arranging the match in the first place. So Maotou went to report, and even sent a palanquin over to bring him for the encoffining. But he didn't come! He said there was no one at her house, and he himself wanted no part of the business. But that was just a pretext. Maotou, you mustn't be headstrong about this! Go see him today."*

Da Mao, head lowered, bit his lips and chopped away vigorously at the tallow seeds without saying a word. In one burst of energy he stripped the tree of its fruit, then jumped down and walked over to

---

*In traditional China, it was important that the death of a woman be reported to her natal family. Usually, her family members would come to inspect the body to ensure that there had been no foul play.

another tree. He turned his head and said, "If I go, I'll go in a few days. Who has the time today?"

Auntie was about to say something, when she turned and noticed that Baby had grabbed two paper ingots and, eyes wide with interest, was about to fold them. She rushed back in a panic and tried to seize them from him: "Didn't I tell you not to touch them! You disobedient child!"

The child was like an alley cat, obedient if you petted its fur with the grain, but quick to bite if rubbed the wrong way. The two ingots had been twisted flat as pancakes, and it was impossible for Auntie to get hold of them. The child's fierce little face was yellow with anger, and his two dull eyes stood out. After glaring a moment, he reached into the basket for another handful.

"This child! Ai! Ai!"

When Da Mao saw this dispute, he strode firmly over to the child, stopped and glared with sad, angry eyes at his son's ferocious little face. In it he saw again the fierce visage of his dead wife. She had had a flat round face, with a ball of dirty white flesh like the fruit of the tallow protruding from one blind socket. The other eye winked hugely, suffused with a fiery red color. "Do you hate him? Then kill him!" Her sharp, cutting voice was like a stream of needles shot into his ears.

"Let go of them!" he shouted.

Like his mother, the child thought little of his father. Here was someone, he felt, whom he could afford to ignore and even insult, someone powerless to control him. Sometimes his father would say, "Look at that snot dripping down your face!" Mother would immediately come running from the house: "He offends you? Go look at your own stupid face in the latrine! You aren't worth dog's meat!" At this Daddy's face would tremble in anger; he'd circle the room once and leave without saying a word. Sometimes when Mother wasn't close by, the child would crook his neck and say, "I'll go tell Ma!" It was only when Ma's bad temper came down on the child's head, when she'd force him down on a bench and, grinding her teeth, strike and slap him over his whole body, that he'd think to cry for his father. But Father would just watch from afar, his lips trembling with rage; then he'd circle the room once, take up his hoe, and walk out. Only after his mother's death did the child begin to realize that this was his own father and even begin to accord him a measure of love and respect. But that was forgotten now, and his old attitude had returned. He racked his little brain for a curse to denounce this tall figure glaring down at him.

"Chicken-seller!" He flung away the rumpled ingots in his hand and contorted his face in hatred.

"Oh, this child!" Auntie cried in surprise.

Da Mao's eyes shot forth fury, and his lips trembled. He threw down the scythe and dragged the child off toward the building. The child opened his throat and let out an ear-splitting, shrill cry, then wrestled himself down to the ground. Finally Da Mao lifted the child up by the waist and carried him, hands and feet thrashing and mouth biting in all directions, into the building.

"I'll lock you in the pigpen!"

"You'll frighten him to death!" Auntie stood by flustered for a moment, then followed after them with healthy strides.

"Auntie," Brother Flatfoot called, waving his hand and laughing, "let them go. The child's been hiding behind his mother's skirt since he was little, and doesn't have any fear of his father. Let him take care of it."

"No, he's still small, after all, and his mother just died." But as she spoke, she hesitated, then picked up the crumpled ingots and returned to her stone. Turning the ingots over delicately in her lap, she grumbled, "Such expensive tinfoil! And we had to trade for it at the mill. Like they say, 'Dragons give birth to dragons, phoenixes to phoenixes, and a rat's child will go digging.'"

"It will get better, Auntie. When his mother was alive, tch! He's been learning behavior like that since he was an infant."

Auntie continued to fold the ingots, but anxiously kept one ear turned toward the house. Baby's cries gradually quieted, and only Da Mao's scolding could be heard.

"The little monster only understands a metal whip; a broom is no use with him!"

"You know, Auntie," Brother Flatfoot tapped out some ashes on the ground, filled his pipe again and promptly lit it. Puffing on it, he said, "Da Mao's uncle made few mistakes in his life, but when he arranged that match, he blundered royally!"

"That's for sure! I told him from the start: you are a sparrow, don't try to fly with phoenixes. Our kind needs a daughter-in-law who can suffer and work hard. Don't do Da Mao a bad turn. That family's descended from a successful provincial examination candidate.* True,

---

*The civil service examinations in imperial China recruited successful candidates for political office. There were several levels of examinations. Those who passed at the provincial level acquired the title of *juren*. The next level was the metropolitan examinations. The graduates acquired the *jinshi* degree and became eligible for the post of county magistrate. Relatives of degree holders often wielded power in their communities by association.

the bean curd's turned in the mud, but the frame's still standing. We used to be their tenants; why, then, even a maid at their place wouldn't marry the likes of us. How could their daughter ever get used to living here?"

"Descended from a successful examination candidate, hmpf! A worthless blind daughter, raised in a gambling den and never properly educated. When she grew up, they couldn't marry her off, so they forced her on Da Mao!"

"My brother was a well-meaning man. Of course he knew the circumstances from the start. He saw her with his own eyes in the village, smoking cigarettes, quarreling, and making scenes right out in the street. He came back and told us, her bad eye was a small thing, but that depraved behavior of hers! Really, not the least like the daughter of a good home! He kept shaking his head, and sighed so as to shake the building, you've no idea. But that Mr. Fang San is a real harpy eagle, even the county head knuckles under to him. When he showed up to make the match, how could Second Brother say no? Even if it's a mouthful of dung he brings, you'd best brace yourself and swallow it! What's more, they tried to win him over with fine talk, saying the marriage would elevate him in society. They wanted to bring some glory to our ancestors, they said, make something of our family so everybody'd look up to us. Our Second Brother was a simple man, and he'd seen what happened to that bit of land we got from our ancestors, dike water stolen on one side, boundary markers dug up on the other. He really thought we'd benefit from the match. So he paid a hundred dollars wedding endowment to buy us that boil! What a fine contribution to the family!"

"I hear most of it was pocketed by Mr. Fang San with the old man only getting twenty dollars."

"It's true! Otherwise why would he force the match? The old man's a worthless lout, and Mr. Fang San has him in his pocket."

"A devil from hell has had his fall. That day I carried the soybeans into town, his wife was out in the streets, asking anybody and everybody in to try their luck at a game of mahjongg. For a person of consequence to be acting like that, without the least sense of shame, Auntie!"

"How true that is! Da Mao acquired from the old man the right to farm 13.8 *mu* of Mr. Fang San's land; of that, 11 *mu* have been sold in the past three years. The two *mu* and some left over were mortgaged when the rent came due this year, and then the crops from the mortgaged fields were reclaimed to make up for the interest. How long can people go on like that? He had a streak of luck for a few years, kicking up such a fuss in the courts. But in times like these who can afford to take anyone to the courts? Besides, the new commissioner doesn't fall for his bribes. Where are his days of glory now? Once you've been a swan, you can't be happy as a duck. He and his wife, and the concubine too, the three of them puffing away all day on their opium pipes! Think of it, in times like these!"

"You're a regular *Encyclopedia of Ten Thousand Treasures*!" Brother Flatfoot chuckled, tucking his pipebag in his belt. He rubbed his hands together and then roughly stroked his wrinkled face. Rising, he started toward the field to bundle the tallow branches Da Mao had cut down. He carried several bundles in turn to the threshing ground, where he beat the twigs on the side of a basket.

The house was quiet now. A line of dark smoke emerged through the slanting reeds on the roof.

"Maotou, are you boiling water?"

Auntie looked up, gathered together her tinfoil and basket, and headed toward the hut.

Inside thick smoke enveloped the room. The cooking range was at the foot of the door on the right. In the corner was an untidy pile of pine needles and kindling. Next to the cistern a stove made of a kerosene barrel (two holes had been opened in its side, and the inside coated with mud) was burning with a furious flame. On top of this was set an earthenware pot. Da Mao sat in the courtyard on a short-legged bench, holding his high cheekbones in his hands and staring blankly at his feet.

Auntie wiped her eyes with a corner of her vest and looked about the room. Baby was nowhere to be seen. She walked across to the latched door of the closet that served as her bedroom. She peeped in through a crack in the door and saw the fierce little child lying on the plank bed.

"He's asleep, poor thing!"

She untied the rope that held fast the door and walked in.

The earthenware pot had started to whistle and steam. Da Mao stared ahead in silence, his eyes stung by the smoke. He rubbed them and looked about absently. The beams and rafters were stained a scorched black color. Spider webs and dust covered everything. From the eaves bunches of *gaoliang*,* corn, rice, soybeans, and red peppers dangled, their withered leaves and branches tied fast with rice straw. The sun shone in obliquely from the courtyard, its golden light permeating the dark smoke. On either side of the door were piled vari-

---

Gaoliang is a sorghum grown in north China. It is used to make a strong wine.

ous farm implements: hoes, harrows, and sickles, both new and worn thrown together in piles in the corners. The front hall was crammed with large measuring buckets, winnowing sieves, and rice baskets. Several sheet-metal benches were stored to one side. On the ground were heaped scores of large, flat northern gourds. Such was his home. Humble and shabby, but how calming to look at, how bustling and cozy it felt! Still, it all seemed a bit unfamiliar: for the past six years or so all he had known was that piercing, needle-like voice and that savage blind eye with its protruding dirty-white flesh.

He couldn't help letting out a sigh in the direction of the skylight, and the vague pressure on his spirit lightened a bit. He stood up and went toward his bedroom. Scooping out a handful of rice crusts, he lifted the rattling cover off the pot and tossed the crusts into the water.

"Aunt," he called. "Don't spoil him. I should have disciplined him long ago."

Then he called Flatfoot in for a rest and some tea. Flatfoot had been talking to someone outside, who now followed him into the house: a twenty-year-old youth with narrow eyes and a broad mouth, whose cotton jacket was open to reveal his sturdy, dark, oily chest.

"Master Mao, Little Dou's come to swap work. He's planting turnips the day after tomorrow."* Flatfoot was smiling, showing much of his dark-red upper gums.

"When will all the tallow be cut, Brother Mao?" Little Dou coarsely wiped the sweat from his chest and neck with his shirttail and charged over to the table, from which he took a porcelain bowl and helped himself to some tea from the pot at the foot of the stove.

"I just started yesterday. It'll take at least three days. Why don't you call Yemaotou over, or have you got something to do?"

"Shit! I mowed two *dan* of hay today. Yemaotou went with me, but I showed that bastard up. My basket had just two *jin* short of 190; he didn't even cut one and a half *dan*." He opened his mouth and poured a large helping of tea into it. Burning himself, he screwed up his eyes and hastily swallowed it. "Aiya! Dammit!"

"Call him over and tell him to bring his scythe. Bring yours, and the four of us will divvy up the work."

Auntie came to the door with her folded ingots and said in a concerned tone of voice: "Da Mao, if you swap work like that, when will you have time to go see your father-in-law?"

---

*It was common in traditional China for families who could not afford to hire farmhands to exchange labor and animals among themselves in order to finish agricultural tasks in time.

Little Dou pursed his lips and blew into his bowl, then opened his eyes wide. "So that gem's back? You won't find me falling for his tricks. Last year he swindled me out of twenty cents for one of those lottery tickets, and I didn't get so much as a hair back. The fraud! All I got was a red and green stub with a few characters written on it—fit to wipe your ass with. Anyway, his daughter's gone now, Brother Mao, and you should make a clean break with him. To irritate an ulcer like that's no fucking use."

Everyone looked at the straightforward young man and laughed. Auntie said, "You're young, little brother. Keep your anger to yourself. The rules mustn't be ignored. If you don't report his daughter's death to him, he'll use it against you."

"Didn't Brother Mao report it to Mr. Fang San? If he doesn't come, is that your fault? Goddam that Mr. Fang San! They give me a knot in my gut here. Those Fangs are all sons of bitches!"

"How's that? What's he done to you?" Auntie asked, puzzled.

"What's he done? Nothing good, I'll tell you."

Flatfoot took the teabowl from Little Dou's hand and said laughingly to Auntie: "In these last two years Mr. Fang San has taken control of one of the Fang ancestral halls. Little Dou and Master Yemao have been planting several *mu* of the hall's land. As soon as Mr. Fang San took over, he raised their rent twenty *jin*. When they paid off this year, he refused to accept cracked or overripened husks. They'd weighed it carefully at home, but when Mr. Fang San weighed it, he found it lacking more than ten *jin* to the *dan*. I'll tell you a joke, Auntie: Little Dou and Master Yemao have tied knots on their belts."

"You can't see the knot in my gut, so I've tied one on my belt!" Little Dou mugged a serious expression. At the same time he thrust out his abdomen and pulled on the blue belt at his waist, lifted the knot, and shook it. Then he dashed from the room.

Everyone was still laughing when suddenly the broad-mouthed, narrow-eyed youth reappeared, gesturing and calling, "Brother Mao, you have a visitor."

Flatfoot and Da Mao stood at the door to look: from behind the barn there was indeed someone approaching the threshing ground with a wobbling gait. He was carrying a white cloth bundle and wearing an old cotton gown stained yellow. Beneath his Western haircut, his grayish-blue triangular face displayed a pair of droopy, swollen eyes and a scraggly yellow beard that stretched from his chin to the base of his ears. With dragging steps he stumbled to the door, then twisted his brooding face into an embarrassed smirk.

"Are you all fine?" he asked in a muffled, nasal voice, his eyes settling on Da Mao.

This was the last thing Da Mao had expected. He stood speechless in shock, gazing at the rat-like creature standing before him.

"Oh, it's Father-in-law," Auntie came out and exclaimed in surprise.

Father-in-law coughed and cleared his throat, snorting through his nose, and then walked into the hut. They all followed him in and watched suspiciously from the side. Da Mao, his brow wrinkled, took a bench out from under the table and offered the old man a seat. Then he stood silently to one side. He had never known how to deal with this man.

"We just heard today from the oil mill that you'd returned," Auntie spoke with a studied politeness as she poured him a bowl of tea and set it on the table. Then she told him that Da Mao had intended to go visit him, but had been delayed by the tallow picking.

"Has my daughter gone out? I've come to see her," Father-in-law said with a snort, not waiting for Auntie to finish. He placed the package on the table, lowered his head and coughed dryly.

This speech and his bizarre manner left everyone at a loss. Auntie glanced in Da Mao's direction, and said: "Didn't Master Fang San tell you? Your daughter passed away two months ago."

"Passed away!" His swollen, expressionless cheeks stiffened into a look of astonishment. He suddenly lowered his head, then clenched his hand dramatically in a fist, struck the table, and cried out in a tearful voice, "A death concealed! A death concealed!"

Everyone was struck dumb by this sudden outburst. Da Mao stared, the veins on his temple stood out, and his lip trembled. After a moment he said, "What do you mean by that, old man? You think I plotted to kill her?"

Father-in-law seemed not to have heard him, preoccupied as he was with snorting through his nose and hacking tearfully. He kept beating his fists on the table, shaking the tea bowl and sprinkling tea everywhere.

"Your pa's brought you these sugarcakes, but you'd passed on unbeknownst to me! Hehe . . . hehe . . . Your death's a foul affair! Ai! Ai!"

He stood up, blinking repeatedly. Wrinkling his swollen, bluish-gray face together, he called wildly as if to the air: "Ill-fated one, I feel your spirit nearby. How did you die? Tell your old father. May your eleven ancestors who wore the silk hats of officials protect you! May the certificate of assignation given your grandfather, the Honorary Provincial Candidate, protect you! Ill-fated one, your father will redress this injustice for you!"

Cursing loudly, he turned, took up the tea bowl and tossed it toward the skylight. With a crash, fragments scattered throughout the room.

"Return my daughter to me! I demand you return her! I won't leave till I see her." He struck the table and gasped in exhaustion.

Auntie had been watching him anxiously, wringing her hands. Now she let out a sigh, "Oh, the things he says!"

Little Dou and Flatfoot stood at the door, at first winking and smiling slyly at each other, as if watching a scene from a very interesting flower-drum opera. Later they stopped smiling and glanced with looks full of concern and outrage at Da Mao, who stood by stiffly. His lips had turned white, and his nostrils flared, opening and closing perceptibly with each breath. From experience, he had come to recognize these contemptible dramatics as part of his father-in-law's repertoire of tricks. His heart sank, and he felt suffocated. He had a sudden impulse to storm over and pummel that swollen, sottish face a few times, but his body was immobilized. He stood there as before, numb and staring.

Little Dou walked over and tugged at Da Mao's sleeve. His broad mouth twisted in hatred, he said, "He's just trying to get your goat! It's all a sham."

"Who are you?" Father-in-law lifted his exhausted head and tried to assume an imposing posture, but his nasal voice was low and breathless.

"I am Little Dou Huang, look closely and you'll recognize me." He touched the bridge of his nose with his second finger. "Last year I bought a lottery ticket from you, don't you remember? What are you pretending for? I've got a matter to settle with you!"

Auntie quickly pulled Little Dou back and pushed him out the door. "Little Brother, get a scythe and go cut some tallow."

She turned and looked at Father-in-law. He hadn't changed his expression at all, but sat breathing with an effort, his head down as before. Somewhat reassured by this, Auntie strode resolutely to the bedroom and dragged out Baby, pushing him towards Father-in-law: "This is Grandfather, Baby. Say 'Grandpa.'"

Baby sleepily opened his two tiny red eyes and looked blankly at the strange swollen yellow face before him, then turned his head and glanced at Daddy. He wiped his upper cheek with his sleeve and was silent.

"Father-in-law," Auntie stepped back a couple of paces, clasped her two hands before her breast, and said politely, "Marriage is a holy contract. If there were any failings on our part, you must graciously forgive them! From the first we always thought Your Honor had favored

us, being willing to marry your daughter to farmers like us. Our Maotou here's a simple man. All he knows is to work all day with the hoe.
At times he's not courteous enough. Your daughter was to give birth in
the seventh month. As you know, her temper was always a bit impul-
sive. That of course is pardonable. The month before she was to give
birth they performed the Dragon King plays in town, and she went
to see them seven nights in a row. It's quite a distance, and there was
a lot of dew on the ground. A delicate creature like that, and late in
her term, you know, it was natural she caught a cold, and her whole
body swelled up. Add to that, her eating was a bit irregular: never
anything but bean curd and peanuts. She liked to eat cold, raw things,
and watermelon at bedtime. She slept on a bamboo bed at the door
and refused to pad the bed with a quilt. When the time approached,
her hands and feet swelled up bright red, and her face puffed up
like a lantern. We asked Mr. Hoardcash from the oil mill to take a
look at her, and he brought medicine, but she refused to take it. She
was always quick to anger, and she'd blow up if everything wasn't just
so. A farmer like Maotou, and in a bad year, where could he get the
money? The bit more than ten *mu* he inherited from his ancestors,
plus the rented ones, didn't bring in enough. When you think of it,
they're one's own fields, but we're eating tomorrow's rice today, and
more often than not, there's not a single grain of rice in the canister.
The rice doesn't bring in enough to pay the bill at the oil mill. Your
daughter was used to a delicate life; Maotou's a simple man, and there
were things he couldn't supply her with. Really, if you must blame
someone, blame his father, a sparrow wanting to fly with a phoenix!"

Auntie spoke in a stream, getting increasingly worked up. She
quickly let out an extended breath, composed herself, and continued:
"On the morning of July 16, your daughter had a pain in her stomach
and kept running to the outhouse. I went to fetch the midwife and
Mrs. Flatfoot, and the three of us looked after her. Actually the second time is not as easy as the first. She kept turning on the cot, in a
terrible state, and wouldn't listen to us at all. In pain like that for three
days and three nights, and still her vagina wouldn't open. We hung
three paper fertility dolls in the room, opened the doors and drawers,
broke all the blue and white porcelain bowls in the house, and even
bought some bowls from the oil mill on credit. The whole courtyard
was covered with broken porcelain, but still her vagina wouldn't open.
On the 20th, your daughter looked weakened. I sent Maotou to Mr.
Fang San to report, but he refused to come. Your daughter passed
away on the 21st at the time the lamps are lit. That night Maotou sent
a sedan chair for Mr. Fang San, but he said he wouldn't handle this

matter. Father-in-law, farmers like us, we're simple folk. Since we were elevated by this match, we've passed the years in great fear. We've done all we could. A barrel-sized calabash can't be hung on a small stem; it's bound to fall!"

Flatfoot's broad face was rigid with anger. When Auntie finished speaking, he pursed his lips and protested: "How many heads has Master Mao got on his shoulders? Would he dare murder your daughter? You've a nerve to talk like that! What kind of woman was your daughter anyway? The whole village, and the town too, knows Mao served her like she had him on a leash. He didn't dare speak a harsh word in her presence. Even an old woman like Auntie suffered from her kicks! Was Da Mao like a real husband, trailing at her heels listening to her chorus of 'Headless ghost!' and 'Hangman's fodder!'? If the least thing crossed her, she'd pull his hair and scream, 'You and your family of bogtrotters! Offend your mistress and I'll see your whole clan sent up the river—they'll vanish like ants off a hot stove!' No wonder, seeing whose daughter she was; of course she was offended by our filthy feet. At first didn't Mao treat her like a princess? But over the course of days and months, there comes a time you can't bear it any more. How can you tolerate someone making every day impossible for you? Bother the least hair on her head, and she'd drag out a knife or rope and threaten to kill herself! Has Mao got the guts of a tiger? Would he dare offend her in anything? I'm only a neighbor and haven't anything to gain from talking like this, but how could what you say have the least basis in fact? Go to Mr. Hoardcash at the oil mill and ask him."

Father-in-law still sat blankly with his head down, as though half asleep, making no response to their speeches. His behavior astonished them: it was hard to believe this was the same person who had made the wild outbreak of a moment before.

Footsteps approached from outside. Little Dou came in bare-chested, repeatedly wiping his face with the vest he had removed. At the same time, Yemaotou appeared at the door with two scythes in his hand and peered into the room; he had two round staring eyes and buckteeth. Several other villagers followed them.

"Is that bastard still here? What's he want?" Yemaotou asked, sticking out his tongue.

"Selling lottery tickets," said Little Dou, "but you won't get wealthy from *his* tickets. You'd better get your ass out of here as fast as possible!"

"He thinks they killed his daughter? Tell him to dig up her coffin and investigate the corpse!" said another of the villagers.

Da Mao had stood there frozen, but now his gaunt cheeks trembled and he drew up his body: "What do you want from me, tell me straight!"

Father-in-law lifted his head and looked about him, then suddenly jumped up as if bitten by something in a dream, gave the table in front of him a push, and waving his arms wildly cried out: "How cruel! How cruel! I'll just have to go to town. I'll just have to take you to court! I'll have Fang San draw up the papers." His nasal voice broke and started to rasp. His hands shaking, he took up his bag and hobbled out with his back hunched. Suddenly he turned, and through his tears pointed at his son-in-law, caught his breath, and croaked:

"You'll regret this!"

But in the middle of his threat, his voice cracked and fell.

Da Mao seemed to have understood everything. He grinned and said in a coarse voice: "Fine, we'll do just as your Mr. Fang San proposes."

Everyone crowded to the door to watch the dingy, rat-like figure limp and swagger across the threshing ground.

"That one's a pustule. You can bet it was Fang San who told him to come here and make trouble."

"If it weren't for the opium attack, he might not have gone today."

"Take you to court! I doubt he could! Just trying to frighten you."

"Today he came for nothing, but I bet he'll come again tomorrow, and maybe bring old Fang San with him."

They all chattered away. Da Mao knit his brows in silence, took up his knife from the ground, and walked toward the fields. Little Dou and Yemaotou had already climbed the tallow trees. Just then Little Dou stuck his head out of a treetop and called loudly towards the road:

"Hey, ticket-seller! You bumbling wart! Ask your Fang San over tomorrow. We'll be waiting. That motherfucker, I'll make him eat pig-shit as I'm a man!"

Auntie led Baby out by the hand to the threshing ground. She sighed to Flatfoot as he beat down the tallow fruit, "Ai, truly! What's to come of this?"

Flatfoot pursed his lips, and then smiled, exposing a mouthful of dark red gums. He shook his head but said nothing.

In the light of the setting sun, the fields were buffeted by the wind. The white clouds, layered like fish scales, had massed together and, suffused with sparkling and translucent colors, were shining with unusual freshness and beauty on the fields and huts. Near the barn a cock was standing on a pile of dung. It flapped its wings and raised its practiced voice in a loud cry.

Xiao Hong

On the Oxcart

//// Late March. Clover covers the banks of the streams. In the early light of the morning our cart crushes the red and green grasses at the foot of the hill as it rumbles through the outskirts of Grandfather's village.

The carter is a distant uncle on Mother's side. He flicks his whip, but not to strike the rump of the ox; the tip merely dances back and forth in the air.

"Are you sleepy already? We've only just left the village! Drink some plum nectar now, and after we've crossed the stream you can sleep." Grandfather's maid is on her way to town to visit her son.

"What stream? Didn't we just cross one?" The yellow cat we're bringing back from Grandfather's house has fallen asleep in my lap.

"The Houtang Stream."

"What Houtang Stream?" My mind is wandering. The only things from Grandfather's village still visible in the distance are the two gold balls on top of the red flagpole in front of the ancestral temple.

"Drink a cup of plum nectar, it'll perk you up." She is holding a cup of the dark yellow liquid in one hand as she puts the lid back on the bottle.

"I'm not going to need anything . . . perk me up? You perk yourself up!"

They both laugh as the carter suddenly cracks his whip.

"You young lady, you . . . you sharp-tongued little scamp . . . I, I . . . ." He turns over from alongside the axle and reaches out to grab

Xiao Hong wrote this story while residing in Japan; it was first published in *Wenxue* (Shanghai) in May 1936. Translation by Howard Goldblatt; reprinted by permission of Indiana University Press from *Born of the Same Roots*, ed. Vivian Hsu (Bloomington: Indiana University Press, 1981).

hold of my hair. Drawing my shoulders back, I clamber to the rear of the cart. Every kid in the village is scared of him. They say he used to be a soldier, and when he pinches your ear, it hurts like the dickens. Sister Wuyun has gotten down off the cart to gather a lot of different kinds of flowers for me. Now the wind blowing in from the wildwood has picked up a bit, and her scarf is flapping around her head. I pretend that it's a raven or a magpie, like the ones I saw in the village. Look at 'er jumpin' up and down, just like a kid! She's back in the cart now, singing out the names of all kinds of flowers. I've never seen her so happy.

I can't tell what those low, coarse, grunting noises from the carter mean. Puffs of smoke from his short pipe float back on the wind. As we start off on our journey, our hopes and expectations are far off in the distance.

I must have fallen asleep, but I don't know if it happened before we crossed Houtang Stream, or just where it happened. I remember waking up once, and through the cobwebs of my mind I thought I saw the boy who watches over the ducks beckon to me. There was also the parting scene between me and Xiaogen as he straddled his ox. And I could see Grandfather again taking me by the hand and saying, "When you get home tell your maternal granddad to come on over during the cool autumn season and visit the countryside . . . you tell him that your old Grandpa's quail and his best *gaoliang* wine* are waiting here for him to enjoy with me together . . . you tell him that I can't get around so well anymore; otherwise these past couple of years I would have gone. . . ."

The hollow sound of the wheels wakes me up. The first thing I see is the yellow ox plodding along the road. The carter isn't sitting there by the axle where he should be—there he is, behind the cart. Instead of the whip, he's holding a pipe in his hand. He keeps stroking his chin with his other hand; he is staring off into the horizon. Sister Wuyun is stroking the yellow cat's tail in her lap. She has wrapped her blue cotton scarf around her head below her eyebrows, and the creases on her nose are easier to see than usual because of the dust that lines them.

They don't know that I'm awake.

"By the third year there were no more letters from him. You soldiers . . . ."

"Was your husband a soldier too?" I couldn't hold back. My carter-uncle pulls me backwards by my pigtail.

"And no more letters at all after that?" he asks.

Gaoliang is a sorghum grown in north China. It is used to make a strong wine.

"Since you asked me, I'll tell you. It was just after the Mid-autumn Festival*—I forget which year it was. I had just finished eating breakfast and was slopping the pigs in front of the house. 'Soo-ee, soo-ee!' I didn't even hear Second Mistress from the Wang family of South Village as she came running up, shouting, 'Sister Wuyun, Sister Wuyun! My mother says it's probably a letter from Brother Wuyun.' She held a letter right under my nose. 'Here, let me have it. I want to see. . . .' I don't know why, but I felt sick at heart. Was he still alive? He . . . . My tears fell on the red-bordered envelope, but when I tried to wipe it dry with my hand, all I did was smudge the red border onto the white paper. I threw the slop down in the middle of the yard and went into my room to change into some clean clothes. Then I ran as fast as I could to the school in South Village to see the schoolmaster. I was laughing through my tears. 'I've got a letter here from someone far away; would you please read it to me. . . . I haven't had a single word from him for a year.' But after he took the letter from me and read it, he said it was for someone else. I left the letter there in the school and ran home. I didn't go back to feed the pigs or put the chickens to roost; I just went inside and lay down on the *kang*. For days I was like someone whose ghost had left her."

"And no more letters from him at all?"

"None." After unscrewing the lid from the bottle of plum nectar, she drinks a cupful, then another.

"You soldiers, you go away for two or three years, you say, but do you return home? . . . How many of you ever do? You send your ghosts home for us to see. . . ."

"You mean? . . ." the carter blurts out. "Then he was killed in battle somewhere?"

"That's what it amounted to; not a word for more than a year."

"Well, was he killed in battle or wasn't he?" Jumping down from the cart, he grabs his whip and snaps it in the air a couple of times, making sounds like little explosions.

"What difference does it make? The bitter life of a soldier doesn't allow for much good fortune." Her wrinkled lips look like pieces of torn silk, a sure sign of a fickle nature and a life of misfortune.

As we pass Huang Village, the sun begins to set and magpies are flying over the green wheat fields.

"Did you cry when you learned that Brother Wuyun had died in battle?" As I look at her, I continue stroking the yellow cat's tail. But she ignores me and busies herself with straightening her scarf.

The carter scrambles up into the cart by holding on to the handrail

*The festival takes place on the fifteenth day of the eighth lunar month.

and jumping in, landing right above the axle. He is about to smoke; his thick lips are sealed as tightly as the mouth of the bottle.

The flow of words from Sister Wuyun's mouth is like the gentle patter of rain; I stretch out alongside the handrail, and before long I've dozed off again.

I awake to discover that the cart is stopped alongside a small village well—the ox is drinking from the well. Sister Wuyun must have been crying, because her sunken eyes are all puffed up and the crow's-feet at the sides of her eyes are spread open. Scooping up a bucketful of water from the well, the carter carries it over to the cart.

"Have some—it's nice and cool."

"No, thanks," she replies.

"Go ahead and drink some. If you're not thirsty, at least use some of it to wash your face." He takes a small towel from his waistband and soaks it in the water. "Here, wipe your face. The dust has clouded your eyes."

I can't believe it, a soldier actually offering his towel to someone! That strikes me as peculiar, since the soldiers I've known only know how to fight battles, beat women, and pinch children's ears.

"That winter I traveled to the year-end market, where I sold pig bristles. I stood there shouting, 'Good stiff pig bristles . . . fine long pig bristles . . . .' By next year I had just about forgotten my husband . . . didn't think about him at all. But all that did was make me mad at myself, because he might still have been alive. The following autumn I went into the fields with the others to harvest sorghum . . . here, look at my hands—they've seen their share of work. . . .

"I got a more permanent job in the fields the next spring, so I took the baby with me, and the whole family was split up for two or three months. But we got back together the next winter. All kinds of ox hairs . . . pig bristles . . . even some bird feathers, we gathered them up . . . during the winter we gathered them all up, cleaned them, and took them into town to sell when the weather turned warm. If I could catch a ride on a cart, I took Little Baldy into town with me.

"But this time I went in alone. The weather that day was awful—it had been snowing almost every day—and the year-end market wasn't very crowded. I wouldn't have been able to sell all my pig bristles even if I'd only brought a few bundles. I squatted there in the marketplace from early morning till the sun was setting in the west. Someone had put a poster up on the wall of a large store at the intersection, which everyone stopped to read. I heard that the 'proclamation' had been put up early in the morning . . . or maybe it had only been there since around noontime . . . some of the people read several sentences aloud as they looked at it. I didn't know what it was all about . . . they were saying, 'Proclamation this' and 'proclamation that,' but I couldn't figure out just what was being 'proclaimed.' I only knew that a proclamation was the business of officials and had nothing to do with us common folk, so I couldn't figure out why there were so many people interested in it. Someone said it was a proclamation about the capture of some army deserters. I overheard a few other tidbits here and there . . . in a few days the deserters were going to be delivered to the county seat to be shot."

"What year was that? Was that the execution of twenty-odd deserters in 1921?" Absentmindedly letting down his rolled-up sleeves, the carter rubs his cheekbone with his hand.

"How should I know what year it was . . . besides, execution or not, what business was it of mine? Anyway, my pig bristles weren't selling so good and things were looking bleak." Rubbing her hands together briefly, she suddenly stretches out her hand as though she were catching a mosquito.

"Someone was reading out the names of the deserters. I looked over at a man in a black gown and said to him, 'Read those names again for me!' At first I was holding the pig bristles in my hand, then I heard him say Jiang Wuyun . . . Jiang Wuyun . . . the name seemed to be echoing in my ears. After a moment or two, I felt like throwing up, like some foul-smelling thing was stuck in my throat; I wanted to swallow it . . . but couldn't . . . my eyes were burning . . . the people looking at the 'proclamation' crowded up in front of it, so I backed off to the side. I tried to move up again and take a look, but my legs wouldn't hold me. More and more people came to look at the 'proclamation,' and I kept backing up . . . farther . . . farther. . . ."

I can see that her forehead and the tip of her nose are beaded with perspiration.

"When I returned to the village, it was already late at night. Only when I was getting down from the cart did I remember the pig bristles . . . they'd been the farthest thing from my mind at the time . . . my ears were like two chips of wood . . . my scarf had fallen off, maybe on the road, maybe in the city. . . ."

Now that she has removed her scarf, we can see that her earlobes are missing.

"Just look at these; that's what it means to be a soldier's wife. . . ."

The ends of her scarf, which she has fixed tightly over her head again, move slightly when she speaks.

"Wuyun was still alive, and I felt like going to see him; at least we could be together as husband and wife one last time. . . .

"In February I strapped Little Baldy onto my back and went into town every day. . . . I heard that the 'proclamation' had been put up several more times, though I never went to see that God-awful thing again. I went to the yamen* to ask around, but they only said, 'That's none of our business!' They sent me to the military garrison . . . ever since I was a kid I've had a fear of officials . . . a country girl like me. I'd never been to see one of 'em. Those sentries with their bayoneted rifles sent shivers up and down my spine. *Oh, go ahead! After all, they don't just kill people on sight.* Later on, after I'd gone to see them lots of times, I wasn't afraid any longer. After all, out of the three people in our family, they already had one of us in their clutches. They told me that the deserters hadn't been sent over yet. When I asked them when they would be, they told me, 'Wait another month or so!' But when I got back to the village I heard that the deserters had already come from some county seat or other—even today I can't remember which county seat it was, since the only thing that mattered to me was that they had been sent over—and they said if I didn't hurry and go see him, it'd be too late. So I strapped Little Baldy onto my back and went back to town, where I asked around again at the military garrison. 'Why all the impatience?' they asked me. 'How many more hundreds of times are you going to ask? Who knows, maybe they won't be sent over at all.' One day I spotted some big official riding in a horsedrawn carriage with its bells jingling as it came out from the garrison buildings. I put Little Baldy down on the ground and ran over; luckily the carriage was heading toward me, so I knelt down in front of it. . . . I didn't even care if the horse trampled me.

"'Venerable sir, my husband . . . Jiang Wu—' Before I even got his name out I felt a heavy blow on my shoulders . . . the carriage driver had pushed me over backwards. I must've been knocked over. . . . I crawled over to the side of the road. All I could see was that the driver was wearing a military cap.

"I stood up and strapped Little Baldy onto my back again. There was a river in front of the garrison, and for the rest of the afternoon I just sat there on the riverbank looking at the water. Some people were fishing out on the river, and some women were washing clothes on the bank. Farther off, at the bend in the river, the water was much deeper, and the crests of waves passed in front of me, one after the other. I don't know how many hundreds of waves I saw passing by as I sat there. I felt like putting Little Baldy down on the riverbank and jumping straight to the bottom. Just leave that one little life behind; as

*The office of the county magistrate.

soon as he started crying, someone would surely come and take him away.

"I rubbed his little chest and said something like, 'Little Baldy, you go to sleep.' Then I stroked his little round ears . . . those ears of his, honestly, they're so long and full, just like his daddy's. Looking at his ears, I was seeing his daddy."

A smile of motherly approval spreads across her face.

"I kept on rubbing his chest and said again, 'You go to sleep, Little Baldy.' Then I remembered that I still had a few strings of cash on me, so I decided to put them on his chest. As I reached over . . . reached over to put . . . when I was putting them on his . . . he opened his eyes . . . another sailing boat came around the riverbend, and when I heard the shouts of 'Mama' from a child on the boat, I quickly picked Little Baldy up from the sandbank and held him . . . against my chest. . . ."

Her tears flow along with the motion of her hands as she tightens the scarf under her chin.

"But then . . . then, I knew I had to carry him back home. Even if I had to go begging, at least he would have his mother . . . he deserved a mother."

The corners of her blue scarf quiver with the movements of her cheekbones.

Our path is being crossed by a flock of sheep, herded by a shepherd boy playing a willow flute. The grass and the flowers in the wildwood all blend together, bathed in the slanting rays of the sun, so that all we can see is a vast jumbled patch of yellow.

The carter is now walking alongside the cart, raising trails of dust on the road with the tip of his whip.

". . . it wasn't until May that the people at the garrison finally told me, 'They'll be coming soon.'

"Toward the end of the month a big steamship pulled up to the wharf in front of the garrison. God, there were a lot of people! Not that many people come out to watch the river lanterns on the July Fifteenth Festival."*

Her sleeves are waving in the air.

"The families of the deserters were standing over to the right, so I moved over there with them. A man in a military cap came over and pinned a kind of badge on each of us. . . . I don't know what they said, since I can't read.

"When they were about to lower the gangplank, a troop of soldiers

*This is often the time when families make offerings to appease the hungry ghosts and when community exorcism rituals are performed.

came up to those of us who were wearing the badges and grouped us into a circle. 'Move a little farther back from the riverbank, move a little farther. . . .' They pushed us back some thirty or forty feet away from the steamship with their rifle butts. An old man with a white beard stood next to me, holding some packages in his hand. 'Uncle, why did you bring those things along?' I asked him. 'Huh? Oh, I have a son and a nephew . . . one package for each . . . when they get to the next world it wouldn't be right for them not to have clothes to wear.'*

"They lowered the gangplank . . . some of the people began to cry as soon as they saw the gangplank being lowered . . . me, I wasn't crying. I planted my feet squarely on the ground and kept my eyes on the ship . . . but no one came out. After a while, an officer wearing a foreign sword leaned over the railing and said, 'Have the families move farther back; they're going to be leaving the ship now.' As soon as they heard him bark out the order, the soldiers herded us even farther back with their rifle butts, all the way back to the beanfield by the edge of the road, until we were standing there on top of the bean shoots. The gangplank came crashing down, and out they came, led by an officer, their leg-irons clanking along. I can still see it: the first one out was a short little man . . . then five or six more . . . not one of them with broad shoulders like Little Baldy's daddy . . . really, they looked wretched, their arms hanging stiffly in front of them. I watched for a long time before I realized that they were all wearing manacles. The harder the people around me cried, the calmer I became. I just kept my eyes on the gangplank. . . . I wanted to ask Little Baldy's daddy, 'Why couldn't you just be a good soldier? Why did you have to desert? Look here at your son; how can you face him?'

"About twenty of them came down, but I couldn't spot the man I was looking for; from where I stood they all looked the same. A young wife in a green dress lost control and busted through the rifles holding us back . . . they weren't satisfied with just calling her back; no, they went out and grabbed her, and she started rolling in the dirt and crying out, 'He hadn't even been a soldier for three months . . . not even . . . .' Two of them carried her back. Her hair was all mussed up and hanging down in her face. After about the time it takes to smoke a pipeful, they led those of us wearing badges over . . . the more we walked, the closer we got, and the closer we got, the harder it was for me to spot Little Baldy's daddy . . . my eyes started to blur . . . the weeping sounds around me scared me. . . .

"Some of them had cigarettes in their mouths, some were cursing

*The packages probably contained paper clothing to be burned for the dead.

. . . some were even laughing. So this was the stuff soldiers are made of. I guess you could say that soldiers don't give a damn what happens to them.

"I looked them over; Little Baldy's daddy wasn't there for sure. *That's strange!* I grabbed hold of an officer's belt: 'What about Jiang Wuyun?' 'What's he to you?' 'He's my husband.' I put Little Baldy down on the ground, and he started to cry. I slapped him in the mouth, then I began hitting the officer: 'What have you done with him?'

"'Good for you, lady, we're with you. . . .' The prisoners were shouting from where they were crouching. When the officer saw what was happening, he quickly called some soldiers over to drag me away. 'It's not only Jiang Wuyun,' he said. 'There are a couple of others who haven't been sent over yet; they'll be over in a day or two on the next ship. Those three were the ringleaders of this group of deserters.'

"I put the child on my back and left the riverbank, with the badge still pinned on, and walked off. My legs were all rubbery. The streets were filled with people who had come over to watch the excitement. I was walking behind the garrison buildings, and there at the base of the garrison wall sat the old man with the two packages, but now he only had one left. 'Uncle, didn't your son come either?' I asked him. He just arched his back and stuck the ends of his beard into his mouth and chewed on them as he wept.

"He told me, 'Since he was one of the ringleaders, they carried out their capital punishment on the spot.' At the time I didn't know what 'capital punishment' meant. . . ."

At this point she begins to ramble.

"Three years later, when Little Baldy was eight, I sent him to the bean curd shop . . . that's what I did. I go to see him twice a year, and he comes home once every two years, but then only for ten days or a couple of weeks. . . ."

The carter has left the side of the cart and is walking along a little path, his hands clasped behind his back. With the sun off to the side, he casts a long shadow which divides with every step he takes.

"I have a family too. . . ." The words seem to fall from his lips, as though he is speaking to the wildwood.

"Huh?" As Sister Wuyun loosens her scarf a little, the wrinkles above her nose quiver momentarily. "Really? You're out of the army, and still you don't go home?"

"What's that? Go home, you say! You mean go home with nothing but the clothes on my back?" The carter sneers as he rubs his nose hard with his coarse hand.

"Haven't you put a little something away these past few years?"

"That's exactly why I deserted, to make a little money if I could."
He cinches his belt tighter.

I put on another cotton jacket, and Sister Wuyun throws a blanket
over her shoulders.

"Um! Still another mile to go. Now if we had a harness horse . . .
um! We could be there in nothing flat! An ox is no good. This beast
just plods along with no spirit, and it's no good at all on a battlefield."

The carter opens his straw bag and takes out a padded jacket from
which pieces of straw fall off and swirl in the wind. He puts it on.

The winds at dusk are just like February winds. In the rear of the
cart the carter opens up the wine jug that my mother's father had
given my father's father.

"Here, drink! As they say, 'In the midst of a journey open a jug of
wine, for the poor love to gamble.' Now for two cups of wine." After
drinking several cups, he opens his shirt and exposes his chest. He is
chewing on some pieces of jerky, causing frothy bubbles to gather at
the corners of his mouth. Whenever a gust of wind blows across his
face, the bubbles on his lips expand a little.

As we near the town, through the gray overcast we can tell only
that it is not a patch of open country, nor a mountain range, nor the
seashore, nor a forest. . . . The closer our cart comes to the town, the
more it seems to recede into the distance. The pores on our faces and
hands feel sticky. Another look ahead, and this time even the end of
the road is lost from view.

The carter puts the wine jug away and picks up his whip. By now
the ox's horns have grown indistinct.

"Haven't you returned home or even received a letter since you
left?" The carter hasn't heard her. He blows on his whistle to urge the
ox on. Then he jumps down from the cart and walks along up front
with the animal. An empty cart with a red lantern hanging from its
axle comes rolling up to us.

"A heavy fog!"

"It sure is!"

The carters are calling out to each other.

"A heavy fog in March . . . that either means war or a year of
drought. . . ."

The two carts pass on the road.

Sha Ting

The Way of the Beast

//// It was an autumn day marked by intermittent wind and rain. As the situation worsened, I was summoned to the city by my uncle, Ji Xianmo, to stay with him. Indeed, even on the surface, all was not well in the city. Not only were the iron-shaped helmets apparent everywhere, but so were gangs of bandits and brotherhood members dressed in civvies.* As for the local gentry and landlords, those who were the least bit famous, the likes of Golden Calf Mao, for example, had already skipped town as soon as reports of the Red Army entering the Fu River Basin had been confirmed. Those who remained were packed and poised for flight, making sure they had teams of porters and coolies around, sleeping fully clothed, and generally behaving like a bunch of scared rabbits. In short, it was sheer chaos, as if everyone knew a great change would soon fall upon them, a change that would turn the whole world upside down.

My uncle, a salaried scholar who taught language in a girls' school, was considered a decent man. Mostly, he enjoyed closeting himself in his study, where he indulged in fits of violent sneezing. His household was simple enough, just my aunt and himself, plus a not-so-young serving-woman whom everybody called Old Woman Wei. From start to finish, my stay in the city totaled three months, but the much-heralded coming of the Red Army never did materialize. On the other hand, the different troops who kept saying that when the Red Army showed up everything—property and wives included—would be communally shared, had certainly caused some unforgettable upheavals.

This story was written in May 1936 and published in the first issue of *Guangming* (Shanghai) in the same year. Translation by Ellen Lai-shan Yeung.

*Members of secret societies, local militia, and bandits were closely associated in the minds of ordinary people at the time.

Just take our little circle, for example. My uncle's hair has turned almost completely white; even his sneezing has lost its former vigor. My sickly aunt has grown more frail, and the slightest mention of the dishes and beddings that she lost in the ordeal sets her sniffling and lamenting until she is choked off by her own asthmatic coughing. As for Old Wei, that poor serving-woman, she eventually lost her mind and took to wandering about the streets all day, naked from the waist down. The sight of her in this already traumatized city only added to the desolation.

Of course, Old Mother Wei was fine at first. Even on the day I came to the city, she was still her usual self, cheerful and talkative. In fact, compared to those preoccupied with evacuation, she appeared extremely at ease, as if all the rumors and fears had nothing to do with her. She had been in my uncle's employ for ten whole years.

Old Mother Wei was short. Some people called her the "Uppity Pepper," but in reality her disposition was most agreeable, to the point of being a little childish. Sure she was garrulous; especially after she had had a few, she'd set to thinking that someone was out to get her and would lash out, weeping and cursing, at anyone and anything. Yet she managed to live through all of it, brought up her son single-handed, and, on top of everything else, found him a wife. Having been widowed early, she had probably seen more hardship than the run of poor people. She was native to the area and had always lived in that wretched alley beside the city's west wall. Her husband had been responsible for patrolling the night watches.

Her daughter-in-law was from a peasant family, used to hard times and hard work. Her son was working as a porter and made frequent trips to the provincial capital to buy sundry goods for the residents of the city. Now and then he would make a trip for himself, heaving a load of salt over his shoulder and peddling it along the river, then returning with medicinal roots for sale. Traveling in these unsettling times was not easy, and her son, Wei the Elder, ended up having to stay over in Chengdu. With him away and her daughter-in-law having just given birth, Old Woman Wei talked my aunt into letting her spend her nights at home, the better to keep an eye on the new mother and baby. To me, however, on my first night in the city, her reason for going home was to make it easier to run.

Later, when I suggested this to her, she broke into delighted laughter.

"Aiiie!" she cried. "What's there to fear? After all, what little food I have is in my belly, and what few clothes I have are already on my back."

Then she told me the real reason, adding, "One has an explosive temper and the other is still wet behind the ears. If anything should go wrong, why, people will hound me to my grave!"

Obviously pleased with herself, she pursed up her wrinkled lips, then lit that contraption that she called her oil lamp and headed out to the street, which was bustling with people and horses. I followed and helped my uncle bolt the main door. The next morning she came especially early, and in the few days that followed, she almost always arrived in time to prepare breakfast. She worked with more alacrity than before, as if she was taking part in some sort of game rather than doing chores. At the same time, she grew even more talkative, and almost without fail, the topic turned to her grandson and her daughter-in-law.

"Young people nowadays are not worth a damn!" she said, scrubbing away energetically at the stove top. "The little one's butt is almost pickled in his own pee!"

"Why do you keep on so?" Sometimes my aunt would try to stop her.

"Why?" returned the old woman. "You should come and take a look. So damn lazy she won't lift a finger. People often say: 'Man may be down and out, but there's always water aplenty.' Washing one more diaper is not going to break any sacred taboo, is it?"

Occasionally she repeated for us bits of news she had heard outside: Pockmarked Jiang's daughter-in-law was ravaged by some soldiers; Third Master Chen was robbed on the stone steps, and so on. One morning, when even my sickly aunt was up and about, there was still no sign of Old Woman Wei. Ordinarily, my aunt could have managed to put together a meal, but having stayed up the past few nights, she was not in good shape. Besides we were supporting five to six laborers in the house, and to feed those fellows one had to do some real cooking, which she was simply not up to. After a while, everybody became a little impatient.

My uncle finally lost his temper and shouted. "This is all your doing, giving in to these ungrateful wretches and spoiling them!"

"And all you ever do is yell," my aunt shouted back. "Why don't you send someone around to check."

Naturally, my uncle was not about to go out himself. As for the laborers, half of them knew where Old Mother Wei lived, but my uncle couldn't bear to let them show their faces on the street for fear of losing them to army press gangs or having them lured away by more generous offers from other families. In the end, after another interval of anxious waiting, I was told to put on a militia armband and go out to take a look.

The army horses usually kept at the front door had been taken outside the city to graze. Horse droppings and straw lay strewn about on the street. The lantern hanging from the eaves of the Forever Prosperous Store was still shining pale and ghostly. Only one of the city gates was open. In one corner a stack of wood had been set ablaze, and several soldiers had gathered around it enjoying its toasty warmth. Old Woman Wei was nowhere to be seen and her dilapidated door was padlocked from the outside.

I called a couple of times and hammered on the door with my fists. A good while passed before someone in a bright yellow felt hat poked his head out from next door, mumbling, "Go on, hammer away! As if last night's ruckus wasn't bad enough. . . ."

It was an old man with one good eye, his face wreathed in big fat wrinkles. After sizing me up carefully, he blew his nose, rubbed his hands together, and dragged out the following story. The daughter-in-law of Old Woman Wei had hanged herself at dawn. As for the old lady, she was screaming for justice in front of the yamen* right at this moment, attempting to press charges against those soldiers for gang-raping a woman barely out of pregnancy. This terrifying bit of news left me clasping the back of my head in shock. I turned and rushed home.

The distraught serving-woman outside my uncle's suite was easily recognizable. She looked even smaller than usual, her face streaked with tears, holding the baby in her arms. Standing at the foot of the steps, encircled by my uncle, my aunt and the coolies, she presented a pitiful figure as she narrated the whole incident. She sobbed, at times stamped her feet and cursed. Her coiled-up hair had long since come undone and hung in disarray down her back.

When Old Woman Wei bent her head to pacify the screaming baby, my aunt suddenly pulled a long face and interjected, "But you, you should have told them. It has been less than a month since she gave birth."

"What else could I have said?" wailed the old woman, stung by the unjust accusation. "I told them: 'She's not clean. She just gave birth to a baby.' I even said: 'I'll do it with the lot of you.' . . ."

My aunt gasped. Suddenly realizing that she had said something wrong, the old woman fell silent, but almost immediately resumed her tearful cursing, "Bastards . . . good only for cannon fodder . . . !"

Then, as if she had lost her memory, she ceased her normal rampage and gave way to tears.

Heartbroken, she wept hard and long. For one brief moment I

*The office of the county magistrate.

couldn't believe that she who was standing before me was the same strong and vigorous woman I had known. But on thinking of her utterance "I'll do it with the lot of you," and of how she must have felt when she said it, I knew it was real. Equally convincing were her tears of despair. We watched her in silence, for none of us could find the right words to comfort her.

My uncle heaved a deep sigh, and, his voice choking with emotion, said, "To think that such a heinous thing could happen! No wonder we are all doomed!"

My uncle was not in favor of her taking her grievance to the magistrate again, but the old woman simply refused to let matters rest. The soundness of my uncle's judgment was quickly borne out, for the government never did accept her written accusation. All they did was to order the headman of the ward to help her procure a coffin and to lecture her at length about how she must not fabricate such immoral tales to disrupt society. It was three days before she showed up for work again, after having entrusted her grandson to the care of another family.

However, the old woman did not forget the insult and the injury done to her. Although her back seemed more stooped than before, and she had developed such a way of squinting at people you'd have thought she was peering directly into the sun, she had a mouth that could still talk, and could talk as tough as before. Whenever she was on her break, she would blast away with her curses, beginning with the army and proceeding on to His Excellency the magistrate.

And yet, as abruptly as she had begun, her anger ebbed to be replaced by despondent tears. "Damned bastards . . . fit only for the executioner's ax . . . How am I going to break the news to them?"

What worried her most was her son and her daughter-in-law's family; she didn't quite know how to deal with them when the time came. Then, one day at noon, my uncle was by himself in the main suite, fuming. His granary had been confiscated by the provincial government and turned over to a troop of bandits. Some of the coolies were sunning themselves on the steps. A pockmarked man with a flat chubby face was sucking on his pipe and spinning a tale. In Zengzichang, a group of soldiers dragged a young girl into a field and took their pleasure with her. Half a month later, the girl gave birth to three babies. They were only two inches or so long, one was red, one black, and one white, all born with army caps on their heads . . . .

I listened, fascinated by this strange, vengeful tale made up by country folk. Suddenly, a woman with green leggings up her shins came through the door, three timid-looking companions following in the shadow of her broad frame. Old Woman Wei stood up, her hands trailing water. Alarmed by the sight of these people, she dropped the laundry she was doing.

"Sister, how are you?" Nervously, Old Woman Wei came out with a greeting.

But the other party just strode up, grabbed her, and started to pull her toward the door, saying loudly, "Let's go! We don't want to quarrel in somebody else's house."

"Hey, hold on. Let's talk things over calmly." One of the coolies stood up and attempted to play peacemaker.

"There's nothing to talk about," said the woman with the green leggings. "Even if you had cooked me like a chicken and eaten me up, there would have been at least some bones left."

"Sister! How can you be so unreasonable?" said Old Woman Wei, who was becoming a little angry herself.

"What? You have the gall to call me unreasonable? You bitch!"

A resounding slap landed on Old Wei's cheek, and soon the two women, arms flailing, were tangled in a heap. Actually, Old Woman Wei hardly retaliated. All she could do was to shield her head with her elbows. The three companions from the village made only half-hearted attempts to stop the fight. Knowing full well that it would be a thankless task, they never really got involved. The two women continued their noisy brawling until my uncle chased them out. As soon as they were out the front door, they went at each other again with blows and profanities, fishwife-style.

By then quite a crowd of idle spectators had gathered, and they followed the mini-drama with all the seriousness of connoisseurs, now and then breaking into applause to show their approval. Later, it was also the consensus of the crowd that directed the two parties to sit down and talk peace over a cup of tea. I was unable to squeeze my way into the teahouse and had to stand behind the group, but I could still hear the women arguing back and forth. It took them forever to get back to the main issue, though not for lack of trying on the part of Old Woman Wei, whose explanations were perversely interrupted again and again.

She had finally gotten round to describing the savagery of the soldiers when the woman with the green leggings launched herself at her, wailing, "Didn't you bother to tell them? You have a cunt for a mouth or something?"

"What else could I have said?" Old Woman Wei protested indignantly, her eyes bulging with the effort. "I said: 'She's not clean.' I even said: 'I'll do it with the lot of you.'"

At that point, raucous laughter erupted. I wheeled around and ran home. Uncle, who was standing at the door, asked me how the peace talk was progressing. I could only shake my head and went straight to my room. It was almost dark when the old woman returned, her collar ripped, her forehead crisscrossed with scratches. Without a single word, and ignoring all our questions, she walked toward the stove, her head bent so low that she looked like a single shadowy mass.

From that day on, her usual uninhibited swearing was seldom heard again. Now, with her eyes reddening, she would occasionally mumble.

"The longer you live, the stranger the world becomes. Even my husband never raised his fists against me. . . ."

The only thing that could bring her comfort was her grandson. Any spare time she had, she would go to see him, but she always came back, looking disconsolate. At times she was moody and silent, and at times as she trudged along the passageway that led to the kitchen, without warning she would fling out her hands in a resigned gesture and moan to herself. "Poor motherless baby!" Her grandson's condition seemed to trouble her a great deal.

Once she walked straight up to my aunt and said plaintively, "He's down to skin and bones!"

"Then why don't you get someone else to take care of him?" suggested my aunt.

"In times like this, you think it's easy? . . . With all this fighting going on?"

Not long afterwards, the young life ended. Old Woman Wei had not enjoyed a moment's peace the whole time he was ill. As soon as she finished the cooking, she would rush off. When questioned about his condition, she would usually shake her head, and her eyes would brim over with tears.

It was early one morning that her grandson died. When the news reached her, it sent her reeling. She straightened up before the stove in a state of shock, her voice trembling. "What am I going to do?"

At first, she showed no emotion and spoke as if in a trance. But immediately she was racked by sobs, and like a woman possessed, her hair dusted with ashes from the stove, she tore away to see her grandson. It was as if she thought she had the power to snatch him from death.

However, Fate was not quite finished with her. The finishing touch, in the form of a little incident, was waiting for her when she came back that afternoon.

There had always been this woman living across from my uncle—the wife of some company commander. Fat, heavy body, hair cropped short, she could be often seen sitting in the doorway with her thighs spread wide, nibbling on melon seeds as she looked out on the world. Whenever she spied Old Woman Wei passing by, she always tried to have a little fun at her expense.

There was so much malice in this woman. She instructed her young son to spread open the crotch of his pants and run around Old Woman Wei, crying, "Hey, I'll do it with you. . . ."

Usually, Old Woman Wei would simply walk by with her head lowered, fearful that any response would get her into trouble. But on this particular day, she had reached the end of her endurance.

"You low-down, no-good, short-life son of a bitch!" Sobbing and cursing, she turned around and went after the boy, who easily eluded her by scurrying up the steps. At the same time, the protective mother had already hurried over, glaring threateningly at the old woman. "Who do you think you are? How dare you curse him?"

"Every time I pass by he badmouths me. . . ."

"Badmouths you? How?"

Watching the old woman stutter and stammer, the commander's wife gave an evil smile and pressed on with her questioning. "Come on, tell me! What kind of bad things does he say about you?"

"You are all doomed to hell . . . No good will come to you! . . . Go ahead, insult me! . . ."

Old Woman Wei threw all caution to the wind and let herself go, giving vent to her anger and pain. Immediately, she felt the commander's wife grab her hair and box her ears hard, once, twice, several times . . . .

From that day on, the old serving-woman withdrew into silence. She constantly made mistakes in her work, and as soon as my aunt scolded her, she would sulk and retreat to a corner where she would sit and weep. My uncle kept threatening to fire her, but finally her son came to take her away. By this time, calm had returned to the city, since all the uniformed troops had pulled out to continue their "seek and destroy" mission in other districts.*

One rainy afternoon, we were all inside clearing up odds and ends, taking stock of what was missing, unwrapping neat packages, and removing what was needed immediately. Baskets and bundles were scattered all over the floor, and the main suite was so disorganized and messy it looked like a loading dock. Every now and then my aunt would heave a sigh, or burst out with an oath as more and more unexpected losses came to light, and the injustice of it all slowly overwhelmed her.

---

*These were extermination campaigns conducted by the Nationalists with the intention to root out the Communists.

Rummaging through a dust-covered bundle, she kept grumbling, "I bet it would have been better if the Communists had really come and communized everything."

"Why are you just standing there?" My uncle was yelling at Old Woman Wei. "Go search inside the walls again!"

Slightly taken aback by the rebuke, the poor serving-woman started for the door. With her head topped by a blue kerchief and her face covered with dust, she looked like a beggar. She had just shuffled across the threshold when once again she stopped dead in her tracks. Her son had appeared at the top of the steps in front of her. We were all taken by surprise. Immediately all noise and activities stopped.

The solid bulk of the porter drew near the door. His voice, when he spoke, was sullen.

"Come, let's go!" Without so much as a glance at anyone, he plucked off his bamboo hat.

The old woman threw her apron over her face and started sobbing.

"Don't you start in on me," she said, peevishly. "I've had about all that I can take."

"Me start in on you? What on earth for?" Wei the Elder retorted in a similar tone.

"Wei the Elder," intervened my aunt, trying to be sympathetic. "What's past is past. Nobody ever wanted it to happen. And if you don't mind my saying so, it hasn't been exactly an easy time for your mother. . . ."

Wei the Elder just gave a strange sort of chuckle.

He soon grew impatient. "People don't like to hear about unpleasant things. If you want to weep, do it in your own home. Look at me. I'm not sad at all. Go get your things, and be quick about it. . . ."

In an oppressive silence, the sobbing old woman went into the room next to the kitchen. We all felt stiff and ill at ease, as if we were in a Catholic church. Wei the Elder turned his face toward the small court-yard. The rain was still coming down softly, the sky was low and grey. All of a sudden, my uncle's face became all contorted, but it was merely a false alarm and the sneeze never came.

The serving-woman finally reappeared, a bulky bundle under her arm. Without saying good-bye, and without even a backward glance, she walked out, head bent low, closely followed by Wei the Elder. I wanted to ask whether they needed something for the rain, but I said nothing, as if I had a lump lodged in my throat. We just watched the fine drizzle come down and sighed . . . .

Two days later I left my uncle's house. When I next visited the city during the first lunar month, Old Woman Wei had been insane for quite some time. One day I ran into her on West Street. Her hair falling about her face, she had nothing on but a garishly embroidered jacket. The street was almost deserted except for the few women who had been standing at the door watching the world go by. When they saw her approach, they retreated back across the threshold, disgust written all over their faces.

Swaying and tottering, Old Woman Wei came over, carrying her trousers in one hand, and brandishing a battered bamboo pole in the other. After advancing ten paces or so, she stopped, and with a dreamy gaze, surveyed her surroundings.

Finally, tap-tapping on the cobblestones, she cried in a long drawn-out voice: "Hey! I tell you she's not cleean . . . I'll do it with youuu . . . !"

For a moment I stood stock-still. Then, burying my head low to keep myself from screaming, I fled.

Ai Wu   Rumbling in Xu Family Village

//// I

On the streets of Xu Family Village, there were no stalls, no vendors ringing little bells, no people walking with baskets dangling from their arms, looking to and fro. Only an air of desolation and fear hung over the place.

The door panels of the shops were all firmly shut. The tattered, earth-red New Year's couplets, medicine posters, and the sign with a round-faced gentleman contentedly smoking a cigarette stood out more than usual.

A dusty wind blew from the plains, brushed across the horse and camel dung on the street, at times emitting a coarse, mournful sigh.

Men hid in their homes. With arms folded across their chests, they frowned and paced back and forth. Every few moments, they fixed an eye to a crack in the door and peered out anxiously, as if trying to see through the mysterious fog that enveloped the town.

Old women clasped incense sticks in their hands, knelt before the statuette of Guanyin,* and chanted their prayers in nervous, hushed voices. In the past, they had cushioned their knees with thick reed mats; now these were the least of their concerns.

Young women rummaged through baskets, trunks, and cupboards, looking for their valuables, unaware that their foot bindings had become undone and were dragging about snakelike on the floor.

This story was written in 1931 when Ai Wu was in jail and published in 1933 in the first issue of *Wenxue* (Shanghai). Translation by Wendy Locks; the editor has made substantial changes in the translation.
     *The goddess of mercy, a popular deity.

Watching papa here and grandma there, anxious children timidly tailed them crying "mama," as if sensing that they were about to be abandoned.

The clatter of Japanese horse hooves, leather boots, and officers' swords on the cobblestones passed through the streets in waves. This symphony of sounds had not been heard in the town for thousands of years. Now each sound trampled upon the hearts and souls of the people in the houses and spattered the thick black blood inside. Fearfully the villagers held their breath and silently awaited the first knock on the door. Once they heard the knock, they would understand that death had come to visit. Yesterday, the head of the village, Master Feng San, had ordered someone to strike the gong and to announce that the Japanese were there to exterminate bandits. No one should be frightened. So everyone felt a little easier. But it was difficult for these harmless folks, who really had never seen a Japanese soldier, not to feel worried, especially after hearing many frightening tales. In the end all were swept away by a tide of fear.

The clatter of horse hooves, leather boots, and officers' swords on the cobblestones flowed like a current through the village toward the Guandi Temple.* There, in front of the temple, was hoisted a pole with a white cloth flag. A large red soup dumpling was painted smack at its center. Unfurled against the grey sky, the flag fluttered noisily in the chilling spring wind.†

Slightly across from the Guandi Temple was the Feng residence. In front, a white cloth flag emblazoned with the red soup dumpling was also hoisted, only it was smaller.

Master Feng San stood respectfully beneath the flag with a small retinue, as if they were awaiting the arrival of distinguished guests. But the nose on the broad, lumpy face was not very dignified. It was necessary for him to wipe off a handful of snivel every once in a short while.

Very soon, a short military officer followed by four soldiers on horseback trotted toward them.

As soon as the officer dismounted from his sweaty horse, he was greeted by Master Feng San, who vigorously bowed his round head covered by a brimless hat. He wiped off a handful of snivel, cleared his throat, and said: "General Yasuzaka, my good sir, you have come just in the nick of time. In one or two days, the bandits in the mountains will arrive." He wiped his nose again. "I humbly represent all the

*Guandi is the god of war and also protector of the community.
† The Japanese military started its aggression in northeast China in the early 1930's.

villagers in expressing our deepest gratitude." After he finished, he feigned another bow.

Captain Yasuzaka, donning the title of "general," handed his whip to one of his men and, as was his habit, smoothed out the thin mustache curled above his lip. He then stuck out his chest and answered curtly in proficient Chinese, "It is my unshirkable responsibility."

The Feng residence was soon filled with an atmosphere of revelry between China and Japan. Milk squeezed from the fertile Manchurian soil, aged sorghum wine, passed through the lips of those happily socializing.

II

The sound of a gong spreading peace could be heard up and down the street. Wang Laosan, the night watchman who walked about with an arched back, beat his gong vigorously and called out as loudly as he could. His wrinkled sallow face appeared both excited and anxious. Because Captain Yasuzaka had given him one yuan, Wang changed his lazy old ways of tapping the gong.

At the sound of the gong, many shops half opened their doors, and heads with startled looks peered out. Clutching the incense sticks for the gods, Old Woman Zhang hurried toward the door. Tugging at her son who had arched his body forward, she asked anxiously: "Laoer, Laoer. What is Third Brother Wang calling? . . . Eh, I'm old. I can't hear. . . ."

Without looking back, her son merely replied, "Business as usual, he says that the Japanese soldiers also give—Hey, Proprietor Liu, are you going to open your wineshop? . . . Prosperous business to you. . . ." The last phrase was for the chubby face peeking out through the half-opened door across the street.

As soon as the round-faced man heard the greeting, he squeezed his fat body through the door. Wiping his forehead (a habit whenever he was troubled), he said, "Eh, it's hard to say, well, . . . we'll see. Your cigarette shop, keeping it open? Second Brother Zhang!"

After he spoke, he turned his fat face to look left and right.

At this moment, a few people dashed across the street, as if fearing that if they did not, their backs might be pierced by bullets. Some women and children pressed their faces against the window lattice and peeked out. A few small hands stuck out through the windows. . . . All in all, traces of life finally returned to the street.

Old Woman Zhang understood what her son had said. Relieved, she happily chanted the sutra, "Amituofu!" Suddenly realizing that she was holding onto the incense sticks that should have been placed in front of the deity, she scolded herself, "Aiya, what an old fool . . . an old fool. . . ."

With the half-burned incense in her hand, she quickly turned around. A seven-year-old boy unexpectedly ran forward and smashed into the incense. In pain, he let out a startled cry.

"Fuck, what has gotten into you?" The man called Laoer jumped back, frowning as he cursed.

"Aiya . . . Puppy, where did you burn yourself? Stop crying, stop crying. . . ." Old Woman Zhang patted him with her six-fingered hand. "Eh . . . grandma's no good . . . grandma's no good . . . the Japanese soldiers are no good . . . don't cry, don't cry."

"Ma, be your aged self . . . Be careful what you are saying!" Laoer rushed back to the door, fearing that someone else might have overheard. Unexpectedly, a man wearing a black woolen uniform and a cap tilted to the side burst in right under his nose, calling loudly: "Any cigarettes? Give me two packs of Forts."

For a moment, the startled Zhang Laoer was dumbfounded. He just hiccuped, stammered, and frowned.

This customer with a local accent was known to all as the village bum. In the first half of the year, he was unable to pay his bill and was stripped of his clothes by Butcher Cai in the middle of the street. He disappeared afterward. But that aroused as little attention as when a mangy dog dies. Now, wearing clothes that shocked the common folk, he unexpectedly reappeared with arrogant airs. This definitely made people look twice.

Laoer instantly understood. He swallowed, affected a smile, and was just about to speak. But someone who came over from next door interrupted.

"Lao . . . Laomo?"

Laomo pushed his cap higher, revealing the entire scarred forehead. He made a low chuckling noise out of the corner of his contorted mouth without saying a word.

"Oh, I was just thinking . . . cigarettes? They're on me." Laoer promptly took out a pack of cigarettes.

Fatty Liu, the proprietor of the wineshop across the street, also hurried over, his stomach protruding in front. He grabbed Ma Laomo's shoulder with his pudgy hand and greeted him loudly, "Hey, Brother Ma, I heard that you were working in a Japanese company. . . ." He was then lost for words, because he had always looked down upon Ma Laomo and would never have called him "brother." He just wiped his forehead and continued in a halting voice, "That's . . . great. Oh, you, brother, you've struck it rich . . . great!" Having finished, he looked him over from head to toe. For three minutes, his eyes were glued to the pair of glossy black leather shoes. One of those who had crowded around to see the excitement grabbed Ma by the hand to look at his gold wristwatch and asked, "This must cost a lot of foreign money. Ah, you have struck it rich."

Ma Laomo took the pack of cigarettes Zhang Laoer handed to him. After a few puffs, he swept a glance at the people all around him and gave an arrogant smile, as if to say, "Look, after all, our Laomo has his day, in the past you . . . ." He then blew a ring of blue smoke into the air and spoke slowly, "No, I didn't make a fortune, nor am I rich. This is nothing!" His mouth contorted by a hideous smile, he continued in a solemn tone, "Nonetheless . . . I do get on well with a few Japanese friends."

On hearing this, the envy on people's faces glossed over with awe. But Butcher Cai, the short man standing behind Proprietor Fatty Liu, instantly sank into a mire of regret: a few months before, he should not have embarrassed the big-bellied thug over a half-catty of meat right in the middle of the street. Gasping silently, he was about to sneak away.

Just then, a hairy chin suddenly emerged over Cai's shoulder calling, "Eh, Brother Ma, the Japanese soldiers won't be reckless, will they?"

Butcher Cai could not get out of the way. He found himself directly in Ma's sweeping line of vision. Ma Laomo at that instant appeared much more forgiving than what Butcher Cai had imagined. His gaze rested on him coldly only for an instant before shifting elsewhere. Squinting his right eye, he dismissed it, saying:

"Humph, reckless? They're ten times better than Lao Zhang's soldiers!"*

Having listened attentively, everyone let out a sigh of relief. Not that they believed his words, but his comment affirmed their hopes.

Ma Laomo took a few drags on his cigarette and blew three rings of blue smoke. Squinting his right eye once again, he threw a cold sidelong glance at Butcher Cai again and then turned to the others saying, "However, Captain Yasuzaka said that in dealing with bad Chinese, don't expect him to be courteous."

Butcher Cai shivered, as if a death sentence had been declared. As

---

*"Lao Zhang," or "Old Zhang," is either Zhang Zuolin (assassinated in 1928) or his son and successor Zhang Xueliang, the warlords in control of Manchuria and the Beijing region until the Japanese invasion in 1931.

he was trying to slip away, Ma Laomo blocked his way, grabbed and shook his shoulder, and said gently, "Hey, master, I've got a good deal for you. Tonight the Japanese want to slaughter a few pigs. As you can see, I'm not looking for anyone else. I want to take care of an old friend." He let go of Cai's shoulder and blew a puff of smoke in Butcher Cai's face. He then raised his hand to reveal the shiny gold wristwatch, took a proud look at it, and announced: "Oh, I have to go to Fatty Feng San's residence for dinner." He squinted his right eye and gestured at the crowd, saying, "So long, folks." Then he straightened his back and strutted noisily in his glossy black leather shoes in the direction of the Guandi Temple.

At the Guandi Temple, soldiers walked about gaily in two's and three's, their bayonets shining behind the black helmets.

The crowd dispersed immediately, slipping behind half-closed doors. But the head with the brimless hat remained outside and stared with curious apprehension.

"Puppy, do you want to get killed? Hurry, come inside quickly." Only the hoarse voice of Old Woman Zhang rose and fell in the momentary silence on the street.

III

Six or seven Japanese soldiers, helmets tilted on their heads, laughed and joked merrily as they walked over. They stood at the head of a lane, looked down it, exchanged knowing smiles, and then disappeared into the lane, pushing and tugging one another.

Along the lane, women's pink garments, a snow-white cotton shirt, blue striped pants . . . were drying on a line. The clothes swayed gently in the cool spring wind.

The pink blossoms of some peach trees fanned out brilliantly above a dirty old limestone wall.

A flock of sparrows was pecking around for food beside the wall. At the sound of leather boots, they skimmed past the Japanese soldiers and landed noisily on the tree branches.

The night before, the soldiers had reminisced about the cherry blossoms in their hometowns. They felt a bit intoxicated by the springtime in this foreign land.

Under the eaves of a house, they caught sight of a girl of fifteen or sixteen. Looking tense, and frightened as a mouse, she was hurriedly taking the laundry off the line. The soldiers stopped, stared at her, and smiled greedily. A soldier with pustules on his face pulled a roll of paper bills out of his pocket and deliberately counted them.

"Girl, you want to die out there!" Her face all contorted, an old woman shouted as she ran to the door. As if she were yanking some-one out of the water, she pulled the girl inside the house and slammed the door shut. A pair of women's pants fell from under the girl's arm on the doorstep.

The Japanese soldiers had not expected this snub. One of them angrily spat a big wad of saliva on the ground. Stuffing the paper bills back into his pocket, the soldier with the pustules on his face lifted the abandoned pair of pants with the tip of his bayonet. Catching the angry soldier by surprise, he dropped them on his head. The sol-dier cursed and grabbed the pants, ripped them in half, and threw them on the wet ground beside the steps, which was stained by blue soap-bubbles and a few coral-colored earthworms.

Grinning, the other soldier again lifted the pants with the tip of his bayonet and hung them on a nail on the old woman's door. He shouted, "I've hung up a Chinese flag for you." Everyone broke into raucous laughter.

At the noise of the laughter, the door of another house jerked open halfway, revealing a man's frightened face. A spirited black dog shot out from between his legs and barked loudly at the foreign sol-diers, who were wild with laughter. The dog's master shouted at it distraughtly and cursed, fearing that the animal would get him in trouble.

These soldiers, who had no way of amusing themselves, lifted their boots and began kicking the barking dog as if it were a soccer ball. Startled by the attacks, the dog snarled and attempted to run away. It unfortunately ran right into the soldier with a bayonet, who gave one handy stroke. Blood and intestines spilled out as the blade was yanked from the dog's stomach. Yelping, the dog disappeared from the lane with his insides dragging and blood dripping. The dog's master was so frightened that he slammed the door shut, as if he too had been stabbed in the stomach.

The sound of boots moved away toward the main street. An assistant in the tailor's shop stuck his head out the door, spat in the direction of the soldiers' backs, and quickly withdrew. He grabbed a piece of thread off his shoulder, passed it through his mouth and said, "Humph, those dogs!"

At the blacksmith's next door, Ah Long—that heavy fellow—swung his hammer more ferociously, as if to let his anger out on the iron scrap on the anvil.

The wind from outside also seemed to howl with anger.

Seeing the bloodstains on the ground and the pants hanging on the door, people were stricken with fear, sadness, and anger. The spring on the lane a moment ago seemed to have vanished along with the foreign soldiers.

By the time the brave dog-killers turned down the main street, shops had begun to open one after another. In a good mood, they wanted to drink and so walked into Fatty Liu's wineshop.

When he saw these foreign guests entering his shop, Fatty Liu did not know what to do except to nervously wipe his forehead. Not until he saw them laughing and cajoling like innocent children did he calm down. He quickly ran to greet them, cleaned the tables and chairs himself, and tried his best to be solicitous. He called back to his helper, "Xiaoer, bring some wine quickly. Bring the good kind." He then swung around, put on a cheery face, and respectfully awaited the orders of the foreign guests.

The soldier with pustules on his face mockingly ordered in broken Chinese, "Go, cut up a plate of Chinese pig for us to eat."

The soldiers who understood Chinese broke into a loud laughter. Fatty Liu was baffled, but he continued to force a smile on his face. Another soldier who had a little mustache smacked the acne-faced one on the back and said, "Stop your nonsense!" He then turned to Fatty Liu and ordered, "Hurry and bring us good wine and meat. The more the better!"

The sumptuous Chinese food made these foreign guests eat and drink to a stupor.

When they left, the soldiers politely settled the bill. What they paid was not cash, however, but a round of bullets from a 38-caliber gun instead.

How would Fatty Liu dare to accept the bullets! Nervously wiping his forehead, he immediately understood what this all meant. Restraining his grief, he returned the bullets with both hands with a forced smile his face, saying, "Gentlemen, if you don't have any money, don't worry about it. I would not dare to take the bullets." If he had said, "Gentlemen, I am honored by your coming; please accept my humble offer of the wine and meat," he could have avoided any grief. However, he lacked the necessary eloquence and intelligence to pull it off. Not only did he lose money, but he was insulted as well. The soldier with a small mustache scolded him with a stern red face, "How dare you! We, the soldiers of the imperial house of the Great Japanese Empire, are not freeloaders."

As he spoke, a few soldiers staggered across the street to the Zhang family shop to buy some cigarettes.

The soldier with the small mustache finally took the bullets from the pleading Fatty Liu as if he were doing him a favor. Then he strode out of the shop. At this moment, Zhang Laoer in the shop across the street re-enacted a similar farce.

As soon as the Japanese soldiers were out of sight, Fatty Liu and Zhang Laoer threw a glance at each other from afar without uttering a word. Abruptly they slammed their doors shut.

The news of these incidents traveled faster than the wind. Instantly, the shopkeepers hurried to close their doors tightly. The banging noises followed one another like exploding firecrackers. The street, which had just come alive, was again reduced to a desolate wilderness.

A dusty wind coming off the plains moaned and wailed as it blew over the horse and camel dung.

IV

The desolation in Xu Family Village lasted well into the afternoon —an overcast spring afternoon. A gray mist hung over the peaks of distant mountains. A south wind wailed and howled over the plains and through the forests. A sorrow never known in ages shrouded the village. Fear ripped the hearts of the villagers, shedding thick dark blood.

Because Captain Yasuzaka and Master Feng San wanted to revive commercial activities, the households of Fatty Liu and Zhang Laoer were driven out into the desolate street. The doors of the two shops were each sealed shut by a notice with a vermillion seal:

The unauthorized closing of this shop has impaired the public order of this town. It is hereby sealed as a warning to all.
> Headquarters of the 11th Detachment of the Northeast Army
> of Great Japan stationed in Xu Family Village.

Clutching an old hen, Old Woman Zhang grabbed Ma Laomo, who had posted the notice. "Laomo, Laomo, please don't . . . don't bring us harm . . . remember, I nursed you when you were a child . . . Laomo, Laomo, in the name of your mother . . . oh, my entire family!" She cried hoarsely, twisting her wrinkled mouth. Ma Laomo pulled his arm away and yelled, "What do you think you are doing? Tugging at me."

But his heart softened when the old woman reminded him of his mother, who had died of consumption and in poverty. He sighed and pointed to a row of foreign soldiers in the middle of the street leaning on their rifles and said, "What can I do? It's their . . . ."

Ma suddenly looked as if he had remembered something important. He quickly raised his wrist and looked at his shiny gold watch.

He pushed aside the old woman who was nagging him and said impatiently: "Don't waste my time."

Fatty Liu handed the baby he had been holding to his wife—a woman who sat on a large bundle at the side of the street crying uncontrollably. Wiping his forehead, Liu rushed up to Ma Laomo, grabbed his hand, and pleaded, "Brother Ma, Master Ma . . . I beg you to be kind . . . have pity on me." He raised his chubby hand and pointed, "Please look!" Ma Laomo threw a sidelong glance in that direction and saw three chubby-faced children sitting fearfully beside a sobbing woman holding a baby. He chuckled out of the corner of his mouth and snorted as if to say, "Your family eats pretty well!"

"Please don't board up the shop, even if it means paying." Fatty Liu did not let go of Ma Laomo's hand.

Only at the mention of money did Ma Laomo stop. Squinting his right eye, he asked in a low voice, "How much?" Then feigning sincerity he said, "We're old friends. I, Ma Laomo, wouldn't think of not helping you out." But what he was thinking to himself was, "Today you come and beg from me. Why didn't you ever let me have a cup of wine on credit in the past? Fuck."

"You set the price. I'll pay." Sensing that he might have a little room to maneuver, Liu finally raised his hand to wipe his forehead. This time, there was real sweat.

The Japanese soldiers marched away. Without raising his arm, Ma Laomo stuck out three fingers, looked out of the corner of his eye and said, "This much."

Fatty Liu stammered, "Thirty yuan? . . . I'll borrow it right away."

Ma Laomo snorted and sneered. Squinting his right eye, he stared at Fatty Liu and said, "You think you can get off so cheaply?" He paused for a second and then said seriously, "You must understand, the Japanese are in control!"

More sweat appeared on Fatty Liu's brow, but he did not wipe it. He asked nervously, "Eh, eh . . . how much do you want after all?"

"Three hundred yuan!" Ma said curtly. "It may still not be enough. Perhaps General Yasuzaka will want 400 or 500 yuan—" He drew the last syllable out especially long.

Zhang Laoer had rushed up beside the two men and was about to plead for something. But as soon as he heard what Ma Laomo said, he was dumbfounded. Ma Laomo knew exactly what he was going to ask. After glancing over Zhang's general store and his mother, wife, and child, who were huddling together and crying, he said gently, "For you, 100 yuan will be just fine." Seeing that the two men did not continue their pleading, he gestured to the crowd and noisily followed after the Japanese soldiers in his glossy black leather shoes.

"If one doesn't burn incense every day, what's the use of hugging the Buddha's feet when in need?" Old Woman Zhang started crying loudly.

Zhang Laoer crossed his brows and cursed angrily, "So a villain gets the upper hand, and . . . . Proprietor Liu, what shall we do?"

Fatty Liu was silent. He sat dejectedly on the street, his head in his hands, motionless. Only his fat cheeks twitched uncontrollably.

The children in the two families suddenly burst into a loud wail.

Carrying their possessions like refugees, the two households finally walked down a lane to the homes of relatives for the night, crying as if they were in a funeral procession. Fatty Liu's family went to stay at the blacksmith shop with the big sign "Zhou Hongxing," and Zhang Laoer's family went to Li Jiachang's tailor shop, which had no sign.

The shops were finally reopened. Round-faced Master Feng San hobbled along with the mustachioed Captain Yasuzaka to take a look around the town. They exchanged knowing smiles. All was in order in Xu Family Village.

After the inspection, the gong began to signal another announcement. Hunching his back, Wang Laosan shouted excitedly, "On the orders of Master Feng San, the village will reward the Japanese soldiers with food and drink this evening. Those who have chickens send chickens, those who have ducks send ducks, and those who have pigs send pigs. . . ."

When the women heard the news, they pressed their hands to their bosoms and grieved, "My heavens! . . . My heavens! . . ."

The men leaped back into their houses and swore loudly, "Fuck your ancestors for eight generations! . . . Reward!"

V

In a spring night in North China, a deep chill filled the air.

Occasionally the helmets of a few foreign soldiers flashed under the dim lights on the main street. The deserted side streets were immersed in a silent darkness. Although a few weak rays escaped through the cracks in the doors, they appeared all the more wretched.

There were no moon and no stars. The boundless sky was raven black, reflecting immeasurable sorrow.

Heavy footsteps were heard coming down the lane. Two assistants in Li's tailor shop put down their needles and thread and tiptoed to the door. They opened it a crack and slipped out to take a look. Gradually they made out the form of a man in the darkness. He was not wearing a military uniform. They could already tell that he was not wearing leather boots. They gathered up their courage to ask, "Who is it?"

"Fuck your mother." The shadow swore loudly.

Catching this not altogether unfamiliar roar, several doors swung open. People and light streamed out, and the man's angry face became more visible. It turned out to be Butcher Cai.

People eagerly asked: "Did you make a fortune? . . ."

"I was just saying, 'We're all down on our luck. There's only one person doing well.' "

". . . ."

Butcher Cai did not respond. Everyone figured out that things were not the way they had expected. So someone said, "At least you must have eaten your fill. . . . You slaughtered for a whole afternoon."

"Fuck! Who had the appetite," Butcher Cai again exploded. "My stomach was bursting with anger!"

At first everyone had been jealous of his good fortune. But now they began to pity him. Several rushed to ask what had angered him. But he was speechless. It appeared that the sympathetic questions finally caused his pent-up feelings of the afternoon to explode. He gave the cobblestones a violent swack with the iron rod he used to kill pigs and roared: "Fuck Ma Laomo's mother! Fuck his ancestors for eight generations!" Then, fuming, Butcher Cai rushed into his house.

His distraught state nonetheless amused the crowd a bit.

Proprietor Zhou of the blacksmith shop stroked the short whiskers on his pointed chin and said with a sigh to Fatty Liu, who stood there dazed, "Cousin, it looks like he didn't benefit at all. Ay, only Fatty Feng San and Ma Laomo would."

"Those sons of bitches, they're more despicable than the Japanese." Fatty Liu cursed and then wiped his forehead as if it would relieve his own suffering a bit.

"Humph. Drag them here and cut them up into pieces with a pair of scissors. . . ." An assistant of the tailor interjected excitedly.

"No, put them on the anvil, and hammer them into pulp." The assistant at the blacksmith's shop insisted loudly.

An assistant named Ah Long joined in, "That's not tough enough! I say . . . I say. Take the red-hot iron poker from the furnace and brand their naked bodies all over."

Old Woman Zhang, who was leaning against the door and listening attentively, burst out childishly: "Let everyone take a bite out of them!"

"Ha, ha, ha," Proprietor Zhou began to laugh, the short whiskers on his pointed chin shaking. "Old mama, are you going to break your vow [not to eat meat]? Ha, ha, ha. Without teeth, how are you going to take a bite?"

The crowd joined in the mirth. It sounded like a mountain waterfall crashing on pebbles. For a moment, the desolate lane regained the liveliness of spring.

Suddenly the clatter of leather boots could be heard at the head of the lane. Startled, everyone snuck away to their houses. The laughter ceased as abruptly as the snapping of a *huqin** string. Doors shut quickly one after another. All the lights were extinguished in an instant.

The marching noise of some dozen leather boots broke through the silent darkness on the lane. There were also noises of people staggering and stumbling.

All the peaceful citizens on the lane held their breath and listened. Their pounding hearts were strung together by a long thread of fear.

Everyone heard the footsteps stop in front of the old washerwoman's house. Then several boots kicked on the door.

Bang! The door was kicked down. Everyone shivered.

"Help! Help! Hel—" the old washerwoman cried out in a raspy voice.

"Ma! Ma . . . ma—" Her crying daughter let out a shrill, trembling scream.

The cries of the two women suddenly stopped. It was as if struggling chickens had had their necks wrung.

The women sank to the ground hysterically and cried, "Bodhisattva, bodhisattva!"

Men shook with rage. "Ai, the bastards, the bastards!"

Children clung tightly to the adults, too frightened to cry.

VI

One minute passed . . . Two minutes passed . . . Half an hour. . . .

The door of another house, no two, three houses, was being pounded . . . pounded . . . pounded . . . .

Ah, the sounds of fists pounding on doors echoed through the lonely chills of a spring night.

Ay, again there were the pleading cries of women that were suddenly broken off.

---

*A musical instrument with a small soundbox and a long neck, usually with two strings. The bow passes between the strings.

Ah, horror . . . horror . . . horror.

A thought suddenly struck Proprietor Zhou of the blacksmith shop. He jumped up calling, "Laojiu, Ah Long, quickly add two bars across the door . . . Right, that's fine . . . ." Turning around, he shouted, "Xiaoqi's mother, you and Cousin Liu must hide."

While they secured the door with more bars, Ah Long and Laojiu angrily yelled, "Heck . . . if we only had guns, if we only had guns . . . ."

The two women were scared stiff. Holding a baby each in their arms, they asked each other, "My heavens, where shall we hide?"

Fatty Liu wiped his forehead as he searched for a place to hide.

Thump, thump, thump . . . Someone suddenly kicked the back door. Everyone froze with panic.

"Quickly, under the bed, quickly . . . quickly . . . ." Proprietor Zhou's voice trembled, as he pushed his wife under the bed. The wife of Fatty Liu followed.

"Waa . . ." The child hit his head under the bed and started to cry.

"Ah, sweety, don't cry, don't cry!"

"Damn. Don't make a noise." Proprietor Zhou nervously scolded. He could no longer care if she was a cousin or not. "Pinch the baby's mouth shut."

Then it went silent under the bed.

Thump, thump, thump . . . Someone was kicking the back door more fiercely, and then lunged at it with his entire body.

"Curse his mother! Who cares about this fucking life!" The three fellows, Laojiu, Ah Long, and Fusheng, rushed over. Two held knives and one a club.

"Oh no! Oh no! You'll ruin me! I can't afford this!"

Proprietor Zhou ran madly to block their way. Fatty Liu, his belly shaking, tried to hold them back.

The back door suddenly fell in. A short, sturdy man tumbled inside. He shouted repeatedly, "Save me, save . . . save . . ." He was choking with words.

When they pulled him off the floor, it was that poor bastard Butcher Cai! They caught their breath and examined him closely. His shoulder was bleeding profusely. His collar was dotted with bright red spots.

"What happened?"

"Who tried to kill you?"

"Who did it? Who did it?"

Butcher Cai did not seem to notice his wounds nor hear what they were saying. He just yelled, "My wife, my . . . give me a . . ." He caught sight of Fusheng's knife, grabbed it, and rushed out. The three assistants of the blacksmith, each holding a weapon, dashed into the darkness after him.

Proprietor Zhou ran to the door and shouted nervously, "You've gone mad . . . you'll get into trouble . . . you . . ."

"Don't . . . quickly . . . hey!" Not knowing what he was saying, Fatty Liu hurriedly picked up the door panel.

Proprietor Zhou turned around abruptly and slumped into a chair. His face was ashen, his muscles twitched and his mustache quivered. He muttered, "I'm finished . . . finished . . ."

Liu placed the door panel on the ground and with his belly shaking, ran with difficulty to Zhou's aid. At the same time, he called under the bed, "Cousin Zhou, Cousin Zhou, come out quickly! (Everyone was panting.) Look! Look!"

The two women, who were nearly frightened to death, crawled out from under the bed, covered with cobwebs and dust. When Cousin Zhou saw the state her husband was in, she was mad with worry. "Goddess Guanyin, the most efficacious Goddess Guanyin. Have pity on us . . . ." She then started to wail.

Proprietor Liu's wife took a look at the baby in her lap: his lips pinched black and blue; he was gasping and his eyes were rolling. Trembling with panic, she grabbed Fatty Liu and cried, "Baby's daddy, baby's daddy . . . look, Oh, baby, baby." She held the child's face close and sobbed.

Fatty Liu was so nervous that he wiped his forehead uncontrollably, as if by wiping he could produce a trick for the emergency.

No one had thought to close the back door. The light that shone through attracted a handful of Japanese soldiers, who stumbled in. The room was instantly filled with the strong stench of alcohol.

VII

A drunken Japanese soldier was leaning beside the door of Butcher Cai's house. Looking up, he hummed the tune he used to sing under the cherry tree in his hometown. The pistol that protected him was hanging loosely in his hand.

Butcher Cai eyed his target, clenched his knife firmly, charged forward, and plunged the knife into the soldier's stomach. The man sank to the ground without a struggle as if he were made of rubber. Butcher Cai quickly pulled out his knife, and instantly finished him off with another skillful cut to the throat.

When he rushed into the house, he saw his son Ah Yang crawling on the floor and crying hysterically. Ah Yang's mother, who should have been holding, kissing, and consoling him, was struggling with a short man in uniform who had pressed her onto the bed. Clenching his teeth and clutching the knife with both hands, Cai mustered all his strength and plunged the knife through the man's back. Using the weight of his entire body, he pressed down on the knife, trying to push the entire handle into the body. The man howled with pain, struggled, and became motionless.

Feeling that the man was dead, Butcher Cai straightened his back in order to pull the body off his wife. But it seemed stuck. He looked closely. Ahh, his wife's stomach was pierced through by the knife driven into the bed. Warm blood from the two bodies was gushing onto the bed and dripping from the bed to the floor.

His wife's mouth was still tightly bound by a white handkerchief. Blood and froth trickled down her cheek. When he saw her, Butcher Cai felt sick. His arms went limp. Paralyzed, he sank on the bed and began to sob.

"Daddy, daddy . . . hold . . ." Ah Yang had stopped crying. He stretched out both hands and called pitifully. But when he saw that his father kept sobbing and did not comfort him as he always had, he was confused.

At this moment, Laojiu, Fusheng, and Ah Long made their way into the room. Butcher Cai jumped up instinctively. He thought they were Japanese soldiers, but as soon as he saw who they were, he sat down once again and wept. The three men were struck dumb by the sight of the bloody scene. Finally, Ah Long rubbed his hands and came up with an idea. "Brother Cai. She's dead. Crying won't bring her back. The Japanese soldiers won't leave you alone. Leave quickly."

"I don't want to live! I don't want to live!" Butcher Cai shouted, steaming with anger. He appeared to be bursting with energy. He jumped to his feet and pulled out the knife that was stuck in the two bodies. He gritted his teeth and said, "I'll fight to the bitter end," and started to rush out of the house.

Ah Long dropped his knife and grabbed him. "You want to die, on your own?"

"Don't you want your Ah Yang? Hey, call for your daddy, call." Laojiu picked up the child and held him in front of his father. The child was still crying, but stretched out both hands to his father. Cai looked at his child, then looked at his wife lying in a pool of blood. Tears welled up in his eyes. He dropped the bloody knife on the ground, instinctively picked up his child, and sat down on the white wooden bed. Two warm streams of tears trickled down his cheeks.

Ah Long rubbed his hands together again and pricked up his ears. The door pounding and the cries for help had disappeared. Yet near and far the hysterical crying of babies could be heard. Ah Long said to Fusheng, "We shouldn't stay here. First let's hide the bodies of the short devils.* Let me see. Yeah, under the bed."

He helped Laojiu and Fusheng drag in the body of the Japanese soldier who had fallen right outside the door. They were about to hide the two bodies under the bed when Ah Long stopped and said, "Wait a minute. Aren't we foolish!" He then removed the pistols and bullets from the two bodies. As if to scold himself and the two others, he said, "What a fool not to take the treasures right in front of your eyes!"

"You're not afraid? Where can we hide them? The Japanese will . . . ." Laojiu took the revolver and dropped it on the floor, his eyes wide open with horror.

"Haven't you been a blacksmith long enough?" Ah Long barked as he picked up the gun.

"Buddy!" Laojiu was startled when he heard Ah Long's question. "You want to give up our trade?"

"You think you can survive in these times?" Ah Long pointed with his revolver to Cai's wife lying in the pool of blood. "Brother, it has all become clear to me tonight. Look at her. . . . Now is not the time to be well-behaved."

Laojiu suddenly felt despair. "Where can we go? Then . . . ."

"It doesn't matter. Anywhere without Japanese soldiers," Fusheng responded. He had already agreed with Ah Long's idea, but only now revealed his feelings.

"There is a place. There is a place. I'll tell you." Ah Long handed Fusheng a gun and placed the other securely in his belt. He thought a moment, rubbed his hands, and said, "Over there in the mountains." His voice was extremely low. "I'll tell you when we get on the road. Hey, Brother Cai!" He raised his voice again. "Don't be upset. Hurry, pack a few things together and come with us."

Stirred by these words, Butcher Cai also felt that escape was the only way out. But he was in a difficult bind because he did not know what to do with his child. Should he escape with him? Inconvenient. Should he leave him behind? He wasn't that cruel. He could not leave his child, just as he could not leave his wife, who had died so tragically. He looked wretchedly at Ah Long and said, "But my child." But before he finished his sentence, he heard the short devils calling for their companions. The voices and the sound of leather boots were approaching the door.

*A derogatory term used by many Chinese to refer to the Japanese.

Everyone jumped up with a start. Ah Long immediately grabbed his revolver and loaded it. He ordered Fusheng, "Quickly." Laojiu hesitated for a moment and then made up his mind. He spit into his palms twice and again took hold of his knife—a knife he had hammered out with his own hands in Zhou's blacksmith shop.

Butcher Cai became resolute. He plopped the child on the bed where the mother was lying, leaped forward, and picked up his knife from the floor. The knife was still dripping with the blood of his wife and enemy. He ran to the door, gritted his teeth, and muttered, "I'll fight to the bitter end." It was as if he were reciting some charms in order to conjure up the necessary strength.

The face and body of the abandoned child were immediately smeared with warm, thick blood. He struggled to get close to his mother, stretching out his bloodied hands and crying, "Mama, mama . . . Yangyang . . . hold."

Blood pumped quickly through the veins of the four men.

The air was so tense it was about to explode.

The sound of leather boots drew closer every second.

Finally a drunken short devil rushed into the room. Butcher Cai kicked him. The drunk staggered a few steps and tumbled over. Butcher Cai leaped forward and whacked him. With one stroke of the knife, the helmet-covered head was severed from the body in black uniform.

"Splendid! What a pig slaughterer!" Ah Long could not refrain from shouting his praises. He sighed in relief.

Another Japanese came rushing through the door. But as soon as he saw the blood and the corpses, he turned around and dashed out. Ah Long would never want to miss this chance. As swift as the wind, he chased after him and shot the man in the back. The soldier fell to the ground in the darkness.

The Japanese soldiers, deeply intoxicated on this spring night in a foreign land, were startled by the gunshots. They hurriedly buttoned up their uniforms as they rushed out of the houses.

Facing the light, the four armed fellows pounced upon the dark outlines of the fleeing soldiers.

The dim streets, steps, and corners soon became the battleground for the oppressors and the resisters.

The families of those who had been abused angrily rushed out to look for the half-dead short devils. They either clubbed them on the head or added a few stabs in the small of the back with their kitchen knives.

Two assistants from the tailoring shop each carried red-hot irons and pressed them onto the soldiers' back.

"Fuck, you burned me." A person who was bending over in the dark jumped up and shouted.

"It's one of ours, one of ours. Let go, you devils." Those nearby could hear that the men wrestling in the dark were cursing in Chinese. They pulled them apart.

. . . .

In the end, all sixteen short devils were killed in the dark. Ah Long rubbed his hands as he supervised the distribution of the sixteen guns and rounds of ammunition, all fitted to the belts of good men—tailor's assistants, bricklayers, handcart pushers, and horsemen.

Ah Long had suddenly assumed the status of elder brother. He spoke decisively and solemnly. "Brothers, let's go to the other side of the mountain. It'll be too dangerous by daybreak. Let's be off!"

"No!" Everyone shouted. The families of the abused shouted most fiercely: "We want revenge!"

"We'll fight to our death against the Japanese soldiers!"

"Yes. Fight to the bitter end!" Butcher Cai shouted angrily, grinding his teeth. He looked for corpses of Japanese soldiers, which he hacked wantonly.

"Are you out of your mind? . . . There are so few of us. Let's leave with Brother Ah Long." Laojiu spoke with a sharp voice, warning the excited crowd.

"No. We would rather die here."

"We'll shoot anyone who wants to escape!" Butcher Cai scolded and gnashed his teeth.

"Right!"

Ah Long rubbed his hands and abruptly pulled out his gun. He shouted, "All right! Let's go and round up more supporters. We'll exterminate the patrol and collect a few more guns. Everyone, please listen to me . . ."

At this moment, a Japanese patrol, which had heard the gunshots, marched over. Their leather boots could be heard entering the lane.

"Brothers. Get ready! The short devils are coming." Ah Long shouted and retreated to the steps where he stood loading the gun.

Suddenly someone shouted in the darkness. "A large troop is coming." Half the crowd holding cleavers and wooden clubs panicked and ran helter-skelter into their houses.

"Cowards. Those with guns, load them and lie low." A Long swore. The sound of boots suddenly drew nearer.

"Fire!"

Ping, ping, ping. More than a dozen guns went off.

The five members of the patrol entered the line of fire and slumped into the darkness.

The shooting stopped. Someone shouted, "They're dead! We've killed them all."

Those holding clubs and knives again stormed out of their houses and eagerly finished off the dying soldiers.

VIII

Landmines in the Manchurian plains exploded.

Xu Family Village was rumbling.

Everywhere the angry roar of the oppressed was surging.

The Guandi Temple and the Feng residence were ablaze.

Bright red tongues shot up into the sky, as if to engulf the boundless darkness.

Part II   The Force of Dogma

Introduction

////   About the time the cosmopolitan and independent-minded writers had been cowed by party discipline in Yan'an, a new generation of writers emerged on the literary landscape. In many ways, their careers were closely linked with party ideology and organization. This section begins with "The Widow Tian and Her Pumpkins" ("Tian guafu kangua"), written by Zhao Shuli in 1949. Born to a poor peasant family in Shanxi in 1906, Zhao acquired a taste for folk art and music early in life. At the age of 19, he managed to attend a teacher-training school. He was jailed once for his participation in leftist politics and, after his release, taught in village schools for many years. In 1937, he joined the resistance and the Communist party, and carried out rural propaganda work in the Taihang District. Zhao was known for portraying the conditions of life under socialism in a "folk" style colored by a strong local flavor and an intimacy with rural daily life. In 1943, his short story "Blackie Gets Married" ("Xiao-er-hei jiehun") attracted the attention of literary critics in Yan'an. He then published the novels *The Rhymes of Li Youcai* (*Li Youcai banhua*) and *Changes in Li Village* (*Lijiazhuang de bianqian*). Mao praised his work as politically correct and accessible to peasants. His stories became model pieces for a sinicized revolutionary literature, and his style was made popular by fellow Shanxi writers.[1] After the revolution, he spent time in rural areas to observe the collectivization campaigns. In the end, he was purged as a "traitor" during the Cultural Revolution and died in 1970.

Kang Zhuo (pen name of Mao Jichang) was born in 1920 in Hunan and attended school in Changsha. The war cut short his senior middle school education. Like many others, he went to Yan'an in 1938 to join the Communist party. After graduating from the literature department of the Lu Xun Art Institute (Lu Xun Yishu Xueyuan), he spent many years in rural propaganda work. After the revolution, he held the post of deputy chair of the Artists League in Hebei and Hunan. His writings continued to focus on rural transformation. In the 1950's, Kang expressed sympathy for those peasants ambivalent about a revolution conducted in their name. In his writings, he tried to expose the "dark side of life" that continued to exist in the new society. He opposed totally politicizing the characters in his stories and instead advocated "middle characters" (*zhongjian renwu*), a tactic that allowed for distance from and doubt about the government programs. *Dripping Water Wears away the Rock* (*Shuidi shichuan*), published in 1957, centers around the rape of a widow by a village cadre. It is a biting critique of the corruption and the growing power of cadres. "The First Step" ("Diyi bu"), written in 1953 when the collectivization of agriculture began, conveys a positive and hopeful view of the future of socialism, though the ambivalence of the protagonists is very noticeable.[2] Kang was persecuted during the Cultural Revolution and rehabilitated in the late 1970's.

Fang Zhi (pen name of Han Jianguo) was born in Hunan in 1930 but spent most of his early years in Nanjing. His family moved back to rural Hunan during the war. When he returned to middle school in Nanjing after the war, he became an underground member of the Chinese Communist Party. He was nineteen years old when the Communists took power. Instead of entering a university as his unit recommended, he plunged into the land reform and the collectivization campaigns. Despite his youthful enthusiasm for the revolution, he came to realize the complexities on the ground. In 1955 and 1956, he and many others opposed the prescribed political formula for literature. He joined Gao Xiaosheng and Lu Wenfu in organizing a literary association, the Tanqiuzhe. Its goal was to examine life in its complexities, free from dogma. As a result, he was denounced during the Anti-rightist Campaign. Although his subsequent writing bore the mark of an "invisible political shackle," he found ways to express what the peasants felt.[3] "Taking Charge" ("Chu shan") was one of the first stories he wrote after the disastrous effects of the rural communization movement forced the party to relax its political grip. The story had the explicit intent of picking up the pieces, but it allowed readers to ponder over the source of the trouble.[4] Fang Zhi was silenced during the Cultural Revolution. He died shortly after his rehabilitation, taking with him his dreams of revitalizing a critical literature.

Hao Ran (pen name of Liang Jinguang) was born in 1932 in a mining town in Hebei. His father died when Hao was eight. Hao and his mother then stayed with her brother in rural Hebei. He had three and a half years of education and joined the Communist party at the age of sixteen. For many years, he participated in youth and rural organizational work. He started publishing in the mid-1950's and became a member of the Chinese Writers Association in 1959. In 1961, he was an editor of the party journal *Red Flag* (*Hongqi*). He rose to prominence during the decade of the Cultural Revolution. *The Bright Sunny Sky* (*Yanyang tian*; 1964) and *The Bright Golden Way* (*Jinguang dadao*; 1972) were held up as "models" of worker-peasant-soldier literature. In these works, even the most intimate sentiments are defined in terms of the class struggle and the correct revolutionary line. Their socialist heroes, determined and uncontaminated, always win in the end. There is little ambivalence. "Firm and Impartial" ("Tiemian wusi") was published in 1971 in this ideological environment.[5] Such writing was devalued if not entirely rejected in the liberalized political climate of the mid- to late 1980's, but Hao's voluminous works have colored the taste of a younger generation.

In the large pool of post-revolutionary literature, the four pieces presented here represent the efforts of a new generation of writers with a tremendous faith in the party. The majority of them were condemned in the end by a political machine that had assumed a monopoly of ideological control. They were charged with not toeing the party line closely enough. The four pieces indicate crucial turning points in this process of losing ground.

The authors differ in background and in political conviction from those included in the previous part. Whereas the urbane, Westernized intellectuals of Mao Dun's generation fought Maoist orthodoxy and attempted to maintain independent voices, these four writers represent those who accepted and thrived on Maoist principles. Their exposure to Western thought and literature was limited because by the time they matured as writers, the revolution had turned narrowly nationalistic. Under Mao Zedong the party had also gained ideological dominance. As members of propaganda work teams, they spent years in the base area around Yan'an and later in the countryside as it was undergoing collectivization. During that period, their concern with the peasants changed from exposing the dark side of the Republican era to reflecting on the positive effects of the socialist programs. By the early 1950's, these writers arrived on the literary scene with official blessings. Their works have formed the bulk of the post-revolutionary literature on peasants and socialism.

Their political enthusiasm was real. Despite excesses in the land reform and in policy debates, the mood of the country in the 1950's was one of faith and confidence. Ironically, the dilemma for these committed socialists arose directly from their rural work.[6] The party expected them to expose the backward cultural values and the private economic interests of the peasants. Instead, participation in the land reform and the collectivization campaigns made them see the adverse consequences of even the most well-meaning policies. They were troubled by the mistakes of a growing party bureaucracy and by the arbitrary power of party cadres. The mission they assumed was to chastise the party for its excesses. Yet just as the peasants were confined to collectives dictated by rural cadres, the writers found their choice of subject matter increasingly circumscribed. The ambivalence of their peasant protagonists reflected their own. The question of how to maintain faith in socialism and in the party without turning a blind eye to the peasants' misgivings became a major though subdued issue in literary debates. It was difficult to be society's conscience. In the Anti-rightist Campaign of 1957, when they and a host of others were condemned, it was all too clear that the political apparatus to which they had devoted themselves had ruled out a loyal opposition.[7] As the party became embroiled in severe factional struggles in the 1960's and 1970's, the opportunities for writers to voice their conscience contracted. Most became unwilling accomplices in a "proletarian" literature that ignored the peasants' plight, denied human complexities, and condemned ambivalence. The characters in the literature of this period embodied political dogma.

Literary images of the peasant have changed over the thirty years of socialist transformation. When Zhao Shuli wrote "The Widow Tian and Her Pumpkins," he had little doubt that the Communist party would bring peace and prosperity. Widow Tian takes the trouble to mark all her pumpkins until she realizes that even the village vagabond, whom she suspected of theft, has enough food of his own after the land reform. Kang Zhuo's stubborn peasant in "The First Step" is an honest man, but he needs a devastating drought to be convinced of the worth of the collectives. When the story was written, the image of local cadres was still positive. It was no longer so when Kang was writing in the mid-1950's, determined to expose the harsh realities in the rural areas. *Dripping Water Wears away the Rock* is a devastating indictment of the corruption of cadres. By the time Fang Zhi wrote "Taking Charge" in 1962, it was clear that the Anti-rightist Campaign had left its mark. He was cautious in the choice of subject matter. In the end, the reluctant village cadre emerges from his doubts to take on the task of rebuilding. But the first sentence of the story contains a not-too-subtle condemnation of the communization movement: "Although

Lesser Wang Village is small, it is known far and near and for one reason only: poverty." Hao Ran exerted himself during the Cultural Revolution to create peasant characters that lived up to Maoist political principles. In the 1971 "Firm and Impartial," neither the writer nor the peasant was allowed his own voice.

The four stories reflect the predicaments of this generation of committed party writers. Unlike the older authors, who upbraided power-holders from the stance of an independent moral authority, they accepted a political power that claimed to represent moral authority. Little could they foresee that they would be persecuted for challenging its excesses. In the end, it was not left to them to judge whether the system was acceptable to them or to the peasants. The party-state defined what was possible. Nevertheless, they held on to the intellectual tradition and continued a losing dialogue with the powerful political order they felt they were part of.

Zhao Shuli

////

The Widow Tian and Her Pumpkins

South Slope Village was full of poor people. Pumpkins and peapods disappeared from the fields, and the hiring of cropwatchers didn't solve the problem; everybody still had to look out for his or her own. One called Qiusheng* was the worst offender, for he had a wife and five children to feed but no land of his own. In fact they got by almost entirely on wild greens, stealing just a few pumpkins and peapods as opportunity allowed. Widow Tian feared crop theft the most, for the pumpkins and peapods on her land came out early. South Slope Village had but thirty or forty families, and of them only Mr. Wang and Widow Tian were landowners. Mr. Wang had ten *mu* or so, but he was imposing. No one dared steal from him. Widow Tian had only half a *mu*, yet since no one bothered Mr. Wang, all the bad luck fell on her. Every year, then, during the summer and autumn harvest seasons, she went down to her field to watch over it.

In the spring of 1946, South Slope Village underwent land reform. Mr. Wang was classified as a landlord; his ten *mu* of land were divided up and given to the poor. Widow Tian was a middle peasant, so she got to keep her half-*mu*.† That summer the vines on her land bore

---

This story was first published on May 14, 1949, in *Dazhong ribao*. Translation by Jeffrey C. Kinkley.

*Qiusheng (autumn born) is possibly a pun on *qiusheng* (to struggle for survival). The richness of the language allows writers to work in such details.

† In the 1940's, the Communists conducted some land reform and organized mutual aid teams and cooperatives in the areas they controlled. Before a village's land was redivided, villagers were classified into broad categories of landlords, rich peasants, middle peasants, poor peasants, and landless laborers. Land and resources classified as "exploitative income" (i.e., resources used to exploit the labor of others) were taken from the landlords and rich peasants and divided among the poor peasants and landless laborers. Middle peasants were left relatively undisturbed.

fruit particularly early again, so Widow Tian went down to her field as before to guard them. The children in the village told her, "You don't need to guard them this year. Now everybody has his own." She didn't believe them. Having never been out to any fields but her own, she didn't have a clue about Mr. Wang's former holdings.

No wonder she was skeptical. She knew what she'd been through. For the past several years, Qiusheng and his flock had seemed to be deliberately teasing her—something would be missing from her field the minute she left it. Once, after she'd gone home for a bowl of rice, she caught Qiusheng advancing toward her field just as she returned. "Sister," he begged piteously, "Spare me a tiny pumpkin! My children are starving." In a bad mood, Widow Tian retorted, "What makes you think any are left? A thief has stolen them all!" Knowing that she meant him, Qiusheng couldn't very well answer back. He just kept on pleading. Widow Tian didn't want to send him off mad because she was afraid he'd steal from her again. She looked over her ripe pumpkins. There wasn't a one she could bear to let go. After an interminable search, she finally picked for him one that was the size of her fist. "What a shame," she said, "it was still growing." Then she sent him packing. Just then Mr. Wang happened to be strolling by, fanning himself. Pointing at Qiusheng's backside far off in the distance, he said, "It's terrible, isn't it! Such people this village has produced —you can't ever rest easy about them, not till you're in your grave." He kept on going without a hitch in his stride. He'd expressed exactly what was troubling her: she wouldn't forget those words for the rest of her life. So when the children told her, "You don't need to guard them this year," she refused to believe it. But facts were facts, whether she believed them or not. One day she got a heatstroke and stayed home for three days without losing a single thing. She said she'd go back to her field when she was well, but there were lots of things to do. A few more days passed without her guarding them, and her vegetables were still there. Ten days passed, still without any losses. Finally she marked the pumpkins she was saving for seed by cutting little crosses into them, having decided not to watch over them any more.

When the autumn harvest was nearly over, she went over to Qiusheng's courtyard and saw a dozen or so pumpkins stored there, two of which had crosses cut into them just like hers. She was suspicious and had a mind to ask him about it. But she was afraid to raise a ruckus without proof, so off she went to her field to check. She ran straight there, without even stopping at home on the way. Halfway there she ran into Qiusheng himself, driving an oxcart loaded with pumpkins. "Qiusheng!" she asked, "Whose pumpkins are those? Where did you get so many?" "They're mine," he said. "I overplanted!" "Why did you plant so many?" "In the old days, my kids drooled at every pumpkin they saw, so this year, when I was allotted my own half-*mu*, I planted the whole field with them. Who would have thought these bulky old things would grow until they got out of hand, till there was no way on earth of eating them all? How much better it'd have been if I'd planted grain." "Can't you sell what you don't eat?" "Sell them? Who has any need of them this year? Where can I go with them? There are still more in the field! If you want some, ask the kids to tote a load over to you, just like when I ate yours in the old days!" So speaking, he drove the oxcart forward. Widow Tian had no heart to go inspect her pumpkins.

Kang Zhuo

The First Step

//// I

After the Dragon Boat Festival* every year, the village gradually became a mountain of green. From a distance, neither the village nor even the plumes of smoke from mealtime fires could be seen. Wave upon wave of crops thronged together like undulating plains; phalanx upon phalanx of green trees circled the village like an unbroken mountain range. In such a fertile region, rejoicing at a rich harvest was almost a certainty. No one even considered the possibility of flood, drought, or pest.

That was how the harvests had always been. Only this year there was no mountain of green, even six and a half months into the lunar calendar. The trees could not screen the village, and every morning the villagers could be seen craning their necks as they looked up at the sky. Some of the crops were doing reasonably enough. In some places there was corn half a man's height, with rich green leaves, but elsewhere it was no more than a couple of feet high, and sparse as rabbit whiskers.

The heavens seemed to have forgotten how to rain. The sun shone relentlessly from an unchanging blue sky. Such clouds as had appeared had been chased away by scorching gusts of wind, and any paltry drops of rain there had been had evaporated before they reached the ground. The village wells were almost dry. Drinking water would soon be in critically short supply, and water for the fields would be out of the

---

This story was written in June 1953 and published in *Renmin wenxue* in August 1953. Translation by Richard King.

*The fifth day of the fifth lunar month.

question. Even old-timers in their seventies and eighties had seldom seen such a drought.

Fortunately the villagers had constructed an irrigation system the previous winter. Just after the formation of an agricultural cooperative, co-op members had joined forces with some mutual aid teams and peasants who were farming on their own, borrowed money from the government, and developed the system.* Water was directed from holding tanks along ditches into a channel, and sandbanks were faced with concrete so that water was saved that would otherwise have seeped away. The winter's snow and ice had been hoarded like treasure. Now the channel had become their lifeline. When people saw its water flowing into their fields, they felt as if they were themselves drinking nectar.

But even in the channel, the water level was dropping. It was now so low that it would take several days to water all the fields of the shareholders even once. The earth was parched and gasping just when the first crop of corn and millet was ready to go into ear, and everyone wanted to water his own fields first. That wasn't possible, and the old system of rotation wasn't working any more. As a result, the villagers argued with each other from morning till night over the allocation of water.

Late one evening they met on the threshing ground at the edge of the village. Party Branch Secretary and Co-op Chairman Xu Mancun took charge of the meeting.† He had been trying to devise a new water-sharing system with the other cadres and party members and had discussed the issue with many of the shareholders. Since his new system wasn't fully worked out, he spoke only briefly, then hobbled away and leaned by a tree so that everyone else could have a chance to speak.

First came co-op member Liu Tiegen: "I'm not speaking on behalf of the co-op," he said, "but we co-op members did the most work when

---

*Soon after the land reform, the government had rural cadres mobilize villagers to organize mutual aid teams and agricultural producers' cooperatives. Mutual aid team members exchanged labor and tools to work on one another's land. The members of cooperatives supposedly pooled their land and other resources, and the government promised various credits and aid. The organizing of these cooperative forms varied in pace, and enrollment was rather voluntary. By 1956, many villagers continued to be independent households (*dan'gan hu*). It was not until 1957 that almost all villagers were made to join collectives.

† After the land reform, the Communist party recruited peasant activists to staff local government at the levels of district and township or large village. Villages had a party branch with a secretary, often a salaried post. The political leadership of a village consisted of the party secretary and the cadres in charge of the cooperatives and militia, most of them party members.

the channel was being constructed, and we never demanded equal effort from everyone else. That's like it was in the old days when we were fighting the war, in the vanguard of the attack, in the rearguard of the retreat!"

Liu Tiegen was the young cadre who commanded the village militia. Five or six years earlier he had gone south with the Red Army for a few months in the war against Chiang Kai-shek and been in two battles. This had become his "capital," and every time he opened his mouth, he always got something in about "the old days."

He went on at some length, then suddenly scowled and gestured with his arm: "I don't mind if the co-op's land gets watered a bit later. But there's one condition—our high-yield land can't be left until last. That has to be watered first!"

Perhaps his words were ill-advised. Certainly they silenced the assembly for quite a while. Then, just as Xu Mancun was getting ready to speak, he heard a blurted question: "Our mutual aid team has high-yield land as well, do we have priority too?"

Someone else joined in: "I'm farming on my own, and I don't have any high-yield land. I do have a share in the channel, though I didn't do much of the work. I guess you'll just use the water however you see fit! But I tell you this, Tiegen—it won't do you people in the co-op any good if you just look after your high-yield land. Do you think you're going to get a thousand *jin* of maize from every *mu*? Fat chance!"

"Who said we were going to do that?" Tiegen was quick to anger when challenged. His neck thickened, the veins pulsating. "Who said we were only going to water the high-yield land?" he shouted.

Other people joined in, yelling at Tiegen: "Who's arguing about your high-yield land? We're trying to decide how to share out the water!" "You're always going on about doing the most work! We've got a right to the water too!" "If you want to argue about your high-yield land, do it with the other people in the co-op!"

Tempers flared as the meeting disintegrated into a shouting match. Someone jumped up and called out: "Hey, what's going on? Is this a free-for-all or a meeting?" Hardly anyone seemed to notice. Xu Mancun stumped into the melee: "Okay, okay, let's talk about sharing the water. There's no need to go on about the high-yield land, or work out who did the most work, all right . . . ?"

His words didn't have much effect. No sooner had he got someone settled down and moved away than that person would be back on his feet. Tempers were getting hotter and disputes more acrimonious. Nobody could make out what anyone else was saying, or even remember what they were fighting about. Xu Mancun couldn't control the ruckus, so he thrust himself into the huddle where the shouting was loudest to find out what was going on.

Someone else was observing the melee from the roof of a house nearby. He lay on a mat spread on the roof, his eyes to the heavens and his ears on the meeting. Once in a while he would turn and watch the proceedings through the sparse leaves.

This was Liu Laishun, a peasant farming on his own who had no share in the irrigation channel. He wasn't the only villager in this position, but his case was an unusual one. He had been in a mutual aid team, but had come to the opinion that collective farming wasn't much use. He didn't go to village meetings and kept to himself. Still, he kept a stealthy watch on other people's affairs. Seeing the meeting erupt as it had made him a little nervous, but more than that he felt happy. He murmured to himself: "Huh! I might have known! The channel water will all be dried up before they get their act together!"

He couldn't make out all the voices at the meeting, but he had a sense of how things were going. When he heard people arguing with Tiegen about high-yield land, he felt like cheering. What possible connection did high-yield land have with sharing the water? What idiocy! Look at you, Liu Tiegen, hanging on to your high-yield land for dear life when the air is parched and the land is cracking! Look at you, co-op members, all depending for survival on your high-yield land! Fuck the lot of you! Liu Tiegen, you deliberately decided to call the field next to my best plot your high-yield land—now let's see if you can get a thousand *jin* of corn from each *mu*!

Murmuring to himself, he rehearsed his arguments with Liu Tiegen. When he had calmed down, he looked back to the meeting and saw Xu Mancun yelling at everybody. The meeting was still in an uproar, so Laishun couldn't hear exactly what was being said. But he had words in his mind for Mancun: "Stir it up, Brother! You're going to make things worse whatever you say!"

Laishun and Mancun were old friends and old partners. They had worked for the same landlord before the war against Japan, and slept on the same *kang*. Even now, Laishun still felt sorry for Mancun when he was in trouble. But the two men had gone different ways. Mancun had joined the Eighth Route Army* early in the war, and returned, hobbling on a crippled leg, to become a cadre. Now he didn't seem to care about his home or making a living for himself, and he didn't even take time off at New Year's or festival days. It wasn't that he'd neglected to come round for a drink and a chat with Laishun every once in a

---

*The wartime Communist army.

while. It was just that when they talked, the two men weren't as close as they had once been. Mancun was always trying to get Laishun to take a lead in work, or to be more progressive politically, which didn't interest Laishun much. For his part, Laishun would urge Mancun to show more concern for his family and livelihood, and this didn't please Mancun particularly. By the time they were halfway through their drinks, someone would invariably come round looking for Mancun, who would then have to wipe his mouth and leave.

Suddenly Mancun's voice made itself heard again. Laishun glanced up to find that everyone at the meeting had settled down. Mancun was leaning against a tree and holding forth in his best parade-ground voice: "The question which Tiegen raised about high-yield land is one the co-op will have to resolve for itself. If, as Tiegen says, the co-op members did more work, they did it of their own free will, and this has no bearing on the allocation of the water. What we have to concentrate on is how to share it out. Let's listen to the people who've been working on developing a new system!"

Other voices took over in a leisurely way, some too soft for Laishun to hear. Strain his ears as he might, he could pick up only a sentence here and there, something about watering in rotation, something else about nobody losing out, but he couldn't hear the details. Later the meeting became more animated, with factions arguing with each other, but this seemed more like group discussions than a fight. Presently more speeches were made, but again there was nothing Laishun could hear clearly. Then Tiegen was on his feet again! Every shouted word reverberated to the roof: "I was wrong just now . . . let's forget about what I said . . . I'm sorry . . . anyhow, compared with those years. . . ."

Hearing this, Laishun realized that Tiegen had been criticized by Mancun. That Tiegen, he'll pick a quarrel with anyone, but he can't stand up to Mancun! It's bizarre. . . .

The meeting drew to a close, and people started to go their separate ways. But for some reason, they didn't go home. Instead, they brought out tables and set oil lamps on them. Villagers who could write and do arithmetic sat down at the tables, with the others clustered around them, though it wasn't clear what they were doing. Laishun lay on his mat, sometimes watching, sometimes gazing up at the sky. Late as it was, the assembly didn't break up. For reasons he couldn't understand, Laishun started to feel nervous. The contentment he had felt when the meeting was in uproar now ebbed away. An awful thought nagged at him—what if they really do come up with a good way to share out the water? His own land was suffering desperately from the drought, and if there were no more rain, he'd be facing disaster. Was it possible that he might not surpass the co-op and the mutual aid teams, and might even fall behind those individual farmers who had shares in the channel?

From the house below him came the sound of braying. Laishun's black mule had finished its feed bag and wanted more. "Blast the animal," cursed Laishun silently. "All it wants to do is eat! eat! I'm damned if I'll feed you!" Still, he heaved himself to his feet and prepared to go down. He hadn't worked out if the meeting had come to any kind of consensus, but anyway his wife had given birth not long before and wasn't too well, so he had to go down and check things out. He rolled up his mat and felt his way down the ladder.

After he fed the mule, he went inside. The room was in darkness except for a glint of silver from the harmonica he had given his son, Bingxiao. The boy was asleep by the window; beside him on the *kang* lay the baby girl and her mother. From their even breathing he knew they were sleeping soundly. Laishun himself felt stifled by a heat in his soul that he couldn't dispel. Maybe he should go back and sleep on the roof . . . after all it was cooler there . . . and then perhaps he might also see how the meeting turned out!

"Still up, Dad?" He heard his son's soft question. Startled, he responded: "Uh? You're still awake?" "I just woke up." After a little while, Bingxiao asked again: "Dad, is that a co-op meeting outside? I heard them quarreling for ages." "It's nothing to do with you!" retorted Laishun. "Go back to sleep!" Bingxiao rolled over. "Dad, I . . . I . . . aren't there any clouds in the sky? I was just thinking . . . our land. . . ." His arm brushed the windowsill and knocked down the harmonica. Laishun picked it up. "Don't worry! Our well's not dry yet! And even if there's no more rain, can land die of drought?"

His wife rolled over and sighed drowsily. Laishun didn't want to disturb them all, so he lay down on the *kang* without another word. But he couldn't silence the voices in his heart. His mind heaved and tossed, a sea of nagging doubts.

II

Liu Laishun was of poor peasant stock, an honest man and a good farmer. In ten years of Communist control he had managed, by dint of hard work, to build up a smallholding of five *mu*. Then during the land reform he had been allocated four *mu* of prime land that he had previously rented from the landlord for many years. He had also been given the well that stood beside it. He had joined the village's leading mutual aid team, which was headed by Xu Mancun and also had Liu Tiegen as a member. In two years he was able to provide himself with tools, fix up his house, and replace his donkey with a mule. Then, two winters ago, after a good harvest, he had pulled out of the team. He bought a waterwheel and some furniture, and the harmonica for Bingxiao. As soon as Bingxiao graduated from primary school, Laishun had insisted that he stay home to work. With a wife who was a good worker as well, his became one of the most prosperous families in the village. They had food and drink and everything else they needed. When there was nothing else to do, he could amuse himself listening to his son playing the harmonica. It could never be said that he'd lagged behind in community spirit—he'd been unstinting in his support for public works and the war in Korea—but on one question his mind was made up. Despite all the propaganda about the socialist society of the future, and numerous discussions with Mancun, he was determined that he would have no part of collectivization. He reasoned: "I should be able to harvest three or four thousand *jin* of grain from those four *mu* of prime land alone! What use do I have for your mutual aid team? You may have lots of manpower, but so what? They're a mixed bunch, and anyway I've got all the workers I need. Why should I hand over my good land and my mule? I'll see about joining in due course." When the villagers were digging the channel, Mancun had come along to enlist his support, but he would have none of it. He had no need for an irrigation channel, he just wanted to be left alone to go his own way.

At the previous year's autumn harvest when the movement to form cooperatives came to the village, he'd been pressured by Mancun to attend the enrollment meeting. Lots of people registered in the co-op there and then, including almost all the members of his former team. Someone came right out and asked him if he intended to put his name down too. Almost before the question was out, Tiegen butted in and answered for him: "I can tell you what Uncle Laishun's going to say." (Tiegen and Laishun were distant relatives.) "Some people haven't joined because they want to see how it works first. But Uncle Laishun doesn't need to see! His answer is a hard-and-fast no! Am I right, Uncle Laishun?"

Mancun immediately criticized Tiegen: "Cut that out! Membership is entirely voluntary. What right have you to speak for anyone else?"

At that, all the other cadres started grumbling about Tiegen. But Laishun stood up at the back of the meeting, face uplifted, his domed forehead thrust forward, and shouted: "There's no need to get mad at Tiegen, he's right! That's exactly how I feel!" With that, he pushed his way out of the crowd.

Mancun had some harsh words for Tiegen after the meeting. Tiegen was prepared to admit he'd spoken rashly, but he certainly hadn't given up on the idea of Laishun's joining the co-op. He and some of the other youngsters who had joined the co-op had looked forward to using Laishun's prime land as a high-yield plot for the co-op and to having Laishun's waterwheel and mule at everyone's disposal. He'd said what he had at the meeting as a ruse to try and force Laishun's hand. The next day he was on Mancun again to go round to Laishun's house and persuade him to join.

Mancun was none too keen on Tiegen's scheme, but he couldn't resist his youthful enthusiasm. "I might just as well have another try at educating him," he thought. So he agreed.

He and Tiegen had no sooner got to Laishun's courtyard when they bumped into someone else. Mancun warned Tiegen not to do anything foolish, then wandered off for a chat with the other visitor, saying he'd be along later. Tiegen went in on his own.

Laishun was cleaning up his tools in the yard. When he saw Tiegen, he put down what he was doing, squatted on the ground and said: "You wouldn't come here for no reason. Say what you have to!"

Tiegen restrained himself for a moment, then grinned: "Uncle Laishun, what I said last night was just a bit of a joke. Actually I know you appreciate the advantages of a co-op, right?"

"Sure," said Laishun, "if Chairman Mao points the way, how could I not believe him?"

Tiegen hurried straight to the point: "In that case, why won't you join?"

"Aha!" Impatiently, Laishun sat himself down on a bench, thinking: "This again! I really ought to teach this jerk a lesson!" But he forced a smile and said: "Tiegen, you're not asking the right question!"

"How's that?"

"Sure I'd like to join the co-op and work with you all. Ha, ha!"

Astounded, Tiegen blurted out: "You want to come in with us? Well, that's not all there is to it, Uncle Laishun. You mustn't think you can just take it easy! We have to get organized, everyone has to exploit his full potential, and push ahead with production, that's the only way we can have a better life. Have you heard of the Soviet collective farms and their tractors? In those days, when I was in the campaigns down south, I remember our officers saying . . . ."

"Of course!" Laishun looked up with a grin. "Tiegen," he said, "there's a point I'd like to make. You talk a lot about potential. Well, to my mind, the potential for production depends on the people doing the work. Don't you agree? If all the co-op members were as advanced and as hardworking as Mancun, of course I'd join up without a second thought."

Tiegen's face showed his disappointment; at the same time, his neck bulged involuntarily. "Huh," he sneered, "if that's how you feel, you'll never join in a hundred years!"

Laishun just laughed: "Well, you're the one that said it!"

Laishun's son, Bingxiao, came running in. Laishun pulled the harmonica out of his pocket and said to him: "How can you be so careless, tossing this in the straw? Come on . . . ." The boy took the harmonica, hung his head, and stood silently to one side.

Mancun hobbled in, found himself a rush mat and sat in the sun. After a while he limped over to Bingxiao, took his harmonica, and blew into it. "What's new?" he asked.

Laishun laughed: "Tiegen came around to try and talk me into joining the co-op. Tiegen, why don't you go through it again for Mancun's benefit? I'm really serious about wanting to join. I think I'd be willing to put in all of my land except for those four *mu* of prime land. Just one other condition—neither I nor my mule will work for the co-op. Is that okay?"

Bingxiao jumped up and down. "Great! I'll work for the co-op!"

Ignoring his son, Laishun smiled at Tiegen. This was not what Tiegen had been hoping to hear, though he couldn't quite work out exactly what was wrong with it. So he glanced across at Mancun, who just laughed heartily and said to Laishun: "That's not such a bad idea! You want the co-op to provide you with farm workers. You want to exploit the co-op's labor force. Is that what you're after?"

"You got it!" said Laishun, and laughed.

Tiegen and Bingxiao's hopes were dashed. Bingxiao looked dejectedly at Tiegen. Tiegen's neck tightened with anger. Laishun's wife saw how things were and came bustling out of the house. "Mancun, Tiegen," she said, "he talked to me about it as well, and he never said he wouldn't join." Then, in an attempt to calm the atmosphere, she tried a different tack: "It's just that we don't have much manpower in the family, really only Bingxiao's dad! Bingxiao's worth half a worker at most, always going on about taking exams and going to middle school. As for me, I'm not much use, with the baby! The mule eats more in a day than all of us put together. We'd be a burden on you! Mancun, you want people joining the co-op who can provide manpower, so we're no good to you at all!"

Bingxiao ran over to his mother and whispered: "Ma, do you . . . does that mean I can go to middle school?"

Laishun scowled, but before he could get a word in, Tiegen hurried up to her and launched into an explanation—they wouldn't be a burden on the co-op, they weren't so weak on manpower really, they'd be certain not to lose out if they joined . . . .

Mancun limped over and listened in. Laishun just squatted down, head bowed, and said nothing.

Tiegen went earnestly through his explanations; Laishun's wife answered, "Hm, hm," glancing furtively at her husband. After a while, Laishun glowered at her to stop the conversation. When Tiegen saw this, his voice rose angrily. Laishun got up abruptly, faced Tiegen, and said: "Forget it! Don't waste your breath!" Tiegen stuck out his thick neck and snarled: "What the hell are you playing at?" Both men's faces were flushed. Laishun's wife backed away in alarm. Mancun chuckled and pushed the two men apart. Laishun pushed back, his forehead almost bumping into Mancun's nose, protesting vehemently: "Mancun, it's just . . . I . . . what's so wrong if I want to have it a bit easier? I've suffered all my life, and I've only now got land and livestock to call my own. Those four *mu* of prime land have given me good yields the last couple of years, but I've poured more sweat and blood into them over twenty years than I've had grain back in the last two! And the mule—I've only used it a bit, I'm hardly even used to feeding it, to walking along beside it; my wife hasn't ridden on it, and I've never taken it to market, how can I . . . ."

"No one's going to force you to join!" said Mancun hastily. "Don't worry, Brother Laishun! Tiegen's an excitable fellow, he wants to achieve socialism right away, you know that, don't you? Let's forget it for now. Tiegen, off you go now!"

"I'm not saying Tiegen's wrong, I just didn't . . . I . . . ." Laishun's face was blood red, and his eyes were getting red too. Tiegen's neck was bulging even more. As he was leaving, he said: "Uncle Laishun, I was wrong again today, I was stupid to say what I did. Go your own way, farm on your own! I just hope you don't turn into a rich-peasant capitalist, that's all!"

"Don't talk crap!" Incensed, Laishun strode up to Tiegen and yelled: "What have I got to do with rich peasants? How am I going to turn into a rich peasant? Bah!"

Mancun bundled Tiegen out of the courtyard and hauled Laishun back in, urging him to cool off. Laishun's wife gave Mancun a light for his pipe, while Laishun himself bent over the water vat and gulped down some of its bone-chilling water. When peace was restored, Mancun admitted, in a voice suited to a formal self-criticism: "Brother Laishun, it's my fault for bringing Tiegen here today. Still," he continued after a pause, "some of what Tiegen said makes sense. If you keep on working on your own and you don't become a poor peasant again, it'll be hard for you to avoid becoming a rich peasant. . . ."

"Don't you worry about that!" interrupted Laishun.

"It's not a question of whether I'm worried or not! It's up to you. . . ."

"I promise you! Brother, I . . . as long as I live, I'll work with you for socialism!"

"Okay then, let's see how it goes!"

Yet again, their discussions came to no real conclusion. It was by no means the first time the two of them had talked about this matter, and every time it had ended like this. Mancun dropped the subject and tried something else. He again urged Laishun to join in the work on the irrigation system.

Laishun wasn't going to have anything to do with that either. He said: "Building the channel is all well and good. But there's something I have to tell you, Brother!" He edged up to Mancun. "Tiegen just said that collectivization was something to do with tapping the potential for production. Potential, he said! If you ask me, our potential is all people! Isn't that so?" He leaned in toward Mancun, his domed forehead almost striking Mancun on the nose. Mancun hastily agreed: "Absolutely! Yes, sure!"

"I'm right? Well, Brother, it's not that I don't trust you, or that I don't believe in what you're trying to do, but you have to realize that not all of these people are up to scratch! The more you collectivize, the more trouble you're letting yourself in for. Tiegen said there were people who wanted to take it easy. Am I taking it easy? I work all day and never dare to take a rest, I'm lucky if I eat decently ten times in a month, I . . . Just look around, there's plenty of people taking it easy, slacking off, looking for a free ride. You can see it right in your co-op. Me, join up? No chance!"

"I don't think you're quite right there, Brother Laishun," said Mancun. "Sure there are people in the co-op who aren't very progressive, but if we get organized and have the Communist party to lead us, surely they can gradually reform themselves? Just think, hasn't everyone made progress over the last ten years?"

"Okay, so there's been progress! I was just saying . . . oh damn!"

Laishun couldn't find the words to express himself, but he wasn't going to give up his opinions either, so he strode back and forth muttering "damn." Mancun saw it was getting late, so he said: "Let's talk again some other time," and hobbled out. Laishun didn't hold him back.

But when Mancun reached the gate, Bingxiao was blocking his way. "Uncle Mancun, put in a word for me about taking the middle school entrance exams."

"I have, and I will again when I get the chance," Mancun agreed as he hurried off to work.

But after this he was busier than ever, and didn't get back to Laishun's house for quite a while.

Laishun didn't seek Mancun out either. He had even less than usual to do with anyone else and concentrated all his efforts on his farming. He seemed driven by some inner force that made him compete with the rest of the world.

He was mainly competing with the co-op, of course. Every problem the co-op had had in the past half-year had seemed like a victory for himself and had sent him rushing home to report it to his wife. When those problems were solved, he went into a sulk, his frustration making him work even harder.

That spring, motivated by Tiegen, the co-op had designated the plot right next to his four *mu* of prime land a high-yield plot; they manured and tended it assiduously, and they bragged that they would get at least a thousand *jin* of corn from each *mu*. Clearly they were out to challenge Laishun. Furious, and becoming increasingly at odds with the co-op, Laishun worked all the more intensely on his own land.

He was growing wheat, corn, and millet on those four *mu*. The co-op was growing only corn. By the wheat harvest, there was little to choose between the two. But with a month of drought after the harvest, the balance started to shift. Laishun had been planning to plant beans in the wheat stubble, but he couldn't get them into the rock-hard ground. Worse still, it was obvious that his millet and corn wouldn't be a match for the co-op's yield. Laishun was distraught. Then he heard the squabbling over the sharing out of the channel water. First he had been anxious, worried that they would argue so much that the water would be wasted, but this anxiety had been displaced by a hope that he couldn't really articulate, but which meant that he would have been quite content if the arguments got even fiercer. . . .

III

There was no way of knowing if the dispute over sharing the water had been resolved. The morning after the meeting, Liu Laishun and his son sneaked out to their land at the crack of dawn to avoid their neighbors.

First they went to check on the few *mu* of dry land in the ravine. It was a lost cause. The savage sun had baked great cracks into the soil, which gaped like thirsty mouths. Then he went to his four *mu* of prime land. This too was doing poorly. He hitched his mule to the waterwheel, but the well was dry before he'd drawn enough to water even one *mu*. He did manage to plant a few beans in the wheat stubble, but the millet and corn could not be watered. He slumped down by the well, too depressed even to look at his son.

A work song echoed from the co-op's high-yield land beside him. Tiegen was singing as he watered the crops. Did this mean that their differences over the sharing of water had been resolved and that a system had been agreed on? The channel flowed by the high-yield land, was diverted round the edge of Laishun's land, and flowed off to the south. Looking southwards along the watercourse, Laishun could just make out people watering their land. More anxious than ever, he looked away to the northwest . . . and there the co-op's flourishing millet crop assailed his eyes like a bolt of lightning. He wanted to look away, but he didn't seem able to avert his eyes. Helpless, he stared transfixed at the rich growth.

Bingxiao called out to him: "Is that it, Dad? Let's go home." He didn't hear. Bingxiao called to him again: "Dad, let's go home! We were up early, and Ma's not well!" He shook himself out of his reverie and, still avoiding the other villagers, drove the mule back home. . . .

When they got in, his wife was moaning and the baby was crying. There was nothing left in the house for him to make her a decent meal—the hens had died of neglect, and the oil jar was empty. Laishun measured out a peck of grain, went to the store, and traded it for some eggs, vermicelli, oil, and soy sauce. Back at the house he busied himself cooking. The water vat was empty too, so he had to shoulder his carrying pole and fetch water.

The drought was affecting the family's supply of drinking water. Even when he let his buckets down on three lengths of rope, he could only half fill them with muddy water. While he was carrying the water back, he met the co-op field workers on their way home. Tiegen strode by, his shovel over his shoulder, looked at the bucket, and asked: "Uncle Laishun, why waste your energy drawing well water? Why don't you just get some from the storage tank by the channel?"

Laishun didn't answer. Distracted by his pent-up anger, he tripped as he went through his gate and spilled some of the water. Behind him, Tiegen stuck out his tongue and made a wry face. Mancun happened to be passing. He chuckled: "Hey, Brother Laishun, what are you doing pouring away water?"

Laishun still didn't answer. Mancun stepped into the courtyard and went on, "Look, you only drew half a load in the first place, and now there's only half a bucket left. You've wasted half your water!"

Laishun said, "Brother, everyone knows how easy-going you are. How can you be so petty about a little bit of water?"

"Things are different now!"

Mancun went indoors to take a look around. When he came out, he suggested Laishun should call the village midwife in to check on his wife. Laishun said that he hadn't called her in for the delivery and didn't see much point in calling her now. Mancun also told Laishun to draw his drinking water from the storage tank by the channel in the future. That water was for public use, he said, and those without a share in the channel could also use it. Laishun made no response.

Mancun saw that Laishun was stubbornly determined to be independent, but he kept cool. "How are your fields doing?" he asked. "I've been so busy lately I haven't been over."

"Nothing out of the ordinary," Laishun replied. "There's still water in the well." Then he asked Mancun: "You as busy as ever, Brother? Still working on how to share out the channel water?"

"We've worked it out," Mancun replied. "Proposals were made and discussed, and we've agreed on which of the plots owned by the co-op, the teams, and the smallholders most need water and which can be done later. Now we can do them all in turn. We talked last night almost till cockcrow, and today we're getting started."

Laishun felt a twinge of alarm, as if he had suffered a personal defeat, but he said, "That's great. How come you're still so busy?"

Mancun said, "We've made the decisions all right, but there are still lots of things that might go wrong! There may well be people who agreed that their land could be watered later, but they won't be happy when it actually happens. They'll complain that it's not fair, that they're being cheated, and so on. And then there are the co-op members too—they all agreed to share income based on the labor and land they invested, didn't they? But if you suggest the land they brought in to the co-op should be watered last, do you think they'll agree to it? It's not that they think they'll get less when the grain's shared out, it's just that they hate to see their own land parched. People get tense when there's a drought like this."

"You're right there." Laishun frowned. "But why do you have to be responsible for everything? Didn't I talk to you about this before?"

"You're wrong about that! If I'm the one in charge, I have to feel responsible, don't I?"

"You're in charge of too much! Why should you run the party branch and be co-op chairman as well?"

"Would I stop feeling responsible if I weren't chairman? I'm a party member!"

Laishun had no response. Mancun paced up and down in the courtyard, and then said, "What state is your land really in? Are you in trouble?"

"Why do you keep on about me being in trouble?" asked Laishun. "Isn't everyone in the same position in a year like this?"

"Not really," Mancun replied. "Even in a bad year like this, there are some that are better off than you are. Like us in the co-op. We organized and dug the channel, so we have more ways of coping than you have."

"So you're doing a bit better! Okay. . . ." Laishun still seemed unconvinced, though he couldn't seem to find the words to justify his opinions. Mancun pressed on: "It's obvious we're better off, isn't it? Just take our high-yield corn. I admit it was partly to needle you that we decided to have our high-yield plot right next to your prime land. Still." Steadying himself against Laishun, he squatted down. "Think about it—the soil of our high-yield land simply isn't as good as the soil in that plot of yours, but the crops . . . even if there hadn't been a drought, we'd have done as well as you, if not better! Do you believe me?"

"Huh!" said Laishun. "Let's see what happens next year!"

"You don't believe me? Okay, we'll see sure enough!"

Mancun still had a lot to say, but he knew that at times like this it was better if he didn't talk too much. He'd be better occupied finding practical ways to help people. So he brought the conversation to an end: "I've got things to do, Brother Laishun. If you have any problems with your land, just come and see me!"

Mancun left without getting any response from Laishun.

Bingxiao was there again as he got to the gate: "Uncle Mancun, you've got to talk Dad into letting me take the entrance exams!"

"What? Okay, don't worry."

Mancun hurried off to work. Bingxiao went back inside the house. The midwife came round, examined Laishun's wife, and advised him to go to the district clinic to fetch the doctor. Laishun said he didn't have time. The midwife offered to go herself, but Laishun just said he'd think about it. The midwife told him in no uncertain terms what she thought of that and stamped out.

Inside the house, his wife was still groaning, and the baby was still crying. Laishun called out: "Soup's on! I'll serve up!" He bustled over to the stove, picked up the pot, and set about the unaccustomed task of cooking dinner.

IV

Days passed without rain. Water from the irrigation channel had saved some of the crops, but even that water was on the verge of running dry. Mancun decided to make an inspection along the channel. With a group of cadres in tow, he started at the source of the channel. By mid-morning they had reached the high-yield land, just as Liu Tiegen was watering it.

The other cadres stood beside the plot. Mancun squatted down, picked up a fistful of the soil and sniffed it, then pressed his hand into the earth that was being watered to see how deep the moisture was penetrating. He stood up and ventured the opinion that the water was being used wastefully.

"Wastefully?" Tiegen was annoyed. "This is high-yield land! We're being a lot more sparing than we were in those days with our bullets!"

"This wouldn't have been considered wasteful in past years," said one of the cadres.

"That's true enough," Mancun agreed. "Tiegen, don't keep on about it being high-yield land. We have to be economical even on high-yield land." Nudging Tiegen's arm, he continued: "And you don't need to go on about those days either. You were given thirty bullets when you joined the militia. When I was fighting the Japanese, we'd only get five bullets to last us a year or more, and one of them would be a dud. You have to consider the actual situation, Tiegen!"

Tiegen still wasn't persuaded. "If that's how you feel," he said, "we might just as well hide the water away and not use it! Then maybe we could get the co-op members to piss on the land! I can't think of anything much more economical than that!"

Still, Tiegen picked up his hoe and adjusted the break he had made in the channel dike to reduce the flow; then he joined in the cadres' discussion on additional ways to save water.

Not far to the southeast, an enraged Liu Laishun was out hoeing. In normal years the soil in this, the best plot in the village, would be black and glossy, rich and moist, springy as yeasted dough, rich as a slab of fat pork. Everyone said that all you needed to do to grow corn in this soil was to scatter seeds and sleep till autumn; that alone would get you four or five hundred *jin* from every *mu*. In years gone by, Laishun had managed six hundred, and in the past two years he'd exceeded seven hundred. This was a patch of land that deserved its nickname of Old Bountiful.

But now, it seemed, a change had come over the land; it was bountiful no longer. Planting the beans had been a waste—not a single one had come up. The millet shoots grew few and far between, like wisps of hair on a scabby head, like a man dying of plague. The stalks were withered, bare as chopsticks, with never a leaf to be seen. The corn was a little better, but it wasn't yet in ear, and without water it too would wither. In the blistering sun, the anguished crops gasped for air, their breath baking hot. It was so hot that the men at work in the fields felt dizzy, their feet burning if they stood still.

The mule couldn't draw enough in a day from the well by the plot to water even half a *mu*. By the time the whole plot had been done, the soil watered first would be parched again. More alarming still was that the supply of water was diminishing day by day, so that soon there'd be none left to draw. The well was already dry for today. Even his great strong mule had collapsed in the shade of the tree to the north of the well and was blinking blearily at its master in a plea for deliverance. Laishun felt more like rushing over and giving the brute a thrashing —it did no work, then it just lay under the tree and blinked at him! To hell with it! . . . But he was too exhausted to lift his head, how could he raise the energy for a show of rage? As he looked at his crops, Laishun felt that his own life would last no more than a few days, that his eyes, dried of tears, would weep blood. Then he remembered the old-timers saying that "hoeing again brings on the rain," so he summoned up all his strength and commanded Bingxiao to hoe with him as hard as he could.

But where was the rain? Steam rose from the ground as the hoes fell. When the hoes got within a couple of inches of the millet, the shoots would quiver at the impact as though they were on the verge of collapse. Before two rows were done, Laishun hurled down his hoe.

Bingxiao was only too pleased to follow suit. He put down his hoe and walked over to the shade of the tree by the well, patted the mule, and settled down to take a rest. Laishun came into the shade as well, pursing his lips as he looked up at the sky.

It was still the same blue sky, with its motionless sun. Laishun thought of another of the old-timers' sayings: "Red sky at morning, a clear day is dawning; red sky at night, rainfall's in sight." The eastern sky had been edged with red cloud every morning—maybe today those red clouds of morning would make their way westwards! There was still time! He twisted his head round. But there was not a trace of cloud in the west. To the west lay the co-op's crops, and he had no desire to look at them.

"Bingxiao, if you've read so many books, did any of them say anything about why it rains?"

"Sure they did." The boy recited: "It rains when hot air rises and encounters cold air."

"We've got hot air rising all over the place! Why don't we have any rain?"

The boy was helpless before his father's scorn. Laishun sneered: "And you think you should go to middle school? Could you make the rain fall if you did?"

Bingxiao rose abruptly to his feet and went back to work with a frown. Laishun, realizing how futile his sarcasm had been, went heavy-heartedly with him.

As they were hoeing, Laishun overheard Mancun talking to Tiegen. They weren't far away, just the other side of the co-op's plot. The crops were dense and unbroken, so that the speakers could not be seen. Still their voices were perfectly clear. Bingxiao cocked his head to listen, but when he saw Laishun glowering at him he returned frowning to his hoe, hating his father.

What was being said was hardly out of the ordinary and had nothing to do with Laishun. Still he felt embarrassed and angry as he stood eavesdropping.

Why did he feel like this? It was hard to say. Mancun was only saying he didn't want the water to be wasted, which was fair enough. Mancun was always considerate and sensible. But the more he thought how sensible Mancun was, the more upset Laishun felt.

Naturally Laishun wasn't happy with Mancun, and he was jealous of the co-op. Silently he expressed the resentment he felt against the co-op: "What's so great about you? You have the government to lend you money, you have the channel, the manpower . . . Huh! If I had all your advantages, I'd reap a thousand *jin* from each *mu* or my name's not Liu Laishun! So much for you!"

His fit of jealousy subsided. The high-yield corn stood fresh and vibrant in front of him, its stalks dwarfing him, glossy leaves basking in the sun like eyes flashing mockery. Dispirited, he turned away. But even though he wasn't looking, he knew that the corn was coming into ear, the pods wrapped in fresh tender skin, crammed with seed like pearls of dew. The very year Old Bountiful's crops perished, here they were with a record yield. Even without the drought, his own prime land might well have suffered defeat. . . .

The sun was approaching the hills to the west. Another day would soon be over. An evening breeze stirred in the arid heat. It was that most stifling moment before the cool of evening. There was not much hoeing left for Laishun and his son to do, and the two of them were almost stupid with exhaustion. Bingxiao's sunken eyes stole bitter glances at his father. Laishun felt a little sorry for his son, so he sat down with a sigh: "Bingxiao, you go home now. I'll do the rest."

These were the words Bingxiao had been longing to hear. But now he was simmering with anger, so he kept at it for a while longer, silent and apparently unhearing. Laishun added: "Take the mule back and give it a decent feed. Then warm up the pot and make some gruel for your mother." At the thought of his sick mother, Bingxiao straightened up. Laishun continued: "You can make the gruel a bit thicker than usual, and ask your mother if she wants you to poach an egg for her as well."

Bingxiao's anger dissolved as he thought of their situation. Full of pity for his parents, he asked, "Dad, did you have anything to eat last night?"

"I'm fine, I had some gruel. If you're hungry, heat up a couple of flatcakes. And if your mother asks about the land, tell her there's no cause for concern. Remember!"

Bingxiao led away the sunken-eyed mule. Laishun was assailed by grief at the sight of the departing forms of his son and his mule. He felt that he'd failed his son, that he shouldn't have prevented him from going to middle school, that he shouldn't have cooped him up to suffer with the rest of the family. Bingxiao was a good boy, and at fifteen he was at the age when he should have been studying and getting ahead, yet here he was being dragged down. Laishun hadn't joined the co-op, and now it seemed that his son was ashamed to meet anyone! The harmonica had amused him for a day or two, but for the last half-year he'd just left it lying around and not played it. . . . Wasn't it for the boy that he slaved from morning to night? . . . He even felt he'd failed the mule, hadn't given it a square meal in a month. . . . His strength left him. Everything was finished. . . .

He heard the voice of Xu Mancun not far away. First there was a throaty chuckle, then: "Look, if we're careful with the water, we'll never use it all up. Do you believe me?"

"Okay, okay, I believe you. How could I doubt any plan made by Chairman Xu?" was Tiegen's response.

"Then it's settled. Finish watering here, and we'll do another plot

tonight." Mancun was speaking again. "If we get a move on, we'll finish this round before morning. Then we'll have nothing to fear even
if it doesn't rain for a month."

"Do you want me to water tonight?" asked Tiegen. "I can be economical!"

"Haha, there are some who can be even more economical than you!
You take it easy!" Mancun paused briefly, then as if something had just
occurred to him, he continued: "Do you know how Laishun is doing
with Old Bountiful over there? He may still be there. Brother Laishun!
Laishun!"

As he heard Mancun calling him, Laishun's stomach knotted, and
he wished the ground would swallow him up. But there was nowhere
to hide. His ears burning, he bowed his head and hoed the remainder
of his plot. He heard another of the cadres say, "Maybe Laishun isn't
there. I thought I heard his mule heading home just now!"

"I was just wondering what state his land was in," said Mancun.

"Need you ask?" sneered Tiegen. "Isn't it prime land? Huh, I
wouldn't be surprised if it turned out to be a prime case for disaster!"

"Really?" said Mancun, "Too bad . . . it's been a while since I went
over . . . if things are that bad . . . ."

"It's night," said Tiegen. "What's the point of looking now! Forget it!"

Mancun agreed: "You're right, let's talk about it tomorrow. You're
through here, let's go!"

Tiegen, Mancun, and the other cadres headed for home, singing a
work song.

When they got to the entrance to the village, Mancun took Tiegen
on one side: "Don't bother with the watering tonight, take charge of
patrolling the channel. Pick a couple of militiamen to help you out."

"Do we still have to patrol?" asked Tiegen. "Is there a risk of sabo-
tage?"

"Who can tell? The most important thing is that there might be a
crack in the dike, which would lead to water being wasted."

"Good thinking! Okay, leave it to me!"

"I'll be off now. Tiegen, there will be a big meeting tonight of the
shareholders in the channel. There's no need for you to come! Just
look after your own job! Who knows, I might just be along to check
up on you."

"Fine! Be seeing you!"

The two men parted and headed back to their homes.

Back at Old Bountiful, Laishun laboriously finished his hoeing and
prepared to go home. He noticed Bingxiao's harmonica lying by the

well, so he picked it up. His legs almost too weak to walk, he plodded his lonely way home.

Finally he arrived, and served himself a bowl of rice gruel. His wife asked him: "There's no hope for Old Bountiful, then?"

Flaring up again, he glowered at his son: "What do you mean, no hope? Has Bingxiao been talking crap again?"

Bingxiao shouted, "Me?" The mother butted in: "Bingxiao never said a word. You've no cause to go blaming him!" Laishun slammed his half-eaten gruel down on the table and yelled: "Who says I'm blaming anyone?"

"There's no need to take it out on me and the baby," said his wife. Their argument had started the baby crying. She put her nipple into the baby's mouth and went on, weak but still angry: "It's not our fault. I kept telling you not to be so stubborn, first when you pulled out of the team and then when the co-op was looking for members." Laishun was so furious that he stuck his head forward as if to butt her. "Fuck you!" he swore. "If you want to join the co-op, go ahead! Join! I . . . I was doing it for you, and this is all the thanks I get!" He slumped to the ground. "Was I the only one who wanted out of the team?" he demanded. "Who was it that didn't want to join the co-op? Didn't you have a say too? Weren't you concerned that other people wouldn't farm Old Bountiful properly, weren't you worried about letting other people use the mule? Damn it, you said it too!"

"Go on, shout at me!" she wailed. "I'll be dead soon!" She sobbed convulsively. Laishun's heart softened, and he fell silent.

His wife too said no more. Bingxiao took off his shoes and lay down on the *kang* to sleep. Laishun went out into the yard to feed the mule, went back indoors, and gulped down some cold water from the jar. Then he went out into the blackness of the yard again and sat on his front steps, his anger smoldering.

His mind wandered to Old Bountiful. The land was withering, and the well was dry. But the channel water gurgled merrily as it flowed by his land, and as it flowed, it jeered at him. In his anger he saw Mancun run over, look at his land, and call out in astonishment: "Hey, you haven't saved your best land! Why don't you water it?"

"This is no time for sarcasm! Water it! What with?"

Mancun slapped him on the shoulder: "What's wrong with you? Are you crazy, Brother Laishun? If you leave the water in the channel and don't water your land, you'll . . . it's not as if the water belongs to any one person! It belongs to us all!"

That's right, he thought, I ought to have a share too! He slapped his own face to chastise himself for his foolishness; then he picked up his shovel and drove it into the dike of the channel! A hole opened up, just a small one, but a strand of water flowed from it into the earth of Old Bountiful. Then suddenly the parched and gasping soil, the burned and sallow crops, all became human, opening their mouths wide, prostrating themselves before him and laughing. . . .

In the yard, the mule brayed. Laishun awoke with a start, rubbed his eyes and stared about him. Where was Old Bountiful? Where were the laughing crops? The courtyard was pitch-black. Listlessly he fed the mule, then went into the house and slumped down on the bed.

But try as he might, he couldn't get to sleep. As he heard the soft snoring of the three people lying beside him, he felt even less like sleeping himself. In the past few years, his fortunes had improved steadily, like the sun rising over the mountains. Everything had been going so well! His one regret had been that he did not have a daughter, and then his wife had become pregnant and borne him the girl he wanted . . . who could have guessed that there would be a disastrous year like this one! The girl had brought no happiness to their house, just another hungry mouth, which deprived him of the labor of his wife! To hell with it! He tossed over to face the window.

It was the twentieth of the month by the lunar calendar, and the moon, still almost full, shone directly overhead. Its silver light poured through the window, bright enough to bother his eyes, disturbing enough to drive sleep from his mind. Why were there no clouds for the moon to hide behind? Clouds! Clouds! Where had the clouds run to? For the last ten years and more, it had only been others who had been defeated by natural disasters, never him. Could it possibly be that in this drought he would be the one to be brought down and fail more terribly than anyone else?

One fall of rain would be enough! One shower would save maybe half the crop on Old Bountiful and get him through the year. This year, just this one year, it wouldn't matter if there wasn't a decent harvest. Next year he'd try again! But what was the point of thinking about a decent harvest, or even half a yield! After putting some grain in storage, buying the waterwheel, and getting the tools he needed, he'd precious little left over. Would he have to sell the mule to survive?

No, he couldn't! Even if they had to go hungry, they mustn't sell the mule, the waterwheel, or the tools! Anyway, they did have some seed grain, so they wouldn't starve. . . . As long as they didn't go under! If only there were water for sale somewhere, he would use up all his seed grain to buy some! He wouldn't mind even if he went hungry!

Laishun turned over again. In the silver moonlight, the faces of his wife and child were pallid gray . . . how could he have allowed this to happen? Damn it, the mule was braying again! It had just eaten! Fuck it! If I have to tighten my belt, why can't you lay off a bit!

He dragged himself up and gave the mule a niggardly feed. He wandered up and down the yard, getting more and more agitated. It was cool, the best time for sleep, but Laishun couldn't sleep, his body was feverish from the anger that burned within. Again and again he thought of Old Bountiful, of water . . . he mustn't let himself be ruined, mustn't let himself go under. . . .

In a flash, he remembered Mancun and their long friendship, he remembered what Mancun had said to Tiegen that evening, that they'd never use all that water on their land! Never use it all! . . . His mind made up, he shouldered his shovel and strode into the street.

V

Silver moonlight shone in every corner of the village, illuminating the street. Liu Laishun was out of the village in no time, blundering ahead like a drunkard. But he was still in control of himself, stealthily taking a detour, so that he walked neither along the village boundary nor along the channel, but kept close to the tall crops on the co-op's land. His heart was pounding so much it seemed to be leaping out of his mouth. His teeth were clenched, his head hunched in, his eyes popping out as he looked furtively around. It was only a walk of one *li* to Old Bountiful, but his route took him three or four times as far. When he finally got there, he sat under the tree by the well.

His racing heart slowed down. Calmer now, he cocked his ears and listened all around him. All was silent. The evening breeze had died down, leaving only the moon looking down on him. Although that held no terror for him, he still couldn't relax. He held his breath and listened.

There was a faint sound. From the northwest of the channel, among the dense and undulating crops of the co-op, came the slightest popping noise. That was nothing to fear either. It was the corn, which, having drunk its fill, was forcing its way upwards and bursting forth. Indeed, this was an encouragement to Laishun. It was a sound he longed to hear! He longed to hear it from his own crops!

He climbed into the tree and peered all around. Then he slipped lightly down and tiptoed to the channel. There, with one thrust of his shovel, he opened up a tiny hole in the dike. And with that simple movement, a jet of water burst from the channel and sped toward Old Bountiful. . . .

Laishun's heart began to pound. He scurried back to the tree and huddled down, his shovel under him, but, try as he might, he couldn't stifle the sound of his wheezing breath. His ears picked up sound everywhere—human voices, animal noises, even the voices of his wife and son, of Mancun and Tiegen . . . he trembled, as he felt a hand on his shoulder! But when he clambered to his feet and looked around him, there was no one there! All he could see was water flowing onto the land before him, and the gaping earth that gulped it in as he had done, crouching feverishly by the water vat, mindless of anything else! And as the land slaked its thirst, it murmured its contentment. The parched yellow stalks colored like a man's face when the blood rushes, turning green, soft and tender, breaking into a smile. . . . Laishun felt a coolness that refreshed him to the core of his being. Involuntarily, he too smiled.

Then came the shock, with the force of a flash of lightning and a clap of thunder. The shout came from within the crops to the northwest:

"Who's there?"

Laishun was as terrified as if a bomb had exploded. He shook convulsively and collapsed against the well. If only he could have hidden by the well, or even jumped down. But he didn't jump, he just tucked his feet under him as he lay there and wondered if he could leap up and run away. But he was too slow, as the man who had called out burst out of the dense crops, leaped over the channel, and rushed toward Old Bountiful. There was a rifle in his hand. He looked all around him for a moment and then rushed up to the tree by the well and pointed his gun at Laishun.

"Who are you? Speak up!" The rifle bolt snapped back.

"I . . ." Laishun's voice was feebler than a fly's buzz. But in the absolute stillness, the other heard quite clearly. Without lowering his gun, he asked: "Uncle Laishun! What are you doing here?"

Laishun recognized Tiegen as the holder of the rifle. Helpless, he stood up, stammering: "I . . . it was late, I went to sleep here, what are you . . . ?"

"Eh? Sleeping here? You're a strange one!" Tiegen's voice softened. He lowered the gun, looked toward the west, and prepared to leave. But in that instant his eyes fell on Old Bountiful, and he too seemed to have been struck by a bomb blast. "Hey!" he roared. "What's this?" Without another glance at Laishun he rushed over to the channel. . . . Everything was revealed to Tiegen with utter clarity in the whiteness of the moonlight—the hole Laishun had cut in the dike, and the channel water flowing onto Old Bountiful.

"So that's it!" Tiegen stamped back to the tree. It was all he could do to restrain himself from kicking Laishun to kingdom come. Pointing his rifle at Laishun again, the pulse in his neck throbbing, he roared: "You . . . what do you think you're doing? Talk!"

Resignedly, Laishun answered: "What can I say? I was stealing your water!"

When the words were out, he picked up his shovel and trudged over to the channel. For an instant Tiegen was caught unawares, but then he trained his rifle on Laishun and shadowed him as if he were taking a criminal into custody. Laishun dug up a shovelful of earth and plugged the hole he had made in the dike. Old Bountiful's supply of water was cut off.

"Let's go!" Tiegen barked out the order as he snatched the shovel away, his rifle aimed at his prisoner.

"Are you taking me to district headquarters, or are you going to hold a meeting in the village to denounce me?"*

"Don't dawdle!" ordered Tiegen. "We'll see what Mancun says."

Someone else emerged from the crops to the northwest, and a voice like a parade-ground drillmaster's shouted, "Who's looking for me? Here I am!" It was Xu Mancun. He was chuckling as he walked over. "Looking for me, Tiegen? You're very thorough with your night patrol! I was looking for you everywhere! Looking after your high-yield land, eh? How . . . ."

He saw Tiegen's murderous expression and Laishun's defiant look. With a look of astonishment, he limped back a pace and asked: "What's going on here? Brother Laishun, what are you doing?"

Then he stepped forward and pushed Tiegen's gun aside. Standing between the two men, he said:

"Who'll speak first? Eh?"

Laishun's head sank down. Tiegen pointed to the spot where the dike had just been closed up again and to Old Bountiful, which was still waterlogged, and briefly explained the matter. Mancun stumped about, staring first at Tiegen and then at Laishun, and scratched his head as if he couldn't believe what he heard. After a while he hobbled off to take a closer look at Old Bountiful, then walked back to the channel. There he stood, staring intently at the heavens, his face stern and somber.

The sky was absolutely still. The only sound was the pounding of the two men's hearts beside him. Mancun snatched the shovel from Tiegen's hand and demanded: "What's all this? Brother Laishun, did you make the hole here?"

---

*District headquarters was the executive branch of the county government. It was one level above the village.

With one thrust of the shovel, he reopened the hole. He asked again: "Is this how the water was flowing?"

The gurgling waters raced their way to Old Bountiful. Laishun looked up: "Yes, that's it. I confess, I did it!"

"Aha. You weren't finished, were you? Take some more!" With a flicker of a smile, Mancun handed Laishun his shovel. "Now we're doing it, you'd better make sure the water flows evenly!"

"What?" The two men exclaimed at the same instant, each of them grasping one of Mancun's arms. Mancun guffawed with laughter; he grabbed Tiegen's rifle and hoisted it over his own shoulder, then he took back the shovel and hobbled off to the eastern corner of the plot. He called over his shoulder to Laishun. "If you're going to let the water onto your land, you could at least do a little digging to regulate the flow!"

Mancun stuck the shovel into the ground and leaned on it, jiggling it back and forth; then he jumped over onto another dry patch of land to even the flow there, and jumped back again. The other two men again seized his arms. Tiegen recalled the lifelong friendship between Mancun and Laishun, so he thrust his head forward and shouted: "Xu Mancun! Don't play favorites here!"

Laishun was shouting too: "Brother . . . what are you doing?"

Mancun's expression was as solemn as ever. He led the two men over to the well, sat them down and said: "You're right to criticize me, but not for favoritism. Do you know why it was I told you yesterday to go easy with the water?" Mancun leaned against Tiegen and looked him in the eye. "I wanted to save it so that we could help out the people who didn't have shares in the channel."

"What?" yelled Tiegen.

"Hear me out. We made the decision to do it at the shareholders' meeting this evening, and we were going to start implementing it in the morning. You missed the meeting, Tiegen, I'm not blaming you. I'm just telling you what happened."

"But . . ." Tiegen objected, "he stole it!"

"Don't get upset, Tiegen!" Mancun turned to Laishun: "Brother, what you did was wrong too! Didn't I tell you to talk to me if you were in difficulties? Why didn't you come and see me?"

Laishun collapsed to the ground, deflated like a burst balloon. Beside him Tiegen was still fuming, but he had nothing more to say. The moonlight shone through the trees and dappled the ground, so that it seemed they were sitting in a giant sieve. Leaves and crops rustled in a cool breeze. Soon there came the popping sound of the growing corn. But the three men were deaf to it all. They sat unstirring on ground bathed silver-gray by the moonlight. Silence reigned.

Then Mancun heard a choking sound from Laishun's chest. As he was about to speak, Laishun took his arm in one hand and Tiegen's shoulder with the other and looked remorsefully at them like a hurt and pleading child. Moonlight twinkled on the tears in his eyes. Suddenly he slumped forward, quietly sobbing. In the silence of the night, in the emptiness of the fields, they heard his tears splashing to the ground.

Tiegen seemed upset as well, though he couldn't put his feelings into words. Feeling awkward, he took his rifle from Mancun's hand and said: "I'll get on with the patrol. You . . . you head home now!"

Tiegen padded away. Mancun helped Laishun with his watering and went back to check on the co-op's land. He talked to Laishun a while longer and then urged him to go home.

By the next morning everyone knew all about Laishun's stealing the water. But Laishun acted as if there was nothing out of the ordinary. He was out early, buckets hitched to his carrying-pole, to fetch drinking water from the tank by the channel. At midday he went to see the midwife, then headed to the clinic to fetch the doctor for his wife. Next day he asked someone going into town to pick up some medicine for her. After a couple of days her condition had improved considerably. There was a change in his son Bingxiao as well—all of a sudden the harmonica he had ignored for so long was never out of his mouth, and he was walking around playing it everywhere. A few days later Laishun steeled himself and sent the boy off, satchel on his back, to the county town to take the entrance exams for middle school. One evening a few days later still, there was a village meeting. Laishun went early and voluntarily made a full confession. Satisfied with Laishun's speech, Tiegen asked him: "Tell me, Uncle Laishun, what do you plan to do from now on?"

"Me? I promise to go along with everyone else in the future." Pushing to the front, his head held high, he said: "I'm asking to take a share in the channel and applying to join one of the mutual aid teams. In addition, I promise to attend village meetings, and I guarantee I won't fall behind in my work. Mancun, everyone else, you've forgiven me, I'm truly grateful, but I . . . I can't . . . I can't go all the way yet."

No one spoke. Then Tiegen asked: "You're not planning to join the co-op?"

"I know how good the co-op is," said Laishun, "and I'll join sooner or later, honestly I will, but I . . . just let me join a team first! I promise to work hard! I . . . Bingxiao's gone, I couldn't hold him back, so I can't count on him any more. Mancun said that if we don't get organized, some of us are bound to finish up as poor peasants. I know that only too well. I don't want to be poor again."

"Okay, Brother Laishun! As you like!" said Mancun. "But you only said the half of it! If we don't get organized, there will be others who finish up being rich-peasant oppressors. You should bear that in mind as well!"

"Yes, yes, of course. I'll never forget!"

Having said his piece, Laishun left.

Some people at the meeting were still none too happy with Laishun. Tiegen confronted Mancun: "He's still as stubborn as ever! Why didn't you teach him a good lesson?"

"Don't get upset, Tiegen!" said Mancun. "Laishun has taken a step forward, don't you think? And it's no small step either!"

"You call that a step forward? Don't make me mad!"

"Don't get so worked up, Tiegen! Even if Laishun had joined the co-op, what would that have achieved? If you ask me, it's just as well he didn't. We've only just taken a first step ourselves, so it's only to be expected that he doesn't have confidence in us. If he can't trust us, what good does it do anyone if you get upset? I was a bit nervous myself, but if I'd been in the state you're in, I'd have messed the whole thing up for sure." Stumping up and down on his game leg, he said: "Look at me! It's all I can do to keep walking steadily. If I got too anxious, I'd fall flat on my face! Isn't that so, Tiegen?" He chuckled: "We have to go forward steadily! Our steps must be firm before they can be fast!"

Tiegen's eyes were glazed. Before he could speak, someone beside him said: "You're right! That's what we have to do!"

"That's what you say," said Tiegen. "Well, I think you're wrong. Chairman Xu's leg will be lame all his life! As for us, even if we've not done too well so far, we'll improve with every step we take! Us, like your leg? No way!"

Mancun hastily agreed: "You're right! Tiegen, I accept your criticism," he said with a laugh.

Everyone else nodded agreement and laughed along with him.

Fang Zhi Taking Charge

////   Although Lesser Wang Village is small, it is known near and far and for one reason only: poverty.

When they were readjusting the makeup of production teams, a few of the surrounding villages were unwilling to take the Lesser Wang villagers on.* Some said, "Unless a family measures their gold by the bushel, they can't arrange a match with a Wang."† And others were even more direct, telling the brigade party secretary, "Secretary, I'll give it to you straight. If you're going to order us to take them on, we'll agree right away, but if you're going to talk it over with us, you can talk for three days and three nights and you'll just be talking to the wall!"

These words spread to the ears of the members of Lesser Wang Village, and the people clenched their fists until the sweat dripped from them. They cried out in unison, "If we're going to be poor, let's be different. If we're going to starve, let's fight! We won't beg anyone; we'll have our own team." The commune and brigade all showed their support by praising them for their high aspirations.

Morale blazed high. All they lacked was a leader.

This story was published in *Shanghai wenxue* in August 1962. Translation by Margaret H. Decker.

*In 1958, the communization movement imposed by Mao Zedong organized villages into a three-tiered administrative structure. A commune consisted of several large villages named brigades, which were subdivided into production teams. The communes and brigades operated industrial and agricultural enterprises, and the land remained in the teams. Team income varied because of the different economic resources assigned to them, and the higher levels tried to equalize the disparity with their resources. The movement and its accompanying chaos brought much hardship. In the early 1960's, the government relaxed centralized control and reorganized the villages according to more natural social divisions.

† Wang is a family name, but it is probably a pun for "king" here.

In order to choose a team leader, the members met for an entire day and considered every nominee as carefully as parents comparing their children's horoscopes for a marriage match. They sieved and selected, selected and sieved, but there was no one who fit completely what people had in mind. Then one member suddenly thought of someone. As soon as the name was mentioned, all the people in the room raised a shout: "Right, he's it!"

This person was one Wang Ruhai, who lived in the village and worked for the brigade's fish-catching group.

But Wang Ruhai himself was not at the meeting place. Someone said that didn't matter, Old Wang was a go-getter. He was sure to agree. And there was someone who said, no, if he wasn't present, it was no good counting on him. Upon hearing this, Wang Ruhai's son, nineteen-year-old Xiaohai, thumped himself on the chest, opened his mouth wide, and trumpeted: "No problem, I guarantee it."

"Wow." His little sister, Xiaocui, was sitting behind him and she curled her lip slightly. "Just like the real thing! When Pa's not here, there's still Grandpa and Ma, but you start strutting!"

Wang Ruhai's woman was always very meek and docile. She simply said to everyone, "I follow him," and having said that, she went on as before stitching the shoe sole in her hand—it was for her niece Xiaoqing.

Upon this people fixed their eyes on Wang Ruhai's father. Although the old man was nearly seventy and could no longer work, he was still a "person of authority" at home. He always spoke with spirit, and his son was completely filial and obedient to him.

"Old man, speak! A word!"

The old man liked to keep face, and so, seeing everyone waiting for him, he answered straightforwardly. "All right! Since you've seen fit not to overlook me, I'll take responsibility for my son's word. But I must add, Ruhai is like me. He's a boorish fellow good only for poling a boat, caring for ducks, catching fish, or working the earth. He was never a cadre. 'It takes a thousand spokes to hold up an umbrella.' All things require your favor! And in addition, if there is anything offensive in his words henceforth, ai, I hope you will be gracious enough to forgive him a few times."

The old fellow generally liked to listen to storytelling and knew how to parse a phrase or two. Hearing him, the team members laughed and said, "We're all neighbors, so what's the need for such polite talk. With us as determined as we are now, no matter what comes up, if Big Brother Wang just gives a sign, we'll all vie to take care of it. We guarantee we won't make him waste his words!"

The sun was level with the west horizon, and the new team leader had been selected. Everyone agreed to hold a meeting the following night and ask the team leader to take up his post.

Quite unexpectedly, without waiting to be called, Wang Ruhai returned that same night. He had come home to get some provisions.

As soon as Wang Ruhai entered the village, it was as if a wind had come up and blown open every family's door. People ran out one after the other, some with their bowls in their hands and others holding babies. Together they filled Wang Ruhai's house. They each used their separate way to pour out the words in their heart, shouting, cursing, laughing, and wishing only that Wang Ruhai could grow a few more ears.

Hearing how the neighboring villages had made fun of them, Wang Ruhai arched his eyebrows; but upon hearing that everyone had elected him team leader, these eyebrows knit together tightly. As he went on listening, his face grew calmer, and only the two blue veins at his temple pulsed, like two boring earthworms. After a long time, he lightly slapped the table with his big, rough palm, and the entire room of people fell silent. Who could have guessed that he would utter just three words, "Bring me supper!"

The woman served him. With a bowl on the left and one on the right, he merely lowered his head and pushed the rice into his mouth. When he finished eating, he wiped his mouth and people thought he wanted to speak. Instead he called his daughter to fetch water for washing his feet. First he washed his left foot, and then his right, one by one he finished washing them and one by one wiped them clean. Then he stood up and said to everyone, "It's late today. If you have something to say, we can talk about it another day!"

Everyone was astonished. They fell silent, and then their voices rose, higher and higher.

"Dad!" Xiaohai's mouth fell open. "What's the matter with you? If we can't get rid of this label of poverty, all the men, women, young, and old of our village can just go fall headfirst into the pond and drown! You—"

"You!" Wang Ruhai pointed with a finger, "You throw out the water from washing my feet!"

He pulled out one cigarette, then another, and another. In a manner neither hasty nor slow, he smoked three cigarettes, and after the voices grew quiet, he reiterated firmly, "It's late today. If you have something to say, we can talk about it another day!"

One day and then another passed, and Wang Ruhai's mouth remained firmly closed, as firm as iron or rock. The atmosphere of the village was at a low ebb, and the old rooster's crow seemed unusually ear-piercing.

Wang Ruhai's family had also become very depressed. Of course the most upset was that Xiaohai, so fond of giving guarantees. He really couldn't understand: with people's hearts as one on the matter, the wheat sprouts looking this good, and those above giving their support, what was his father's difficulty? "Hmph! If you won't do it, I will!" He thought angrily. Unfortunately, no one had elected him. He really wanted to argue with his father, but one glance at his father's face, and he didn't dare open his mouth. He went to plead with Grandfather. But the old man said he'd caught a cold and was lying in bed. He didn't want to see anyone from either his family or the village. The old man was holding in a stomachful of resentment. For his son not to agree to be team leader was equivalent to spitting in his face in front of everyone, but his son was already forty-odd. He couldn't beat him if he wanted to, nor could he scold him. It was no use urging him gently, and to push too hard might lead to a fight. If they started to argue, it would just give people something to laugh at, and if they didn't argue, the people still would have something to laugh about. So all the old man could do was catch a cold. When Xiaohai came to plead with him, he not only took no notice of him, but [gave] his grandson a big shove. "I'm old. Don't know when Death is going to issue me an invitation. Who cares about your infernal affairs—scram!"

Xiaohai went to plead with his sister. She was his father's spoiled darling, but his sister said, "It was your boasting that got you into the frying pan. It wasn't me!" She was more clever than her brother and knew one had to watch for the occasion to act like a spoiled child.

However, Wang Xiaohai's worries weren't half as deep as his mother's. She was frightened no matter whom she saw. She was afraid of the team members because she felt she had let them down. She feared her husband because she had a mind to urge him a bit, but was afraid this would add to his worries. These last two nights Wang Ruhai hadn't slept well. He would get up, smoke a cigarette, and lie down again; lie down and then get up and smoke a cigarette. She was the only one who knew about this. She was also worried about her father-in-law, son, and daughter, fearful they would start a fight with her husband. All day the woman acted as if she had lost her soul. In the morning she forgot to let the chickens out of the coop, and at night she scraped a repair patch off the cooking pot.

Wang Ruhai was very calm, as if nothing had happened in the family. During these two days he sometimes went to look about the village, sometimes wandered about the fields, and sometimes went who knows where. When people ran into him, some turned their faces away, some gave him a curious look, and some, strange to say, felt inexplicably embarrassed themselves. He, however, was noncommittal. He was still himself, still wore that same expression.

On the third day, when it was time to turn on the lights, he returned from who knows where. Once home, as usual, he ate, wiped his face, smoked a cigarette, and washed his feet. The woman sat dumbly by the door of the stove, the old man lay in bed coughing, and the son and daughter sat in the shadows with their backs to the light whispering about something. This went on for a while, and then suddenly Xiaocui cried out peevishly, "Ouch!"

"What's the matter?" Startled, the mother looked toward her daughter.

"Nothing!" her son immediately replied. He sat up ramrod straight, like a wooden stake.

The sister covered her mouth, stifling a laugh. After a while she cried out again, "Ouch! That really hurts!" Angrily she shifted her body and, purposely raising her voice, said, "Don't you have a mouth under your nose? Dad won't eat you!"

The woman moved nervously over to her son. "Look how big you are, and you're still picking on your sister. If you're bored sitting, then go buy me some matches. Hurry up. If you delay, the store will be closed!" As she said this, she secretly gave her son a spank.

Grumbling, the son got up to go. Who could have guessed that the husband would choose that moment to open his golden mouth?

"So what if it closes. Here are some matches!" Smack! a box of matches was thrown on the table. The woman was stupefied. Without waiting for her to recover her senses, Wang Ruhai shouted toward the inner room, "Dad, are you asleep?"

Two coughs from the room indicated that he was not yet asleep.

Wang Ruhai stood up and gave instructions, "Bring the lamp to Grandfather's room, and all of you come with me!"

All three, wife and children, looked at each other, then together stared at the back of his tall silhouette, and slowly got to their feet.

The old man rolled himself up in bed. His son immediately placed a pillow behind his father's back and draped a padded jacket over his shoulders. He said, "Dad, take care you don't get cold."

The old man gave his son a look and mumbled something that the others couldn't understand and that he could hardly understand himself.

Wang Ruhai turned up the lamp a little. Except for the niece Xiaoqing, who was at school studying, the whole family, the entire battalion, was there. He waited until everyone was settled before opening his mouth. "I know," he swept the entire family with a glance, "everyone's been complaining about me behind my back these past two days. And I've involved the family, so that you're ashamed to see people. The team members are all waiting for a word from me. Will I take the position or not? Actually these last two days I've been waiting for a response, too. If you say I can serve as team leader, I'll do it; if you say I can't, I won't. . . ."

Before he could finish, the whole family burst out, popping and crackling as if a handful of salt had been sprinkled over a flame. With a wave of his hand, Wang Ruhai carefully questioned them one by one. First, he asked his father. Just as the old man opened his mouth, Xiaohai interrupted, "You still need to ask? Grandpa agreed long ago, otherwise he wouldn't have gotten so mad he got sick!"

"You talk too much!" his mother glared at him.

"This . . . ," the old man gave a dry cough and said, "Ruhai, you know me! The people didn't pick any Zhang or Li, they picked you. How can you not try to do them credit!"

Wang Ruhai then asked the woman, who still murmured that "three-word Classic":* "I follow you!": "And if I don't agree, you'll still go along with me?"

The woman, again stupefied, got flustered and then said hurriedly, "When did I tell you not to accept the position? Tell me clearly!"

"Yes, we must speak clearly. So do you or don't you actually want me to accept?

"Why not? If you don't, won't everyone criticize you?"

"You want me to accept?"

"Yes!" The woman finally squeezed this one word out through a crack between her teeth. Then she turned her face away and said angrily, "Hmph! As if I were hanging on your leg and holding you back these last two days!"

The whole family laughed.

One by one he asked each person, but then didn't stop there. After a while, he sighed and said, "Still, it's really not easy to be team leader. Two skinny oxen, one incomplete waterwheel, a soil of gray sand and white snails, and, counting young and old, fifty to sixty mouths to feed!† 'When you use a bow, the arrow doesn't turn back.' If I accept,

---

*The *Sanzi jing* (Three-word classic) was a popular traditional text recited by children in village schools in the past. Each of its lines had three characters.

† It was the responsibility of the team leader to plan production and assign work for the team members. Since income was shared, a bad decision could mean hardship for the entire team.

I can't change my mind halfway. So let's talk now behind closed doors. It's better to have people curse you outright than to have them criticize you behind your back. Think about it again. If I won't do as team leader, it's still not too late to say so." Having said this, he took a long drag on his cigarette and through the smoke examined the people in his family.

Everyone was silent for a while, then they all started to shout.

"The arrow has already been shot, what turning back is there?"

"Dad! If you really don't accept, I won't have the face left to live in this village. You come back and till the land, and I'll go take your place catching fish!"

"You really make something out of nothing and can't give up until you've pushed someone to the wall! Ai, in these last two nights you've used up half a month of my lamp oil!"

"All right!" Wang Ruhai laughed. "Then let's save a little lamp oil! Since you say I should accept, I will, but—"

"What more 'but' is there?" Xiaocui pouted her lips and declared, "Dad, hurry up and look at yourself in the mirror. You've become Mr. Long-winded!"

Wang Ruhai couldn't help laughing outright. Then he put his hand on his daughter's shoulder and gave an order, "Xiaocui, on the seventh you and Zhou Ersao and the two girls from the Chen family will go to Sleeping Ox Mountain and cut wood. Our team has only 500 *jin* of straw left, at most enough for the oxen to eat for ten days. Once you come back with the wood, we can exchange it for the straw people are burning to cook, and then we can feed that to the oxen. In seven days you want to cut five and a half tons of wood. The older girl of the Chen family can be your group leader. Even though she's the same age as you, you must obey her. People will only obey your father if you're willing to obey others. While working, take on the heavy tasks. When sleeping, sleep on the outside and let the others sleep inside. You must be able to suffer, and while suffering not always be mentioning it. Your father, of course, will know. . . ."

The mother listened silently, and at the end she couldn't keep from sighing, "Ai, why don't you send men?"

"Men will be put to men's use. I've already planned it out."

Wang Ruhai then proceeded to talk about the production plan he had thought up over the last two days. How many people had to be assigned to this task and how many for that, when they should begin and when they should be finished, even how the work points should be determined.* He had it all figured out.

*In a team, members were allocated a certain number of work points for finishing their assigned work. The value of work points was calculated by dividing the net in-

"Then," the woman looked timidly at her husband, "then I'll go in Xiaocui's place. Anyway, there are no infants in the house, and Xiaocui can do the cooking. . . ."

"And what about the Chen sisters? Can they find two mothers to replace them?"

The woman was silenced, and the old man hadn't opened his mouth, although he was actually very worried about his granddaughter. At this time, the most cheerful one in the family had to be Xiaohai. He deliberately stuck his tongue out at his sister and said softly, "Little darling! There are wolves in the mountains!"

Infuriated, Xiaocui flipped back her two three-inch-long braids and said. "Wolves, hmph! There are tigers, too!"

"That's daddy's good girl!" Wang Ruhai smiled slightly. Then he added, "There's another thing. The brigade has given us credit to buy fifteen hundred *jin* of ammonia water. The team has a bad shortage of manure buckets. This is something else in which I'm going to have to rely on you. . . ."

"What am I supposed to do about that?"

"Since there aren't enough manure buckets, you'll have to shoulder the nightsoil buckets. If you can do as I say . . . ."

Xiaocui didn't listen to the end but shook her head and shouted, "I won't! Carrying nightsoil buckets! People will laugh so hard their teeth will fall out!"

"You're not even afraid of tigers," her brother said with great seriousness. "So how come you're afraid of carrying a nightsoil bucket? If you're unwilling, how can you expect the other women to listen to Dad's orders?"

Xiaocui was silent a moment, and then suddenly stuck out her chest and said, "All right, I'll carry it!—but Dad, let me ask you, what are you going to have this big guy shoulder?" Having said this, she jabbed her finger at her brother.

This really struck home. Immediately the brother sobered up, his two eyes focused anxiously on his father.

"Don't worry," Wang Ruhai laughed. "Of course I have plans. This team leader was not only elected by the village, but also by the family. Whether I serve well or badly, everyone in the family has a share in it. For cadres to talk themselves dry without getting their own family members going isn't worth much!—Mother of Xiaohai, what do you say?" The woman was caught off guard and made no rejoinder. Wang Ruhai went on speaking, "For example, our team hasn't enough farming tools, and our waterwheel is incomplete. So isn't it like grabbing

---

come of the team by the total number of work points earned. Each laborer's share was determined by the work points he or she had accumulated over the year.

a stone to smash heaven to talk about fighting drought or draining flooded fields! To make the farm tools, you need wood. We can't buy it, so we can only rely on people making contributions. Naturally, price would be set according to value. After the fall we would pay, and no one would lose a single copper. But there always needs to be a leader, wouldn't you say? For instance, how about using those scholar trees and elms in our backyard? . . ."

Before he had finished, the woman burst out, "What! You want to cut down my two scholar trees? Those are for making our niece Xiaoqing's trousseau. Have pity!" And with that "have pity," her tears flowed. "My sister died young and only left behind this solitary shoot, Xiaoqing. Just before she breathed her last, she grasped my hand and said, 'Sister, sister! Life is cruel for this child Xiaoqing. Her father's life was short, and I'm not going to make it either. I can only entrust her to you. For you it will mean raising an extra daughter. Later, when you have nurtured her to adulthood, find her a decent person. I'm not hoping to climb high, I only want him to have three to five *mu* of land. If he has some poor tea and plain food to eat, that's enough. And for her trousseau, I don't want a lot, just a few basics. Just so that she doesn't go empty-handed to be laughed at by her in-laws! . . .' Those were my sister's very words. Have pity! When I brought Xiaoqing into our family, I planted those scholar trees in our backyard. Even through the hardships before the Liberation, I couldn't bear to touch them. And now, you, you, you . . . ." Crying, the woman ran into her own room. One could hear her through the wall, scolding and crying, "As an uncle, you have the heart of a wolf! Hmph, I see. Tonight, all your sweet words and beating around the bush, what was all that fancy footwork for? You just had your mind set on my scholar trees! . . ."

Wang Ruhai laughed and said, "I see now that it's not going to be easy to save a few ounces of oil for the lamp. Ai! Fortunately I haven't yet accepted the job!"

Like a puff of wind, the son and daughter blew into their mother's room.

"What are you crying about!" This was the son's trumpeting voice. "And just now you spoke so firmly. Aren't you afraid of looking bad?"

"What's there to be afraid of? If you think I look so bad, get your old man to find another wife!"

"Xiaohai!" Wang Ruhai roared. "You come here!" His son came out obediently. Wang Ruhai scowled at him and, pointing, said, "Sit down, and sit up straight! It's you who's not afraid to look bad, speaking to your mother that way!"

The sound of crying through the wall of the other room ceased and turned into sobbing.

"Second Daughter!" the old man called to his daughter-in-law on the other side of the wall according to the old customs.* "Ai! Things aren't what they used to be! I ask you, your sister wanted you to find a man with three to five *mu* of land for Xiaoqing, and can you find one? There are no longer families working their own land. You couldn't find one if you went out with a lantern! Don't take it so hard. Come on out!"

"Ma!" This was Xiaocui's voice. "So what if a girl doesn't have a trousseau. All she needs is work points! If she wants something, doesn't she know to go to the department store and pick it out? And so what about her mother-in-law? What can she do about it? Sister Xiaoqing can work hard and has education. What mother-in-law would dare laugh at her? And as for that mouth of Xiaohai's. Even if you scold him, could you shut him up? Dad's already spoken to him—come on, come out!" Following this was the sound of tugging.

"Xiaocui! You come out too."

Given no choice, Xiaocui came out, and in the room on the other side of the wall there remained only the mother. Xiaocui took a look at her father and wanted to say more, but Wang Ruhai took no notice of her. Serenely he smoked a cigarette. He had passed through thirty years of wind and rain with his wife, and he knew her temper completely.

Both rooms fell silent. There was only the hiss of smoking and soft sobbing.

A moment passed like this, and then the sobbing in the room next door stopped. After another while, there was the sound of light footsteps. The steps approached the center room, approached the door, then stopped. The woman had come round of her own accord.

She turned her head to the side and stole a glance about the room. Her husband's brow was knit, and the wrinkles on his forehead were as deep as plowed furrows. He didn't move at all but only sucked in one big mouthful after another of thick, bitter, and acrid smoke. The woman's heart tugged so it quivered. Ah! He was troubled! How could he not be? Having said all right, she had then put on another face. So how would you have him answer the others? These last two days he had already suffered enough. He hadn't slept well, had flipped and tossed in bed, just like a fish that had jumped onto a sandbar. Others didn't know about that, but didn't she know? Ai, ai, husband and wife

---

*Traditionally there was a strong taboo against fathers-in-law and daughters-in-law communicating directly; this is one way of addressing the problem.

for thirty years. No matter what she might say, it was only for those two precious trees! . . .

The woman hurriedly used a corner of her clothes to wipe away the traces of tears, straightened her blouse, and then walked into the room and sat with her back to the lamp.

"All right then." It took a great effort before she could open her mouth. Originally she had planned to say something gentle, but for some reason the words came out, "I don't care, you go ahead and chop away. Then you'll be satisfied."

The husband sat silently as before. The old man couldn't very well say anything. Son and daughter didn't dare speak.

He was angry! The woman thought in a panic. How could she expect him not to be angry? He hadn't allowed his own daughter to study, but had sent Xiaoqing to school, and yet she had said that as an uncle he had the heart of a wolf. It was all well and good to scold her son, but she had to drag her husband into it by saying such an ugly sounding thing as "get your old man to find another wife then." And just now she had spoken so aggressively, ai, ai! . . .

"Father of Xiaohai!" the woman's lip trembled once. "It's not that I can't bear to part with those two trees. If Xiaoqing had a father and mother and you wanted to chop them down, fine, you could just chop them down. I . . . it's so sad . . . I'm just trying to be faithful to my sister's wishes!" Having said this, her eyes grew red again.

"Mother of Xiaohai!" Her husband suddenly opened his mouth, and much to her surprise, he spoke considerately, very gently, without the least trace of anger. "I wasn't plotting to get those two trees of yours. I need that faithful heart! It's not going to be easy for Lesser Wang Village to reverse its fate. Do you think that all it will take are those two trees of yours? No, there are plenty of difficulties, ones you can imagine and ones you can't, lots of them!" His voice gradually grew excited. "Both year before last and last year our village's harvest was poor. And this year? The wheat seems to be sprouting well at the moment, but 'the crops only reach home when they're in your mouth.' If by any chance this is also a famine year, what will we do? It's easy to struggle for one breath, but hard to endure a hundred days of hunger! When that time comes, you can't hold a grudge or cry or run elsewhere. You can't dump manure only on your private plot— it's not strange that it would take a while for me to find something to say. If we don't talk over the difficulties thoroughly, completely, and to the end, then later we'll have trouble! I tell you, if I'm going to be a good team leader, our entire family must be given to the cause, not to mention those two trees. For instance, what if this home—" he pointed at the ceiling, "were burned down by a bolt of lightning, and I didn't have this heart of a wolf? Don't go beating my gong ahead of time. If I didn't have this heart of a wolf, I would let everyone down. With this sort of heart, and the entire family with it, each and every family the same, one season, two, one year, two, even if Lesser Wang Village were poorer . . . ."

Before he had finished speaking, a hot kernel popped out of the cold pot, and Xiaohai cried, "I guarantee it! If we don't take off this label of poverty, all the men, women, young, and old of our village really can just all go fall headfirst into the pond and drown!"

"There you go again!" Wang Ruhai gave him a sideways glance. "One minute giving guarantees and the next jumping in the pond, and you still want to drag everyone else in with you! Jumping in the pond! What are you, a woman or a man?"

Except for Wang Ruhai, the entire family laughed. Xiaocui laughed the loudest, and even Xiaohai himself laughed loudly and foolishly.

Was there anything else he needed to say to them? No. Very happily, Wang Ruhai stood up and told everyone to go to bed—the lamp oil was about used up. But Xiaohai still couldn't be sensible. He looked at his father idiotically and said, "What about me? Dad, you still haven't told me what you want me to do!"

"You still need to ask about that! You go open up your guarantee shop." His sister never let an opportunity slip by. "You!" his father said, "From now on you do more work for me and set off less fireworks! A real man's chest is easy to pound! If you go on being so rash and careless, be careful I don't take the willow switch and thrash you!" Having said this, he couldn't help turning his head away and smiling. Sons and daughters are different. You had to be harsher with him.

Satisfied, the son left. The wife and daughter also went to sleep. Wang Ruhai stood up and then sat down again and called softly, "Dad!"

The old man leaned forward and looking in his son's eyes asked, "What's the matter? Go ahead and speak. Ruhai, I just thought of something. The cattle shed is no good. Would you like me to give up this room?"

His son shook his head and said, "Dad! As team leader I'll have to roll along with the brigade. In busy times there will be busy matters to attend to, and in times of leisure there will be matters of leisure to attend to. In the past I was able to go fishing when I had time off and find enough money to get you a couple of bottles of liquor. From now on—ai, don't take offense . . . ."

The old man didn't say anything. He could give up the room, give up anything except his cup of liquor.

The son hung his head and didn't look at his father.

"All right!" the old man suddenly sighed and looked up. "I won't die from drinking a little less liquor! There's an old saying, 'One can't be both completely loyal and completely filial.' Put your mind at rest and go ahead boldly!"

Early the next morning Xiaohai flew out the door and went to report the happy news of the night before. His father, however, did not immediately take up his post but asked for one day off.

As the glow of sunset covered the earth, Wang Ruhai returned carrying his fishing spear and taking large strides. When he reached home, he pulled out two bottles of good, fragrant, jade green liquor and set it on the table in front of his father. Then he turned his head and shouted fiercely, "Xiaohai!"

"Here I am!" The son shot through the door like an arrow.

"Inform the village," Wang Ruhai waved his big, dark hands, "we're having a meeting!"

Hao Ran

Firm and Impartial

////   During the course of a night and half a day in the Hou family home, three things happened that gave me a bad impression of my landlady.

Yesterday I set out from the county seat, and the sky was already dark by the time I arrived at Reed Bend [Weiziwan] brigade. The party branch secretary, Zhang Zisheng, greeted me warmly, briefed me on the conditions of the brigade, and then personally escorted me to the home of Lao Hou.

This was a three-room brick house with tiles, facing north; the west room was already prepared for me, and the landlady lived in the east room. The old woman was out visiting, and only a young boy named Qingming sat under the electric light doing homework. He told me that his parents worked in the city, but he and his grandmother remained in the village. Because I was curious about my new surroundings, I very much wanted to chat with my landlady. But after waiting a long time for her return, I decided it was best to go to bed.

These several years I had lived in the city. It was not easy to get a chance like this to go to the countryside. On thinking that I was about to begin a new life, to confront new problems, and to attain new gains, I was in an excited mood. I tossed and turned before finally falling asleep. Suddenly, I woke up with a start at the sound of knocking on the door.

"Comrade, comrade, are you asleep?"

I heard the voice of an old woman. Guessing that it was my landlady, I was about to get up and open the door.

This story was written on November 29, 1971, and published in *Beijing ribao* on January 25, 1972. Translation by Kate Sears; the editor has made substantial changes in the translation.

The old woman outside then said, "If you are already in bed, don't get up. I came to see you several times, but hearing no sound of activity thought you were working!"

I thought, the landlady is so warmhearted. She should come in for a chat. So I threw some clothes over my shoulder and got off the *kang*.

The landlady continued: "If you are not reading or writing, then turn off the light. Don't sleep with the light on, it wastes electricity! I called you just about that matter, so go back to sleep."

She left, and I immediately turned out the light. Falling asleep the second time was even more difficult. Just when I was soundly asleep, I was again awakened by a noise. I opened my eyes and discovered that the sun had already reached the window lattice. The landlady was shouting loudly in front of my window: "Who told you to climb over my wall and pick my peaches? Are they fully ripe? Can you eat them? Huh!"

A boy answered her in a husky voice: "Don't make a fuss. Next time I won't pick them, ok!"

"Take them all out! Do you still have any? What's in that pocket over there?"

"It's a slingshot. . . ."

"The slingshot must also be confiscated. This will all be sent to your teacher so he can see whether his students are diligent in their studies or are specialized in breaking civil discipline!"

This was followed by the child's pleading and the landlady's obstinacy and scolding, until I put on my clothes and went outside. The small boy seized the chance to run off, and this storm in a teacup was reluctantly brought to a close.

The landlady was over fifty years old, tall, thin, with large hands and feet.* Probably because she had just been angry, her wrinkled face was ruddy and there was a taint of severity in her look. She placed the two half-ripe peaches on the windowsill and turned around, gave me a smile, and said, "You're up, didn't you sleep well?"

I also smiled at her and made a few of the usual polite remarks when meeting someone for the first time.

Gesturing with a hand as big as a small cattail leaf fan, the landlady cut me off, saying, "Don't mention any additional trouble, still less is it an inconvenience to me; cadres come to Reed Bend from all over for the revolution, and those who do so are members of the family. Whatever you need, just ask me. If I don't have it, I'll borrow it for

*There is an implicit double entendre here; the characters for "large hands and feet" also mean "wasteful" or "careless."

you. Things to be mended and washed, just put on the *kang* in my room."

I then introduced myself, saying I was there for a short period to "temper myself through physical labor," and asked for her help.*

The landlady listened, smiled a little, and when I had barely finished speaking, she said earnestly, "When two people come together, they won't be similar; each has strong points and shortcomings, so any help is mutual. Writing a letter, reading the paper, explaining national affairs, I shall be asking a great deal from you."

· · · · ·

That noon the third incident occurred.

Having gotten off work and eaten, I returned to my room. As I was about to open a notebook to write a few notes, I again heard a loud commotion in the courtyard. Since this time there were two people quarreling, the noises were loud and confusing. Not sure what I was hearing, I hastened outside to look. I saw Qingming standing at the doorway holding a rice bowl, and so I asked who his grandmother was arguing with.

Qingming said, "With the person from the south courtyard, nicknamed Small Hand Hou!"†

I then asked him why his grandma was making such a fuss.

Qingming said, "Small Hand Hou reaches out everywhere, that walled compound of his inches its way outward every few days, always pressing toward us!"

The terrain of Reed Bend is low; except for the two main streets, most of the homes and grounds border on the reed pond by the bank of the Jian'gan River. They are narrow, small, and very irregular. The spot where my landlady lives is next to the riverbank, and there are only two families, front and back. That two families are such close neighbors but are so disharmonious is indeed uncomfortable. I thought of going over to mediate but decided there wasn't much point in it and paused indecisively in the doorway.

From the looks of it, the landlady had just returned from the fields. One hand gripped the handle of a hoe on her shoulder; with the other hand she gestured forcefully as if ready to fight anytime. She continued to shout: "How much space have you seized? What kind of heart do you have? If you don't grab something for yourself or cause

---

*Mao Zedong called on intellectuals to go to the countryside periodically and labor with the masses in order to purify their class stands.

† Another double entendre; the characters for "small hand" also mean "prone to stealing."

hardship for other people, you don't feel right. What sort of itch you got there in the palm of your hand?"

The old man nicknamed "Small Hand Hou" was small in stature, humpbacked, and sharp. He had one foot in the freshly dug ditch, the other firmly planted on the wet earth. Grasping a shovel in his hand, he retorted in a similar manner: "You keep on saying that I have seized your spot, where does it say, where is the record?"

"First tell me, was the *chun* tree [ailanthus, or tree of heaven] at the base of the west wall planted by me or not? Yes it was, right? So, open your eyes wide and look. If according to the ditch you just dug you go directly to your compound, which side is the tree on?"

"Uh . . . uh doesn't it fall short by less than half a foot?"

"Half a foot? Even if it were an inch or a lump of earth, I would not yield to you! You draw back your small hand right this instant, or else we'll immediately go find Party Secretary Zhang!"

"Is it worth the trouble . . . ?"

"If you won't admit the mistake, we'll go right away! Go on, go on!"

"I, I won't get entangled with you womenfolk, I shall shift the banks of the ditch toward my courtyard, OK?"

"This ditch you just dug should not be filled in!"

"I'll fill it in for you, then we'll consider it finished. . . ."

"You stay put, just stay there! I want to call the cadres and brigade members to take a look, to analyze, to sharpen vigilance and learn!"

"Old sister-in-law, we are neighbors, is it necessary?"

"It's no use to soften up after being tough, I won't buy it!"

"What a nuisance, you won't let me live in peace?"

"I'll let you live socialist. No more nonsense, that's the way it is!"

. . . . .

I returned to my room feeling a bit uneasy. I remembered yesterday when Zhang Zisheng described the landlady's situation to me, he had said, "That old woman is firm and impartial." I now felt that "firm" was true, but there was no evidence of "impartial." In order to save the household a unit of electricity, she could rudely awaken a guest she had never seen. For the sake of two peaches, she could make a small child so miserable. Although it was of course wrong of another person to encroach upon her property, the mistake was admitted and was to be corrected; for her to insist on pursuing the matter was truly going too far. I could not reach a verdict on the landlady this early, but, in order to genuinely receive an education, to become familiar with the peasants' new life and new outlook, and later to eulogize them in writing, I had hoped to find a good landlady with advanced thinking, a noble character, and a strong revolutionary spirit. . . .

In the afternoon, I was again weeding the rice fields with Party Branch Secretary Zhang Zisheng. During a rest on the ridge between the fields, I tactfully suggested moving to another house.

He gave me a look and said: "Why would you move? The home of Old Woman Hou has only a few persons, it is spacious and quiet. . . ."

I told him that for the time being I was not writing anything, my primary purpose was to come into contact and learn about the masses.

He said, "Compared to party and youth league members and activists, Old Woman Hou would not necessarily be considered first-rate, but she is representative of the average commune member, particularly the older generation, which endured the old society. . . ."

I could only frankly state my own impression of the landlady and use as an example her argument with Small Hand Hou.

The young party branch secretary suddenly laughed out loud and said: "Comrade Liang, you are completely misled. Old Woman Hou cherishes that small courtyard she lives in, that is true. That small courtyard has a history of blood and tears and enmity! Originally the courtyard was as low as the reed pit at the back. The Hou family didn't have a pinprick of land, let alone a place to take shelter from the wind and rain. The two of them—one a farmhand, the other a wet nurse —worked for a landlord for two years with the promise that he would give them a slice of his land. The result was that the rapacious landlord only gave them half a reed pond. There was nothing they could do but work themselves to the bone during the day for the landlord and at night fill the pond with mud, basket by basket. They worked for two more years until the ground was level with the riverbank; they built a small shelter, and the whole family made it their home. . . . Now, that courtyard is the best site for the brigade to teach our young people about class struggle. That fellow Small Hand Hou has a lot of tricks. His courtyard grows legs, the wall moves; not only does he encroach upon Old Woman Hou's courtyard, but also on inspection, I see that he also occupied some of the collective land on the east side. Old Woman Hou has sharp eyes; it's very important to be able to discover this problem promptly! We are planning to hold an 'on-the-spot meeting' there tomorrow noon to educate the masses."

I was shaken by his words. I was convinced that I was mistaken. In the evening, feeling apologetic, I returned to the most precious little courtyard of my landlady.

The old woman and Qingming were picking peaches. Two small baskets had been filled, and some were piled up on the ground.

The old woman, busily working with both hands, said to me: "Eat some, pick the ripe ones."

I asked her why she did not hold off picking them until they were fully ripe.

The old woman said: "Originally I intended to let the peaches grow a few more days, but I'm afraid they always attract mischief from the children, which does not have a good influence on their thinking, and they will cause more trouble if they fall. Don't harm the large for the sake of the small." Carrying a basket, she came over from the foot of the tree and said to Qingming, "Take this basket over to Grandpa Wang of the 'five-guarantee family'* on the east side; that basket I will deliver to the soldier's dependent, Grandma Liu."

Each carrying a basket of large peaches, they happily left home and returned only very late, one after the other. As soon as the old woman saw me writing notes in the house, she said: "Move the small table into the other room for your writing. Qingming does homework in this room and may disturb you."

I said I would share one light with Qingming in order to save electricity.

The old woman said, laughing: "When you should use it, then use it; when you should save, then save. Don't be too inflexible." She then said, "Our village is different from the city, a brigade has one central meter for electricity. With many families sharing, even though costs are calculated according to the light sockets, one really shouldn't waste unnecessarily. Tell them that a few times, and they take note. You see, our village is now vigorously building small factories, adding many machines; electricity is in demand everywhere so we should save some for their use. This is to bear in mind the interest of the larger collective. . . ."

It was as if the landlady was engaged in daily small talk, naturally, without the least bit of self-assertiveness or of lecturing others. As I listened, my heart beat vigorously. My so-called impression of her had completely reversed. The old woman was truly a "firm and impartial" commune member. I had chanced upon a good landlady. At the same time, her daily behavior was a mirror that reflected the dust covering my thinking. It revealed the ignorance I had of the new qualities of the laboring masses in China's villages today.

Three days later a rainstorm came down. After the rain the area was impassable. In the vegetable patch Qingming and I straightened out the cucumber trellis and tomato seedlings blown over by the wind. As we were working, we suddenly heard the sound of whipping and shouting in back of the compound.

---

*The commune guaranteed food, clothing, medical care, housing, and burial expenses to elderly people who were childless or on their own.

Qingming first looked blank, then said: "Oh no, another cart is stuck!" As he spoke, he ran outside.

I followed him.

A newly repaired road stretches from the west across a temporary bridge over the Jian'gan river to the western wall of our village, where it turns north. Then it turns to the east and runs along the northern wall before turning south along the eastern wall. Finally, it extends directly east at the newly constructed small factory and granary. This part of the road, because it is obstructed by the two homes, zigzags in the shape of the character for bow [弓]. The part of the road at the back of the house is worse, for the south side is the slope and the north side is the reed pond. Because it is low, water remains after the rain and the reed pond often overflows, so it is very muddy.

Sure enough, a large cart loaded with lumber was stuck there. The cart driver was sweating in agitation. He shouted and whipped in order to drive the draft animals in the shafts of the cart. Another person was helping to lift the cart's wheel—this person's body was practically lying in the mud, and due to the exertion, the white shirt was tightly stretched across the back, a rip at the shoulder was opening into a large tear, and a scarlet bloodstain oozed amid the sweat and mud. . . .

Qingming cried "Grandma!" and flew over to help push the cart.

I also hurried over, and only then discovered that the person pushing the cart was my landlady.

The old woman lifted her head, wiped at the sweat, and panting heavily, hurriedly said: "You two replace me, lift this wheel upwards and don't let go. If you let go, the wheel will sink deeper, and the animals in the shafts will be hurt!"

The two of us replaced the old woman.

She ran home and in a moment ran back carrying a door board on her shoulder and a shovel in her hand. She threw down the door board close by. Brandishing the shovel, she began vigorously digging in front of the wheel. Then she called out to the anxious and touched cart driver: "Don't bother about the animals, quick, slip the door board over where I dug out, move, move!"

After the cart driver had put the door board in front of the wheel, the landlady said to him, "You go tend to the animals, steady them so they conserve energy." The landlady then told me and Qingming: "I'll stand on this side, you two stand over there. Listen to me shout one, two, three, and when I get to three, the cart driver will drive the animals and we three will lift upwards—be certain to use our strength in unison. So long as the cart wheel gets on top of the door board, things will be fine!"

Faced with the situation, I was dazzled. Recounting it now, I feel even more inarticulate. To put it simply, just as the party branch secretary, Zhang Zisheng, hurried over with several commune members, we exerted our energy together at the command of the old woman and rolled the wheel, with a whizzing sound, onto the door board.

The cart driver, emerging from his anxiety, finally remembered to utter a few words of gratitude.

Zhang Zisheng said, "There is no need for thanks, this is something we ought to do. After a few days we should think of a way to fill in this section of the road. No matter how difficult, it should be repaired; otherwise it will be even more dangerous for carts in the future!"

When the cart driver looked around for my landlady, she had disappeared.

For several days after this event occurred, I found that my landlady's mood seemed especially withdrawn; coming and going, she always seemed to have something on her mind.

One morning I was awakened by a strange sound outside my window. I scrambled out of bed, put some clothes on, and went out to take a look. I was struck dumb.

The landlady and Qingming were in the courtyard sawing down the big peach tree. They sat on the ground one on each side pulling a small saw, as its lustrous silver teeth sparkled and gnawed at the purplish red tree trunk. Golden sawdust, flowing out like flour, piled at the foot of the tree. . . .

Flustered, I asked why they wanted to cut down such a good peach tree.

The old woman smiled at me, but before she could speak, that luxuriant peach tree fell with a crash. Broken branches and smashed foliage were thrown throughout the courtyard, breaking the cucumber trellis and flattening the tomato seedlings. The few peaches that had not been picked tumbled in all directions.

The landlady, patting away the sawdust on the front of her jacket, said to me: "Go quickly and brush your teeth and wash your face, then help me sort out the vegetable seedlings and tree branches. I borrowed two pickaxes. In a while the three of us can tear down the top of the wall. . . ."

Confused by the commotion, I did not know what the landlady wanted.

The old woman called loudly: "Don't stand there in a daze, hurry up and move! Oh, you still don't understand? It's like this: I don't think there is any way to fill in that road at the back of the house. It might be done, but the brigade would expend a lot of labor and it couldn't be permanent. With carts coming and going, endlessly turning curves, it will always be troublesome and dangerous as well! I want to give up this half of our courtyard to straighten out the road! . . ."

There was no way to describe my excitement and respect for the old landlady upon hearing this intention. Because things had happened suddenly and had come out contrary to my expectations, I went so far as to clumsily remark, "It would be a pity to destroy this courtyard. Isn't it possible to think of another solution that would satisfy all conditions?"

Upon hearing what I had said, the "firm and impartial" landlady shook her head with disapproval, and then said with seriousness: "In order to make the road unimpeded, if it means destroying this small bit of family property, or even cutting out flesh from my body, I should not hesitate."

The old woman's words at once set my heart ablaze, and I hastened to help her by doing everything she wanted me to do.

The eastern and western walls were pulled down so the road passed through the middle of the courtyard, forming a perfectly straight thoroughfare. The roadbed was filled in with pieces of stone and earthen bricks so that it was level and solid.

The sound of the cart whip and car horn. Carts, cars, the production brigade in a line, all passed through the courtyard, heading due east where the sun rises!

Part III Critique and Ambivalence

Introduction

//// In the 1980's, Hao Ran was left to carry the Maoist legacy, but the majority of writers enjoyed an unprecedented "thaw," at least up to June 1989. For the peasants, the economic reforms produced mobility and an explosion of entrepreneurial energies. Many of those who believed that they had been wronged ventured into Beijing in order to appeal to the "higher-ups."[1] "Call it a second liberation," they said.

For the intellectuals, there was ambivalence. The old "rightists" and "counterrevolutionaries" were rehabilitated. Many were determined to work feverishly in order to recover the twenty-odd years that were lost. Not all of them had the chance. Lao She, a contemporary of Mao Dun and Ba Jin, committed suicide after being publicly struggled against during the Cultural Revolution. Zhao Shuli died in 1970 after much suffering. Younger scholars were not spared. When Yang Jiang departed for the cadre school in 1970 to join her husband, Qian Zhongshu, she bore the grief of their only daughter, whose husband had taken his own life a month earlier. Gao Xiaosheng sadly remembers that his wife's death was due partly to a lack of medical care in the rural area where he had been sent for fifteen years. His friend Fang Zhi survived until 1979. But a combination of harsh labor, a poor diet, and an excessive intake of sedatives over a long period physically crushed him at the age of 49. "Tell me how much time I shall have," he pleaded with his wife when he was hospitalized. "If I have three more years, I shall plan for three years; if I have a month, I shall leave the hospital right away to finish the most urgent tasks." He barely lived another 30 days.[2]

The younger generation had its own problems. Those sent to the countryside returned to find a new society not ready to take them back.

They were out of school too long to meet the competitive requirements for higher education in an era that stressed technical expertise. They were beyond the age to find suitable spouses. From the government's point of view, they were also politically unreliable. Most important, they found it difficult to forget their part in a political drama that denied human compassion and shattered dreams.

It was up to the survivors to remember and to reflect. The literature of the 1980's was torn with anguished condemnations of the past and desperate attempts to leave the memories behind. Among other trends were the literature of the wounded, the exposure literature, obscure poetry, the new literature on sexuality, the efforts to find cultural roots, and experiments in modernism. They blossomed despite the fluctuating political winds. However, the ideological presence of the party-state was not reduced to a mere shadow. In 1981, there was the campaign against underground literature and the Bai Hua Incident.[3] In 1983, the party imposed the anti–spiritual pollution campaign. In 1987, the campaign to curb "bourgeois liberalism" caused leading critics to lose their party membership.

The controversy over social responsibility and self-expression emerged in the midst of ideological redefinition. Although the works included in this section were not directly involved in the debate, they illustrate how the issues were represented and resolved. In the literature on rural life, there was a rush to expose the horrors of the Maoist era. The impetus came from middle-aged writers who were silenced for a long period. "A Gift of Land" ("Song tian"), written by Gao Xiaosheng in 1985, satirizes the system that made arbitrary abuse by rural cadres the normal state of affairs. This story is but one of Gao's many biting portrayals of peasant life under socialism published since his rehabilitation in 1979. His comic hero, Chen Huansheng, who appears in a series of stories, has all the pathetic qualities of a narrow-minded, calculating, self-demeaning peasant trying to make the best of his circumstances. Yet one cannot help sympathizing with him. Born into a middle-peasant family in 1928 in Jiangsu, Gao spent many years in the country, including fifteen years when he was labeled a rightist. A master of critical realism, Gao uses satire not unlike that of Lu Xun to expose the irrationalities of a political system that continues to twist human character.[4] At the same time, he forces readers to reflect on their acquiescence.

Gu Hua is a slightly younger writer. Born in 1942 in rural Hunan, he graduated from a prefectural-level agricultural school. He became a village teacher during the commune movement in 1958 and started publishing in 1962. In 1980, he joined the Chinese Writers Association and was elected an executive of its branch in Hunan. He is known for his *A Town Named Hibiscus* (*Furong zhen*), a love story that exposes the devastating power of a stratum of village poor turned party cadres. "An Ivy-Covered Cabin" ("Pa man qingteng de muwu"), published in 1981, has a similar theme. It probes the issue of how Maoist politics dovetailed with the most ignorant and backward-looking cultural attitudes in rural society to create a stratum of local bosses who formed the basis of the party's power.

Younger writers have also exposed the nature of a political system that has paralyzed peasant livelihood. Li Rui was born in Beijing in 1950. He graduated from junior middle school in 1966. At the official conclusion of the Cultural Revolution in 1969, he was sent down as an educated youth to settle in the Leiliangshan District of Shanxi. He stayed for six years. Afterward he worked as a laborer in a steel factory for two years before becoming an editor of *Shanxi wenxue* (Shanxi literature) in 1977. His volume of short stories, *Thick Earth* (*Hou tu*, 1988), consists of seventeen pieces that capture the flavor of peasant life in Leiliangshan.[5] "Electing a Thief" ("Xuan zei") describes how some peasants turn the tables against a hated brigade leader. When the laughter is over, fear overwhelms them. Their gestures of reconciliation reveal the haunting complexities surrounding compliance and complicity.

If the goal of a realist writer is to portray life truthfully, the sharpness of his or her sensitivity to life is an important asset. Critical self-reflection, the second theme that has emerged in the 1980's, addresses the issue. The new-style writers examine the threads that bind the divergent fates of the peasants and themselves. Yang Jiang was born in Beijing and educated in Shanghai, Suzhou, and England. She is a noted translator and professor of English literature, and has been an established playwright since the 1940's. *Six Chapters of My Life "Downunder,"* published in 1981, reveals a dignified and resilient human spirit quietly resisting the dehumanizing labels imposed upon her and the peasants alike.[6]

The critical energies come largely from writers in their thirties, who regard cultural reflection as the root of literature and art. Han Shaogong was born in Changsha in 1953. After graduation from junior middle school in 1969, he was sent to the Hunan countryside. He was transferred to a county cultural center in 1974 and graduated from the Chinese department of Hunan Normal College in 1982. He has been an executive of the Hunan branch of the Chinese Writers Association and recently moved to Hainan Island. He is a representative of a group of young writers identified as the Xun gen pai (Back to the roots school). In an article entitled "The Roots of Literature" ("Wen-xue de gen"), he argues that writers must be sensitive to the ways in which the cultural and historical unconscious informs their art.[7] He is also noted for combining imagery and the real in his own work. The story "Déjà vu" ("Gui qu lai") describes his eerie return to the village to which he had been sent down as an educated youth. Memories of the web of human relationships twisted under political pressures continue to haunt him. But through the memories, he explores the amoral forces that underlie love and hate, greed and guilt, and that join his fate to that of his fellow beings.

Jia Pingwa* was born in 1954 in Shaanxi. He graduated from the Chinese department of Xibei University and worked as an editor for Shaanxi Renmin Chubanshe (Shaanxi People's Press). He started publishing in 1973 and is known for his intimate portrayals of rural life in his native Shangzhou. He is an executive of the Chinese Writers Association and the vice-chairman of its branch at Xian. In the story "Floodtime" ("Shuiyi"), the daily conflicts between members of two generations in rural Shaanxi are windows into the subtleties of individual emotions, cleansed of ideological shadows. The matter-of-fact tone of the story quietly captures what the new-style writers consider to be the "life force" (shengmingli) of the Chinese cultural tradition. Their mission is to give this force the artistic expression it deserves.

Ah Cheng (pen name of Zhong Ah Cheng) examines this "life force" in painful detail to show how creative and destructive energies are intertwined. Born in Beijing in 1949, he is the son of the famous film critic Zhong Dianfei. An active young artist, he is a founding member of the avant-garde artists club Xingxing Huashe (Stars Art Club). He wrote the screenplay for Gu Hua's A Town Named Hibiscus and is identified in China as a member of the Xun gen pai. He became known in literary circles outside of China after publishing a stunning series of short stories, "King of Chess" ("Qi wang"), "King of Trees" ("Shu wang"), and "King of Children" ("Haizi wang"). Critics compare his literary style to that of Lu Xun and describe him as "a soul famished but not fallen."[8] He has resided in the United States since 1988 and has written several short stories for the Hong Kong journal Jiushi nian-dai. In "Chimney Smoke" ("Chui yan"), he uses the trauma shared by the geologist and the peasant to depict the haunting complicity of victims, a complicity that touches the core of human existence.

*Jia uses the pronunciation "Pingwa," not "Ping'ao."

Gao Xiaosheng   # A Gift of Land

//// In Southern Zhou Village even people who don't know the first thing about bookkeeping understand that in this day and age farming is the most demanding and least profitable line of work around. After living in the same village and having traveled the same road to prosperity for many years, what was life like for factory workers? What was it like for workers in the stone quarry? For tradespeople? For transportation workers? For contract laborers? For the cadres? And what was it like for the farmers? Nothing could be clearer: the blind may not be able to see and the mutes may not know how to talk, but even they understand.*

Anyone could tell at first glance that Southern Zhou Village was a prosperous village. A look at the homes said it all: the new houses had driven the old ones into the ground, right through the cracks.† Those sad old buildings had once housed people, and the ones that had the good fortune to remain in existence were happy to live the degraded lives of pigpens and woodboxes. Their owners had moved into new homes, until only a few people remained in the old places,

---

This story was written on August 2–4, 1985, in Changzhou and published in *Jiushi niandai* in February 1986. Translation by Howard Goldblatt; reprinted from *Ba fang* by permission of that journal's editors.

*After the collectivization of agriculture in the mid-1950's, farmers were confined to their villages and made to grow grain to be sold to the state at a fixed price. Compared to urban workers, rural residents were disadvantaged, but household registration policies, rationing, and the need for work permits made it difficult for them to work in town. The situation lasted until the early 1980's, when procurement quotas were lifted and the communes were dismantled. Farmers have since diversified their sources of income and now sell their goods in revived markets and enjoy a degree of prosperity.

† In traditional China, owning a house in a community meant settlement rights for oneself and one's sons. Even in some prosperous areas today, it is difficult for young men without an inheritable dwelling to marry.

not because they wanted to, but because they hadn't yet built their new ones. Naturally, their numbers were dwindling fast, which meant that the overall situation was improving daily. More wondrous was the fact that some people who had already built their new homes got the itch to add on to them every three or four years. Take Zhou Xilin, for example: he was the first person in Southern Zhou Village to build a new house, a single-story, two-room place seventeen meters long by seven meters wide, with a total of seventy-five square meters of living space. Three years later, with all the other people building new homes, he found himself becoming just one of the crowd, seemingly no longer any better off than the others. Okay, tear this place down and build a two-story house! Looking ahead, he figured that within a few years two-story houses would be pretty common, so he invested some extra money in laying a foundation that would accommodate as many as five stories later on. Just as he'd predicted, within two years there were lots of two-story buildings, and it was a simple matter for him to add a floor to his own, increasing it to three stories. When, as time went on, a number of three-story buildings began to appear, he calmly added a fourth floor to his house. With all this building going on, the homes were getting taller and taller, better and better, and the situation had improved not just noticeably, but dramatically. The tallest and the best, of course, was Zhou Xilin's. Amazing! True heroes are never lost in the stream of history.

Now how did the people in Southern Zhou Village earn the money needed to build those houses? Simple, from the very beginning it was nothing more than a matter of a few rocks. Now rocks are things you encounter every day, and it takes some imagination to see how someone could live a good life on the strength of a few rocks. Southern Jiangsu is blessed with many factories, rich soil, and lots of ways to make a living, so who would give a second thought to something as hard, as cold, as heavy, and as frightfully dull as some rocks? Fengyu Xiang, the township where Southern Zhou Village was situated, was nothing but a bunch of desolate hills that were as bare as bald pates, where the soil was anemic, and whose sparse vegetation made them look like scabie-heads. They were a miserable lot: a tree wouldn't grow there if it was planted by hand, so there was nothing to do but write them off. For more years than anyone could count they were cursed by the people. During the Great Leap Forward in 1958, although no one proposed that rocks be the key to the future, with all the bridge-building, road-building, and factory-building under way, not to mention repairs of the scars made on heaven and earth by all those heroes, rocks became like the staff of life overnight, the foundation of foundations, a treasure among treasures.

Good lord! This is no Sichuan, with its Mt. Emei. Rocks are the one thing we're missing in this neck of the woods. The rocks here are sleeping the big sleep beneath the people's feet. What rotten luck! And so the desolate hills that had been written off suddenly became gold and silver mountains whose riches could never be depleted. The township* opened a stone quarry, to which every village and unit assigned workers, whose annual wages were three or four times that of the farmers in the production teams. The only pity was that not everyone could go; given the agricultural base with rice as the key product, someone had to tend the farm. We can't pay attention only to economics and neglect politics, after all!†

So then, who was to go and who was to stay? A good question, for which there is no clear answer.

But then, that's not unusual, for there are far more questions for which there are no clear answers than those for which there are clear answers. And among the latter there are many for which there should not be clear answers or cannot be clear answers, and even some unclear reasons why some questions should not or cannot have clear answers. Such things are better left unspoken. After all, going or not going, lucking out or striking out, are domestic issues that have nothing to do with outsiders.

We can begin with two representative types. Zhou Xilin, for example, was destined to be among those who went. Not only that, he was even a man with some responsibilities. As a person with high levels of consciousness and experience, no matter where he went, he made it known that he could take on more and more responsibilities. That's how it was in the village, that's how it was at the stone quarry, and that's how it was later on when he was reassigned elsewhere. After all, a tiger of a father never produces a dog of a son, and the door latch of a wise man's home is a pestle that can husk rice.

Their prospects were excellent, for neither his two sons, his two daughters, nor his two daughters-in-law ever so much as picked up a farm tool. Members of this family were involved in nearly every line of work—leadership, commerce, accounting, technical fields, and labor. So it didn't matter whether or not government policy allowed for certain people to get rich before the others, for on the road leading to

---

Xiang can be translated as township or large village.

† During the Maoist era, farmers were made to grow food grain at the expense of everything else.

wealth for all, he had early on placed himself at the head of the line. What more proof is needed than the matter of his house. If his family had been out in the fields struggling to make ends meet, how many years would it have taken him to get where he was? The proverb "good money, no work; good work, no money" says it all. Who says that culture and intelligence mean nothing? This requires class analysis—it depends upon who has the culture and intelligence. For a member of the bourgeoisie to spend all his time memorizing dictionaries is like farting in the wind. Zhou Xilin knew only about half the words used in the *People's Daily*, and still there wasn't a soul in the village who dared offer up a challenge. The legendary Zhao Pu brought order to all the land with his knowledge of only half of the Confucian *Analects*.* With the amount of ink running through Zhou Xilin's system, there was damned little he couldn't turn black if he was of a mind to. Which goes to prove the saying that "with the stroke of a man's pen a general is kept busy all day." A life of leisure has great appeal, although in the winter the turtle draws into its shell, making it difficult for anyone to see what it's up to, while in the summer everything is out in the open. In the evenings, after everyone in the family had washed up from head to toe until they looked and smelled as clean as could be, they'd sit on the rooftop and have their dinner. Made of reinforced concrete, sporting railings on all four sides, and decorated with plants and flowers, it was a real rooftop garden. After dinner they enjoyed the cool evening air, with Zhou Xilin seated in his specially made chair, whose four legs were nailed to two arched boards, so that whenever he shifted his weight slightly, the chair rocked back and forth; while he was making the trip from one end of the arc to the other, all the stars in the sky and the lanterns on the ground fell under his gaze. It was like watching a procession of radiant flowers, until he was so comfortable and peaceful he didn't even want to think. Such a happy life, even the immortals never had it so good! The height of the building did more than lend it an impressive appearance: the wind was strong enough up there that there were few mosquitoes (since there was blood to be had down below, why waste all that energy to fly high?) and, if that weren't enough, one could see way off into the distance (as they say, "to see the horizon, one need only climb a single story").

What I'd like to emphasize here is that the situation I've described so far is normal. Zhou Bingnan never complained about the way things

*A.D. 916–92. A high official under the first two emperors of the Northern Song dynasty (960–1126). He was a devoted student of the *Analects* and once remarked to the second emperor of the Song: "With one half of this work, I helped your father gain the empire, and now with the other half I am helping Your Majesty keep it."

were. Now you can call him an Ah Q if you like,* and encourage him
to fly out from under Ah Q's wing, if you like (I don't know when Ah
Q grew wings. At first all he had was a pigtail, if I'm not mistaken.
I wonder where it's gone. You haven't grabbed hold of it, have you?
Or jerked it clean off?), or even go so far as to heap scorn upon him
and say he doesn't deserve to be written into the story. I don't care.
But don't ever try to jump to his defense, because you'll jump in vain;
besides, he doesn't need it. He followed along with everyone else and
lived all these years in the new society without taking a back seat to anyone. He gave a reasonable account of himself, letting the good things
pass him by so he could pick up the bad. He worried before the world
got worried and only felt happy after the world was happy. He knew
that boats rise at high tide, and he was, after all, on the boat. What,
may I ask, is wrong with that way of looking at things? Now it was his
turn to get rich and build a house.

Zhou Bingnan got rich and built his house by working at the stone
quarry. The Cultural Revolution had no sooner breathed its last than
people stopped giving all the reasons why Zhou Bingnan "should not
go" (which goes to show that everyone has a sense of right and wrong),
but an absence of reasons why he should not go was not the same as
saying he should go. No, the reason why he should go lay elsewhere:
the township had built factories that were better than the stone quarry
—safer and cleaner, with livelier work and better pay. All the stone
quarry workers who had something going for them quickly wriggled
their way into the new factories; in Zhou Xilin's family, for instance,
three people had once worked at the stone quarry, but now the number
was zero. Finding itself with a manpower shortage, the stone quarry
raised wages to recruit workers and still came up short. Too many
people wanted to avoid hardships, tiring work, and dirt, not to mention the possibility of serious injury—who needed to get buried under
an avalanche after one of the blasts! That was when Zhou Bingnan
showed up, and he was welcomed with open arms.

A little more than three, but less than four, years later, Zhou Bingnan and his son, by saving the wages they earned on the mountain,
had enough money to build a two-room, two-story house. Every dime,
every penny they earned was figured in. But how much sweat had it
cost them?

Who measured? Who counted?

And yet, earning enough money to build a house was not the most

---

*Ah Q is the pitiful, self-deceiving village bum in Lu Xun's classic story "The True
Story of Ah Q" ("Ah Q zhengzhuan").

significant consequence of Zhou Bingnan and his son's working in the stone quarry for all those years; what mattered most was that two peasants had been turned into workers.* The family's primary source of income was no longer the planting of a few *mu* of land in the production unit's farm, but their stone quarry wages. This resulted in changes in spirit and temperament; they now did things with a flair. In the past, if Zhou Bingnan had been able to save up this much money, he would not have used it to build a house. What if, he would have wondered, there were some sort of natural disaster? What if Mother took sick? What if my son Liangliang found the girl of his dreams? What if I underestimated the costs and had to borrow money to build the house, then couldn't pay it back? But these things no longer bothered him, for now he had a permanent source of income and there was no need to keep a reserve. He was not afraid to risk everything.

"To hell with all that, let's build the house first, then see what happens. If we need money for something else, we can always borrow it and pay it back later." That was the sort of confidence Zhou Bingnan had these days.

"Hurry up and build it!" the other villagers encouraged him. "Look around! How many people are left who haven't built their houses yet? It ought to be your turn by now."

"Ha-ha, the sun will soon be shining down on the front door of my house." Zhou Bingnan was a happy man.

He had never been one to do things without planning. When plots of land had been distributed and production contracts signed some years back, he had considered a site for a new house then. Less than fifty meters from his old house there was a plot of land not quite one and a half *fen* in size, 6 *li* of which already belonged to him as a private plot,† while the remaining 9 *li* were Zhou Xilin's private plot. Zhou Bingnan had originally asked the production unit to redistribute Zhou Xilin's portion to him as the site for his house, but his request could not be approved, for there was, it turned out, a requirement that land earmarked for a house site must be built upon within a year.‡ Zhou Bingnan had not had the money back then, so he gave up the idea.

---

*A peasant is often tied to the land by grain procurement quotas imposed by the state as well as by the responsibility to feed himself. A worker is entitled to buy grain from state grain stations at a subsidized price.

† Even when most of the village land was collectivized, each household was given a small strip of private land.

‡ In the 1980's, when the communes were dismantled, each village reassigned its land and production resources by contracting them out to individual households. Sites for houses were restricted because the government feared that the amount of land devoted to agriculture would be affected.

Some people laughed at him: "You would have been better off building your house on every inch of the land that was already yours. That would have given you nearly forty square meters of living space." Zhou Bingnan then asked that the land be turned over to him for use as a personal plot, but Zhou Xilin withheld his consent—naturally. "My friend," he said, "if you wanted it to build a house, I'd have to go along with it. But why should I turn it over to you as a private plot when I can work it myself? Besides, I'm used to working it, so why let you have it?" There was nothing Zhou Bingnan could say. He lost again.

By this time houses covered nearly all the usable land in the village. That one piece of land, of which two-fifths belonged to him and three-fifths to someone else, was about the only vacant plot left. Just that one piece of land—spacious, well irrigated, and far enough from neighboring plots to avoid the problem of blocking other people's light or summer breezes. So Zhou Bingnan brought up the old arguments once more, asking for help from the village committee.

Without question, the land belonged to the collective, so the village committee was obliged to act favorably upon Zhou Bingnan's lawful request. But nothing in this world happens that doesn't involve a good many other things. Sure, the land belonged to the collective, but its operation was the responsibility of individuals. The village director, Zhou Guoping, who was very young and new on the job, not only was no match for Zhou Xilin, but couldn't even stand up to Zhou Xilin's son.* So the agenda called for a reshuffling of individual and collective ownership, rights of operation, and rights of possession. He was very polite in dealing with "Uncle Bingnan," saying things like "The village committee has no objection to your request for that piece of land, but it's necessary to talk it over with Zhou Xilin and get his approval."

"Then please go ahead and talk it over with him," Bingnan said.

"You do it. It's best for the two of you to hash it out."

"No, you do it!"

"No, you do it!"

Back and forth it went, the polite give-and-take. Now Bingnan was no fool, and the more polite the village director became, the more Bingnan knew there was trouble ahead. This increased his resolve to avoid confronting Zhou Xilin head on, for if they reached an impasse, there would be no way to get the discussions moving again. "Director," he pleaded, "I need your help. You must talk to Zhou Xilin for me, no matter what. If you bring him around, fine; if not, that's okay too.

---

*Decollectivization forced many old cadres who had dominated the countryside for decades to retire. However, the new cadres were often young and inexperienced and acted more as mouthpieces for the retired cadres.

Even if you only get a sense of his intentions, I'll be in your debt. You can tell me what he says, and that will help me plan my strategy before talking things over with him. If this piece of land is turned over to me, you have my word that I'll meet any conditions within my power. I'm not looking for a free ride. No one will be the worse off because of it."

At this point the village director nodded his head to show that he agreed to do as he was asked.

Three months passed, with no news. Running into someone in the village was never all that difficult, but since Zhou Bingnan was working on the mountain during the day, he could only see the director at night when he was attending to village matters. He knew the wisdom in the saying that "the emperor never sends hungry troops into battle," and that the only way to bring the "summer rains" was to produce some "eastern winds." The village director was in a difficult position, since he couldn't put things off indefinitely, and he couldn't gain a reputation simply by fishing for it, so he had to row with the current. But "everyone in a village is as busy as everyone else." "Whenever I'm free," he said, "he's tied up, and whenever he's free, I'm tied up. I went to his place twice, but he was out both times. Twice I asked him to drop by, and he came over both times, but I was out. We met twice on the street, but he was on his way to work and had no time to talk. But don't panic, I'll keep trying."

One day, as the fourth month was drawing to a close, Director Zhou rushed over to see Bingnan. "I've talked with Zhou Xilin," he announced, "and there's no problem. He doesn't want a thing from you and has no desire for you to suffer any loss at all. You can go over and discuss it with him yourself."

A load fell from Zhou Bingnan's heart. Only in a new society could something be resolved so easily.

"That's right, a new society." Zhou Xilin received Zhou Bingnan in his four-story house. After the pleasantries were dispensed with, Zhou Xilin outlined the situation: "If this were the old society, I wouldn't have given in if you and I were born of the same mother, let alone share the same surname."

"Naturally," Zhou Bingnan said in a tone that revealed his deep gratitude. Even though they lived in the same village and were both named Zhou, this was the first time Zhou Bingnan had been in this house, and it was an eye-opening experience. "Wow!" he thought to himself. "All they ever say is, 'People are dressed in clothes, Buddhas are dressed in gold,' but that doesn't say it all. It's only proper for a Buddha dressed in gold to live in a magnificent temple. What comfort! This is the way a house is supposed to be built, the ultimate in prestige." He was not in Zhou Xilin's league.

"Land for a house is worth its weight in gold," Zhou Xilin said casually. "If you try to buy it, you'll find that it costs three times as much as ordinary rice-paddy land, and even that's like giving it away."

"That was in the old society. Building a house was beyond my means then."

"I'm talking about the old society," Zhou Xilin declared, then added with the tone of an expert, "In matters like this, altruism seldom enters the picture. The six-room house belonging to Hong Fu in East Village is just a run-down old building now. When his grandfather built it, about 8 *li* of the land was reclaimed from rice-paddy fields, and he wound up paying several times what it was worth just to build a wall on it. But the people who owned that land—their pride and joy—didn't want to part with it and wouldn't even set a price. Do you know what Hong Fu's grandfather wound up doing? He placed a silver coin on every single rice stalk. Now that's class!"

"That *is* class," Zhou Bingnan agreed, nodding his head. It was an often-told story.

"There are more awkward situations like that than you'll ever know. When Liu Gen built his house, the land in front of his gate belonged to someone else, and when he wanted to make an access road, he paid dearly. Then there was Wu Zhihong, whose father built a two-room house, then had to sell a hundred kilos of rice to pay for two banquets, just because water from his eaves ran off onto someone else's land. Now that's land worth its weight in gold!"

All Zhou Bingnan could do while these examples were being reeled off was say "uh-huh" now and then; he had no chance to talk business. By the time Zhou Xilin had exhausted his repertoire, it was getting late, and Zhou Bingnan had to be on the job early the next morning. "Thank you, Elder Brother," he said as he made ready to leave.

"Why thank me?"

"For agreeing to turn over the land for my house."

"No need to thank me for that. You go on over and iron out the details with Director Guoping."

"Guoping said he had no objections, that all I needed was your okay."

"Hasn't he gone over the details with you?"

"Such as?"

Zhou Xilin smiled. "You go talk to him. I've already told him how I feel. I wonder why he didn't say anything to you. I guess he's too young to know how to handle matters. Go ask him."

After he'd been seen out and the door had closed behind him, Zhou Bingnan's heart sank. He knew that it had not gone well.

What could it be that made everyone keep skirting the issue? Until he got to the bottom of this, sleep was out of the question, so there was no use lying in bed. He went over to see Guoping that very night.

"He doesn't want anything of yours," Guoping said to him awkwardly, weighing every word as he stood in the doorway, a jacket thrown over his shoulders. "He has 2.3 *mu* of land under contract over on South Bank that is not being tended. He's agreed to let you have the land you want for the house with the condition that you take those 2.3 *mu* of farmland as well."

"Oh!" Zhou Bingnan gasped. He was speechless.

After a moment, Zhou Guoping sighed softly and said, "Well, what do you think?"

Zhou Bingnan wiped his sweaty palms on his shirt as he answered, "Do you think I can manage?"

"I know the fix you're in," Zhou Guoping replied softly. "So when he wanted me to tell you, I refused. I advised him to tell you to your face. But you see, I was forced to be the one to tell you after all."

Neither of them knew what to say for a long time.

The times change quickly, and all it takes is five or ten years for a complete turnaround. Generation after generation of peasants have tilled the land—the land has been their livelihood. There's no need to go a long way back—ten years is enough. Back then anyone who signed a contract to till a plot of land on his own was a counterrevolutionary; and as recently as four years ago, when production contracts for the land were being parceled out, everyone was afraid of what might happen if they were accused of being unfair. But now the land had become a burden to many, and you couldn't give it away. Zhou Xilin handled the matter the way a businessman would, by sticking slow-moving goods together with fast-moving ones, and forcing the customer to buy a package deal. He was giving something away for nothing, all right, but he was throwing in a great deal extra, so much, in fact, that even he was sheepish about it. But sheepishness or not, opportunities like this didn't come around every day.

Zhou Guoping came to Zhou Xilin's defense. "He's in a fix himself. Who among the six adults and one youngster in the family is free to till the land?"

With a pained look on his face, Zhou Bingnan said, "So he wants to pin the tail on me, but I can't handle it. I've already got 5 *mu* of my own, and if I take on this additional 2.3 *mu*, then either my son or I will have to give up the stone quarry job to work it, and I hate to think how much that will cost me a year."

Zhou Guoping stood there without saying a word and listened.

"Figuring roughly," Zhou Bingnan continued, "A *mu* of land requires about 30 workdays a year, so 2.3 *mu* means 69 days. I make at least 7 yuan a day up on the mountain, compared to the 2.50 yuan a day I can earn on the land. If I lose 4.50 yuan a day for 69 days, it comes to over 300 yuan. And not just for one or two years, but from now on!"

"That sounds about right."

"Not only that, South Bank is a long way from the village, and how much fertilizer can I carry over there every day?"

"That's no problem. It's a good road all the way over, so you can use a tractor."

"Am I supposed to mechanize for a little plot of land like that? I don't have that kind of money. What's wrong with just going up on the mountain and making a good living?"

"So what are you going to do?"

"Right, what am I going to do?" Zhou Bingnan answered in exasperation.

When you don't know what to do, you do nothing. Isn't that what history is all about—doing nothing? It's enough to make you sick!

Zhou Bingnan had not been blessed with the doggedness of Zhou Xilin. Sure, he was in the right, but Zhou Xilin was in the driver's seat, so the outcome was never in doubt. Blame it on fate, if you will. Well then, if he couldn't build his house on this plot, he'd have to find another. Why not? All he had to do was put in a request with village director Zhou Guoping.

Who would have guessed that this road would be blocked too? Zhou Guoping assured him there was no problem, but one day led to another, then one month led to another . . . and nothing happened. Several months passed before Zhou Bingnan got wind of something in the air. There'd been a change in the situation. Now it was no longer a question of whether or not he wanted that plot of land, for Zhou Xilin had sunk his teeth into him and wasn't about to let go. Who was Zhou Guoping going to listen to, Zhou Xilin or Zhou Bingnan? Do I have to tell you? Hm?

Who said that doing nothing was getting nothing done?

Nonsense! Doing nothing is the only way of getting something done.

Zhou Bingnan had no choice but to bite the bullet and accept defeat with bowed head.

> Mountains gone, waters ended, where is the road?
> Willow shade, flowers bright, another village at hand.

In contemporary speech, this would mean something like "though there are twists and turns in the road, the future is still bright."

Following delicate negotiations, everyone obtained what they needed, with no casualties, major or minor, on either side, not even a red face. The results could be compared to a Shaolin Temple master fighting a three-year-old child,* the outcome of which is predictable, yet does not cause a ripple of protest among the populace or have any effect on public order.

But the process took nearly a year from start to finish, from late fall of one year, when the standoff occurred, through the following summer, when Zhou Bingnan ultimately accepted the other party's "peace offering of ceded territory." He chose this particular time for good reason—by then the crops were mature enough that Zhou Xilin would have to take in the harvest before it was Bingnan's turn to plant the next crop, a strategy that earned him a six-month reprieve.

Now that the land was his, Zhou Bingnan could build his house whenever he felt like it, and his two-room house was completed before the crops in the field were ripe. It had cost him a tidy sum, but the money wasn't wasted. He took on the appearance of someone who was prepared to spend as much as necessary in order to demonstrate—to the surprise of others—that he was now reasonably well off.

The autumn harvest was completed before the frosts came, after which Zhou Xilin had Zhou Guoping inform Zhou Bingnan that it was time to plant the new crop on the South Bank land. Naturally, this required no formal ceremony, but was a simple matter of transferring the rights of operation to him.

It was, after all, the new society! In the past who would have done what he did?

Zhou Bingnan, a man of his word, took possession. But even after the first snows had fallen, no crops had been planted.

Was he going to just let the land lie fallow? No, everyone knew that Zhou Bingnan was not that kind of man. Zhou Guoping came to persuade him not to let his sense of having been wronged make him act rashly, but Zhou Bingnan only smiled and said, "What do you mean, act rashly? It's still early!"

"Early?"

"Right, it's early for what I'm going to plant."

"What are you going to plant?"

"What am I going to plant? Well, I can't compete with Zhou Xilin. You recall that the South Bank land was converted from a dry field into a paddy, don't you? But can land really be converted just like that? During all these years, it has produced meager harvests. The land

*The monks at the Shaolin Temple and their disciples were known for their skills in martial arts.

can't hold the water, which keeps running off. If it were a cooperative, who would care? If it were Zhou Xilin's, who would care? They can absorb the losses. But not me. I'm going to convert it back."

"Dry land is harder to work. You have to irrigate it every summer and fall."

"Not me."

"If you don't, the crops will die."

"Not necessarily. I'm going to plant trees."

"Plant—trees—?" Zhou Guoping could hardly believe what he was hearing and didn't know what to do. How could he plant trees? Wasn't the land accustomed to producing rice? What difference did it make how good or bad the harvest was?

But he didn't object. That wouldn't have been right. Times had changed, and besides, it wouldn't have done any good to object. Zhou Bingnan had a bellyful of responses ready for that eventuality. If he refrained from objecting, those responses would stay right where they were.

With his mind made up, it was time for Zhou Bingnan to spring into action. Whenever he had some free time, whenever he could find a break in his busy schedule, sometimes even if he had to ask for time off from the quarry, Zhou Bingnan and his family went out, braving the bone-chilling winter winds, to dig holes in the icy ground, add some fertilizer, and plant saplings. It took them a full winter of hard work, but they managed to cover the 2.3 *mu* of land with 3,000 saplings. A bit dense, perhaps, but since not all of them would survive, he needed some reserves.

It was no easy matter for the family to complete an undertaking of this magnitude, and when they were finished, there was nothing but row upon row of bare branches—not much of a sight. But when spring came, when the weather turned warm and a few rains had fallen, then there would be fresh green branches, followed by tiny buds and tender green leaves, and the whole place would look like a nursery with lots of children, all lively and jubilant, and lovely to behold.

An entire family was kept busy all that time, never quite aware that the wheel of history continued to turn and that, without their realizing it, "another village" had come into view. It never ends.

Not long after the saplings had been planted, shortly before the New Year's festival, Zhou Bingnan and his son had just gotten off work late one afternoon and were heading home from the stone quarry. Just as they turned onto the road home, they heard someone off in the distance hailing "Younger Brother Bingnan." When Zhou Bingnan looked up, he was surprised and bewildered. Wasn't that Zhou

Xilin? But how could it be, with such a gentle tone of voice! Yet if it wasn't him, Zhou Bingnan's eyes were failing him. He was still wondering when Zhou Xilin walked up alongside them. No doubt about it, it was him all right. He had been blessed with a pleasant voice and good looks, but Zhou Bingnan had never been exposed to them.

"Younger Brother Bingnan," Zhou Xilin said warmly, with a twinkle in his eye, "I've been looking high and low for you, and when someone told me you were here, I didn't believe them. It's nearly New Year's, and here you are out working every day. Why be so tough on yourself?"

"What else can I do?" Zhou Bingnan had never known how to handle sweet talk, and he was starting to fidget, not knowing what was expected of him. "You . . ."

"But there is something you can do, there *is* something," Zhou Xilin interrupted him. "As long as there's leadership in the Communist party, there's always something you can do. When you felt like building your two-room house, didn't you go ahead and build it? Just like that, without owing anyone a penny?"

"Elder Brother Xilin, what did you want to talk to me about?" If Zhou Bingnan didn't try to get in a word edgewise, the conversation would never turn in the direction it was meant to head; and the sooner he found out what was up, the sooner he'd be back home. It was nearly year's end, he was busier than ever, and he was famished.

"Nothing in particular. Let's walk together," Zhou Xilin said as he fell into step with them. "Really, there's nothing," he repeated. "I'm just on my way home. Why don't we all go to my place and have an end-of-the-year meal. That includes my esteemed nephew here." Everything was topsy-turvy here. Zhou Bingnan was damned if he accepted and damned if he didn't. After a moment's hesitation, he said, "I can't do that, Elder Brother. It should be me asking you over instead of the other way around."

"What's the difference?" Zhou Xilin quickly interrupted him. "We're like brothers. There's only one way of writing the surname Zhou, so it's all the same who treats whom. Tonight you come to my place, and tomorrow night I'll come over and sample some of Sister-in-law's cooking. Why treat each other like strangers? I'm sure you're not afraid of having me over for a meal!"

Zhou Bingnan was a decent man who didn't have a deceitful bone in his body; but decent though he was, age alone had made him wise enough to know a few things about the ways of the world, and he had a sense of what was going on. But like a criminal who's been thrown into prison, there was no way of avoiding the shackles, so he tagged along like a puppy dog, raging inwardly over his inability to get out of situations like this. At the very least, he figured, he should have been able to find a hole in the net for his son to escape through; but even that was beyond his power, and so now they'd both fallen into brother Xilin's grasp.

"What kind of talk is that? Are you afraid that the food at your uncle's house is no good? No, even if you only taste it, that's better than nothing. Or if that's still too much, then at the very least you have to come in and sit for a while. Don't worry, if my stools take a bite out of your rear, you won't have to spend your money on medical bills, don't you worry!"

Father and son just stood there like bumps on a log, neither managing to break free. Actually, there was nothing to worry about. Getting dragged along was a stroke of luck, for they were met by a solemn sight: there seated in the room were six people. In addition to Zhou Xilin's eldest son and his wife, there were four local officials, among whom Zhou Guoping was the most junior. As for the other three, since Zhou Bingnan shied away when he ran into them on the street, he didn't dare say anything now. But when Zhou Bingnan and his son walked into the room, they were unexpectedly greeted with smiles and nods, which made their bones feel heavier than ever; they were afraid to move a muscle for fear of being laughed at, so again they stood there like bumps on a log. All they could think of was how to avoid having these people look down on them. All other thoughts had vanished.

What a hypnotic spell was cast over the two of them: a resplendent room, noble guests, exquisite table settings, and a sumptuous meal; the combination turned Zhou Bingnan and his son into a couple of marionettes nailed to their chairs at the table. Zhou Xilin knew all about this sort of mental state, and he liked it. He'd long since found all the rationalizations he'd ever need for his customary hypocrisy, and naturally he wanted people to take his various poses as genuine feelings.

"Brother, let me toast you," he said, rising solemnly and raising his glass to Zhou Bingnan. "Come, come, let's not stand on ceremony. Tonight you are the honored guest. The party secretary, the director, they're all here to help me entertain you, so you must drink the first toast. Brother, this is a chance for me to do some atoning, and your acceptance of the toast will show that you forgive me."

"Elder Brother, you . . ."

"Now be reasonable. I have my shortcomings. I didn't think things out clearly enough, never dreaming that you didn't want the land in the first place. If I had known, that would have been the end of it, but you never said a word. Then when you took it over, planting rice wasn't showy enough, so you decided to plant trees, which stirred up public opinion . . . but stirring up public opinion was a good thing, for I did treat you shabbily."

"Brother, I never . . ." The two marionettes' strings had been pulled.

"I know, you never intended to cut the ground out from beneath me. Other people seized upon the incident and made an issue of it. But as kin, we can't let other people exploit us. I admit I made a mistake, so now you must let me take that land back, then no one will be able to say I took advantage of you."

"Brother, you . . ."

"Brother, all I ask is that you trust me. The party secretary and the director are here to serve as witnesses that my only concern is to salvage my reputation. It never entered my mind to plot for any personal gains, and I certainly never expected to hear some of the things people have been saying. So I've suffered a bit, but now you let me take the land back. Even if I have no time to do any planting and have to leave it untended for a year or so, making it necessary for me to pay out 10, 20, 30, or more yuan to make up the quota, what does that matter? A couple of friends could spend that much on one good meal at a restaurant."

The longer Zhou Xilin talked, the more emotional he became, and the more he showed that he was truly speaking from the heart. All of this made Zhou Bingnan feel quite ashamed and begin to wonder if he might have misread Zhou Xilin all along. Maybe he hadn't really tried to use up some of his grease after all (not that Zhou Bingnan had any grease to speak of—and Zhou Xilin hadn't actually taken any money), but had only been interested in saving a little trouble. He felt, after all, that he was guilty of "sizing up a gentleman's belly with the eyes of a beggar," and when his thoughts reached this point, he said plaintively:

"Why didn't you tell me this at the beginning, Brother? I've already planted the land with trees!"

"Not to worry, I've already thought that out, and I'm not going to let you lose a thing. How much did the saplings cost you? And the fertilizer? And how about the labor? Just give me a figure, and I'll take care of it."

Now that's what's called clear thinking, fair business tactics, and the application of humanity and duty. Is there a brother alive who could refuse?

Just then, Zhou Bingnan's son, who hadn't dared to open his mouth up to this point, said, "Uncle, we have receipts for everything else, but how are we supposed to figure the labor costs?"

"Not to worry, I'll be as generous as possible. We can arrive at a figure. Ask someone else to give an estimate and I'll up it by 10 percent. And for wages, we'll use the salary scale at the stone quarry."

My god, how could anything be more wonderful than that? Who could believe that such things were possible?

"Ai! It's me who was in the wrong." Zhou Xilin, who knew exactly what was going through the other man's mind, turned solemnly to the party secretary and the director and said, "It was contrary to documented internal policy. Now we must abide by it."

"Ah!" exclaimed Zhou Bingnan and his son just then, as everything suddenly became clear.

"If we work this out, I won't forget you. Young nephew, the stone quarry is a tough place to make a living, and there's no future there for someone as young as you. As soon as the opportunity arises, I'll find you a job in a better factory," Zhou Xilin said with a note of concern. Then he turned to Zhou Bingnan: "Don't you have a daughter at home? How old is she? I'll find a factory job for her when I can, too."

. . . . .

It worked. The earth revolves in accordance with the will of the Zhou Xilins of this world.

Zhou Bingnan had planted the trees very conscientiously. When spring came and the flowers began to bloom, green buds appeared on nearly every one of the 3,000 saplings.

Not long after that, all of South Bank, a total of 38 *mu*, including the 2.3 *mu* on which Zhou Bingnan had planted trees, was taken over as a site for a huge new factory, for which the village committee was given a sum of appropriation money and an allocation of 39 worker slots for the villagers. The people who had production contracts for the land were given the equivalent of a year's output value as compensation, which satisfied everyone. Zhou Xilin was as good as his word, for he turned the two worker slots allocated to him over to Zhou Bingnan's son and daughter. The previous misunderstanding was now but a faint memory, and relations between the two families had never been better.

Not many months later rumors began to surface that the 3,000 trees on Zhou Xilin's 2.3 *mu* of land had been compensated for by the new factory on a per-tree basis. Some said that the figure was 5 yuan a tree, others said 10 yuan, and some said 20, 30 . . . as much as 50 yuan.

The talk spread, stirring up waves of public opinion. Zhou Xilin had no choice but to come forward and refute the reports. Zhou Guoping also declared that it was only a rumor and not to be believed. But to his close friends he said in private that it was actually only 10 yuan a tree, not all of which had gone into Xilin's pocket.

It's difficult to say whether he was telling the truth or not.

Naturally, the rumors reached Zhou Bingnan's ears as well, and he had his suspicions. "No wonder my elder brother was so keen on taking the tail back; he must have already known that things were going to work out for him just fine." At first he was indignant over the fact that someone else had made out so well because of the trees he —Zhou Bingnan—had planted. But on second thought, this was precisely Zhou Xilin's skill. If the land had still belonged to him, he would never have come up with a scheme to fleece the government, so the profits were never his to earn in the first place. Zhou Xilin had done him a service, for both his son and his daughter had gotten jobs. Zhou Bingnan was not a greedy man, and he knew he should be satisfied with what he had.

So he had no misgivings. No matter how you looked at it everyone's lot had improved, and what could be better than that!

2–4 August 1985
Changzhou (in a hurry)

Gu Hua   The Ivy-Covered Cabin

////   For years now, there has circulated in the forest area of
Mount Fogline the story of "Naogelaoyulang," the Yao Damsel. It is
said that in Green Hollow, in the center of the innermost reaches of
the quiet, ancient forest on Mount Fogline, there lived a young Yao
woman who worked as a forest ranger. Her name was Pan Qingqing.
She was born in the mountains and grew up there, and when she married, her groom came to the mountains to live with her.* Even such
a faraway place as the headquarters of the Forestry Center, she had
visited only once. All the young fellows in the tree farm had only heard
of the legendary beauty of this damsel, but had never set eyes on her.
Her ancestors had all lived in Green Hollow, in a wooden cabin overgrown with ivy. The wooden cabin was made of pine logs too hard
for an axe to cut and too heavy for a wild boar to dislodge. The section of the pine logs buried underground had rotted to black, with
wave-shaped laces of white fungus growing in thick layers. Behind the
cabin was a stream where clear water flowed all year. Apart from a
little dirt road, the only means of communication between the wooden
cabin and the outside world had been a telephone line installed before the Cultural Revolution for reporting on forest fires. One year, a
heavy snow crushed the line. As the Cultural Revolution unfolded, the
leaders of the Forestry Center came in and out of view like a revolving
lantern. Since everyone was preoccupied with seizing power and pre-
venting others from seizing power in a political flip-flop game where
there could be no winners, no one bothered to have the telephone line

This story was published in *Shiyue* in 1981 (issue no. 2). Translation by Tam King-fai;
the editor has made substantial changes in the translation.
   *Pan is a common name for the Yao people, who now live in the mountainous areas
of Hunan, Guangxi, and northern Guangdong.

repaired. Consequently, the wire that symbolized modern civilization never again reached into the ancient forest. . . . Day in and day out, Green Hollow was as quiet as sleep in the midst of the forest vast and deep, except for the occasional crowing of chickens and the barking of dogs and the crying of babies, and the pale blue kitchen smoke that hovered above the cabin. Even all the noisy chirping of the birds and the blooming and falling of all the flowers in the mountains had not awakened it.

Pan Qingqing's parents died early. Her husband, Wang Mutong, was a Han Chinese. He was tall and robust, with a build sturdy enough to overpower a tiger. Both husband and wife were forest rangers. Before each meal, Wang Mutong enjoyed having a glass or two of maize wine, warmed up by Pan Qingqing. Except for occasional fits of temper after drinking, when he would beat his wife until she was green and purple all over, he was not a bad husband. He knew how to look out for his woman's comfort. Qingqing never had to gather firewood in the mountains since the logs were already stacked beside the door; she never had to tend the fire lanes because there had not been a forest fire in Green Hollow for more than ten years; she never needed to work in the fields because the large private plot beside the stream was always tended, and provided more vegetables than their family of four could consume. All she had to do was feed the pigs, nurse the children, and attend to the usual household chores of washing and mending. That is why, even in her mid-twenties, Qingqing was as fresh and soft as a maiden. Wang Mutong was illiterate, but he was very sure of himself. In Green Hollow, he felt that he was the true master: the woman was his, the children were his, the house and the grounds were all his. Sure enough, he had to report to the Forestry Center but it had sent him here to look after the forest, he was therefore like the lord of a small fief. Before she had children, Qingqing had wanted to visit the headquarters, over 90 *li* away, but Wang would not permit it—she even received a few slaps on the face and was made to kneel. What he feared was that once his gorgeous wife was exposed to the bustling world outside, she would be dazzled, and then some slick young fellow who couldn't keep still for a moment could lure her away. Not until Pan Qingqing gave birth to a son and then a daughter did he finally feel secure. It was as if Pan Qingqing was now truly his woman, firmly fastened to his belt. The slapping, forced kneeling, and other family disciplinary actions then fell on the children instead. He imposed order in their daily lives. Husband and wife, parents and children, assumed their respective roles in Green Hollow to maintain a semblance of hierarchy. They formed a society in miniature.

Wang Mutong and Pan Qingqing thus lived away from the rest of humanity. Although their marriage was far from perfectly harmonious, they had grown used to each other and shared a life peacefully. Wang Mutong went to the headquarters once a month to claim both their salaries and to carry home the month's supply of rice, oil, and salt. On his return, he would at least share with Pan Qingqing some of the happenings at the headquarters or other rumors he picked up there. Pan Qingqing always listened with her black glistening eyes wide open, fascinated, as if the man were telling tales about some far-away country on the edge of the sky. In the last few years, all that he had told her about was how students in the outside world had turned rebellious and stirred up trouble, how spectacled teachers had been strung together like monkeys and paraded with placards around their necks, and how technician Lin, who had spent half his life in study, had drowned himself in a little mudhole where buffaloes wallowed. So shallow was the water that his back wasn't even drenched. Then there was the campaign against "deers" [scholars]. The deer aren't the same as those in the woods which only bullets can fell. They say, all scholars are deer. . . .* "Ai, life in our Green Hollow is better after all. The black soil shines and oozes out oil fat. A stick would sprout in it. We don't have education; we don't bother others, nor do they bother us. . . ."

What her husband said, Qingqing understood only partly. Confused, she had even worried for the scholars. To know how to read and write means trouble, she thought, how lucky she and her husband were. Having had the line "It is better to live in our Green Hollow" repeated to her so many times, she began to believe it. Now, she did not even think about the headquarters, a chaotic place where scheming and backstabbing ran rampant. She did not have high expectations for her husband; she only hoped that when he lost his temper, he would not slap her too heavily. In the evenings, no sooner had it turned dark than they quickly closed the door and turned in. Half a *jin* of kerosene was enough lamp fuel for six months. Only the moon and the stars in the sky, in the occasional moments when they shone through the window lattice high on the wall, were witnesses to their nocturnal life.

"Qingqing, you must bear me a few more babies."

"We already have Xiaotong and Xiaoqing. Didn't you say that the Forestry Center does not permit people to have more children? And that all the women will have to be fixed up?"

*Since Chinese is largely an uninflected language, it is possible to change voice in the course of a narrative without the use of grammatical markers. I have used a colloquial tone or put in italics passages that clearly contain changes in the voice of narration but do not warrant the use of quotation marks as is the practice in English.

"Who cares? Five more are not too many for us."

"Yeah. You never care how rough it is for me."

"Rough? What is so rough about bearing babies?"

"I'm afraid the people at the headquarters will give us a hard time."

"Afraid, my ass! So what if they withhold our grain ration. We have land and water in Green Hollow. Look, look at my arms! Thick as a rice measure. What's the big deal in raising a few more kids? After the winter, I shall clear out another plot of land for cotton. You take out the spinning wheel and the loom that your mother left you. Clean them up. . . ."

"You, you think I am a pheasant, to be kept in the mountains."

"You are mine."

Pan Qingqing became quiet, tightly tucked under her man's arm amid the sour smell of his perspiration. She was meek and tame. She belonged to her husband, and it was her lot to be beaten and scolded. She was in her prime, and for her to bear children was as natural as for trees to bear fruit. There would be no pain at all. For suckling babies, milk flowed from her firm white breasts like sap from the trees. As for her man, he was young and strong. He could kill a tiger or subdue a wild boar. He held her tightly with his iron-hoop arms, and vigorously did to her what husbands and wives outside the mountains would do, as if he had no other place to release his energy.

In the summer of 1975, there came to Green Hollow a certain "Single-hander." Don't be mistaken: this Single-hander was no comrade with authority.* He was just a young man from the city who had been resettled in the Forestry Center in 1964. His real name was Li Xingfu,† and he had been born in the year of the Liberation. He was tall and slender, with delicate features. He was conscientious in going about his chores and charmed the workers and cadres in the center with his tongue. But the mass mobilization of the Red Guards in 1966 bewitched him.‡ In an attempt to climb aboard a moving train, he lost one arm on the tracks. Since that time, one shirt sleeve had hung loose. After dawdling around in the city for several years, Li returned to the center. His co-workers then gave him the high-flown nickname of "Single-hander." The leaders at the center did not know what to do with him. They tried calling different tree camps and nurseries, but

---

*Diyi bashou (single-hander) is a term for the leading cadre in a unit or office.

† Xingfu means blessings.

‡ The da chuanlian (mass mobilization) was a massive movement of Red Guards from the second half of 1966 to the beginning of 1967. Young people were encouraged to put aside their usual occupation to travel to other parts of China to "exchange revolutionary experiences" with each other. The movement caused so much havoc that it was quickly called off.

nobody wanted him. The answer they gave was always the same: even if they overlooked the fact that Single-hander could not assume his fair share of physical labor, he nonetheless had been a "young warrior of the revolution"! What if he started mobilizing workers in some quiet ravine or gully? Taking him in would be like ending up with a piece of bean curd that had been dropped in the ashes. You can't blow or tap the dust off. What can you do?

One day, when Wang Mutong, the forest ranger of Green Hollow, came to claim the grain ration for his family of four, he was spotted by Political Section Chief Wang, who suddenly had an idea: Yes, of course, why didn't I think of assigning Li Xingfu to Green Hollow to assist the Wangs? The work load would be just right, neither too light nor too heavy. Even better, there isn't another living soul within a hundred *li* radius. With simple folks like the Wangs, can he possibly organize monkeys and pheasants? When Wang Mutong heard that extra help was coming under his leadership, he was delighted. But after finding out that Li Xingfu was the man known as Single-hander, he hesitated. Section Chief Wang clapped his shoulder and said, "Mutong, my old fellow, you've been asking to join the party for years, haven't you? This is a test for you. Li Xingfu has only one arm. What is so difficult about supervising someone like that? I will personally speak to him and make it absolutely clear that he has to obey every one of your orders in Green Hollow, to report everything he does, and to obtain your permission if he wants to step out of Green Hollow. As for you, show some spirit. Educate this errant young man so that he can turn over a new leaf." Only then did Wang Mutong nod in consent, determined to accept this test from the party and shoulder the heavy burden of "educating and reforming people."

Thus Single-hander Li Xingfu came to Green Hollow, and the miniature society headed by Wang Mutong expanded by one important member. At a spot close to the clear, jade-hued stream, twenty or thirty paces from their own ancient cabin, the Wangs put up a low, small cabin for Single-hander, using logs for walls and fir bark for the roof. The two cabins, one big and the other small, one old and the other new, became neighbors. Initially Wang Mutong did not harbor any hostility toward Single-hander; instead he found Li Xingfu's way of addressing him as "Big Brother Wang" rather pleasing to the ear.

New to the place, Li Xingfu was intoxicated by the serene beauty of Green Hollow. Every day, Wang Mutong sent him halfway up the mountain to man the outstation. In the morning, he followed a road that wound about like a snake into the fog of the forest, feeling as if he were moving in a hazy dream. The milky-white fog spread over the hills and valleys. It was deep and thick as moving fluid, as if a man might almost float on it. Especially at about nine or ten in the morning when the sun had barely shown its face and the fog began to disperse, he could see in his outstation halfway up the mountain the thousands of trees engaged in a contest of verdancy. Beneath him spread an ocean of dense fog. Only clusters of tall Cantonese pines and iron firs emerged in its midst. It was like the celestial mountain, the heavenly isles, the jade trees on the Penglai Islands*—definitely beyond the world of mortals. Li Xingfu would certainly not mistake these valleys and forests for fairyland. He felt that the Wang couple were still young. "Sister Qingqing" was so gentle and pretty, with big and glistening black eyes that could speak and sing. He prudently kept his distance. But it is hard for young people to stand the loneliness. In this vast gorge where everything that met the eyes was green, was he really expected to mobilize and befriend monkeys, thrushes, and pheasants?

Wang Mutong had two children: the boy Xiaotong was seven years old and his sister Xiaoqing was five. Initially, the two were a little afraid of "Broken Arm." But the situation changed after Single-hander presented Xiaotong with a few red birds he caught, pinned the wild flowers he picked in Xiaoqing's hair, and then held up the little round mirror when she turned left and right to look at herself. The two children then began to shower him with names such as "Uncle Li" and "Brother Li." As time passed, Xiaotong even shamelessly made himself at home in Single-hander's small cabin. He would not leave even if Pan Qingqing came over to get him. Children of the mountains have their endearing ways. Once, a snake found its way into the small cabin, leaving Single-hander trembling all over. Xiaotong took it upon himself to inform him, "Snakes seldom bite as long as you don't step on them." Gesturing as he was expounding, Xiaotong then spoke of the three main species of snakes in Green Hollow.†

"The green bamboo snake is the laziest of all. It simply coils up in a spiral on a length of bamboo." Xiaotong tilted his face upward, closed his eyes, and pursed his lips, "Just like this. *Fu, fu, fu*, blowing out poisonous vapor to attract the birds. Once a bird gets too close, the snake shoots up and catches the bird in its teeth. It then coils up again in its

*A mythical place where immortals reside.
† In the following dialogue, as elsewhere in the translation, I have modified the paragraphing of the original to conform to English practice. The author strings together lines of dialogue in the same paragraph with no clear indications of the identity of the speaker of particular lines—which is acceptable in Chinese but not in English. I have also changed the paragraphing in other instances for stylistic reasons.

lazy pose and leisurely enjoys its meal. The shouting snake is different. Its scales and skin are the same color as clods of earth. When it moves, it's awesome! The grass falls apart in its path, and its head can come up to one's waist. Just like this . . ." With his eyes bulging, mouth wide open, and neck fully stretched, Xiaotong jerked his head back and forth, "*Hu*! *Hu*! *Hu*! It's real scary. There is also a kind as thick as the handle of a firewood chopper and as long as a carrying pole. My dad calls it '48-rings.' Its head flails around as it moves. Really wild!" Fearing that Xiaotong might do another imitation, Single-hander put his hand on Xiaotong's head and asked, "Where did you learn all this?"

"I have seen the green bamboo snake myself. And my dad told me about the shouting snake and the 48-rings. My dad knows how to catch snakes, and he takes them down the mountains to sell." Single-hander looked at the child imitating the movements of the snakes when he should have been in school and thought of the cold, slimy, long creature that just escaped from his cabin. Sadness overwhelmed him.

Adults observe children; children also observe adults. Single-hander brushed his teeth every morning, and when he did, Xiaoqing would stand half-hidden by the door of her home and stare with curiosity.

One morning, Xiaoqing came over bashfully and asked, "Uncle, does your mouth stink?"

His mouth full of toothpaste, Single-hander did not catch the question.

"If your mouth doesn't stink, why do you use that brush every day?"

Single-hander burst out laughing. He finished washing his face and then told Xiaoqing, "Next time, ask your mama to buy toothbrushes for you and Xiaotong. Brush your teeth in the morning. Your teeth'll be sparkling and pretty."

Xiaoqing was not impressed. "Mama never uses a brush and her teeth are sparkling."

Just to convince her, Single-hander asked, "Does your mama's mouth smell?"

"Mama kisses me all the time. Her breath is so sweet. If you don't believe it, you should kiss her and find out for yourself. . . ."

"Xiaoqing!" her mother interrupted from the cabin. "You naughty girl! What nonsense are you talking? Come back now!"

Instantly, Single-hander felt his heart thump and his face burn. He dashed back into his cabin and hid, as if he had done something improper.

It was an insignificant exchange, but it was overheard by Wang Mutong. Xiaoqing was immediately dragged to the door and made

to kneel. The motive was obvious: it was for Single-hander's benefit. Although so far nothing suspicious had occurred, Wang Mutong
became watchful even when his back was turned!

Life in the two households in Green Hollow was like the clear jade-
hued stream behind the wooden cabins, flowing quietly. At its deepest
part, the water came up to one's calves; at its shallowest, it covered
the arch of one's foot. Shallow though it was, one could see reflections
of the trees whirling in the wind, the clear blue sky, and the drifting
clouds. And now, one more thing was reflected in the water: atop a tall
fir pole erected by Single-hander beside his cabin, a radio antenna.

This, however, was destined to cause trouble. The little black box
in Single-hander's cabin could talk and sing, and it broke the nocturnal silence that had filled the depths of the mountains since antiquity.
At first only Xiaotong and Xiaoqing dared come to the cabin to listen at nightfall, but eventually, on the pretext of fetching the children
home to bed, Pan Qingqing would also drop in to listen. It then became necessary for Wang Mutong to urge his wife and children home
to bed. At times, when Wang Mutong's voice was a bit rough, Pan
Qingqing would even pettishly retort, "It's still early! If you climb into
bed as soon as night falls, what a long while to wait for the sunrise!"
Just listen to that: the woman now finds early to bed hard to take! A
gloomy feeling began to becloud Wang Mutong. This tall and sturdy
forest ranger, who easily consumed two *sheng* of rice at a meal never
went to listen to the wailing music in the black box. He maintained
his manly, unapproachable dignity, watching the developing situation
with vigilance.

A little while afterward, Single-hander led Pan Qingqing and the
two children in doing a thorough cleanup of the ground between
the two cabins. They put firewood and other sundry household items
around the door in neat piles, evened out holes and bumps in the area
between the cabins, and swept it clean of animal droppings. Single-
hander even suggested that they grow flowers there and that he teach
the children to read and to do the radio exercises.* Pan Qingqing was
so delighted that her face beamed with smiles. The two children
now kept close to Single-hander's heels from morning till night. Such
phrases as "Uncle Li said . . ." or "Uncle Li forbids . . ." rolled off their
tongues, as if Uncle Li were closer to them than their own dad was.
These happenings made Wang Mutong even more uncomfortable;
they smarted like thorns in Wang Mutong's eyes. Don't underestimate

*Exercises coordinated to music from a radio program, popularized in schools and
factories during the 1970's.

this Single-hander. Without one's knowing, he was changing life in Green Hollow, just like an earthworm noiselessly turning over the soil.

"That son of a bitch! He does want to act up in Green Hollow, showing off his education to get even with me!" Sure enough, Single-hander came up to Wang Mutong with four suggestions for protecting the forest: first, to request that the headquarters immediately repair the long-defunct telephone line and install a receiver loudspeaker in each of the two cabins; second, to erect painted placards on forest paths, detailing forest protection regulations; third, to patrol the mountains for fire prevention—he and Wang Mutong would each take an eight-hour shift, one in the morning and one in the afternoon; when on duty, they should not dig edible roots, trap animals, or engage in personal business—fourth, to form a study group to study politics and culture; Xiaotong and Xiaoqing would be included. On hearing this, a delighted Pan Qingqing shot a glance at Wang Mutong. Although she kept silent, her crystalline eyes clearly said, "See, when you are educated, you think differently and you say it well."

None of this escaped Wang Mutong's eyes, and it pricked him inside. He pulled a long face and kept his mouth shut tightly, his eyes sparkling with rage: the honeymoon's over; you'd better pack up your bag of tricks! He threw a menacing glance at the woman and then bluntly lectured Single-hander, "You, young man from the city. You must have heard the old sayings—'Follow the local customs in a new place,' and 'Guests should respect the wishes of the host'? Of course you are not a guest here, but neither are you the host. There hasn't been a single forest fire in Green Hollow in the last couple decades. Of all the leaders in the Forestry Center at Mount Fogline, who has not praised my work? When did I ever fail to get the title 'model forest ranger'? I didn't earn that by relying on telephone lines, placards, two-shift systems, or so-called study groups. Go and sharpen your scythe and toughen your arm and legs. The headquarters has given clear instructions: I'm in charge here in Green Hollow. Section Chief Wang of the Political Section has spoken to you about this. Don't you take his warnings as nothing more than a breeze in your ears!"

Wang Mutong stood with both hands on his hips. His eyes glared; his face was severe. Single-hander was dumbfounded, and his face turned ashen. Pan Qingqing felt sorry for him, but in the face of her husband's savage outburst, she dared not interfere in the slightest. In a comforting voice, she said, "Ah Li, don't you mind him. He's an uneducated man, just a bit uncouth. . . ." But, when she saw her husband's ominous face, she shut up at once. Wang Mutong smirked, "So I am a rough fellow, and I suppose he is delicate. In this world of ours, it happens that the uncouth rule over and boss the delicate. As for you, Li Xingfu, don't you forget that the leaders sent you to Green Hollow to be educated and reformed." He then strutted away, swaying his hefty torso in an exaggerated manner, and stamping his feet so heavily that each step could easily have made a ditch in the ground.

Single-hander's four suggestions had crashed smack against the stone wall that was Wang Mutong and failed to leave even the slightest trace. Li Xingfu felt defeated. Indeed, he had been assigned to Green Hollow to be educated and reformed. It is for the uneducated to re-form the educated. This is an invention of this age of ours. He could not help feeling a twinge of fear toward Wang Mutong. He realized that it would be difficult for him to do anything to improve his present circumstances. But, he's full of energy. He mustn't let himself go idle. If he idled, he would feel lonely and isolated, as if there were noth-ing to live for. He might as well jump from a cliff to end his life. He possessed two books from the pre–Cultural Revolution days—one was *An Index to Trees* and the other was *Fire Prevention in Forest Areas*. He carried the *Index* with him every time he went out on patrol. Following the illustrations in the book, he learned to identify several hundred kinds of broad-leaf evergreen trees in the mountains. In order that his time not be spent in vain, he planned to carry out a survey of natural resources in the forest for possible use in timber-felling work in the future. He knew that Pan Qingqing would understand him, so he told her about the plan. Sure enough, Qingqing was as kind and gentle to him as to her own brother.

"What a blockhead you are! If you want to do it, just go and do it. Don't bother to discuss it with others anymore."

"Wouldn't Brother Wang mind?"

"Are you committing a crime? Oh youuu . . . !"

Sister Qingqing let the word "you" linger. Her eyes were glisten-ingly dark, so dark that one could see one's own reflection in them, so dark that they penetrated right into one's heart. He was not sure why, but Single-hander was afraid to look at those eyes. That trailing "youuu" was like music, or a meandering stream, entwining his heart.

The time was autumn. Single-hander had collected in old envelopes seeds of some rare and precious trees, including an uncommon species of fir and the gold-leaf fig. He was thinking of setting up a small nurs-ery to germinate the seeds and then to take them to the headquarters for the technicians to propagate. To set up the nursery, he would need to slash and burn several *fen* of land. Knowing that Wang Mutong would not be interested in the project in the slightest bit, once again he could seek help only from Pan Qingqing.

That day, Wang Mutong went to set up traps in the mountains.

Single-hander and Pan Qingqing picked a piece of land overgrown with wild eggplants by the vegetable plot, which happened to be the same piece of land that Wang Mutong had planned to use for growing cotton. In no time, billows of thick smoke were rolling toward the sky, as the wind hurled the fire across the field. Talking and laughing like brother and sister, Li Xingfu and Pan Qingqing felt happily unrestrained. Who would have thought that Wang Mutong would then storm down the mountains? He swept an icy glance at them, pulled his bushwacker from behind to cut down a small pine tree, grasped it with both hands and beat out the fire. Single-hander hastened forward to offer an explanation. Wang Mutong glowered and roared, "Cut it out —you and your tricks! I have plans for this plot of land. Li Xingfu, how dare you clear the ground without my permission? You'd better write a self-criticism tonight."

"For whom?"

"For whom? You think I'm so illiterate that I cannot supervise you? I am telling you frankly: under me, you'd better behave yourself."

Just listen to this, all such nonsense! Pan Qingqing took a look at her husband and wanted to cry. Enraged, Wang turned to his wife and berated her, "And why aren't you feeding the pigs? The fodder is all burnt!"

Single-hander stole a pathetic glance at Pan Qingqing, who turned without a word, wiping her eyes with the back of her hands as she walked away.

Everyone has self-confidence and self-respect. A small crack untended will eventually grow too large to be repaired. These days, even the earth is opening up with cracks. Wang Mutong felt the immediate challenge of Single-hander. Even his woman was getting wild, no longer tame and obedient as she used to be.

That day, it was time for Wang Mutong to fetch the family's grain ration at the headquarters. He would usually spend the night there. But this time he somehow felt fidgety from the very moment he set out in the morning. He simply could not put his mind to rest. This sturdy fellow gritted his teeth, ignored the fatigue, and returned that very day with the 120 *jin* of rice on his back. He walked well over 170 *li* there and back. When he reached home, he was drenched in sweat. The door of the cabin was closed but unlatched, and the light was on. *Stange, the woman is still up.* When he got inside, no one was there. Then, laughter and music from Single-hander's cabin reached his ears. He felt around the fireplace: the stove and pans were cold. *How could he suppress his rage!* He shot out through the door, stood at the window of Single-hander's cabin, and took a good look. His woman was resting her chin on her hands, with Xiaotong cuddled in her lap. There they were, mesmerized by the whining voice of a female singer in that blasted box. As for Single-hander, he held Xiaoqing in his lap and pressed his cheek against hers. Wang Mutong recognized the song from the black box; that was a Yao love song, something like "Man and woman, the hearts are one."

"What a beautiful song. My mother used to sing songs like that. . . ." It was obvious to Wang Mutong that his woman was staring coquettishly at Single-hander, her eyes glimmering shamelessly. "You Yao people are good at singing and dancing." Wang Mutong could no longer stand watching the meaningful exchanges. Suppressing his rage, he barely managed to keep from bursting into obscenities. He shouted, "Xiaotong! Xiaoqing! Have the two of you learned to hang around singing parlors? Do you think the nights can be shorter this way?" Realizing only then that her husband had returned, Pan Qingqing anxiously hurried out of the cabin, dragging Xiaotong by one hand and Xiaoqing by another, "Aiya! Why didn't you spend the night at the headquarters, you dunce? Look at you, you've worked up such a sweat." Wang Mutong did not reply. He gritted his teeth and restrained himself from saying what was on his mind: "If I were to spend the night at the headquarters, you'd probably end up in his bed."

When they got back to their own cabin, Pan Qingqing hastened to boil water and prepared his dinner. She did not warm up the wine for fear that with a bit to drink, her husband would act rough. But this night, Wang Mutong showed an unusual restraint and a silence that made one shiver. Even the air in the house was frozen. He washed his body and feet, ignored the food his wife had laid on the table, and went to bed without a word. His wife sensed that he felt put upon. She nudged his naked back conciliatorily with her trembling hands, but he just lay there like a heavy barrel of gunpowder. How frightening.

Wang Mutong not only possessed brute strength; he could use his mind as well. He realized that his position in Green Hollow was being threatened, and the source of rebellion came from Pan Qingqing and the children. *How can I let Single-hander lure my woman and children away right under my nose? How can I, a respectable, hard-working "model ranger," be beaten by a lone crippled, sent-down youth? Damn!* He decided first of all to stabilize the situation at home. Early the next morning, with eyes bulging and face glowering, he declared in his thunderous voice, "Xiaotong, Xiaoqing, get down on your knees, both of you! Listen carefully. Starting from today, if any of you, including your mother, go into that cabin, rest assured that I'll poke out your eyes and break your legs." On hearing this new prohibition, Pan Qingqing's face turned ashen. Xiaotong and Xiaoqing, their teeth clattering, knelt down behind their mother, like two young saplings trembling in the chilling wind.

Wang Mutong then went to the small cabin before Single-hander set out to work, and asked to see the self-criticism report he had demanded several days earlier. Single-hander replied that he had not written it.

"So you think I was just muttering to the wind? My words don't count much? Li Xingfu, I'll be frank with you. The leaders of the Forestry Center have placed your fate between my fingers! From now on, you'd better behave yourself! I'll give you one more day. Tomorrow morning, you better hand me the self-criticism report." Glaring, and shaking his huge fists, Wang Mutong laid down three more rules, "Listen! From now on, at the end of each day, you'll make a report to me in this very cabin about your day's activities. For personal business, you must come to me for permission. Don't you hang around my cabin for no good reason. One more thing: if you dare to entice my household again with that blasted box of yours, you are asking for a beating. With one tug of my little finger, I can pull the entire set up, wire, pole, and all, and thrust them over the hills."

Now that he had taken the double precaution of "stabilizing the internal situation and warding off external threats," Wang Mutong adopted one more measure in order to make sure that the rules he laid down were effective. Originally, no matter if he took the dirt road eastward to go to the headquarters or crossed the stream westward to the outstation or to patrol the mountains, Wang had to pass the front door of Single-hander's cabin. Wang Mutong labored hard to clear another path for his family to use. Of course, this meant that no matter if they were to go to the mountains or to the headquarters, a big detour had to be made, adding many more paces.

So that was the situation. Single-hander had to accept it. Wang Mutong's dignity and status in Green Hollow was like that of a tyrant in an ancient forest kingdom, tough, secure, and not to be questioned. He had seldom entered Single-hander's cabin before. Since his wife and children dared not come anymore, Wang made a point of stopping by every night to have Single-hander report the day's activities to him. He apparently savored the power of leadership and made Single-hander as docile as a member of the "five elements."*

*Landlords, rich peasants, counterrevolutionaries, local bad elements, and rightists. These five groups were regarded as enemies of the people in the days of rigid political ideology.

As a result, the small cabin and its occupant resembled a snail withdrawn into its shell. Even the volume from the black box was lowered. Harsh reality once again bruised and cowed Single-hander. Life in Green Hollow sank back into a drowsy quietude.

The weather was unusual that winter. There was hardly any snow but plenty of frost, and the old folks predicted a dry winter and spring. Every morning, the extensive forest of Green Hollow was covered with frost that hung like fangs on the trees. The broad-leaf evergreens donned a silvery coat. The world was a stretch of white that did not disappear until the afternoon. The two wooden cabins at the bottom of the valley, one tall, the other short, wore white crowns of jade way into the morning. The stream behind the cabins lay frozen. Gone was the tinkling sound of flowing water.

On these dry, cold, frosty days, Pan Qingqing had no other chores but to feed the pigs and to cook meals twice a day. She rummaged through some old clothes and used them to mend the soles of the children's shoes. When Wang Mutong took Xiaotong and Xiaoqing to the mountains to play, Qingqing would hold the scraps of cloth and sit motionless by the fireplace for a large part of the morning as if in a daze. Wang Mutong brought back wild rabbits and boars every day. He nailed the skins on the wall and cooked the succulent meat in a pot; the aroma spread for miles around. Strangely enough, when Pan Qingqing smelled the odor of meat, she lost all appetite, as if she were pregnant again. Her heart was heavy, pressing down on something that was still alive. Of late, she was frequently beaten by her man. Her body was covered with patches of purple and blue. All day long, she lived by his mood, and she would not so much as breathe loudly. Even when he raised his hand against her, she could only hope that it would land on some harmless parts of her body such as the back or legs. Her eyes were constantly filled with tears. She cried for her fate and hated her man for being a brute. She felt that only Single-hander would still respect her and treat her like a human being, whereas her husband disciplined her as if she were a criminal. *That young fellow is as pitiful as myself.* . . . But at times she hated him. Of all places, why did he have to come to Green Hollow and upset the life of her entire family. . . .

These days Pan Qingqing dreaded going to bed at night to the pungent smell of sweat on her man. Very often, she wept quietly in the darkness of the night. A rebellious desire began to grow inside her. As soon as she got into bed in the evening, she would stubbornly face the wall, as if nailed in that position. Her man could push and pull as he might, but she would not turn over. Wang Mutong swore and sputtered with rage, "I'll kill you."

"Go ahead. See if I care."

"You bitch. You want that man."

"The more you beat me, the more others laugh at you."

"You slut!"

"Ouch. . . . Stop it or I'll scream! I tell you, I'll scream." Pan Qingqing now had the courage to stand up to her man. But she was puzzled as to why her man was so afraid to have Single-hander find out what went on in their private lives. In fact, she too did not want Single-hander to know that she was roughed up and beaten every night. . . .

This was an abnormal life, and these were abnormal emotions. Pan Qingqing realized that she was changing, but she was not sure it was for the better or the worse. In this cold and dry winter, she paid unusual attention to her own appearance. She took out the silvery gray venetian scarf that she had carefully stored at the bottom of the trunk and wore the rosy red corduroy vest. She dressed herself up all day, as if she was ready to go out for a visit. She also loved to fill up her mother's copper basin with clear water from the stream and gaze at her own reflection. Several years before, she had asked her husband to bring back from the headquarters a mirror that she could hang on the wall and use when combing her hair, but each time he said he forgot. Now that she thought about it, she was sure that he did this on purpose. He was afraid that she would discover her own good looks: *the face is round like the moon; the eyes are glistening; as for the lips, they are like the red petals of a creeping fig covered with traces of morning dew.* And there are the two dimples. They look sweet whether I smile or not. Who wouldn't like me? . . . Does Single-hander like me? Oh, what an embarrassing thought! Her heart started to pound, her head flushed with excitement. She put her hands on her burning cheeks, too embarrassed to look up. Indeed, lately she could not help looking over to Single-hander's cabin. Isn't it strange? The more her man forbade her to enter that cabin, the more she was drawn to it. His radio, soap, face lotion, and news from all over the world—all these composed an enticing new universe. . . . Li Xingfu, ah, even his name promises happiness! But is that lanky and pale man happy? Every day, he cut firewood, washed his clothes, cooked his meals with a single arm, and didn't even dare to cast her a look. Poor fellow. Every time he saw Wang Mutong, it was as if he met a tiger. She pitied him and treated him gently with the enchanting shyness of a Yao girl.

Once, Single-hander returned from the headquarters and secretly gave Xiaotong and Xiaoqing two handfuls of candies wrapped in colorful tinfoil. Xiaoqing knew enough to quickly unwrap a piece with her little hands and stuff it into her mother's mouth. Pan Qingqing hugged her tightly and kissed her repeatedly. Rapturously she asked, "Xiaoqing, is there a bad smell in mama's mouth?"

"No, no."

"Is it sweet?"

"Yes, mama's mouth is very sweet."

Aiya, shameful you, watch what you are saying to your daughter! She recalled the conversation between Xiaoqing and Single-hander about half a year ago when he was brushing his teeth one morning soon after his arrival in Green Hollow. She felt her face burning. Sucking the candy, the sweet juice filled her heart. She continued to cover the little girl's tender pink cheeks with her sweet kisses. Her severe husband saw none of this and therefore could not interfere. Or else he would have instantly beat her to death.

One day, Wang Mutong had gone to the mountains to set traps for animals. Pan Qingqing took a bucket to fetch water in the stream. She saw Single-hander there washing his clothes with his one arm in the piercingly cold water. The arm was reddened from the cold. She put down her bucket and walked over to him. Then she snatched the clothes from his hand and proceeded to wash them. Single-hander stood up hastily, drew back, and pleaded, "Sister Qingqing, please don't do this. If Brother Wang sees this, he'll . . . ."

Pan Qingqing kept washing without looking up. "Why shouldn't I? I am not doing anything improper."

"I know . . . Brother Wang will beat you for this."

Pan Qingqing seemed surprised for an instant and dropped her washing.

"Look, your arms are all purple and blue."

"Shut up, you fool. They were bruised by the pigs in the pigsty."

Tears welled up in her eyes, but she stubbornly fought them back. *How I wish I could hide somewhere and let it all out!* She gave the clothes a few shakes and turns, picked them up and wrung them out perfunctorily, then threw them back into Single-hander's tin bucket in one big knot. She picked up her bucket and went off without even looking back, forgetting that she was there to fetch water. Once she got inside her cabin, she leaned against the back of the door. Her whole body went limp, but her heart pounded with excitement. She did not cry—on the contrary, she found the whole thing a bit amusing. This was the first time she had done anything for a young man behind her husband's back. Everyone must have first experiences like that, where one is left trembling all over. Pan Qingqing was ecstatic long after her heart stopped pounding. In the evening, when her husband returned, he did not notice anything. She had become the victor. . . .

At the year's end, the winter drought and the frost continued. All around Green Hollow, many broad-leaf evergreens had only bald branches left, which reached out to heaven like the pleading, bony hands of famished old men. The slope was covered with thick layers of dry fallen leaves. Whenever a cold wind swept across, the fallen leaves in various shapes and colors tumbled and rustled in a shower of gold and silver. It was quite a brilliant and magnificent sight.

This long period of dry weather made it impossible for Single-hander to hide in his cabin. He got up before dawn every day to patrol the hills, his bushwacker on his belt and the book *Fire Prevention in Forest Areas* under his arm. A few times, he summoned enough courage to suggest to Wang Mutong that they clean out the leaves and repair the fire lanes as soon as possible. But Wang Mutong harbored such a grudge against him that he deliberately ignored all his suggestions. He insisted that in Green Hollow, he was in charge. There was no room for unsolicited opinions nor was there need for Single-hander to be overzealous. This time, Single-hander was quite obstinate. As if sensing that something disastrous would happen, he took some precautions. He convinced Sister Qingqing to lead Xiaotong and Xiaoqing to clean up the leaves, twigs, hay, and firewood around the two cabins. He made use of every opportunity to read to Xiaotong and Xiaoqing from the book *Fire Prevention in Forest Areas*, which was also meant for Pan Qingqing and Wang Mutong. One morning, Wang Mutong listened in as Single-hander and Xiaotong were engaged in a question and answer session.

"Uncle Li, what does 'running against the wind' mean?"

"When there is a forest fire, the only way to escape is to run in the direction from which the fire is coming."

"Uncle, what if our house were on fire?"

"You should crouch in the stream. Crouch where there are no big trees nearby. . . ."

"Bullshit! What an unlucky thing to say." Wang Mutong blurted out angrily. Having scared away Xiaotong, he cursed, "Li Xingfu, are you planning to set fire to the forest in Green Hollow or what?"

Single-hander was dumbfounded by the outburst.

"If not, why are you always thinking about means of escape?"

"But, Brother Wang, a fire can be merciless."

"So, you are sure that there will be a forest fire this year?" Wang

Mutong scornfully snatched the book from Single-hander. He turned the pages contemptuously a few times, as an illiterate would, and threw it back to Single-hander. "This is probably a fortuneteller's book, full of wise advice against misfortunes?"

"Brother Wang. We've had a long drought and the mountains are covered with leaves. There are radio broadcasts every night. . . ." For some reason, Single-hander could not keep from appearing sheepish, pale, and powerless before Wang Mutong.

At the mention of the radio broadcasts, Wang Mutong smirked and cut in, "So your black box still sings those corny 'Oh my darling, oh my love' songs these days?"

Single-hander did not know whether to laugh or to cry, but he persisted in his plea, "Brother Wang, I have an idea. . . . Do you think we should report the conditions in Green Hollow to the leaders at the Forestry Center and request that they repair the telephone line immediately? That way, we would not be cut off from the outside if indeed Green Hollow is endangered."

"If you want to do it, go ahead. I'll even give you two days leave. We'll see whether the center will send a fire brigade to Green Hollow." He threw a scornful sidelong look at Single-hander and yawned with a nonchalant air. "I don't mean to brag. I have been here in Green Hollow for more than 20 years, and I don't know what a forest fire is."

That same night after dinner, Wang Mutong came to Single-hander's cabin as usual. This time, something surprised Single-hander. In the past, Wang Mutong always wore a reproachful look, as if he were speaking to a member of the "five elements." But tonight, Wang Mutong was a different person. He said conciliatorily, "My young fellow Li, didn't you say you wanted to go to the headquarters? Could you do something for me on the side. . . ." He pulled out a blank sheet of paper and asked Single-hander to write for him an application to join the party. Single-hander was still wondering what all this meant when Wang Mutong sank his teeth in a finger. The flesh ripped open, and blood gushed out. He held the bloody finger to Single-hander's face, as if waving a miniature flag, and said, "Come, write the letter with this: Most respected leader of the tree farm, with this letter written in my own blood, I request the honor to be admitted to the party. . . . I am uneducated and uncouth, but my heart is determined to follow the party. . . ." Single-hander was flabbergasted. He hastened to find an old writing brush, dipped it into the blood on Wang Mutong's finger, and wrote out the blood petition as quickly as possible. Oh my! He dreaded the sight of blood. He trembled and was drenched in a cold sweat.

When the petition was completed, Wang Mutong folded it up carefully and put it in the pocket of his undershirt. In the final reckoning, he did not trust Single-hander and would not have depended on someone with an unreliable political background to submit his sacred petition to the headquarters.

The next morning, Wang Mutong, not even bothering to bandage the wound on his finger, set fire to some dead branches in his vegetable field in order to expand his private plot. He was an efficient worker and rapidly cleared out an area of 3 to 4 *mu*. The center had stipulated that the Wangs should raise three pigs. The pork was to be dried at the end of the year to meet a procurement quota. Anything above and beyond the quota they could keep. Wang never gave much thought to such matters as beliefs or ideologies. He believed in the party because he believed in himself. He felt that the party should be made up of people like himself. Wang collected big piles of branches, leaves, rotten roots, and weeds from the hills and burned them for their fertile ashes. Dry as the winter was, he was not going to make an exception this year. Single-hander was extremely anxious over these activities of Wang Mutong, but he dared not interfere. He could not relax in sleep and had nightmares about fires of the strangest kinds —fires as brilliant as the color of the evening mist, fires roaring by like a swollen river. For two nights, he quietly crept out of bed, cut down a small pine tree from the slope, and guarded the embers left from Wang Mutong's fire during the day. There he stood until the night was half over. The wintry wind scraped his hand, feet, and face like a knife. Why should he be guarding the fire? It wasn't he who wrote a petition in blood. Even if he had, who would have believed him? Tongues of flame leaped from the embers, and sparks crackled in the air. It would take only a few sparks on the dry branches and leaves nearby to kindle a fire that could envelop the entire forest. . . . *Shouldn't I go to the headquarters to report on this? I should ask them first of all to send someone to repair the telephone line and then review the fire prevention work in Green Hollow. They'll have to persuade and stop Wang Mutong!* Li secretly told Pan Qingqing about his plan. Recently Sister Qingqing's eyes had been swollen like walnuts. With tears in her eyes, she nodded in agreement. Toward this pitiful person her face showed a mixture of sympathy, disappointment, and resentment, as if she had so much to tell him.

One afternoon, when Single-hander was squatting in front of the stove to prepare some food for his trip, Pan Qingqing suddenly burst into his cabin. *One needs to know that this is blatantly defying the severe rule laid down by her husband several months earlier!* Single-hander stood up in a panic. Sister Qingqing must have just returned from the fields, for she had only a thin shirt on. The shirt was a little too tight, and the button below the collar had popped open, exposing part of her ravishing bosom.

"Sister Qingqing, . . ." Single-hander could not raise his head. He was too flustered to finish his question.

"You idiot. Sometimes you're so smart, and yet at other times you're so foolish. I'm not a mountain demon. . . ." Observing his distraught state, she felt even more affectionate, akin to a kind of maternal feeling.

"Sister Qingqing . . . you . . ."

"I am just asking. When you go to the headquarters, will you do me a favor?"

Upon hearing this, Single-hander finally managed to collect himself. He raised his head to face Pan Qingqing.

"Here is 100 yuan. Please buy us a radio, one like yours, and then a mirror, soap, plus the kind of face lotion you use in cold weather. For myself, Xiaotong, and Xiaoqing, please get a toothbrush for each of us. . . . I would like to have a fir pole put up for an antenna. . . ."

Wide-eyed with awe, Single-hander stared at Pan Qingqing. This daughter of the forest was just like a goddess of beauty. Her breasts were full and round, her limbs well-proportioned, her body strong. She was gentle and demure, exuding a youthful, irrepressible energy.

"You, why are you staring at me? I am just a unfortunate being like you. . . ." Pan Qingqing turned away, her voice feigning anger. Her face was flushed and her eyes cast down.

"Oh, oh . . . yes . . . Sister Qingqing, you are so wonderful! I, I . . . ." For an instant, Single-hander seemed entranced, as if he had discovered something sparkling in Pan Qingqing. But he awoke quickly from his raptures. His face completely flushed, he said, "Sister Qingqing, you're spending so much money at one time. Don't you fear that Brother Wang . . . ."

Facing him, Pan Qingqing was lost in her own rapture. But when she heard the phrase "Don't you fear that Brother Wang . . . ," the honey sweetness in her heart was instantly spoiled, as if a handful of salt had been thrown into it.

"Fear? I've lived with it for more than ten years. . . . In the winter, he goes to hunt, and in the spring he sells the furs and the hides. There are also our wages, which we had little excuse to spend. The 10-yuan bank notes piled up in the bottom of the trunk. . . . He won't spend it and doesn't know how to spend it anyway. . . . I'm not afraid.

Living in this ravine with him, the worst that could happen to me is death. . . ."

Her eyes were filled with tears now, and so were Single-hander's. "Sister, I'll take your money and buy the things you want. Don't cry. Don't cry. We're both to be pitied. I hate myself. I really do. . . . Sister Qingqing, please don't cry. All right? If Brother Wang sees this, you will get a beating and I'll get a tongue-lashing. . . ."

"You . . . you are not much of a man. You can't even measure up to the ivy that climbs over my cabin." Pan Qingqing threw a reproachful look at Single-hander, turned around, and left the cabin.

"Sister Qingqing, Sister Qingqing . . . ." Single-hander stumbled to the door despite himself and, without knowing, reached out both arms as if to embrace something precious—although there was nothing but an empty sleeve hanging at the lower portion of his left arm.

Single-hander arrived at the headquarters of the Forestry Center. All around, people were writing new slogans in large characters: "Rebut the Wind of the Right Deviationists," "Condemn the Capitalist Class in the Party." The spacious office of the Political Section of the headquarters was in a hubbub, with workers and cadres going in and out. Single-hander thought it appropriate to report to Chief Wang of the Political Section, since it was this person who had sent him to Green Hollow. He waited at the door for almost an entire morning and managed to squeeze himself in only as the office was closing.

"Oh, it's you, Li Xingfu! Why are you here?" Section Chief Wang was standing in front of his desk just about to leave. Seeing that it was Single-hander, he had to stop. He stroked the back of his head swollen with work, put his hands on his hips, and turned his trunk left and right to loosen stiffness. He seemed friendly enough.

Single-hander immediately seized the opportunity to state his request to have the telephone line in Green Hollow reinstalled in the most succinct way possible.

"Fix a line that has not been used for over ten years?" Section Chief Wang did not hide his skepticism. "Is that Old Wang Mutong's idea? Oh? So it's yours. Li Xingfu, we count on Wang Mutong for the work in Green Hollow. He might not be educated, but he is politically trustworthy. All these years he has been a model ranger. As for the telephone line, that requires funds and resources. It can't be done overnight. There's a big campaign coming on soon. The whole country is soon to be involved in the campaign against the right deviationist trend, which should take precedence over everything else. You understand?"

Single-hander then requested that the headquarters send someone to inspect the fire prevention work in Green Hollow and reported that despite the unusually dry winter, Wang Mutong kept up the practice of burning branches for ashes. He feared that Section Chief Wang, who was about to leave, would be too impatient to let him finish.

"Oh, my! Li Xingfu, you're really making progress these days, huh?" Chief Wang again acted surprised. Then he pulled a long face and said, "I'll say this one more time: the headquarters trusts Wang Mutong. You must obey his leadership in Green Hollow and accept his efforts to educate and reform you. Don't rock the boat now. Besides, by some accounts . . . uh, his wife is pretty and fresh. Now, don't you go slobbering or itching after her. Otherwise, what'll you do if this only arm of yours gets broken too? Right? You are an educated youth. You still have a future ahead of you. . . ."

Thus, not only did Single-hander fail to report the situation to the headquarters, but also got an earful of scornful lectures. It was obvious the leaders simply did not trust him. He felt that it wasn't worth living like this. He was nothing but a mangy dog, kicked around and shoved away by people. For two days, he wandered aimlessly in the streets, the stores, and nurseries. He hated his parents for sending him to school. He wished that he were an illiterate, uncouth fellow, so that he could join the ranks of the likes of Wang Mutong. In this day and age, it's an honor to be uneducated. The more knowledgeable you are, the more reactionary you are assumed to be. Only people like Wang Mutong can join the revolution, and they are around everywhere you turn. . . . Finally, he remembered Green Hollow, Pan Qingqing, Xiaotong, and Xiaoqing. At least in that utterly isolated part of the world, there were three people who did not look down upon him and who believed in his integrity. So he seemed to come around somewhat. He bought enough oil, salt, and rice for two months from the provisions store of the center. From the supply and marketing co-op, he bought a radio, soap, face lotion, toothpaste, toothbrushes, and a round mirror the size of a small basin for Sister Qingqing. He then went to the cafeteria to buy two *jin* of steamed buns. Early the next morning, he carried the bundle on a pole and headed back to Green Hollow.

He did not reach Black Hill Hollow until sunset. Green Hollow would be one more hill over. Before nightfall, he should be able to reach the little cabin where he was to settle for life. He already saw black fumes coming from the direction of Green Hollow. *Is Wang Mutong still burning branches? Why is there so much smoke? No, this isn't the usual burning of branches. . . .* He was very tired, but disregarding that, he hurried to climb the slope so he could see what was happening. The more anxious he was, the heavier his legs became. A certain ominous feeling seized him. When he had almost reached the top, he smelled the charred odor wafting from the other hill and heard the popping sound of wood burning. *Oh my heavens, is Green Hollow really burning up? The sky has turned dim, but over the hill, it is brilliant red. Can it be the sunset? The evening mist? Or the furious flames of the burning forest?*

He raced along the mountain path, drenched in sweat from head to toe. He pushed himself to the top by sheer superhuman power. Instantly, a vast valley of flames surged right in front of his eyes. He felt faint. . . . *Green Hollow! Oh my heavens! Green Hollow is a sea of fire.* Swept up by the wind, the rows of flames brutally and petulantly scurried across the ridges in all four directions like thousands of giant red centipedes. Thick smoke and flames raged and galloped in the valleys. Each and every one of the ancient trees stood like a burning pillar that lit up the sky. Rocks exploded with loud bangs under the intense heat. The billowing flames, the shooting arrows of fire, the frenzied dancing of red snakes, together with the waves of oppressive heat, formed a strangely enchanting picture of a forest in flames.

"Sister Qingqing—Xiaotong, Xiaoqing—"

Single-hander threw down his baskets at the mountain pass, and ran down into the blazing valley shouting. Faced with this imminent disaster, he couldn't forsake Sister Qingqing, Xiaotong, and Xiaoqing. They were the only three persons close to him in this forest. . . . He kept running, forgetting his own safety, and miraculously did not once fall down. How long he ran, he did not know. He burrowed his way through waves of choking smoke before he saw a woman with disheveled hair, a dirty face, and tattered clothes crawling toward him on all fours.

"Sister Qingqing, Sister. What happened? Is everybody all right?"

Single-hander shouted with joy when he discovered that the woman was Pan Qingqing. Who would have guessed that upon seeing him, Pan Qingqing would extend her arms in a beseeching manner and collapse to the ground. He rushed over and, half-squatting, caught her with his arm.

"Sister! Sister! It's me. Li Xingfu. Sister Qingqing. . . ."

Single-hander's throat was dry, and his voice was hoarse. He kept calling Qingqing as he cried. A full ten minutes passed before Pan Qingqing came around. As soon as she opened her eyes, she murmured, "It's you. I see you after all." She then began to whimper in his lap.

"Don't cry, Sister. First, tell me how this fire started. Where are Xiaotong, Xiaoqing, and Brother Wang?" Single-hander shook her shoulders.

"Let's go. Help me up. . . ." As she talked, she struggled to get up and stumbled toward the mountains. Single-hander quickly helped her up and listened as she said, "That damned scum! What a rascal. . . . In the afternoon after you set off for the headquarters, he discovered that a hundred yuan was missing from the trunk. He insisted that I had spent it on a lover. . . . No matter what I said, he wouldn't listen. Instead, he savagely beat me to a pulp. . . . The scum! He then locked me up in your cabin. For three days and nights, he didn't give me a single drop of water. . . . It was only late last night that I finally managed to loosen a board with my fingers and crawl to the river for a drink. . . . Then I saw the fire. The ashes he was burning . . . So burn! Burn until every creature in the mountains is dead!"

"What happened to Xiaotong and Xiaoqing?"

"That devil. When the fire got out of control, he got hold of the wooden trunk with the money in it and escaped down the stream with the two children . . . the way that you told him. . . ." Pan Qingqing's body went limp. Leaning against Single-hander's shoulder, she stopped crying. Apparently relieved, she gathered her disheveled hair and reached up with her hand to part the sweaty hair on Single-hander's forehead.

The immense disaster left Single-hander stunned out of his wits. They climbed up the hill and found the two baskets he had left. Only then did Single-hander remember that there were two *jin* of steamed buns and a canteen of cold water in his bag, and he quickly took them out for Pan Qingqing. She was famished. It took her only three or four mouthfuls to gulp down a whole bun. When she reached for her fourth bun, Single-hander stopped her and gave her water instead. Pan Qingqing was still leaning against him. She closed her eyes and rested.

Single-hander held Pan Qingqing close to him, dazed by the raging fire and the roaring wind below. Suddenly he remembered something. Over the next hill was Lovers' Gully, where there was a plot of rare fig and fir trees. The technicians in the headquarters had once told him that these two kinds of trees were rare remnants from the minor glacial period. They were fast becoming living fossils, since they were close to extinction in other parts of the world. An idea suddenly came to his mind, and he turned to Pan Qingqing.

"Sister Qingqing, now the fire has only reached the middle level, let's go around to the hill facing us, and guard the fire lane around the peak. If we can protect that patch of forest in Lovers' Gully, we at least can explain ourselves if we ever make it back to the headquarters."

As he spoke, he looked back at the path to the headquarters, but his eyes were unmistakably bidding a final farewell.

"Whatever you say. I will follow you wherever you go." Food and momentary rest had restored energy in this Yao damsel, who had always been strong.

The forest fire in Green Hollow was sighted by a People's Liberation Army radar station more than a hundred *li* away. The station placed a call to the Mount Fogline Forestry Center, sending the leaders there into a tumult. They dispatched a team to put out the fire, but almost a third of the vast virgin broad-leaf mixed forest had been destroyed. What was left were valleys of bald branches and charred trunks, like a throng of condemned souls who had emerged from the underworld.

Seven days later, Wang Mutong came out of wherever he had managed to hide and returned to the headquarters with the two children and his wooden trunk. Pan Qingqing and Li Xingfu, on the other hand, were nowhere to be found. Wang Mutong swore tearfully that the forest fire was the doing of Pan Qingqing and her illicit lover, Single-hander! It had nothing whatsoever to do with his burning branches for fertilizer. For more than ten years, he had been a model ranger, and, to prove his loyalty, he handed over with both hands the petition to join the party written in his own blood. The cadres of the center of course believed his tearful account and sent for the people's militia to track down Pan Qingqing and Li Xingfu. The militia found only carcasses of wild animals in the forest, now covered with black ash. Who knows whether Pan Qingqing and Li Xingfu were alive or dead?

At the time, like every other place in the country, the center was in the midst of a political struggle that was to determine the fate of the party and the country. In order not to interfere with and to diverge from the major direction of the campaign to rebut the right deviationist trend, the cadres at the headquarters submitted a report to their superiors based on the accustomed theory of class struggle, stating that "class enemies had set fire to the forest, but the fire was extinguished by the revolutionary viligant cadres and masses." The case was thus closed. Wang Mutong, however, would not go back to Green Hollow, even on pain of death. At that time, the center also administered the virgin forest at the Cave of the Heavenly Gate at the border of Guangdong and Guangxi. The old ranger there had died. The leaders of the center therefore assigned Wang Mutong to succeed him. Wang was thus able to continue his indefatigable, industrious, and self-sufficient living. It was rumored that he married a Guangxi widow the same year. So they rose to work at sunrise and retired to bed at nightfall, and their energy was boundless. It so happened that the widow had a boy and a girl too. When they grew up, it was only natural and reasonable that they should be matched up with Wang Mutong's children to continue their line in the ancient cabin at the Cave of the Heavenly Gate.

However, after the fall of the evil Gang of Four, quite a number of people at the Forestry Center maintained the view that if Pan Qing-qing and Single-hander were still alive in some faraway place, they must be leading a different kind of life. There were even those who speculated that now that false accusations were being reversed all over the country, one never knew if Pan Qingqing and Li Xingfu would suddenly turn up at the center to demand their rehabilitation. Why not? After all, in the last two years, even the tall and bald trees that had survived the charring fire had again begun to sprout new green leaves and branches!

Li Rui   Electing a Thief

/////   "So elect already!"

The head of the production team banged a rock down onto the mill roller like a gavel, then hoisted his leg up in the air and landed it smack on the millstone in a most imposing manner.

It was stifling, hot enough to addle the brain. The faces of the villagers under the old sandalwood tree went blank one after another. They stood there glued to their places, silent as posts. The team head had become angry.

"Fuck your forebears! You think I'm bullying you even now? We give you self-determination, and you still won't make your move, so what then? Are you gonna make me do even your democracy for you? His Honor the Lord High Magistrate in the city doesn't make such a big deal of things. Elect! If you don't elect a grain thief this very day, there'll be no threshing, which means no wheat harvest this year. Come New Year's you'll just have to fill up on coarse cornmeal cakes! Come on, hurry up about it, everybody pick whoever he wants, but no talking allowed!"

Still no one spoke or gave any hint of what he thought. It really wasn't as easy as all that.

The team leader had been on sentry duty last night. When he checked first thing this morning after awakening, one sack of grain from the wheat harvest was missing. He called in the team accountant and the man in charge of the storehouse; one sack missing it was. The team head began cursing people's ancestors. He swore he'd nab the culprit and bring him to justice. They investigated up and down, but

This story was published in *Shanxi wenxue* in November 1986. Translation by Jeffrey C. Kinkley.

there was only one clue—one sack of wheat was missing. Everybody put their heads together. First, it couldn't have been stolen by one of the women, for none of them could have shouldered the 50-kilo-plus load. Second, it couldn't have been one of the six sissy students from Beijing, because they all lived together in the newly built dormitory.* They had no place to hide it. Third, it couldn't have been the team head, for he'd been on sentry duty all night. It had to have been done by a thief. But a thief was in it for himself; he wouldn't have the courage to give himself up, the bastard. There was nothing you could do about someone who was not only despicable but sneaky. Yet the more people grew philosophical about it, the more the team head cursed out their ancestors. He took it as a serious insult. The grain thief had specially picked that night not on account of the wheat, but to get at him, the team leader. He was so angry he couldn't see straight. He saw the word "thief" written on every villager's forehead. In a fit he assembled them all together. He'd mobilize the masses to conduct an election and solve the case. There was no suffrage for women, so they clasped their babies in their arms and squeezed into a corner to watch the excitement. Students didn't vote, either. After preparing the paper and pens, they just waited for someone to make up his mind, then come on up and lean over to whisper the name in their ear. Then they'd make up the ballot—just writing down the name of the person voted for.

But it was just too hot, brain-addling hot, so hot that the men waiting in the shade couldn't concentrate. Seeing that he couldn't curse them into action, the team head relaxed his taut face:

"Don't be afraid, this is a democratic election, you can pick anyone you please. Elect whoever looks like he might have stolen the wheat." Then he beat his breast: "Pick me for all I care! The one you elect won't necessarily be the thief. What we're going for is a clue. Come on, cast your vote, we'll start with you."

The team head poked his finger at the man nearest the millwheel. He kept pointing until the man had to react. So the first gap appeared in the passel of men all glued together, then a second, and then a third. A magpie alighted on the sandalwood tree and started chirping excitedly, as if it, too, wanted to fly down and cast a ballot.

The voters were very serious about it. One by one they came up and

*At the end of the Cultural Revolution in the late 1960's, millions of youths upon finishing middle school were sent from the city to settle in the countryside. This Maoist policy was designed to make urban youth learn about the peasant revolution. The youths gradually made their way back to the cities beginning in the mid-1970's. The story describes a situation in the early 1970's, when rural cadres had tremendous control over peasant livelihood because of their connections with the state machinery.

whispered into the students' ears, then returned to where they were, still wearing a very grave expression. The election went forward very smoothly. Fourteen ballots were cast; no one gave up his right to vote. All smiles, the students handed the ballots over to the team head. He suddenly frowned.

"All right, you sons of bitches. Is this how low you think of me? Have I been working for you all these years for nothing? You all elected me. If I really wanted the wheat, would I have stolen it from the threshing yard? Sons of bitches, I've been with you all these years without really knowing you. I . . . I fuck all your ancestors! Every one of them! I quit. Whoever wants this lousy job can have it. Come the end of the year, whoever thinks he's up to it can go to the commune and plead for your emergency loan and relief grain. You think you can fart it out of them? We'll see if you get a cent. Sons of bitches, you can fill your bellies with the northern wind for all I care!"

Washing his hands of the matter, the team head withdrew from the polls and stomped off.

The dazed electors were still stuck together.

"Fuck him and his, who would have thought we'd be so unanimous, gosh!"

Somebody or other who couldn't stand the tension sniggered. Suddenly the ground beneath the old sandalwood tree shook with laughter. Menfolk and womenfolk laughed till they were crying, till they had stomach cramps and couldn't walk straight. You would have thought the wheatfield had been hit by a whirlwind.

When they'd had their fill of laughter, some began to worry.

"If he really has quit, then from now on there'll be no one to call us to work and assign tasks. If we mess up, the wheat harvest really will be delayed."

"A man can't walk without his head, and a bird won't fly without a leader. Can the village do without a head man, without someone to manage it?"

Quite out of their depth, the students said, "If he's really gone, we'll pick another leader!"

"Who'll we pick? You? Will you be able to bring us back relief loans and relief grain at the end of the year?"

The villagers under the old sandalwood woke up from their previous mirth; how could they joke about the wheat in front of them, their subsidies at the end of the year, their food, their clothing, their very lives? They'd got a bit slaphappy just now. Their smiling faces were blank again, and now with some lines of worry. From the women's corner came a jabber of complaints.

"You've ruined everything. You've got him mad, so what are you to do now?"

"Whoever causes the problem has to solve it. So why don't you fellows be the team leader?"

"Just a sack of wheat—if it's already lost or eaten then it's too late to do anything about it—was it worth offending him?"

It was stifling, hot enough to addle the brain. Aware that they'd brought on a disaster, the menfolk sheepishly grinned toothy white smiles, but this couldn't hide their rising fear. Nobody could think of how to put an end to this today. With the team leader gone, there was suddenly a space beneath the old sandalwood that couldn't be filled. Under the merciless sun the villagers' fear began to produce resentment.

"The thief, that bastard, if he wanted to steal it, all right, but did he really have to wait until the night the team head was on duty?"

"The son of a bitch did this purposely to ruin us—catch him and don't show him any mercy!"

"I hope that wheat rots out his gut, dissolves it into little pieces."

"Let's get the second-generation turtle-spawn bastard and pulverize him!"

"Search for the grain! We'll go door-to-door and just see if we don't find that wheat!"

And yet, however agitated they became, however full of righteous indignation, the team leader who'd abandoned his flock did not return. Without him, they could only worry in the shade of the sandalwood tree.

"Let's pick a person to go to his house," someone proposed.

But who would go?

Their indignation cooling off, the crowd congealed again—everybody had had a hand in provoking this calamity, so who deserved now to bear the burden all by himself? And what response could he expect? He'd better prepare his last eighteen generations of ancestors for this, at least.

"This concerns all of us, so let's everybody go."

The crowd began to stir. At this point someone decided, "Women in front—they're good with words—their small talk and making-up will keep anyone from losing face."

"Right, women go first."

The villagers' shiny-black faces were offset by toothy white smiles again. The huddled crowd finally set off. Following the cloud of dust they shook off from their behinds, the whole village, women in front and men bringing up the rear, straggled from under the sandalwood into the scorching sunlight. In the twinkling of an eye, there was nothing left but an empty patch of shade and a few bewildered students.

An audacious rooster self-confidently hopped up onto the millstone and pecked some old grains of rice and flour from the cracks. Then, cocking up his magnificent comb and raising his head, he began to crow, as if he had the place all to himself. By bearing and manner, he was every inch a leader.

Yang Jiang

Leisure: Tending a Vegetable Plot

Every member of our company was a hard worker and a hearty eater—I guess we might call this a case of "from each according to his abilities, to each according to his needs."* Of course, this doesn't tell the whole story, since not everyone received the same wages. I didn't eat much, had little strength, and performed only light tasks, but I was paid a very high wage. I guess this could be characterized as taking full advantage of the "superiority of socialism," even though the cost to the nation was considerable. I felt rather awkward about this situation, but no one took my discomfort seriously. So I just toed the line, going about my business of planting vegetables at the cadre school.

There is a great deal of work involved in starting a new vegetable plot. First on the list of things to do is building a toilet. Since we were counting on gathering a good part of our fertilizer supply from passersby, we chose a site just off the roadway on the northern edge of the farm. We erected five wooden posts—one for each corner and

---

This is chapter 3 of *Six Chapters of My Life "Downunder"* (*Ganxiao liuji*), which was first published in *Guangjiao jing* (Wide angle; Hong Kong) in April 1981. Translation by Howard Goldblatt; first published in *Renditions* (no. 16, Autumn 1981: 9–43); reprinted by the Chinese University Press of Hong Kong and the University of Washington Press (1983, 1984); reprinted here by permission of the University of Washington Press. With the permission of the translator and the University of Washington Press, the editor has made minor changes in romanization and capitalization to match the usage in the other translations in this volume. In *Six Chapters of My Life "Downunder,"* Yang Jiang describes life in the cadre school to which she and her husband, the famous scholar Qian Zhongshu, were sent in the wake of the Cultural Revolution in the early 1970's. Mao founded the cadre schools to instruct errant intellectuals and cadres about the class struggle and the proletarian worldview through physical labor and harsh discipline.

*The principle of distribution propounded in Marx's "Critique of the Gotha Programme."

an additional one on the side where the door would go—then made walls out of woven sorghum stalks, and that took care of the enclosure. Inside we buried a large earthen compost basin; in front of that we dug two shallow holes into which we fitted bricks for footrests. That completed our toilet. The only thing we needed now was some sort of curtain for the door. A Xiang and I decided that it should be as neat and clean a curtain as we could make. We settled on the smooth core of sorghum stalks from which we had stripped the outer layer; we then wove them closely and neatly together with hempen cord, resulting in as lovely a door curtain as one could imagine, which we proudly hung in front of the door of what was now a quite unique toilet. We were shocked, to say the least, when we came out early the next morning and discovered that not only had our door curtain disappeared, but even the accumulated compost had been stolen. From that day onward, A Xiang and I had to serve as one another's "door curtain" whenever we used the toilet.

Our vegetable plot was not an enclosed area—to the west, south, and southwest it bordered on three other vegetable plots that also belonged to the Study Division Cadre School. One of them possessed a toilet of such sophistication that all the waste material ran into a detached cesspool, and the hole inside was enclosed by bricks. But most of the compost in that toilet was similarly pilfered, for local wisdom had it that the waste produced in the cadre school was the best around.

We dug a shallow rectangular pit to produce green manure. Then we all went out and cut down large quantities of grass, which we laid in the pit; but in about as much time as it takes to eat a meal, the grass that was steeping in the pit disappeared as if on wings—it was probably put to use as feed for oxen. Grass was in such short supply there that dry grass—roots and all—was used in place of firewood.

The first companies to be sent downunder had constructed three- and five-room dwellings on the vegetable plot site. We hurriedly erected a shed for ourselves on the northwestern edge of the well, first throwing up a wooden framework, then forming a rammed-earth wall on the northern side. The other three sides were closed in with woven sorghum stalks, which also went to make up the roof, on top of which we added a layer of asphalt felt and sheets of plastic for insulation. A brick kiln belonging to the Study Division Cadre School was located just northwest of the vegetable plot; the ground around it was strewn with broken bricks. So we filled up two carts with cast-off bricks, with which we laid a floor in the shed to keep the inside from getting too damp. After all, people had to live there. Finally we hung a sturdy door in the southern wall and even outfitted it with a lock.

Three people were assigned to live in the shed and keep watch over the vegetable plot: the leader of our unit, a poet who worked the plot with us, and "Little Ox." The shed also served as a resting place for the other workers.

One by one we planted seeds in each of the vegetable beds. Mostly we sowed Chinese cabbage and turnips, although we also planted small quantities of things like greens, leeks, potherb mustard, lettuce, carrots, coriander, and garlic. However, all the companies, with the exception of the first few to arrive downunder, had built their homes near the school's Central Compound, which was quite some distance from our plot. So we opened another plot near the newly constructed buildings; some of the stronger men leveled the ground and dug irrigation ditches. And since we couldn't leave the original plot unattended, A Xiang and I were assigned to keep watch there.

We took some Napa cabbages and wrapped them up leaf by leaf, tying each one with vine. Some of them actually grew to look like regular Chinese cabbage, although they weren't as tightly packed as the real thing. A Xiang had strength enough to carry two half-filled buckets of urine on a carrying pole, but I was only able to irrigate the fields a cupful at a time. Our favorite crops were the "ivory turnips" or "Taihu turnips," which were actually long white things. Their tips, which were the size of a ricebowl, only stuck up out of the ground an inch or so. "What we're raising here is the cream of the crop," we confided to one another. So we used all of the plant ash our unit leader had told us to spread among the carrots to fertilize our little darlings instead. And what darlings they were! I was certain that the ground would yield up turnips a foot or more in length, or at the very least half that long. I planted my feet on the ground and tugged for all I was worth, so hard, in fact, that I lost my balance and plopped unceremoniously onto the ground. That was because beneath the surface there were only a few skinny tassels. That was the first time I'd ever seen a "long" turnip *that* flat! Some of the radishes we grew didn't look too bad, although they were no larger than "duck pears."

Then the weather began to turn cold. As we squatted in the vegetable beds pulling weeds, the cold north winds penetrated our clothing. It was invariably dark by the time we returned to the company area to eat dinner. By that December all of the new homes had been completed, so the entire company moved into the Central Compound, and A Xiang was assigned to work in the new vegetable plot. The three people who shared the shed now returned to the old plot to sleep each night, so that during the days I kept a solitary watch.

The unit leader had given me this assignment for my own good;

since Mocun's* dormitory was located a short distance to the north of the brick kiln, it only took me a little more than ten minutes to walk there. Mocun had by then been placed in charge of the toolshed, so our unit leader often sent me over to borrow tools, which naturally had to be returned afterwards. My coworkers giggled like schoolgirls when they saw me walking over and back with unbridled enthusiasm as I borrowed tools, then returned them. Mocun's sole duty as the man in charge of tools was to register the names of users; he also served as roving patrolman on a rotating basis. His official designation was mailman, a job that consisted of going to the post office in town every afternoon to pick up newspapers, letters, and parcels, then returning to camp and distributing them. The post office was southeast of our plot, and each afternoon Mocun followed the meandering stream to the south of our plot, first heading south then east. Sometimes he would skirt around the plot and come over to see me. Whenever he did that, we all stopped work and made him feel welcome. But he dared not spend too much time with us, and he seldom came by, so as to disrupt our schedule as little as possible. While A Xiang was sharing the lookout duties with me, she would sometimes nudge me suddenly and cry out: "Well, look here, look who's coming!" Mocun would be returning from the post office with a sackful of mail, heading straight toward the vegetable plot. The three of us would exchange greetings across the stream and chat for a moment or two. Later on, when I was alone in the plot, the stream had dried up to the point that one could jump across it, so Mocun no longer had to skirt the stream to get to the plot, but could cross it on his way to the post office. That afforded this old couple the chance to be together, a great improvement over the old Chinese novels and operas, where young lovers had to arrange their trysts in rear gardens.

Mocun eventually discovered that it was unnecessary for him to jump across the stream, since there was a stone bridge that would take him to the eastern bank on his way south. Every afternoon I could see him striding toward me as he headed over from the kiln off to the north. When the weather was nice, we often sat for a while on the bank of the irrigation ditch to the south of the shed and just soaked up the sun. Sometimes he came by so late that we barely had time to speak before he had to be on his way again. But first he would hand me a letter in which he had jotted down bits and pieces as they had occurred to him the previous day. I often locked the door of the shed and walked him over to the stream, then rushed back to the vegetable plot

*Courtesy name for her husband, Qian Zhongshu.

to keep an eye on things. I would watch him walk off into the distance, growing smaller and smaller until he disappeared completely.

He didn't dare cross the stream to see me on his way back from the post office, since he was always in a hurry to get back to the unit to deliver his mail and newspapers. But I could still see him as he walked along the road in our direction, and if I had forgotten to tell him something earlier, I could always have a brief conversation with him across the stream as he passed by.

This vegetable plot was the center of my world. There was a mound of earth on the southwest border that the people referred to as "Tiger Mountain."* It was situated directly across from the brick kiln far off on the northwestern border. Mocun's dormitory was located a little way to the north of the kiln. The Central Compound of the entire cadre school was a considerable distance to the west of Tiger Mountain —our unit's dormitory was on the southern edge of this compound. The dining hall belonging to one of the other units was located at the foot of Tiger Mountain, and that's where I went to buy my lunches and dinners. My drinking water I usually got from the people in the buildings on a neighboring vegetable plot to the west. Once in a while I asked for some boiled water from the people who had a stove in a shed south of ours. I had set up a small fireplace with only three bricks, in which I tried to boil water over a fire of dried sorghum stalks, but that was impossible in a strong wind. If I traveled south, I could reach the post office where Mocun made his daily pickups of mail and newspapers. The area east of the stream was lush with green fields and flat fields as far as the eye could see; the few clusters of green trees off on the horizon belonged to the neighboring villages. A place called Yang Village, where I had once stayed, was located to the east of those trees. The vegetable plot was the center of my daily activity, and in that respect, I was like a spider who had settled there to spin a web all around her; several trifling observations and ephemeral emotions were trapped in this web of mine.

I set out alone for the vegetable plot every morning immediately after breakfast. On the road I often ran into the three people who slept in the shed as they headed toward the central compound to get their breakfast. When I arrived at my destination, the first thing I did was reach into the sorghum stalks alongside the door of the shed and fish out the key. After opening the door I'd put down the ricebowls and other odds and ends I'd brought along with me, then lock the door behind me and go out to take a look around the plot. Our car-

---

*An allusion to *Taking Tiger Mountain by Strategy* (*Zhi qu Weihu shan*), one of the eight "model revolutionary operas" promoted by Jiang Qing during the Cultural Revolution.

rot patch was at the eastern extremity, where the soil was so hard and barren that the harvests never came up to our expectations. The few carrots that did reach a respectable size were, as often as not, picked on the sly, and so hastily that the thieves snapped them off, leaving only stumps behind. I'd dig out the stumps, wash them off with well water, and save them to help quench my thirst later on. As for the Chinese cabbages planted alongside the nearby road to the north, no sooner were they plump and ready to be eaten than they would be picked and taken away, with only the newly severed stalks remaining in the soil. I once discovered three or four freshly cut stalks of fully grown cabbages on the ground, while the cabbages themselves, which had been left behind in the rush, were resting there in the vegetable bed as though nothing had happened. We knew we'd better pick the cabbages right away before they were fully grown.

On one occasion I walked around to the rear of the shed, where I caught three women in the act of stealing some of our greens right out of the ground. They got to their feet and ran off, never thinking that I'd take off after them. They tossed the greens away as they ran, and once their baskets were empty, they were no longer frightened by the prospect that I'd catch them. Actually, I was chasing them only because I was expected to; I would have preferred to let them take the greens home and eat them, for my retrieving them served absolutely no purpose.

Those particular women had just been passing by. Normally, the villagers came out in groups of ten or so to pick kindling and various grasses. Their ages ran from seven or eight to twelve or thirteen, and there were both boys and girls among them. They would be led out of the village by a girl of sixteen or seventeen or perhaps by one of the older women of forty or fifty. Wearing brightly colored but tattered clothes, they would be carrying baskets over their arms and small knives or spades in their hands. When they reached a likely spot, they'd split up into groups of two or three and start foraging around. If they came across something worth taking, into the basket it went. They didn't immediately pick up the twigs and branches they cut off the trees in the woods, nor did they necessarily put those they did pick into their baskets right away. They normally just stacked them in piles alongside the roads or on the banks of canals and tied them into bundles. Then when it was time for lunch or dinner, they'd walk back home as a unit, the bundles of firewood and dried grass on their backs, and baskets full of whatever they had found on their arms. Some of the bolder boys even uprooted little saplings, which they also tied into bundles and tossed into a creek; these they retrieved before mealtime and carried home with them.

The sorghum stalks that had been more or less dumped all around the shed had long since been picked clean by these people; the five wooden posts used to construct the toilet had gradually dwindled to two, and before long they too were gone. Even the sorghum stalks on the toilet walls were getting noticeably thinner, a condition that gradually spread to the shed itself. I always waited until the people with bundles of firewood and grass on their backs had passed by and were a long way off before I'd dare to walk over to the dining hall at the foot of Tiger Mountain to buy my meal.

There was once a harvest of cabbages in the neighboring farm to the south of ours. They had more people than we and they were stronger; the quickness and agility with which they worked could not have been more different than ours. Our unit was composed mainly of older and weaker people. We chopped, we picked, we stacked the stuff into piles, which we then weighed, recorded, loaded into carts, and delivered to the kitchen in the Central Compound. . . . We were busy the day long, and our vegetable beds were cluttered with the discarded outer leaves of the cabbages. But the other company had finished their harvest before sunset, leaving the fields swept completely clean of crop residue. An old woman and her daughter sat in front of our shed waiting to go out and pick the outer cabbage leaves. Every once in a while the girl would run over to see how things were going, then return and report on the progress of the harvest. Finally the old woman got to her feet and said: "Let's go!"

"They've swept it clean," the girl answered her.

They spoke so rapidly that I had trouble understanding them. About the only thing I picked up was "feed the pigs," which was repeated several times. The old woman muttered angrily: "Even the landlords allowed us to pick that!"

I asked them how they could eat the old outer leaves of the cabbages.

The girl answered by saying that they first boiled some water, into which they dumped the shredded leaves, then added flour paste and stirred it all together. "It really tastes good!"

I'd seen their steamed buns, which were reddish-brown in color, as was the flour paste they used. I wondered about the flavor of this flour paste that "really tastes good." The tough cabbage and bitter turnips that comprised our daily fare wasn't very tasty, but we never tried that stuff of theirs that "really tastes good," even though we should have.

We never really harvested the lump-vegetables we had planted. The big ones grew as large as peaches, while the smaller ones were no larger than almonds. I had gathered a pile, which I was sorting in order to deliver the large ones to the kitchen. The old woman, who sat off to the side staring at me the whole time, asked me how those were eaten. I told her they could be pickled or boiled. Then I said to her: "I'll keep the big ones and you can have the small ones." She was delighted, saying over and over: "Okay, you take the big ones, and I'll take the small ones." But her hands were too quick for me, and she began stuffing her basket with the larger ones. Since I didn't want to cause a scene, I just waited until she had filled her basket, then relieved her of the biggest ones, swapping them for two handfuls of smaller ones. She offered no resistance and walked off very contented. But I later had cause to feel remorse over the whole incident, since the kitchen help never did use the pile of large lump-vegetables I had presented to them. At the time, however, I didn't dare give things away to anyone I pleased and was afraid to set a precedent.

Whenever I was weeding and pruning in the vegetable plot, some of the village girls would run over to watch me work. Once I had mastered their local speech I passed the time of day with them. I gave them some of the smaller twigs and they helped me do the weeding. They referred to their menfolk as "the big guys." They were all young girls of twelve or thirteen whose future marriages had been arranged by their parents. One of them told me that one of the others had already been accepted by her in-laws. This comment obviously embarrassed the girl referred to, who denied the charge and turned it right back to the first girl. Neither of them was literate. The family I had lived with for a while in another village was better off than the families of these girls; their two sons, who were in the neighborhood of ten years of age, didn't need to tend oxen to make a little money, but were both in school. Their seventeen- or eighteen-year-old sister, on the other hand, was illiterate. Her parents had enlisted the aid of a matchmaker, and the girl was already engaged to be married to a PLA soldier whose age and appearance were just right. The two of them had never laid eyes on one another, but the soldier had written his fiancée a letter and sent her a photograph. Both his level of education and his appearance were those of a simple farmer. The girl's family and I shared the same surname, so they called me "Auntie"; they asked me to write a letter for them in reply. But I sat there, pen in hand, for the longest time without coming up with a single appropriate line, until finally my roommate and I put our heads together and managed to compose a letter. The soldier had to do without a photograph of his intended.

For some reason, the fifteen- and sixteen-year-old boys from the village seemed to loaf around all day long with nothing to do. With large baskets slung over their shoulders, whenever they saw something that interested them, they picked it up. Sometimes they went out in groups of seven or eight and uprooted young trees alongside the road that were no bigger around than a man's arm. Then they would smack the ground with them and shout loudly "Ha! Ha! Ha!" as they hunted around for wild rabbits.

Three or four of them came rushing into our vegetable plot one day, clamoring and yelling for all they were worth. They said there was a "cat" in one of the vegetable beds. "Cats" were what they called rabbits. I told them there were no cats here. The rabbit that was hiding among the cabbage leaves knew instinctively that there wasn't enough cover to protect him, so he darted out like a flash. He was much too fast for any of the dogs chasing him, but under the direction of the young hunters, they split up and went after him from different directions. The rabbit changed course several times until he was surrounded by the dogs. He jumped into the air, as high as six or seven Chinese feet, and when he hit the ground he was set upon by the dogs. I felt so frightened and sorry for him when he jumped that my heart nearly broke. From then on, the coarse, loud shouts of "Ha! Ha! Ha!" held no attraction for me to go take a look.

On one occasion—at about three o'clock in the afternoon of January 3, 1971—some people came up to me suddenly and, pointing to a couple of grave mounds beyond the vegetable plot to the southeast, asked if that was the cadre school cemetery. Just after the first contingent of people from the Study Division had arrived in the countryside, one of the tractors had been crossing a bridge when it flipped over into the water, and the driver was drowned. The newcomers asked me if that's where the man was buried. I told them no, then pointed off into the distance to where the cemetery was located. A little while later I noticed several men digging a pit on the bank of the stream east of the turnip field. A big cart, the bed of which was covered with a reed mat, was parked alongside them. Ah! Were they going to bury a corpse? A few men in military uniforms stood off to the side—they were probably from the Propaganda Section.

I watched from a distance as three or four of them dug the pit, their movements extremely rapid. One of them jumped down into the pit to continue the digging. The others soon followed. Then all of a sudden, one of them ran toward me. I assumed that he was thirsty, but he actually wanted to borrow a shovel, for the handle of his had snapped in two. I went into the shed and got one for him.

At the time there wasn't a local villager to be seen anywhere—the only people around were the men digging the pit, busily, urgently. After a while all I could see of them were their heads and shoulders—

the pit was deep enough. They pulled back the reed mat and lifted a corpse dressed in a blue uniform out of the cart. I could feel my heart thumping wildly as I watched them bury the body off in the distance.

When the man came back to return the shovel to me, I asked him if the deceased had been a man or a woman, and what the cause of death had been. He told me that they were from a certain company, that the deceased was a suicide, thirty-three years of age, a male.

The winter days were short, and night was beginning to fall by the time they began driving the cart away. Not a soul was left on the now bleak and desolate vegetable plot. I trotted over to the gravesite. It was nothing more than an earthen mound that looked like a huge steamed bun, and no one would ever notice that a new grave had been dug on the bank of the stream.

I related this incident to Mocun on the following day and told him to be careful not to step on the new grave, since they had buried the man without a coffin. When he returned from the post office, where there was plenty of talk about the incident, he had not only learned the name of the deceased, but that he had a wife and children and that several suitcases were being sent back to his hometown that very day.

One day not long after that there was a heavy snowfall. I was worried that after the snowfall the ground would loosen and the grave cave in until the body was exposed enough for the dogs to get at it. As it turned out, the ground did give way, but not enough to open up the grave.

I kept a solitary watch over the vegetable plot all winter long. In the mornings when the sun made its first appearance, the clouds in half the eastern sky were bathed in radiant colors. From villages far and near, groups of people of all ages wearing brightly colored but tattered clothes emerged one after the other. When they reached the vicinity of the vegetable plot, they broke up into groups of two or three and disappeared in all directions. They drifted back and reformed into groups at sundown, carrying their loads on their backs as they headed home. I bought my dinner and returned to the plot, where I often stood in the doorway of the shed as I slowly ate my meal. The sunsets would grow darker and darker, the evening mist would become heavier. The vast fields were dim as far as the eye could see; not a single person was out there, and there were no lights to be seen. I went back into the shed, where all I could hear were hordes of rats scurrying around in the sorghum stalks—the dry leaves made a loud rustling sound. I ladled out some water to wash my bowl and spoon, then locked the door behind me and headed back to the dormitory.

Everyone was busy with all the work to be done; I alone had time on my hands, and my idleness nagged at me, frustrated me. Although I wasn't a busy "arms instructor of the mighty Imperial Guards," at least I had the sort of feeling that Lu Zhishen must have had when he went up to the monastery on Mt. Wutai to become a monk.*

While I was living with one of the local families, since my roommates and I worked at different places, it was inconvenient to join up with them for the walk back to the village. So I made the round trips alone, which gave me a sense of freedom and comfort. Besides, I enjoyed walking down dark roads. If I carried a flashlight, which lit up only a small space wherever I pointed it, I never knew exactly where I was. So by walking down dark roads, I got to the point where I knew the surrounding areas well. I walked back to the village along a winding, uneven, rock-strewn path. From the neighboring villages I could occasionally see a flash of light from amidst the trees, but the light I was heading toward was by my bed, that tiny spot of real estate beneath my mosquito net—it was a lonely place to return to, for it wasn't my home. This often reminded me of a painting I had once seen: an old man with a bag slung over his back and a cane in his hand walking step by step down a mountain path directly into his own grave. That's pretty much how I felt about myself.

After New Year's, on Tomb-Sweeping day [the fifth day of the fourth lunar month] to be exact, the Study Division Cadre School was moved to a place called Minggang. Before we made the move, our entire unit went to the original vegetable plot, where we dismantled all the structures we had put up. Everything that could be moved was taken apart. Then the tractors came and leveled the ground. On the eve of our departure, Mocun and I slipped over to the plot to take one last look around. The shed was gone, the well platform was gone, the irrigation ditches were gone, the vegetable beds were gone, and even the small mound of earth had disappeared from sight; all that was left was a piece of empty land strewn with clods.

*A hero in the classic novel *The Water Margin* (*Shuihu zhuan*), nicknamed the Tattooed Monk, who could not become accustomed to the inactivity of monastic life.

Han Shaogong   Déjà vu

////   Many people have said that sometimes, when they go to a
place for the first time, it seems very familiar, and yet they don't know
why. Now I have had such an experience.

I am walking. In many places the dirt road has been washed away by
mountain torrents, leaving behind ridges of dirt and nests of pebbles,
as if flesh had been gouged out to reveal sheaths of muscle and bone
and pieces of dried organs. In the ditch there are a few stalks of rot-
ting bamboo and some lengths of decaying rope leads for oxen; omens
that a village is about to appear. A few circles of motionless black shadows rise above the small pools beside the road. Without giving them
much thought, one might assume they were rocks; but looking closely
I discover these are the heads of small water buffalos, staring furtively
at me. Wrinkled and bearded, they are old at birth; their inheritance,
decrepitude. A square blockhouse rises above the forest of banana
trees in front of me, with icy portholes and walls particularly dark, as
if they had been burned by a smoky blaze or had congealed the black
of many nights. I have heard that this place used to be bandit infested,
that if troops weren't sent in for ten years, the place would have been
entirely deserted. Small wonder each village has a blockhouse, and the
mountain folks' homes are never scattered about but hug each other
closely, all of them solidly built and retiring. The windows open up
high to small eyes, so that robbers can't easily climb in them.

This is all very familiar and very strange; like those times when
you look at a written character, and the more you look, the more you
think you know it and the more you think you don't. The devil, have

---

This story was published in *Shanghai wenxue* in February 1985. Translation by Margaret H. Decker.

I been here before or not? Let me do some guessing; after stepping on that gravel road ahead, going around the banana plantation, and turning left beside the oil press house, I might see an old tree behind the blockhouse, a ginko or a camphor tree, already dead from a blast of lightning.

After a moment, my prediction is in fact confirmed. Even the hollow in the center of the tree, and the two kids at play burning straw in front of the hollow all seem to have been within my imagining.

Nervously, I make another prediction: behind that old tree perhaps there is a low cowshed, with a few piles of manure in front and, under the eaves, a rusted plow or rake. I walk over and sure enough, clearly and distinctly, this is what greets me! Even that crooked mortar and pestle of speckled rock, the mud and two fallen leaves in the bottom of the mortar, I seem to have known before.

Of course the stone mortar in my imagination didn't have mud in it. But if I think about it, since it had just rained, wouldn't the water from the eaves have flowed into the mortar? A chill mounts from my heels straight to the back of my neck.

I have definitely never been here before, it's absolutely impossible. I don't have brain fever, nor am I demented. My mind is still functioning. Maybe I saw it in a movie? Or heard friends talk about it? Or had a dream. . . . Flustered, I try to remember.

Even stranger, the mountain villagers all seem to recognize me. Just a moment ago as I was tying up my pants legs and testing rocks for crossing a stream, a fellow shouldering two trees bound together in the form of an "A" approached. Observing me as I slipped and teetered, he pulled a dry stick from the melon shed beside the road and tossed it to me. Then unaccountably he smiled, revealing a mouth full of yellow teeth.

"You've come?"

"Yes, I've come. . . ."

"Must have been over ten years, huh?"

"Ten years. . . ."

"Come to the house and sit for a while. San Gui is hoeing in front of the gate."

Where was his house? And who was San Gui? I was confused.

He went with me over a small ridge, and a courtyard with tile eaves rose in front of me. A few figures were beating and tossing something in the yard. Their flails whipped with loud cracks, several heavy blows and then a light one. They were all barefoot, with short, even hair, and there was a brown glaze of sweat on their faces, its edges jagged and uneven. When the sun flashed, the patch of sweaty glaze

on their foreheads reflected the light. Their shirts hung short, exposing soft stomachs and navels. The waists of their pants hung loosely
around their hips. It was only when I noticed one of them go over to
a basket and begin unbuttoning her shirt to nurse a baby and then
discovered that they were all wearing earrings that I realized they—
they were women. One of them opened her eyes wide to look at me.

"Isn't this Ma. . . ."

"Four-eyes Ma." Another prompted her. Finding this name very
funny, they all laughed.

"My name's not Ma, it's Huang. . . ."

"You changed your name?"

"I didn't change it."

"Right, you still like to tease and play tricks, huh. Where are you
coming from?"

"From the county seat, of course."

"You're really a rare guest. How's Sister Liang?"

"What Sister Liang?"

"Isn't your wife's name Liang?"

"My wife's name is Yang."

"Maybe I remembered it wrong? No, I couldn't have. She told me
then that she was from my family. My mother-in-law's home is Sanjia-
kou, you know, the Liang family of the She* people."

What did I know? And of what relationship was it to me? It seemed
like I had been trying to find my wife, but had come here instead. I
didn't know how I had got there.

This woman dropped her flail and led me into her home. The
threshold was very high and broad. Who knows how many people had
stepped over it, going from their youth to old age, or sat upon it so that
the center part was already slightly worn down. Yellow wood grain, it
was as if circle after circle of moonlight had spread upon this threshold, gradually hardening into a fossil. Infants crossing the threshold
would have to crawl; adults needed to hook a leg up high before they
could lean over and hobble in. Inside it was very dark. I couldn't
see anything clearly. There was only one high, small window through
which a few rays of light leaked in and divided the damp darkness.
There was also the smell of corn slops and chicken droppings. It was a
long time before my pupils adjusted to the gloom and I could see that
all the walls were dark from smoke and there was some sort of hanging basket, which was also sooty black. I sat on a wood block—oddly
there were no chairs here, only wood blocks or stools. The old and

---

*A minority people originally from Guangdong but resettled in Zhejiang during the
sixteenth century.

young women all crowded at the door chattering. The one who was nursing was not in the least embarrassed as she fished out her other long breast to exchange it for the one in the baby's mouth and smiled at me. The breast taken from the child's mouth still dripped milk. They were all saying strange things. . . . "Little Qin. . . ." "Not Little Qin." "No?" "Little Ling." "Oh, oh. Is Little Ling still teaching?" "Why doesn't she come to visit?" "You all returned to Changsha, then?" "To the city of Changsha or the countryside?" "Do you have kids?" "One or two?" "Does Little Luo have any kids?" "One or two?" "And what about Bear Head? Has he found himself a wife or not?" "And he has kids, too?" "One or two?" . . .*

I realized that they had all mistaken me for some "Four-eyes Ma" who knew a Little Ling and a Bear Head. Maybe that fellow looked like me and peered at people from behind his glasses.

Who was he? Did I have to think about him? Judging from these women's smiling faces, I would have no problem today in getting something to eat and some place to sleep, thank heaven. Wouldn't be so bad to be some guy named Ma. And no big effort answering one or two questions to amaze these women or engage their sympathy for a while.

The sister-in-law from the Liang family brought over a tea tray with four big bowls of a gruel made from fried flour. Later I found out that this signified four seasons of peace. The rim of the bowl was so black that I didn't dare touch my mouth to it, but the gruel was fragrant with the aroma of fried sesame seed and glutinous rice. She picked up some dirty children's clothes from the floor, tossed them into a wooden basin and carried it into the inner room so that her sentence was broken into two fragments. "Didn't hear any news of you for a long time. According to Master Shuigen . . . (a long while and then her voice emerged from the inner room) after you went back, you were put in prison."

Startled, I almost let the gruel scald my hand. "No, I wasn't. What prison?"

"That bedeviled Shuigen, talking like a demon. Did so much harm my father-in-law was scared out of his wits and burned a lot of incense for you." She covered her mouth with her hand and started to laugh, "Aiya, he'll be the death of me."

The women all began to laugh. A mouth with yellow teeth added, "He even went to Mount Daigong to pray to Buddha."

This was really ominous, bringing up burning incense for Buddha. Maybe this guy Ma had actually run into an evil wind and had the

---

*These are probably some of the educated youths sent down to the village with the protagonist.

misfortune to go to jail, and here I was drinking gruel and laughing foolishly in his place.

Elder Sister presented me with a second bowl of gruel, as before with one hand placed across the wrist of that holding the gruel, probably some kind of ritual. But I hadn't finished the first bowl. The broth was gone but the sesames and glutinous rice hadn't slid up to the edge of the bowl. I didn't know how I could eat it with any grace or refinement. "He was always worried about you, said you were righteous and had a sense of justice. He wore that padded jacket of yours for several winters. After he died, I made it into padded pants and the children wore it too. . . ."

I wanted to discuss the weather.

The room suddenly darkened. Turning my head, I saw a black shadow nearly blocking the entire door. I could see it was a man, the top half of his body naked. The bulging muscles had no curving lines but were all edges and corners like pieces of rock. He carried something in his hand. Judging from its silhouette, it was an ox head. The shadow moved toward me, and covered me, without letting me see the face clearly. With a thud he dropped the thing he held, and two big hands grasped mine, rubbing it like a file. "It's Comrade Ma. Aiyoyo, heyaya. . . ."

I'm not a caterpillar, so why did I recoil in panic?

Only when he turned toward the grate of the stove and the side of his face was gilded with a layer of light could I see clearly that it was a smiling face with a big, pitch-black mouth, his two upper arms tattooed with some gray design.

"Comrade Ma, when did you arrive?"

I wanted to say that my name wasn't even Ma, it was Huang, Huang Zhixian, and I hadn't come with some deep emotion like a hero searching for my past.

"You still know me, don't you? The year you left I was still doing road construction in the Luosi Mountains. I'm Aiba."

"Aiba, I know, I know." I answered despicably. "You were team leader then."

"Not team leader, I recorded work points. You still know Elder Sister, don't you?"

"I know her, yes I know her. She makes the best gruel."

"I went with you to chase meat. Remember? (Chase meat, did he mean go hunting?) That time I wanted to pacify the mountain god, and you said that was superstition. In the end, it wasn't, though. You ran into some herder's needleweed and got covered with poisonous sores. That time you also came across a deer, it ran right between your legs, but you missed spearing it. . . ."

"Uh, yea, I missed it, but just by a little. My eyes are bad."

The pitch-black mouth started to laugh. The women got up slowly and, their large rumps swaying, went out the door. The man who called himself Aiba brought out a bottle gourd and offered me one large bowl after another of liquor. The liquor was muddy, with a sweet, hot, bitter taste. It was said to have had some herbs and tiger bones steeped in it. He wouldn't smoke my cigarettes, but rolled his own in the shape of a megaphone with some newspaper. When he took a drag, the paper flared up. Unhurried, he didn't give it a glance, and it was only after I had been anxious for some time that he leisurely extinguished the flame with one breath. The cigarette was still intact.

"With things as they are now, you can go on drinking wine and eating meat, and every family will slaughter an ox at New Year's." He rubbed his mouth, "That year we had to emulate Dazhai,* no one got any good out of it. You remember that."

"There wasn't anything." I wanted to talk about how the overall situation now was good.

"Have you seen Brother Deyou? He's township head. Yesterday he went to Catch Little Sister Bridge to plant trees. Maybe he's back, or maybe not, or maybe he will be." He began talking about a muddle of people and things: so-and-so had built a new house, one *zhang* six feet high; and so-and-so had also built one, one *zhang* eight feet high; so-and-so also wanted to build a house, one *zhang* six feet high; so-and-so was just laying the foundation, maybe it would be one *zhang* six feet or maybe one *zhang* eight feet high. I listened nervously, looking for some kind of logic behind these remarks. I observed some strange things about the talk here; for "see" they said "behold," "say" was something like "saith," "quiet" became "quietude." And there were all these "ji" added to words. Did they mean "to start"? Or was it "to stand"?†

I was a little tipsy, arbitrarily showing pleasure whether for one *zhang* six or one *zhang* eight.

"You still remember us, and you come back to the mountains to see us." Again he inhaled his cigarette paper into a low flame, and again made me silently anxious for a couple of seconds. "I still keep the book you wrote that time you were the local teacher." Clunk, clunk, he went upstairs, and then after a long time, with strands of cobwebs on his head, he came down, slapping a few, very yellowed sheets of paper. It was a small, mimeographed book of a few pages, probably a text-

*In 1964 Mao picked the Dazhai brigade as a model for self-reliant rural development and for correct socialist politics.

†The villagers speak a local dialect, which the protagonist, a city person, cannot comprehend.

book for learning characters. Its cover had already been torn off, and
it gave off a poisonous, camphorous odor. It seemed to contain some
kind of a song for night school, miscellaneous vocabulary having to do
with agriculture, the 1911 Revolution, even Marxist theory of peasant
movements, and some maps. It was printed very crudely, each character extremely big, and there were circles from the oil in the ink. I
suppose I could have written something like this; it wasn't anything
extraordinary.

"You'd come on hard times then, too. So starved there was nothing
left of your face but two eyes, and you still came to teach."

"It was nothing, nothing."

"The snowy days of the last month of the year were really cold."

"Really cold. My nose almost froze and fell off."

"And you reclaimed fields, going out to work with pine torches."

"Uh huh, pine torches."

He suddenly got very mysterious. That small chunk of light on his
cheekbone and a few pustules pressed close to me. "I want to ask about
something, was it you that killed Shorty Yang?"

"What Shorty Yang?" The top of my scalp suddenly tensed and my
throat constricted as I shook my head over and over again. Ma wasn't
even my name in the first place, and I had never seen any Shorty Yang,
so how was it that I was being dragged into this criminal case?

"Everyone said it was you who did it. That guy was a two-headed
snake.* He deserved to be killed!" He spoke angrily and, seeing me
deny it, seemed a little suspicious but also a little regretful.

"Is there any liquor left?" I changed the subject.

"Yes, yes, all you can hold."

"There are mosquitoes here."

"Mosquitoes pick on strangers. Should I burn some straw?"

The straw was lit. Group after group of people came to see me,
hobbling in the door and each time asking such things as Was I well?
and Was my family well? The men accepted my cigarettes and smoked
with loud sucking noises. They sat leaning against the door or the wall;
their eyes narrowed when they smiled and they seldom spoke. Occasionally I heard them make a comment or two among themselves.
Some said I had put on weight, others said I was thinner; some said
I looked much older, and others that I was still "baby-faced," and of
course this was because the food in the city was richer in oil. They
would stay until they finished their cigarettes, and then would smile
and say they were going to fell a tree or spread manure. A few children ran over and took my glasses to inspect for a moment, and then

*A person with divided loyalties.

with intense delight and delicious terror shrieked as they fled in all directions, "There are little demons inside! Little demons!" A young girl stood by the door, chewing on a piece of straw and fixing a silent gaze at me. It seemed as if her eyes swam and glittered with tears. This made me very uncomfortable. I could only assume an earnest expression and fix my gaze on Aiba.

I had already run into a lot of this sort of thing. Earlier I went to see the opium they were growing, and I ran into a middle-aged woman along the way. Seeing me, she appeared terrified, her face like a light gone suddenly dim. She quickly pulled the back part of her cloth shoe up onto her heel and went on her way with her head lowered. I didn't know what it meant.

Aiba said I must also go see Third Grandfather—in fact, Third Grandfather was already dead. Apparently he had died of a snake-bite not long before, and he had left behind only a name in people's conversation. Over by the brick kiln, his lonely hut still remained. It was already half fallen down and seemed about to collapse. Under two paulownia trees, grass flourished waist-high, surrounding the hut from all sides and flowing up onto the steps in a sinister way, blades of grass that wagged narrow tongues as if they wanted to swallow the hut, as if they wanted to swallow the last remaining bones of a clan. Insects had bored minute black holes in the locked wooden door. I wondered whether a house could become as dilapidated as this while the owner was alive. Could it be that people are the souls of houses, and once the souls have flown, their outer form rots as quickly as this? In a thick growth of grass a rusted lantern was planted upside down, with a few white bird droppings on it. There was also a broken earthenware jar. If you touched it, a swarm of whining mosquitoes poured out. Aiba said that this jar was always used to make pickles, and that back then I often came to Third Grandfather's home to eat cucumber pickles. (I did?) The plaster on the wall was peeling, and there were a few indistinct characters painted on it. Only the edges where the brush had touched had not yet faded completely: "With the whole world in mind . . . ." Aiba said I had written that. (Had I?) He pulled out a bunch of plantain and threw it at a bird's nest in a tree. I took a quick look in the window and saw there was half a basket of lime in the room and a big round plate. Looking closely, I discovered it was the weight of an iron barbell, corroded by rust. I was amazed. How could such unlikely physical training equipment appear in the mountains? How was it moved here?

Probably there was no need to ask. I had given it to Third Grandfather, hadn't I? I gave it to Third Grandfather to beat into a hoe or rake, and he never did so. Right?

Someone was calling the oxen from the dike, "Wuuma—, wuuma—" And following this came the faint sound of oxen bells from the forest opposite. The way of calling oxen here is rather special, as if one were crying for mama, crying desolately. Perhaps the brick wall of that blockhouse had been cried black by this call.

An elderly woman was coming down from the mountain with a very small bundle of wood. Her back was bent almost to a right angle and at each step she pulled back with her chin, almost as if she were hoeing. She looked up at me penetratingly, as if she weren't looking at me but at the paulownia tree behind my head. Blurred black pupils held up her eyelids. She showed no expression, only a face covered with wrinkles so deep they shook me profoundly. She looked at Third Grandfather's hut and then turned back to look at that old tree at the entrance of the village, and without making any sense murmured, "The tree is dead too." Then slowly, again as if she were hoeing, she moved away. The wind pressed down a few of her dry silver hairs.

I believed now that I really never had been here before. And I had no way of understanding that old woman's words—a profound and bottomless pool.

Dinner was very grand, with ostentatiously big chunks of beef and pork, pieces the size of a palm and cooked rare. They had a raw, fleshy taste. They were piled up, overflowing the bowl, so a woven grass collar was attached and layer by layer the meat was stacked up, like stacking a brick kiln. Probably thousands of years ago they ate this way. Only the male guests could sit at the table. One guest had not yet arrived, so the host spread a straw paper at his place and as everyone ate a chunk of meat, a piece was placed on the paper, as if he had eaten as well. During the feast I mentioned fragrant rice. They were entirely unwilling to discuss a price and wanted simply to give me some. As for opium, the harvest was good all right this year, but the state medicinal materials center had a purchasing monopoly. I couldn't very well say anything more.

"Shorty Yang deserved to be killed." Aiba sucked in a mouthful of soup and then placed the spoon back on the table in its former sticky place and, eyeing the bowl of meat, rapped his chopsticks. "Such a cocky bastard, with fat soft hands, never worked but half-heartedly. And he was going to build a house, wasn't there something fishy about that?"

"That's right, and who hadn't got a whipping from his rope? I still have two scars on my wrists. Fuck his mother good!"

"When did he die? Did he really run into a blood-stained demon and fall off a cliff?"

"No matter how savage he was, his fate was fixed. You only get one peck of life, and he wanted to eat a bushel of it. Hong Sheng of Xia Family Bend was the same."

"He even ate rats. He really was ferocious!"

"Yeah, he really was. Never heard of such a thing before."

"Bear Head ran into trouble with him, too. Took a couple of Shorty's punches. It was obviously a couple socks of dye. I saw it myself. Couldn't even have used it to dye cloth, only good for painting Buddhas. But Shorty said it was gunpowder."

"That was because Bear Head had a higher class background, too."*

I got up enough courage to interrupt, "The matter about Shorty Yang, didn't the higher-ups send anybody to look into it?"

Aiba bit with a noisy squeak into a fat piece of meat. "Someone came looking. What the fuck can they find! So the day they came to find me, I went to find my chickens! Ai, Comrade Ma, you haven't touched your wine? Here, have some food, eat something."

He pressed another chunk of meat on me, and my throat constricted. All I could do was pretend to go help myself to more rice, then sneak off to a dark corner and pick it off the bowl to give to the dog that squeezed between my legs.

After the meal, they insisted that I must have a bath. I wondered if this were some local custom and had to pretend I knew all about it. There was no tub, only a big high barrel set in the room with the stove, enough to hold several big pots of hot water. The women could come and go as they pleased in front of the barrel, and Elder Sister from the Liang Family even came from time to time to add water with a gourd ladle. It made me very embarrassed and I squatted down again and again in the barrel. As soon as she picked up a bucket to go feed the pigs, I secretly let out a long breath. I had already bathed so that my whole body was hot, and a steamy sweat rose up from me. Probably the water had had sweet wormwood boiled in it. The red marks from the mosquito bites all over my body no longer itched so much. The glass chimney of the boar oil lamp over my head gave out circle after circle of a dim blue mist in the steam, applying a blue layer to my body as well. Before putting on my shoes, I looked at this blue me and suddenly had a weird feeling, as if this body were unfamiliar, strange. There was no adornment here and no stranger, no one to cover up or put on an act for and no conditions for it, only my naked self, my own reality. I had hands and feet so I could work; intestines and a belly for eating; reproductive organs with which I could propagate descen-

*He must have belonged to one of the five bad elements—landlords, rich peasants, counterrevolutionaries, local bad elements, and rightists—to be disciplined by the revolution.

dents. The world had been temporarily closed out. Wherever we go, we're always busy and in a hurry, and have no time to take account of or think about such things. As a result of a chance encounter between a sperm and an egg long ago, I had an ancestor; and through another chance encounter between this ancestor and another, there was yet another fertilization; and only thus, generation after generation, was there the possibility of my existence. I was also a blue fertilization of innumerable consecutive fortuities. What had I come to the world to do? What could I do? . . . Idiotically I worried over this.

I rubbed a scar over an inch long on my calf. I had been stabbed here by a spiked shoe on the soccer field. But at the same time it seemed that wasn't it, instead . . . some short guy had bitten me. Was it that misty rainy morning? On that narrow mountain path? He passed by holding an umbrella and trembled in terror at my gaze. Then he knelt down and said he would never dare do it again, never again. He also said Second Sister's death had nothing to do with him, and it wasn't he who had led away Third Grandfather's ox. Then finally, he resisted and, with his eyes protruding as if they would fall out, he bit my leg. His two hands began to pull at a rope lead for oxen tied around his neck, and then they reached out fiercely, like two crabs crawling on the ground, leaping, and digging into the mud. I don't know when these two crabs finally came slowly to a rest and fell quiet. . . .

I didn't dare think any further, or even dare look at my own hands —Was there a smell of blood and a scar carved out by a rope?

I struggled now to convince myself I had never come here before and never known any Shorty. Never, even in a dream, had I seen this circle upon circle of blue mist. Never.

It was very lively in the main room of the house. An old man came in and stepped on his pine torch to extinguish it. He said he had once asked me to buy him some cloth dye and owed me two bucks. He had come now to return it, and he also invited me to come to his house the next day to eat and "lie down for the night." This started an argument with Aiba. Aiba said tomorrow he was meeting with a tailor, he had already cut the meat to entertain him, so tomorrow without a doubt I should go to his house. . . .

While they were still arguing, I took the opportunity to slip out the door. Stumbling along, I wanted to see the old house where "I" had lived before—according to Aiba, it was the cowshed behind that tree. It had been converted into a cowshed only two years ago.

I passed underneath the paulownia tree once more and again saw the tangle of grass about to swallow the black shadow of Old Grandfather—of the leaning thatch hut. It looked at me silently, borrowing the voice of a crow to cough and the rustle of the leaves to speak with me. I even smelled a faint breath of wine.

Child, you've come back? Pull up a chair and sit down. I told you before, go as far as you can, as far as you can, don't ever come back.

But, I missed your cucumber pickles. I learned how to make them myself, but I can't get that flavor.

What's so tasty about those wretched things? At that time I saw you were hungry, you'd run into bad times. After plowing one length of the field, you would even strip the raw broad beans along the field paths to eat. So I figured out a way to make a little something.

You were always concerned about us. I knew that.

Who hasn't had to be away from home some time? I was just doing what I should.

That time we were carrying logs, we only carried nine loads. You were keeping count, but you always said we carried ten.

I don't remember.

And you also insisted that we cut our hair. You said hair and beards consumed blood so to let them grow long would harm our energy.

Really? I don't remember.

I should have come sooner to see you. I never thought the change would be so great and you would leave so soon.

I had to go. Wouldn't I have become mere essence if I'd lived any longer? I just liked to have a sip of wine, and now I've drunk enough, so I can sleep peacefully and soundly.

Grandfather, would you like a smoke?

Little Ma, make yourself some tea if you'd like.

. . . . .

I left that breath of alcohol. Holding up a pine torch about to go out, thinking about the field labor the following morning, from time to time hearing the frogs by my feet jump into the water ditches, I would return home. But now I had no torch in my hand, and my home had become a cowshed, looking unfamiliar and cold. I couldn't see anything clearly, I could only hear the sound of oxen chewing their cud, and there was the sour odor of warm, steamy manure oozing out the door. The oxen thought their master had come, and they looked out with heads pressed together, hitting the gate railing with a clatter. When I left, the sound of footsteps echoed back from the earthen wall of the cowshed, as if there were another person walking on the other side of the wall, or within the earth of the wall—and that person knew my secret.

The mountain wall opposite was black and gloomy, and it seemed higher and closer in the night than in the day, giving you the feeling that it was difficult to breathe. I looked up at the uneven line of star-lit sky overhead; the earth close and the sky distant. It seemed as if I were about to be dragged by a nameless force farther and farther down into some deep place through this crack in the earth.

A huge moon rose, and, as if they had been startled, the village dogs yelped. I stepped on the moonlight that filtered down through the shadow of the trees, small dots and circles like algae or duckweed, and went toward the side of the stream. I guessed that maybe there was a person sitting by the stream, perhaps a young girl with a leaf in her mouth.

There was no one by the stream. But as I returned, I did see a figure under the old tree.

On such a moonlit night, there should be such a cut paper silhouette.

"Is that Brother Ma?"

"It's me." Surprisingly, I answered without the least exaggeration or lie.

"You're coming from the stream?"

"You . . . who are you?"

"Fourth Sister."

"Fourth Sister, you've grown so tall. If I ran into you elsewhere, I wouldn't recognize you at all."

"The world you run in is big, so you feel everything has changed."

"Is your family all well?"

She suddenly fell silent, looked toward that narrow house, and then her voice became somewhat different. "My older sister, she really hates you. . . ."

"Hates . . . ." Nervously I darted a look at that path that led toward lamplight and the horizon and wanted to flee. "I . . . there are a lot of things which are hard to explain. I told her . . . ."

"That day, why did you put corn in her basket like that? Can you put just anything in a young girl's basket? She gave you a strand of hair, and you knew, didn't you."

"I . . . I didn't understand, didn't understand the customs here. I . . . wanted her to help, so I had her carry out some corn."

I hoped I had given a pretty good answer and could still muddle past this.

"Everybody talked about such things. Were you deaf? I saw it all. You taught her acupuncture."

"She liked to study. She wanted to become a doctor. Actually, I didn't understand acupuncture myself at that time. I just stuck the needle in anywhere."

"You city people, you feel no ties of friendship."

"Don't talk like . . . ."

"It's true! It's true!"

"I know . . . your sister was a good girl, I know. She sang beautifully, and her needlework was very skillful. Once she took us out to catch eels, and she got one each time she put her hand in. I got sick and she cried so hard. . . . I know all that. But there are lots of things you don't understand, and that can't be explained very clearly. My whole life I'll be chasing about and having a lot of trouble, I . . . I have my career."

In the end I chose the word "career" even though it was a little unnatural.

She covered her face with her hands and began to sob. "That Hu, he was really cruel."

I seemed to know what this meant and continued to answer probingly, "I heard about that. I want to find him and settle accounts."

"What's the use? What's the use?" She stamped her feet and cried heartbreakingly. "If you had said something sooner, it wouldn't have turned out that way. My sister has already become a bird, and every day she calls for you here, calls for you. Have you heard her?"

Under the moonlight I saw her thin back rise and fall. At the top was her shining neck, and I could even see distinctly the white scalp in the part of her hair. I had an impulse to wipe her tears, to grasp her shoulders and kiss that scalp, as if I were kissing my little sister, to have her salty tears stick to my lips and swallow them.

But I didn't dare. This was a strange story, I didn't dare break it with a lick of my tongue.

There really was a bird calling in the trees, "Don't do that, brother, don't do that, brother—" The voice was lonely, like a sharp arrow shot into the sky and then suddenly fluttering down among the mountains, down into the green forest, down into that distant daub of black clouds and soundless flash of lightning. I smoked a cigarette, looking at the lightning, as if putting a query to a silent history.

Don't do that, brother.

I left, but before going I wrote Fourth Sister a letter, asking Elder Sister of the Liang family to give it to her. In the letter I said that her sister had wanted to become a doctor but hadn't in the end. I hoped she could realize her sister's desire. Roads were traveled by people. Did she want to sign up for the entrance exam to health school? I would send her lots of review materials; definitely, I would send them. I also said I could never forget her sister. Aiba had captured that parrot in the tree, and I was going to take it back to have it sing for me each day before my window, to become my friend forever.

I fled almost secretly, not saying goodbye to the people of the village and without buying any fragrant rice—what did I want fragrant rice and opium for anyway? It seemed that wasn't what I had come for. The entire village, and my entire unaccountable self, made me feel I was suffocating. I had to flee. Turning my head to look back, I saw again that old tree killed by lightning at the entrance of the village, stretching out dry limbs, like convulsing fingers. The owner of the fingers had fallen in some battle and became a mountain, but he still struggled to raise this hand, to grab something.

I checked into the inn in the county town, and fell asleep to the parrot's murmuring at the head of the bed. I had a dream, I dreamed I was still walking and walking along that wrinkled mountain road. The dirt road had been washed away by mountain torrents, as if its flesh were gouged out, leaving behind sheaths of muscle and bone and pieces of dried organs to bear the mountain folks' straw sandals. One could never reach the end of this road. I looked at the calendar watch on my wrist. I had already been walking an hour, a day, a week . . . but still this road was under my feet. Until finally, no matter where I went, I had this same dream.

I had woken with a start. I drank water three times, pissed twice, and finally placed a long-distance call to a friend. I wanted to ask whether or not he had brought that ugly Cao to his knees at the poker table, but what came out was an inquiry about studying for examinations on one's own.

My friend called me "Huang Zhixian."

"What?"

"What what?"

"What did you call me?"

"Isn't this Huang Zhixian?"

"You called me Huang Zhixian?"

"Don't you call yourself Huang Zhixian?"

I was stunned, my head empty. Yes, I was in an inn. In the corridor mosquitoes flew round a dim lamp and there was a row of cots set up. Just below the receiver I was holding was a big fat head making a whistling snore. But—was there a Huang Zhixian in the world, too? And was I that Huang Zhixian?

I was tired. I could never walk out of that enormous I. Mama!

Jia Pingwa

Floodtime

//// I

This year, 1985 that is, the Zhou River flooded again in August. At first the rain fell in vast sheets, which was not a good omen; and at night, while the lamps were still lit, rats began climbing up the posts to the rafters, first one, then a second, a third, and a fourth. More than anything else, Old Man Shou hated rats. He would take down two traps to catch them and, if he succeeded, would pour kerosene over them and light them, letting them burn themselves up as they writhed about. But this time he felt a twinge in his heart. Three rats stole upward at once. The first and last were big, and the one in the middle was very small. All four of its feet scrambling as it squeaked endlessly, it had to be an infant. To Old Man Shou it seemed to be saying: A flood! A flood! Seeing another of the world's sentient beings crowded together up there on the rafters, he was filled by a surge of sympathy. He didn't feel like sleeping. He carried out wooden boards and logs from the inner room. Braving the rain under the sky-piercing elm in front of his door, he began twining and binding together a wooden raft, using the body of the tree as an axle shaft.

A glance around the neighborhood showed the old folks were all out binding rafts under the sky-piercing elms in front of each house.

"Old Shou, can you manage?"

"Yeah, but I don't have enough strength in my hands. I can't twist the wire tight."

"Just tie it up with kudzu vine. How high could the water get?"

This story was published in *Zhongshan* in February 1986. Translation by Margaret H. Decker.

"There's no telling! The water could be here by first watch, couldn't it?"

"Manman really didn't come home?"

"It looks like he won't be coming."

"Better to plant an elm than raise a kid. . . ."

Old Man Shou didn't make any answer. Squinting his eyes, he looked upward from the roots of the sky-piercing elm. The tree bored up into the sky, so tall you couldn't see the top, shining white in the blackness like a pillar of light shooting upward. That elm had been planted when the house was built; they all planted elms when they built their houses. Just as when you waded the Zhou River, you spotted exactly where you would get out of the water as you went in; or when you built a stove, you fixed the outhouse. The sky-piercing elm in front of each house was a soldier who guarded the home. "Maintain an army for a thousand days and use it for an hour." These sky-piercing elms were used once every year in August.

Old Man Shou finally finished twining the raft together, packed his everyday things into wooden boxes, and moved these onto the raft. Altogether there were eight boxes, all built by Manman. A few years ago Manman would have taken a load of kindling and wanted to put that on the raft, too. Now he ignored the matter entirely, wasn't concerned about any of it!

Old Man Shou took the cash he had saved and put it all in a leather wallet which he tied tightly to his belt. He leaned a wooden ladder against the caves, using a rope to fasten its base to the roots of the elm. Then he took his wife's memorial picture down from the wall, hung it on the crossbar of the door, and gazed at it as he smoked a water pipe.

"The water will come in the first watch," he told her. "Don't be scared. As soon as the water reaches the base of the stairs, I'll tuck your picture in my shirt and carry it up to the roof. Manman didn't come home . . . not just Manman. Seven or eight out of every ten sons of our village didn't come back. Anyway, how bad could the flood be? Every year it floods, and then in half a day the water goes down. Our village is in a lucky spot."

The picture of his wife had been taken three years before she died, and in it she looked kind and gentle. Old Man Shou started recollecting all sorts of things, remembering only her good points. Although they had been man and wife a long time, they hadn't had the fortune to live together very much of it. He was the manager of a medicine shop in Zhou City and only came home once a month. She always treated him like an honored guest. Whatever he wanted, she did for him. He felt that she saw him not as her own man but as her leader, and yet she was always so warm and courteous. He thought that this was because they weren't together very often, and that when he retired and returned to the village, things might change. But then before he had retired, his wife fell ill. Manman brought his mother to Zhou City to see a doctor. This did no good, so Manman took her to the hospital in the provincial capital, saying that in ten or fifteen days, after she was well, they would be back. They were gone forty-five days. Forty-five days later Manman came back, looking dark and thin and carrying a big bundle on his back. Old Man Shou asked, "What about your mother?" and Manman answered, "I'm carrying her." He put down the bundle, which turned out to be a small cinerary casket! Manman's mother hadn't gotten well while she was in the provincial hospital. She had closed her eyes and died. After crying a while, Manman had assumed responsibility himself and taken his mother's corpse to be cremated. Old Man Shou had been good-tempered all his life, but he cursed his son then for the first time! However, the deed was already done, so all he could do was build a wooden coffin, place the casket in it, and then give her a second funeral. He made a burial mound at the foot of his mother's and father's graves. "Since when do peasants have cremations?" Every time Old Shou brought the matter up after this, he would berate Manman, "It's cruel enough that she died away from home, but you had to go and leave her soul to drift aimlessly. Our ancestor's graveyard is in a lucky spot. Burying her here in this good grave would have been good for sons and grandsons!"*

Even though Old Man Shou had been a manager in a medicine shop, several decades of experience had given him only a sketchy knowledge of medicine. Chinese philosophy begins by intuiting the whole and grasping the world through yin and yang and the five elements. Old Man Shou had learned to consider the direction of mountains and streams, the abode of yin and the home of yang, through the primary elements of Chinese medicine—metal, wood, water, fire, and earth. Aside from his belief in the moral wisdom of the phrase "When a leaf falls, it returns to the roots," the only reason for his persistence in wanting to return to this village after retirement was that he couldn't give up this piece of land where he had been born and raised and where his mother, father, and wife were buried.

The rain was still falling, incessantly and soundlessly, and the sky was so black you couldn't see a single star. A few rats ran up from the

---

*In certain parts of rural north China, family graveyards at the edge of the village are important centers for rituals. During the Maoist era, the government tried to prohibit burial and prescribed cremation instead.

rain-soaked earth to the steps. In confusion they sped past under his feet, climbing the posts to the rafters, and an instant later he heard a muffled roar followed by the sound of a bell. The bell was rung by Lower Bend Village. Every year they built the river dikes up high in front of that village, and every year there was a crisis. Old Man Shou imagined the dikes once again crawling with men like ants, as they cut wood and carried sacks of sand to plug the dike. He calmly extinguished the papery ashes of his tobacco and put the oil lamp chimney on a lantern that burned methane made from pig urine. Carrying this, he fastened his wife's picture around his neck, draped a straw rain cape over his shoulders, put on a rain hat, and climbed up the ladder to the roof. The cat, which ate rice but not rats and was so fat it shone, also climbed up by way of the ladder. People were sitting on each house, riding the backs of their homes as if they were playing a game of riding horses. The buildings of the village had not been laid out neatly to begin with because the back of the village leaned up against the Luo Mountains. The main peak of the Luo Mountains was very high, its sides sloping gently downwards like two arms coiled in an embrace. "Leaning up against a mountain," that really made for a lucky location. The mountains across the river were called the Mang Peaks and had five sawtooth-like summits. The abode of the yang, or the southern-facing windows and doors, had to face those peaks exactly in order to be properly situated, but since the wisdom of each geomancer was different, the position of each family's house was different too. Some were set exactly along a north-south axis, some northwest-southeast, northeast-southwest, or slightly west and slightly east. At this time, with a person and a methane lantern on every roof, they weren't panic-stricken, as if facing some great calamity. Instead, they looked casually toward the Zhou River as they called out to each other and carried on a conversation.

"The water is up to the steps."

"It's over the steps, and the rafts are floating!"

"Do you think the dikes of Lower Bend Village will hold?"

"That village is in an unlucky spot. When the river reaches there, it's 'evil water'!"

"Aiya! The rafts are already so high. It's a big flood this year!"

"It won't go over the window tops. . . ."

"Will our earthen walls hold?"

"No problem, even if the water reaches the eaves, it's no problem. It'll still go back down."

"The water had better not reach the eaves! If something really happened, there aren't many strong young people in the village. . . ."

It was lonely on the rooftops. Although the older folks had never in their lifetimes experienced a flood that covered the eaves, the clouds in the sky were unfathomable, and if by any chance the water did reach the level of the eaves. . . . They all held their breaths and didn't speak.

Suddenly Old Man Shou spoke out, "Moon River didn't flood, did it?" The nature of this question was originally to free them from the tension, but there was an immediate answer. "The rain falls from the same heaven, how could Moon River not flood?"

"Then how could they be panning for gold?"

"Even if they aren't panning for gold, they won't think of coming home!"

"Their hearts are hard!"

It was their sons and daughters they reproached. As they watched the rafts floating up alongside the sky-piercing elms, their resentment against their children's unfiliality suddenly intensified.

"Let it flood and drown us all and see whether they come back!"

"They'd be even less likely to come back then."

"The water can't rise any higher." Old Man Shou again changed the subject to ease the tension. "Our ancestors built our village on this spot. A flood won't wipe us out."

"And once the water goes down, we won't have to fertilize our fields."

"The day after tomorrow, when boats can travel the Zhou River, let's go to the sandbanks of Moon River and look for them. Brother Shou, will you go call Manman to come home?"

"I'll go."

The water in fact reached the tops of the windows and then didn't rise any further. But it wouldn't recede until tomorrow after breakfast. This was their experience over the years, and that meant that the people on their roofs would have to ride the backs of their homes straight through until tomorrow morning after breakfast. None of them felt like sleeping. Wide-eyed, they watched the roofs, the rafts already near the roofs, and the wooden boxes on the rafts. Old Man Shou caressed the portrait of his wife he held to his chest, saying to her in his heart, it's nothing, nothing. This place of ours is lucky. Your grave was covered, but once the water recedes, I'll tend to it. Then he watched the cat, which had stayed snuggled close beside him, crying in a very soft and gentle fashion, its eyes shining with a greenish light.

Suddenly someone called out sharply, "Look, a demon woman has come up to the river's surface!"

Old Man Shou, too, immediately looked toward the surface of the Zhou River. It seemed to him that his eyes shone green like the cat's. He looked in the direction of a cliff in a backwater bend. At first there was a ball of light, red inside and bordered with blue. This spun upwards, then following the river's surface moved down until it was almost in a straight line with the village, where it abruptly extinguished. Following it, another ball appeared, and another, flashing and then dying out.

Even those villagers who had not seen it before with their own eyes, all knew about this extraordinary sight. The Zhou River flowed a few thousand miles from end to end, and the whole way it was a big river with big bends. When it reached that cliff, which was also the place where the left arm of the Luo Mountains stretched down and ended in a steep, round-topped hill, it suddenly made a lazy little bend. The village was located on this bend. The terrain there was not at all high, and the soil was extremely fertile. Every year when the river rose, the water flooded the fields and the houses, but there was no history of it washing away the soil or destroying the homes. It was a backwater, so all depended on this steep cliff. The cliff was dark and precipitous next to the river, allowing only strange trees, like coiled dragons, to sprout there. Their foliage wasn't thick in spring, summer, or autumn, but red clouds* would hang on them, like bright drops of blood. Seen from a distance in the winter, the cliff would seem to be cracked with crevices. If you went closer by boat, you could see roots like cast iron, stubbornly twined onto the rock wall, like a relief sculpture. But of any ten wooden boats that went near the bank, eight or nine would not return. Floating smoothly on the surface of the water, the boat would begin to spin as it approached and then suddenly stand on end and sink. Of those who fell in the water, one able swimmer escaped with his life to report that there was a whirlpool there, as fierce as a tornado. The face of the person who spoke was bloodless, as if he were telling of the underworld. After this, cargo boats that passed by never again dared go close to that cliff. And yet there were figures carved in it, which didn't look quite like men or animals, and no one knew what person had carved these figures, or when.

Once, after Manman had been away from the village for some time, he came back and said, "Those figures are called 'cliff carvings.' They were carved by people in ancient times. What's more, there is a book in which someone particularly mentions the carvings here." Of course carvings on a cliff are called "cliff carvings." Who needed Manman to tell him that? Old Man Shou asked Manman what the function of those cliff carvings was, and Manman answered, "In the book it said

*A kind of tree fungus.

that the ancient people used them to pacify the water demons." Manman had gotten glib since leaving the village. Everything was what someone had written in a book. Since it was supposed to pacify the water demons, then why did the water demons still come out each time there was a big flood? No other place had these balls of light, they only appeared at this cliff, and they didn't appear on ordinary days, but only when there was a big flood. Even Manman was baffled. He opened his mouth but couldn't explain it.

Old Man Shou, however, felt deep gratitude toward this cliff and the appearance of the balls of light that were water demons. His knowledge of the principles of yin and yang and the five elements wasn't profound, and he couldn't explain why these water demons existed, but he believed that they weren't a bad thing. In fact, it was just because things were this way that the soil of this bend was so rich and this village had never been destroyed. This was the luckiest spot along the entire Zhou River.

But Manman and this younger generation were ungrateful and looked down on the land of this bend. They looked down on this village!

"These water demons are really strange. As soon as they move in front of the village, they disappear!"

"The water demons protect this bend of ours."

"Our village really is in a lucky spot."

"It's an evil thing that Manman and the others don't return."

"Could the fortune of our location be washed away because they've all run to the outside?"

"It couldn't, could it? Won't they have to return when they get old?"

II

It's all one sky, and there's only one sun. When the Zhou River flooded, Moon River flooded too. The rock base of the hollow dug in the river's sandbank had been revealed and in the first afternoon they had panned twenty-five grams of gold. But just as they were saying their luck was good, water flooded the hollow. Manman swore crudely, and his companions made fun of him, "Manman, city folk don't say 'X his mother'! Be a little more civilized."

"I'll screw his mother!"

Having said this, Manman then laughed himself. They all laughed, but when they stopped, they began to feel bitter and all fell silent. Returning to the household where they were lodging, they drank spirits.

The owner of the house was a hunchback, wretched in appearance but a crafty schemer. Seeing that there was gold in the sand, he kept watch over Moon River, but he didn't have the strength to dig out a hollow and pan for the gold. Besides taking in rent from the outsiders who came to pan, he would collect their sodden grass shoes and wash them out in the gold panning tray. Manman and the others drank themselves into a stupor, pursuing whatever talk suited them. They'd utter a sentence or two and laugh a bit, or if something painful was mentioned, curse resentfully for a while. The hunchback picked up the several pairs of grass shoes at the door and went to the river's edge. After a long while he came back, his face gleeful.

"Uncle Hunchback, did you see color again?"

"I did! I tell you, as long as I have this life, it doesn't matter if I go to sleep only in the middle of the night and have to get up early. It's a stick of gold!"

"A stick of gold?"

It was indeed a stick of gold, gleaming yellow in the bottom of the hunchback's pan, the length of a finger and the thickness of a needle point. It shone but was white in the middle.

"There's not only gold in Moon River, there's quicksilver, too. This is a piece of gold corroded by mercury, otherwise why would it turn white?"

"Uncle Hunchback, you sly old bugger, you always make a cheap profit. We aren't going to let you pick through our shoes any more!"

"I can get gold even without picking through your shoes. In the twenty-fourth year of the Republic [1935], I passed by the riverbank on my way to cut grass and picked up a piece as big as a mung bean."

"Okay, so your fate is good. Let's play a few games of mahjongg."*

"Manman, are you still holding a grudge against me? You're on a losing streak, and my luck is right. You want to give me all the bills in your pocket?"

Without a word, Manman snorted and flung the empty liquor bottle out the door where it exploded noisily. The mahjongg pieces clattered and toppled over on the table.

"Manman, there you go again! Are you drunk?"

The hunchback's daughter, Yunyun, stood in the door, brows raised and eyes fixed on Manman. Yunyun's eyes were venomous, the eyes of a snake. Manman wilted, his gaze falling on Yunyun's white feet clad in plastic sandals. Behind her feet were those two snow-white dogs, docile and obedient.

*A popular gambling game.

Manman left the table dejectedly, climbed the ladder upstairs, bored his way into his own bedding, and fell asleep.

The water in the river flowed on, roiling and seething. Agitated and impetuous, it bit and chewed at the rocks on the banks, chewed at the homes on the banks, and at the outsiders, come to pan for gold, who were lodging in these homes.

Darkness came but Manman didn't get up; he didn't regain consciousness that whole night. The next day at noon, when the big red sun was seeping in through the holes in the ceiling, Manman came downstairs. His eyes were swollen from sleep.

"It's cleared, Manman, the river's gone down!"

"Who cares? Let it flood all it wants to!"

That's what he said, but still a few people stepped out of the house and went to the sandbank to take a look. The difference in Moon River's water level when it rained and when it didn't was dramatic, like the change in the face of a woman or child who is quick to cry and quick to laugh. Already there were a lot of people there opening up new hollows. A stretch of white thatching grass along the bank had been submerged by the water but hadn't been flattened. It stood with leaves and branches vertical and lofty under the sun, and in it one of the two dogs with fur white as snow was lying down and one was standing. Yunyun stood still behind them and looked toward the river.

"Manman's not afraid of anything but Yunyun!"

"He's not afraid, it's the other thing."

"The other thing?"

Manman's face darkened, and giving his companions a dressing down, he told them to drive the hand-tractor down to the sandbank. This tractor wasn't for pulling things. It was used solely to drive the water pump. Manman's fellows picked up the shoulder poles with carrying baskets and the settling basin and went with him. Manman was the leader of this group of panners. He had the ability to see the veins of the river and whether there was or wasn't gold. He went to a backwater, looked left and right, held his breath, closed his eyes, uttered a curse, and then they began to open a hollow. Within an hour, a hollow two feet deep had been dug and water began bubbling up, so they set up the pump and started drawing the water out. Manman was already so hot he had taken off his shirt, exposing the bamboo tube for holding gold that hung from the belt of his pants. He arched his back and caught a glimpse of the woman with her dogs in the patch of white thatching grass.

What was Yunyun thinking about over there? Was she at odds with Old Man Hunchback again? Old Man Hunchback was worried to death about marrying off Yunyun. He had found one family, but Yunyun wasn't willing, so he found another and she still wasn't willing. He scolded her, "You want to grow old and die here and never get married?" Manman knew Yunyun. It wasn't that she didn't want to marry. It was because she was almost going crazy thinking about a husband that she had raised these two snow-white dogs. Yunyun didn't want to become a daughter-in-law here; she had her mind on Zhou City. The hunchback had raised Yunyun, but he didn't understand her. He played the part of father in vain. Manman understood.

"Manman, you're rich!" Yunyun had said once as Manman fished out a large lump of gold. "You're rich. Go back to your village and build yourself a home with a compound of gray bricks and tiled roofs."

"That's not for me. When I have enough money, I'll go to the city, buy a house, and start a business."

"You're boasting!"

"Government policy allows it, so why shouldn't I go to the city?"*

"You're another one with ambitions as high as the sky, but fate as thin as paper!"

After that, Yunyun always came to watch Manman pan for gold and would talk about the buildings in the city, the people, and even the artificial mountain and lake in the city park. Once they talked of their fathers. Manman complained that his father shouldn't have retired and returned to his home, and Yunyun blamed her father for not minding things he should mind, perversely minding things that weren't his business, and fretting all day about marrying her off. Manman got on close terms with those two white dogs. He gave a whistle and enticed them over. He hugged the dogs and thought about a lot of pleasant things.

But while Manman had thought all about it, he kept his thoughts to himself because right now he was only a gold panner.

The hollow had already been opened up. One could see the river's bed in one spot. Manman fixed up the sifting tray and directed the shovelers to shovel the sand. The carriers carried, and the rinsers rinsed. As if possessed, everybody kept to his position and minded his task.

"What did you have for breakfast this morning?"

"Taro porridge!"

"No meat? There must be almost nothing in your stomach!"

"If we see color today, I'll buy a pig's head! Let's work hard. Tonight we'll down some drinks with pig tongue and get drunk."

*From the late 1950's to the late 1970's, few peasants were allowed to live or work in the cities. In the 1980's, this rule was relaxed, and many moved to small towns and cities to engage in business or to be temporary workers.

The mention of wine with pig tongue reminded one of the group of something else, and he told about how a panner lodging upriver had gotten in good with his host's old lady, and they had been seen behind the cattle shed "eating pig tongue"!

"Have you ever tasted any, Manman?"

"Manman has been panning a long time. He's got money, but he's planning to go to the city!"

"Not necessarily. I'll bet that in the future Manman will be eating the best pig tongue!"

The one who spoke gave a sidelong glance at the distant Yunyun, but then seeing Manman cross over from the settling basin, deliberately shut up. On the surface, he shut up to keep Manman from hearing, but actually he meant to make him hear. Manman just swore, "Go eat your mother's pig tongue," setting himself and everybody else off into laughter.

Having been sworn at, the speaker retaliated, steering the talk in another direction. "The water of Moon River floods fast and goes down fast, not like the Zhou River!"

"Our village was probably flooded again this time!"

"Even if the houses were destroyed, how much was the family property worth anyway?"

"It's no big deal for us, but Manman's old man brought back a lot of stuff from the city!"

Manman naturally began to think of his father. The old man was really getting on and getting muddled. He had worked in the city all his life, so why did he just have to move back when he finished? Manman's anger began to rise, and with the infinite strength of rage, he picked up two baskets of sand with his hands instead of using a carrying pole and took them to the settling basin. He dumped them with a thunk, thinking to himself, Dad! You just don't understand me. Or is it me who doesn't understand you?

He pursed his mouth, wanting to whistle for those two white dogs, but Yunyun was talking with someone over there.

"Old Wang, have you come from the city?"

"Just set foot here."

"Are the streets along the river flooded?"

"No, the flood didn't reach them. They've put up big dikes so that even if the river rose another five feet, it wouldn't flood. Yunyun, you haven't been to the city lately? There's a 'New Wave' singing and dancing group from Anhui performing there, and it's really something. Aren't you going to see it?"

"Un-huh."

This Wang was the gold collector, a fiend, an insect. Originally the panners had given their gold to the county bank. Then gold collectors started coming every three or four days to buy it. They gave a high price and bought on the spot. So while Manman was willing to let these fellows buy, in his mind he swore at them for their tricks and wondered how much money they managed to get as the gold passed through their hands.

After Old Wang and Yunyun had finished talking, he came straight to the hollow and called Manman in a high-pitched voice, "Manman, the water's only just subsided and already you're panning! I thought you would have gone home?"

"Nope."

"I hear it flooded there again. Aren't you going to go back to have a look?"

"No."

"You must be happy with your haul! How much color have you seen today?"

"The price of our gold's going up!"

But Old Wang laughed and pulled out some good-quality cigarettes, passing them out to everybody one by one, purposely swearing coarsely to make the atmosphere more intimate.

"Manman, don't you play this fucking game with me! What, are you jealous just cause you see a layer of oil floating in my soup?"

"Old Wang, as you well know, state policy is that the gold we find should be sold to the state!"

"All right, all right. You sell it to the state!" Grinning, Old Wang called Manman over. "I've just about settled matters on the two-room storefront you asked me to buy for you. Their price is four thousand, and they won't drop it a copper!"

"I could open a shop there?"

"Of course, there's even a small back courtyard where you could build a two-room house. When the time comes, your father could live in one and the two of you could live in the other."

"Who else is there?"

"You're not going to get married?"

Manman gave a soundless laugh and raising his head saw that the sun had dissolved the clouds into clumps, making bright and dark strips on the sandbank. The two white dogs in the thatching grass patch were like rocks of white jade.

Manman paid no further attention to Old Wang. Silently he went to the side of the settling basin. He said something to the young fellows rinsing the sand, and they sat down and began to smoke cigarettes. Then all the panners stopped for a rest and got their bags from the hand-tractor. As they fished out steamed bread to chew on and give them a little "filler," they gathered around, eyes big and round, to watch Manman start to clean the settling basin.

When the settling basin was cleaned, all the panners supervised, partly because they hoped that the gods would be moved and a little more gold would appear from this flat, and partly because under everyone's gaze, there was no suspicion that the person cleaning the basin might suddenly steal a piece of gold the size of a rice grain. Manman was in charge of this group, and he was an honest man who never did anything underhanded. He had made it clear beforehand, only he could clean the basin, and when he did, everybody had to be watching.

Manman flushed the sand and rocks from the basin into a pan, then straightened his back, closed his eyes and held his breath. Once more he recited a litany of curses before placing the pan in shallow water and shaking it three times, two times, seven times, eight times. The stones and mud all washed away with the water, and one could see a bright yellow sediment in the bottom of the pan. Everyone grew excited.

"Ah!"

"Ahhh!"

"It's hard work, but Moon River doesn't betray the sufferer. You pan and you get gold!"

"For this half-day's work, everyone can get a share of five yuan, no problem!"

"It sure beats staying at home and growing crops!"

The gold was put in the bamboo tube on Manman's belt. And before everyone's feelings of excitement had abated, a few panners from the other groups came over, greed in their eyes.

"Is this a good hollow?"

"No, tomorrow we're going to have to open a new one," Manman said with an impassive face.

III

Old Man Shou had moved his residence to the countryside, but he still lived off the state.* If it hadn't been for Manman's allotment of land, he really wouldn't have had anything to do.† The water flooded

---

*Workers in state-owned enterprises are eligible for pensions. Those in collective enterprises and peasants usually are not.

†Under the system instituted after the communes were dismantled in 1983, each villager receives land for growing grain for subsistence. These are the *kouliang tian*. The village office also contracts land to villagers to grow other crops.

the land after the autumn harvest and did in fact deposit a good, thick layer of river silt. If you stood at the edge of the field, you could smell a rank, fishy odor. Frost's Descent,* the eighteenth of the twenty-four solar periods, had already passed, but the silt was still soft. It was really a torment not to get the wheat planted. So when Old Man Shou saw others scattering seeds in the silt and then just raking to cover them, he did as they did. That winter he tended this piece of land just as he had tended Manman's mother when she was recovering from childbirth. A few days after the wheat appeared above ground, he took the wood and straw ashes left from heating the *kang* and scattered them on the field. A couple days later he took the nightsoil bucket and splashed that on. The other villagers saw him and called out in alarm, "Old Shou, do you want to flatten your wheat?"

"I didn't put any base fertilizer on it to begin with. This way it should grow strong and sturdy!"

"The river silt is base fertilizer, isn't it?"

So Old Shou didn't spread any more fertilizer. As before, he got up early every morning and went for a walk along the edge of the field to see if the border of rocks at either end was crooked or not, or whether any wild rabbits had spent the night there and dug up a patch of seedlings. If there was a single weed, he would bend down to pull it out. He was as devoted in his attendance to the field as he had been in his several decades at the medicine shop, where he had been the first to arrive each morning, sweep the dust, and wash the window in the door. After touring the field, he would tend meticulously to the flowers and herbs in front of his door, then sit down, steep a pot of tea to sip slowly, and feel completely content.

But Old Shou felt more and more regretful about his house. It hadn't collapsed after the flood, only one end of a gable had fallen in and a layer of the water-soaked wall was peeling off in strips. Often at night, when he got up to relieve himself, he would light the lamp, and the floor would be overrun with pill bugs fleeing like defeated troops. So Old Man Shou made plans to repair the house. He took out his money box and carefully added up all the family savings and his retirement allowance. Then, while chewing on some steamed bread which he would spit out to feed his little cat, he made calculations: to entirely rebrick four walls would take four thousand bricks, five bags of concrete, 100 kilos of lime. Then for fill to raise the foundation, I'll need 20 cubic meters of pebbles; and to repair the courtyard wall and build an archway. . . . By the time he had figured this far, all of Old Shou's money had been used up, and he was still short a few hundred

*Roughly late October–early November.

yuan. No matter what, Manman would have to put up a little of the money!

Manman, however, disagreed. He didn't come home until someone took a letter to him, and then he came dressed very stylishly, from leather shoes to sunglasses. His old father scolded him, "You dress up like a wolf but don't look like one, so you pretend to be a dog but your tail's too long!" Whatever else, he didn't look like a peasant!

"My money can't be touched. I'm buying a house in the city."

"And just forget about this house?"

"As long as it doesn't cave in and there's a burrow to return to, that's enough."

"What bunk! 'As good as Chang'an was, it didn't last forever.' You going to live in the city your whole life?"

"Don't people live in the city?"

"Manman, your father lived long enough in the city. If you roam the whole world, where will you find any place as good as our home? Trees may grow thousands of feet high, but the leaves return to the root when they fall. If you don't keep this place, you'll regret it in the end!"

"I won't regret it!"

"You rootless, baseless thing! You think you've got great ability? You can do without all your ancestors and without your father? Go ahead, then, and don't you ever come back. You just see if I can't get this house repaired without you!"

Father and son quarreled a while, their necks red and faces swollen, until finally Old Man Shou's dander was really up. He boxed Manman in the ear and then took up a spade to beat him. Manman grabbed him by the waist. The old man was really light, and in an instant Manman had carried him to the *kang*, letting his father know that his son was already grown and had considerable strength. Then he went out the door and left.

He had arranged with Old Wang to go to the city to see for himself the house under discussion.

The city was on the upper reaches of the Zhou River, 80 *li* from his hometown and 60 *li* from the place where he panned for gold, going upstream and north along Moon River. The land wasn't level here. A long, flat-topped hill bordered the river, and the city was built on this hill. The buildings spread over ravines and embankments and then across these to a gentle slope. The cityfolk all called it "Little Chongqing." Since Manman had never been to Chongqing, he didn't know what that city was like, but every time he came to Zhou City, he was fascinated by the people, the buildings, the streets, and the alleys! If he ever wanted to be something, he had to come here. Manman believed that he did have ability and that in his village there was no way he could give it free rein. The house under discussion was situated on River Street at the foot of the hill and running along the Zhou River. It was the busiest street in the city. The location was just right, and Manman was very satisfied.

He settled into a hotel so that he could arrange to hand over the remainder of the money and clean up the storefront in a month. At the same time he could select a few purchasing agents and prepare well ahead of time the materials for cleaning up and the goods he would manage in the future. He also invited his liaison man, Old Wang, out for a meal of thanks. The restaurant was on the second floor, where they sat next to a window, eating dog meat and drinking white spirits. Eyes bleary with drink, Manman spied two dogs on the street below, lying in front of the door of a shop. They were white, pure white, unmarred by a single dark hair.

"Aren't those Yunyun's dogs?"

"Yeah, they are!"

"What are Yunyun's dogs doing here?"

Old Wang gave a sly smile and whispered that Yunyun had asked him to find some contract work for her in the city. Only recently he had found her something, a position in a clothing sales department. She had asked him to keep it a secret, and especially not to be the first to tell Manman.

Manman smiled as he gnawed on a dog bone. He gnawed at it with relish, first picking it clean of meat with his teeth, then crunching the bone and sucking out the juice of the marrow.

That night, there was a full moon, and Manman invited Yunyun for a stroll through the city. There were lots of people at the night market. In front of every shop there were lights of five or six colors, flashing on and then blinking out, on a moment and then off again. As the two walked, the distance between them widened. There were so many people that from time to time they were swept apart. At some point, Yunyun took Manman's hand, feeling neither shy nor awkward. Each became the other's little dog. Later they descended the stone steps from River Street and walked to the sand beach.

"Do you know what this beach is called?"

"It's called Iron Chain Beach. I've heard that no matter how high the river floods, this beach won't flood. Is it true?"

"I've heard that it is. Could there really be an iron chain under the beach?"

According to legend, there used to be an iron column on this beach, with an iron chain fastened to it. Once someone had tried to pull it up. He had pulled out several hundred feet of chain before he didn't dare pull anymore. Manman and Yunyun searched for the chain along the beach, but without any luck, so they sat looking at the night scene of the mountain city.

"Manman, have you bought your house?"

"We've reached an agreement, but I'm a little short of cash. Tomorrow I'll go back to Moon River and pan another month's worth of gold. Do you want me to take anything along to your father?"

"Just tell him everything's fine!"

Her tone was aggressive, so Manman knew that when Yunyun left home, she must have had another argument with her father. Yunyun had her thoughts and so did he, so Manman didn't say anything more.

The moonlight was bright and clear. The water murmured. Suddenly, Manman felt as if the beach underneath him was no longer a beach, but rather a reed mat or a cloud, being washed along with the water. He told Yunyun of this impression, and she said that she had the same feeling.

"This is Iron Chain Beach!"

"And there's an iron chain attached to Iron Chain Beach. So the water can't wash it away!"

Afterwards they went up from the beach to River Street, and in a small alley that was all old buildings, they ate a street-peddler's "deep-fried dumplings." These were made from rice flour. First the flour was made into a batter, which was poured into a frying spoon the shape of a half moon. Then some bean curd filling was put in and another layer of batter poured on. After frying it in the oil, it became a little pouch, a half-circle. Giggling, the two ate until their mouths and hands were covered with oil.

They strolled till their bodies were exhausted, but their minds were still restless. After saying goodbye, Manman lay on his hotel bed, half asleep and dreamless but wanting to dream. He felt as if he had gone north again from the city, going upstream along Moon River 60 *li*. The Zhou River was so strong and bold, so rich and vast. Its spirit was entirely that of a man. But Moon River came winding and twisting from 60 *li* away, curving and bending its way to the city, where it converged with the Zhou River. Moon River was like a girl; a girl whose heart was firm but whose nature was yielding. She was like the moonlight, which might be summoned a thousand, or ten thousand, times. Had it emerged or was it still half-covered by clouds? Manman panned for gold in Moon River. The gold was in the sand, and Manman's luck was good, he sifted out everything. . . .

It was this same night that a guest came to the hunchback's house. The guest had come a long way; it was Manman's father. Old Man Shou had come looking for Manman, but Manman wasn't there. He upbraided the youths who panned for gold with Manman, saying that if things kept up this way, their village would become a wasteland. Some ten days ago Widow Wang, who lived at the edge of the village, had died, and there hadn't been anyone who could carry the coffin. Manman's companions didn't like listening to this. They snickered and laughed a while and then went out again to pan. The two fathers left behind talked over human affairs and the vicissitudes of life. They complained of their respective son and daughter, and after this they discussed the old wisdom about how one region nurtures one kind of person. Finding a soulmate, Old Man Shou's enthusiasm for talk was high. He went outside to check the geomancy of this village. He told the hunchback how to look at mountains in a mountainous region, how to watch the mist on a plain, how to distinguish directions where there was a river, or if there wasn't a river, how to watch the runoff from the rain, and if there weren't mountains or river or rain or mist, how you should plant a cane on a level piece of ground and let it fall over naturally. Where the handle fell was the head, or the abode of the yang; and where the end fell was the tail, or the abode of the yin. After this, the two sat silently, without speaking for a long while.

"Let them go. If they don't run off to other places, they won't know the good of the village."

"A few bad times and they'll come back!"

IV

In the ancient books it says that once, by a river, Confucius sighed with deep emotion and said, "What passes is like this!"

He was exactly right. The water of the Zhou River flowed day after day, vigorous and active, but the Zhou River you saw one instant ago was not the one you saw now. Where did the river's water come from? It was always flowing! The homes in the village grew more and more old-fashioned, and the people became fewer and fewer. A year passed. Old Man Shou hadn't seen a play. Nor had he been able to see public fireworks in the first month of the year. He heard some *suona* horns once. The sound was quite pleasant, but when he went out to see, it turned out that Lower Bend Village was out to bury someone. They were taking a wooden coffin up the mountain. Besides the grieving children and their mother, there were fewer people helping to see the dead one off along that dark road or to heap dirt on the grave mound than there were in that band of *suona* players. At first Old Man Shou enjoyed the mourning song, but later, like a fox grieving for a dead rabbit, he sighed deeply and cursed Manman since he missed him.

In the end, Old Man Shou did repair the house. He contracted the entire set of repairs out to a construction team. This was because at first he had bought bricks and tiles from the kiln in a neighboring village and asked the youth of that village to transport them. There weren't many young people, so he asked the children of those villagers who had at least some ties of family or friendship to come help, figuring it would be all right if he just made sure everybody got something good to eat and drink. It never occurred to him that the first thing they would ask about was payment! So the only thing Old Man Shou could do was to contract the work to a construction team. In the village he said, "The ways of the world these days, the ways of the world . . . !" Those who responded only laughed bitterly, shaking their heads as they crossed shoulders with him and passed by. The house was repaired, and to tell the truth, it really was pretty ostentatious and extravagant. The foundation had been raised two feet. No longer would shoes put under the *kang* grow mildew. The pill bugs no longer multiplied and scurried about. The four walls were all gray brick with white mortar in between. He had sealed the roof tiles with concrete, and had two small mirrors set in, one facing north and one south. There was a courtyard wall as well, with an arch over the gate. At last the old man felt at peace. He would return from the field, pick a tender white radish, pinch a couple of bright green scallions, and go into the kitchen to cook them. Then sitting beneath a railing of potted plants, he would pick up a bite of food with his chopsticks and direct it to his mouth or select some soft noodles to feed the little cat. Or else if he turned up a worm in the field, he would fix it onto a hook bent from a needle and go leisurely down to the Zhou River to fish. Of course, this was more likely to end in a poor catch than a good one, but the drunk's purpose is not the wine. In this quiet and beautiful landscape what absorbed him were the old men and women of the village in the fields tending their crops. Although undoubtedly oppressive, these days were not uninteresting. Often his thoughts would stretch far along the river to that city 80 *li* away, but as soon as he thought of Manman, his anger would rise, "Ingrate, what place would suit you!"

Living in the countryside best suited Old Man Shou's state of mind, and this rebuilt house enhanced the contentment of his old age. What a pity there were so few good houses in this village! August arrived, and it was the rainy season. No need for guesswork, the Zhou River would be flooding again. As soon as the rains began, each family started binding together their wooden rafts. As expected, on August 11, the loudspeaker on the wall behind the gate transmitted the county weather station forecast: the floodwaters of the Zhou River were due at 2 A.M. As soon as it grew dark, household goods were moved to the rafts, lots of wheat flatbread were grilled, and people climbed up good and early to sit on their roofs. Old Man Shou, not only took along something to eat and drink, but he also couldn't bear to abandon his flowers. The blossoms were full and brilliant, chrysanthemums, orchids, roses, and crab apple. So he set their dishes and pots up on the rooftop, too. Everything was arranged and in order. He held the little cat in his arms, and by the light of the methane lantern, looked toward the other roofs.

"What sort of fate is this, every year we climb up on our roofs."

"The toad hides every fifth of the fifth month."

"Old Shou, your house won't get washed away this year, will it?"

"Nope!"

"Next year during wheat season, after I've sold my grain, I'm going to do some repairs, too!"

"Yes, you should. After rebuilding, your life in it will be good and comfortable. Much better than living in a house in Zhou City. Where could you find such a big, roomy house as this in the city?"

A house a little farther away picked up the conversation in a tone of voice that was full of envy for Old Man Shou. "Manman hasn't sent any money back?"

"No."

"I hear his business is really thriving. . . ."

Old Man Shou could say nothing. The light from his methane lantern had dimmed some, so he lowered his head to fiddle with it and accidently put it out. In the darkness, Old Man Shou heard someone out there curse his own children. He was saying that before the Liberation there hadn't been many youths in the village, but that was because they had to run from conscription. And at that time, they would still sneak back in the middle of the night to see their old fathers and mothers. Nowadays, young people were all off to make money, and after making some, they didn't think about coming back again. The old folks missed them, but they didn't miss the old folks.

With great difficulty, Old Man Shou got his lantern lit again, shedding a warm circle of orangish-yellow light on the flowers and the little cat cowering among them on the ridge of the house.

"Gold is a good thing, but it messes up the head."

"Did you hear, the panners on Moon River want to pool resources and buy a dredge for collecting gold! A dredge to collect gold, that would be something! All modern, you just drive it along and while it digs up the dirt, it sifts out the gold. Each day you can collect a big handful!"

"Wouldn't that turn Moon River upside down?"

"When they come across a village, they just move it, and when they run into fields, they destroy them."

"Gods in heaven, a person doesn't have to eat or live somewhere?"

"Just rebuild the village and repair the fields! They'll only use the dredge three years. The first year will compensate for the homes and fields; the second year they'll get back their investment in the dredge; and the third year will be pure profit!"

"How much is this dredge?"

"Just to say it would scare us to death! But those youngsters dare do it. Old Shou, your Manman has put in a share. Didn't he tell you?"

"He told me, but I didn't feel like listening."

"They're going to turn all of Moon River upside down, all the way to the foot of the city. . . ."

Old Man Shou's first thought was that this would destroy the geomancy of Moon River's two banks. Then for some reason he thought of that hunchback landlord.

"There's no gold in the Zhou River!" Having said this, he felt somewhat reassured.

This thought might have gone farther, but at that moment the wind came up with a whirl that made a deep roar. The people on the roofs all turned their heads in the direction of the river. It was black as pitch out there, and immediately they heard the sound of the bell at the Lower Bend Village on the bank obliquely opposite. They were reinforcing the dikes there again.

"The flood's here!"

The wooden rafts started to squeak and very quickly rose up from the bases of the sky-piercing elms. This year was unusual; in the time it takes to smoke a pipe, the rafts had already reached the window ledges. Some of the people on the roofs grew alarmed. Then the water covered the tops of the shutters, and the reflection of the lanterns' light gleamed back at them from a spot one foot below the eaves.

"Aiya! We're in trouble. The water is going to reach the eaves!"

"Quick, wash your feet! Everybody wash your feet!"

Washing feet was a traditional method for holding back a flood. But not in their memory had these sixty- and seventy-year-olds washed their feet like this. They had heard their elders say that in the first year of the Republic, 1911, there had been a big flood on the Zhou River, and the water had reached the eaves. Only after the elders had washed their feet did the flood subside. It was also said that when the water had reached River Street in Zhou City three years ago, a lot of the people ran to the city's edge to wash their feet. Amidst the shouting, Old Man Shou could only move himself to the edge of the eaves, take off his shoes, and splash his feet in the water. As he was cautioning the others to be careful, a hoard of rats unexpectedly scurried onto the roof from under the eaves, and in the confusion one of his shoes went off with the water.

The water didn't fall any after the feet washing. On the contrary, it continued to rise, coming to the level of the eaves and then up to the first row of tiles. Old Man Shou retreated to the ridge of the house. The rats were all squeaking, as they piled up and squeezed onto the ridge as well. He looked at those small creatures. They were like birds emerging from the nest waiting to eat, with their front paws in the air and standing on their hind legs in a state of alarm. They frightened and sickened him, but at the same time he pitied them immensely. Old Man Shou didn't kill them. His mind was an utter blank.

On the roof of a faraway house, someone was crying. Immediately the person on the neighboring roof took a ladder which had floated up and held it between the two houses for the other to cross over. But before long, the roof of this neighboring house was also about to be submerged, so they crossed again to another. From one roof to another, and then another, in a little while the sound of crying, shouting, and cursing was everywhere. After that, everybody crossed over to the roof of Old Man Shou's house.

Old Man Shou's roof was the highest and its area the biggest. Fortunately there weren't many old people in the village. With not one left out, they all sat safely on the roof and listened to the sound of their homes collapsing in the distance. Under the light of the methane lanterns, all eyes watched as a few of the rafts tied to the sky-piercing elms overturned or came apart. No trace was left of their household goods. The water climbed up to the eighth level of tiles and then began to hold steady. The eldest were squeezed together on the ridgepole and those slightly younger clustered together along the edges. Countless tiles were smashed under foot, and the roof creaked as if stirring into motion.

"I'm afraid the weight is too much for the roof!" Having said this, Old Man Shou picked up a pot of roses and tossed it into the water. This was followed closely by ten pots, and several tens of pots. All were tossed into the water. Then they took off the tiles and removed the raised roof ends which were built of concrete and brick. Row by row, the tiles on all sides were tossed away and the people clung to the wooden rafters. There remained only one small tiled section at the top, where those with no strength sat. On those bare rafters, both the people and the rats had to stay. A struggle broke out between them, and soon many rats were tossing about and crying frantically in the water, and then they were gone.

"As long as they don't bite anyone, let them stay." Old Man Shou said sorrowfully, his feet tightly squeezed around a rafter as he searched his pockets for a match. In the panic all the methane lamps had gone out. He couldn't find any matches, though.

These old folk were pathetic parasites in this world, a world that was too small, pitch black, surrounded by water, and where no other house could be seen. The fields where radishes, cabbages, scallions, and purple garlic grew couldn't be seen either. Would the water continue to rise, or if it didn't, how long would it be before it receded? Would this roof collapse, or if it didn't, how long would they have to stay here? Suddenly someone called out, "The water demons!"

It was so, the water demons had come out again. Far off in the direction of the other bank a ball of light flew up. It was red inside and bordered with blue. It whirled upwards and then, following the river's surface, it moved down, just as it had the year before.

"The water demon has come down. She'll be in front of the village soon!"

"If she passes the village, that's the end of us! Gods in heaven, have we angered the spirits?"

In order not to take up any space, the little cat had stayed in Old Man Shou's arms. Now, its eyes were fixed on that ball of light, shining green like two bits of will-o'-the-wisp. Everyone's eyes were green; they were a crowd of living ghosts.

But just in front of the village, the ball of light went out.

Old Man Shou was the first to show excitement. Then everyone began to feel hope for survival. And once they had this hope, they began making extravagant plans for their lives. "This village of ours can't be destroyed!"

"How could it be? We lean back against the Luo Mountains, and in front are the Mang Peaks. Up the river is a cliff and on the cliff are figures carved by the gods. So how could the village just be destroyed?"

"Even without our sons and daughters, we still won't die!"

"And when I do die, I want to be buried in the land at this bend of the river. Couldn't have my corpse floating to the mouth of the Zhou River, could I?!"

For some reason, Old Man Shou suddenly thought about Zhou City. "With the river so high, would River Street be covered? Manman's shop was on River Street. . . ."

Immediately he stifled this thought with a long, long sigh.

Ah Cheng

Chimney Smoke

//// I

Lao Zhang had himself a daughter. That's good, Lao Zhang said, as long as she doesn't look like me when she grows up. She'd never get married if she did. So he named his daughter Beauty, Beauty Zhang.

Lao Zhang's college classmates said, There's nothing wrong with naming her Beauty, except it's a little common. Lao Zhang, with an education like yours, couldn't you have come up with a more elegant name?

What's wrong with being common? Lao Zhang asked them. It can't hurt.* In times like this what's most important? Durability.

Lao Zhang's classmates said, Durability? Then call her Iron Ore, or call her Aqueous Rock. Yes, why not Aqueous Rock? That's what people in our field study, durability. Lao Zhang had studied geology in college.

II

Lao Zhang doted on his daughter. Lao Zhang was a smoker. Lao Zhang's wife said, If you want a child, then stop smoking. I read somewhere that smoke has harmful effects on a baby's genes. Lao Zhang took the cigarette he was smoking out of his mouth, threw it on the floor, and ground it out with his foot. He quit smoking. After Beauty was born, Lao Zhang went out and bought a pack of cigarettes. Lao

---

This story was published in *Jiushi niandai* in July 1989. Translation by Howard Goldblatt.

*This is a political comment on the plight of the intellectuals in the Maoist era who were often accused of having elitist tendencies and who were subsequently made "to temper themselves" by laboring with the masses.

Zhang's wife said to him, Do you want Beauty to grow up with black lungs? Lao Zhang was crestfallen. Lao Zhang's wife said, Smoke if you want to, but not around Beauty.

Beauty was born in the fall. When spring came, Lao Zhang's wife carried Beauty outside for some sun. A wind came up, and Lao Zhang said, Can't you tell it's windy, why don't you go inside? Lao Zhang's wife said, If Beauty doesn't get some sun, she won't be able to absorb the calcium she needs. Lao Zhang said, Then take her inside and sit by the window to get some sun. Lao Zhang's wife said, Windows keep out the ultraviolet rays. Ultraviolet rays make it possible for people to absorb calcium. Sunbathing through a window is a waste of time. Then wait till the wind dies down, Lao Zhang said.

Lao Zhang was watching his wife nurse Beauty. Lao Zhang's wife had read quite a bit, too. When she noticed Lao Zhang staring at her, she said, Haven't you seen enough? It's not the first time you've seen them. Who's looking at you? Lao Zhang said. I'm afraid there isn't enough there for Beauty.* They both laughed. Beauty stopped and took a breath. She laughed, too.

III

Fall arrived, and Beauty had grown a bit. She could point to things. She pointed to Mama, she pointed to Papa, she tugged her ear, she tugged Mama's hair, she tugged Papa's nose.

One day Lao Zhang's wife was holding Beauty while Lao Zhang stood beside them screwing up his face and playing with Beauty, who shrieked with laughter and waved her hands in delight. Lao Zhang's wife held Beauty up next to Lao Zhang's face. Beauty stuck her hand into Lao Zhang's mouth.

It takes longer to tell than it did to happen. Lao Zhang raised his hand and sent mother and daughter reeling with a resounding slap. Lao Zhang was in the geology brigade and was always pounding rocks with a pick and hammer. His hands were powerful. The slap caught Lao Zhang's wife by surprise, and she fell backwards. Her maternal instincts took over, and as she hit the floor, she twisted herself enough to cushion Beauty in her bosom.

Beauty was screaming. Blood trickled from the back of her mother's head. She'd never cursed anyone before, but she was cursing now. Lao Zhang's wife was cursing Lao Zhang.

Lao Zhang was dumbstruck. He was shaking from head to toe, he

*Hunger is a familiar theme in Ah Cheng's stories. See the interviews of him by Shi Shuqing (1989) and by Wang Chan (1985*a,b*).

couldn't breathe, sweat streamed down his neck and down under his collar.

Lao Zhang was taken to the hospital. He didn't utter a word for two days and a night.

IV

The famine came in 1960. People starved all over the country, except for Yunnan.* I'd graduated that year and was on a field trip. I went into the mountains to do some prospecting.

I was lost in no time. I had a compass, but it did me no good. I'm hungry, I'm hungry! Panic, I began to panic, and the situation turned desperate. My mind was still clear at first, and I knew I was finished. Without enough to eat, I couldn't keep up my strength, and when the sugar in my kidneys was depleted, that would be it. I began to sweat, then even that stopped. I wouldn't allow myself to think about anything, since the loss of body heat was increased by brain activity. I lay down. The acid content of my stomach was so overpowering my teeth seemed to turn soft.

Then heat began to rise from my stomach, and the soles of my feet, my neck, the tips of my fingers, were getting overheated. Didn't Hans Christian Andersen write a tale about a little girl who sold kindling? That old Dane really knew what he was writing about. People begin to overheat when they're starving. When the heat dissipates, death takes over.

I didn't die. If I had, how could I have married you? How could I have had Beauty?

When I came to, I still couldn't see clearly for a while. Then off in the distance I saw chimney smoke. My only thought was: chimney smoke means cooking. Go, even if you have to crawl.

Let's not talk about how I got there, but I managed. It was a house. Save me, I pleaded in the doorway. Give me something to eat. No one heard me.

*Ah Cheng is describing the famine in the wake of the Great Leap Forward and the communization movement of 1958. During the "three bad years" (1959–61), it is estimated that 15 to 30 million people died of famine-related causes, mostly in the rural areas (Mu Fu 1984). The fact that the state could snatch grain from starving peasants' mouths demonstrated how powerful its ideology and organization were at the time. Although the Great Leap Forward is now recognized as an error, the failure of the intellectuals to criticize the movement and stop the tragedy remains an agonizing issue. The note on Yunnan is ironic. At the time, the only major road out of Yunnan led to Guiyang in Guizhou. Poor transportation facilities prevented grain from being transported out of the province (Ah Cheng, personal communication).

I know, my voice was too soft. I went inside.

A man was standing up against the stove. So skinny his teeth were protruding, a frightening glare in his eyes. Give me something to eat, I said. After a long pause he shook his head. Even if you're my grand-dad, my ancestor, you have to give me something to eat. He shook his head again. Are you saying you don't have anything? Then what's that you're cooking on the stove? A few sips of hot water will do. Tears streamed down his cheeks. Fuck your old grannie in the ear. . . .

I was past caring. I lifted the lid off the pot. Steam filled the air. I saw what was cooking in the pot, it was a child's hand.

Part IV Furrows

Introduction

////   This part summarizes the eventful journey of modern Chinese intellectuals and their use of literature to conduct a continuing political dialogue with themselves, the peasants, and the state. When Lu Xun (1881–1936) wrote the preface to *Letters Between Two Places* (*Liangdi shu*) in 1932, he had already been drawn into the political struggles of the Nationalists and the Communists. His condemnation of the Nationalist government was explicit. He wanted later generations to know what it meant to live under a repressive regime. Except for the letters he had exchanged with his wife, Xu Guangping, and was now publishing, he had burned all his correspondence for fear that it would incriminate his friends. Although he was critical of the Nationalist government, he remained independent from the Communist organization all his life, and his quarrels with such party writers as Zhou Yang and Xu Maoyong confirmed his fears about their surrender to political expediency. Little did he foresee that the movement his work had inspired young intellectuals to join would deny the very human warmth he himself so cherished.

The "Superfluous Words" ("Duoyu de hua") of Qu Qiubai (1899–1935), written shortly before his execution, captured a moment of truthful self-scrutiny of the kind Lu Xun had demanded of himself and of others. After examining the motives behind his political choices, Qu admitted the futility of his participation in the revolution, a conclusion as brutal as the external power that was to end his life.

What Qu Qiubai and Lu Xun feared, Wang Shiwei (1907–47) experienced: his stubborn devotion to a political ideal was betrayed by his comrades. Wang was a friend to Wang Fanxi and Chen Qingchen, both of whom had Trotskyist beliefs. He himself was seen as "a man of strong emotions, quick to lose his temper and fired with a strong sense of justice."[1] Wang dedicated "Wild Lilies" ("Ye baihehua") to a comrade he had loved who was delivered by her own uncle to the hands of the Nationalists and then executed. The essay criticized the changing nature of a movement, to which many idealistic young people had given their lives. The agitation it aroused and its violent consequences marked a turning point in the Communist movement; the position of the writers became increasingly superfluous. Moral authority was no longer a subject for the critical intellectual to define or to represent.

By the time the Communists established a national government in 1949, they had left this generation of intellectuals behind with a hollowed-out sense of mission and with voices that were the lingering echoes of a romanticized past. A new group of Marxist writers ascended the political stage with their own sense of mission. Armed with faith in the party and optimistic about the new nation, they challenged what they believed to be its excesses. Undaunted by the persecution of Hu Feng, Huang Qiuyun put up a valiant fight against party dogma. Born into a well-to-do family in Hong Kong in 1918, Huang finished middle school there. He gave up a scholarship to study in England and in 1936 enrolled in Qinghua University in Beijing instead. He joined the resistance movement and then the Communist party. In 1954 he took up editorial work for a literary journal. "Do Not Close Your Eyes to the Sufferings of the People" ("Buyao zai renmin de jiku mianqian bishang yanjing") was one of the many essays he wrote in 1956 and 1957. He spoke out against "the rigidity of party dogma," the "superficial optimism and the lack of compassion," and "the cowardice behind a concealed reality." For his forthrightness, he "slid to the very edge of being labeled a rightist."[2] He was unable to imagine that only a decade later even total surrender would not be enough. Hao Ran, the next writer translated here, toed the Maoist line more closely than any other peasant writer of the 1960's and 1970's, yet his work was criticized for "not having shown enough faith in the party." For this generation of party writers, who took it upon themselves to shoulder the burdens of building socialism, it must have been difficult to find themselves so dispensable.

For the survivors, there was renewed soul-searching in the 1980's. Ru Zhijuan was born in 1925. Her mother died when she was three, and her father abandoned the family. She spent her childhood in orphanages and in the homes of relatives. With the help of an elder brother, she finally graduated from a middle school in Zhejiang in 1943. They joined the Communists' New Fourth Army in the same year, and she became a party member in 1947. In 1955, she was transferred from the army to the Shanghai branch of the Chinese Writers

Association and became an editor for *Wenyi yuebao* (Literature and art monthly). At present she is an editor of *Shanghai wenyi* (Shanghai literature and art). In retrospect, Ru Zhijuan appreciates the distance she inadvertently created between herself and the political campaigns in 1957; this allowed her to display a glimpse of human compassion for her characters. "Lilies on a Comforter" ("Baihehua") was written in 1958. She had difficulty publishing the piece and was not spared by the politically minded critics.[3]

Li Zhun was born in 1928 and spent his childhood in the Hunanese countryside. He was not able to pursue formal schooling beyond the first year of a junior middle school, but he continued to study on his own. He started publishing in the early 1950's and became a professional writer in Hunan. His works include screenplays, operas, novels, and two collections of essays. His depiction of the struggle between the sexes in "The Story of Li Shuangshuang" ("Li Shuangshuang xiaozhuan") became a popular text. Like many others, he was not spared in the political turmoil. In the four years he spent in rural areas near the Yellow River, he came to appreciate the vitality of the cultural tradition that sustained Chinese peasants as well as intellectuals like himself. *The Yellow River Rushes On* (*Huang he dongliu qu*) symbolizes a common bond between writer and peasants based on an unyielding spirit. Although both were immobilized by the intrusions of state power, they respected one another. The experience made him see what it means to be a victim and what can be done to resist victimization.[4]

However, appealing to the virtues of a cultural tradition to confront contemporary politics does not free the writer from the dominant order. In the 1980's, the Beijing government actively promoted patriotism and cultural pride among its citizens. The task Ah Cheng has set himself is to critically examine cultural roles and expectations that have become internalized and are taken for granted and then to see how the party-state has penetrated and appropriated them for its own ends. In the piece presented here, he concludes that the tragedy of his father's generation lies precisely in the sense of mission they assumed. This compelled them to become accomplices in their own political victimization. Cultural critique starts from such an understanding.

Lu Xun

////

Preface to 'Letters Between Two Places'

This is how this book came to be compiled.

On August 5, 1932, I received a letter signed by Li Jiye, Tai Jingnong, and Wei Congwu, reporting that Shuyuan had passed away at the Tong Ren Hospital in Beijing on August 1 at 5:30 in the morning.* They were planning to collect his writings for a memorial volume and asked if I had any of his letters in my possession. On reading this, I felt a sudden constriction of the heart. First, because I still harbored a hope that he would recover, though I knew full well that this was unlikely; second, because I feared that, in one of those moments when I had allowed myself to forget how unlikely his recovery was, I may have destroyed all his letters—letters that he had composed painfully while propped on his pillow.

It is my habit to destroy ordinary letters as soon as I have answered them, but if they contain something controversial or an interesting

---

This preface was written in December 1932 and published in *Liangdi shu* in April 1933. Translation by Marston Anderson. *Letters Between Two Places* is a collection of Lu Xun's correspondence with his wife, Xu Guangping. It is divided into three sections: Beijing, March to July 1925; Xiamen–Guangzhou, September 1926 to January 1927; and Beiping–Shanghai, May to June 1929. The notes to the translation are largely based on those of the editor of Lu Xun's complete works (*Lu Xun quanji: Liangdi shu*).

*Li Jiye (b. 1904), Tai Jingnong (b. 1903), Wei Congwu (1905–78), and Shuyuan (pen name of Wei Suyuan, 1902–32) were all natives of Huoqiu County in Anhui Province and were, with Lu Xun, all founding members of the Nameless Society (Weiming she). The Nameless Society was established in 1925 in Beijing to encourage the introduction of works by foreign, especially Soviet, authors. Wei Suyuan, who had studied in the USSR, assumed primary responsibility for the group, and it was he who took over editorship of the society's semimonthly journal *Mangyuan* (Wilderness) when Lu Xun departed for Xiamen in 1926. The society disbanded in 1930. Among the works that Wei Suyuan translated were Gogol's "The Overcoat" and, with Li Jiye, Trotsky's *Literature and Revolution*.

anecdote, I sometimes keep them. In the past three years, however, I have undertaken two large letter-burnings.

Five years ago, when I was in Guangzhou at the time of the Nationalist purge,* I often heard that when A was arrested with one of B's letters on him, B would also be apprehended; if one of C's letters was then found in B's possession, C too would be rounded up, and all three of them would vanish without a trace. I was familiar with the "melon-vine seizures" of antiquity in which so many were involved,† but had always thought such episodes were a thing of the past. Reality, however, taught me otherwise: I began to understand that living in the modern world is no easier than in the ancient. But still I failed to take this lesson to heart and was careless. Then in 1930 I joined the Freedom Alliance,‡ and the Nationalist authorities in Zhejiang requested that the central government put out a warrant for the arrest of "decadent literati like Lu Xun." Before leaving home to escape this trouble, I had a sudden inspiration to destroy all my friends' letters. I was not trying to cover the traces of some conspiracy. It just seemed senseless to implicate others for no other reason than that they corresponded with me. And it is well known how terrifying the least contact with a Chinese yamen can be. After having survived this crisis, letters began to pile up at my new residence, and I grew careless again. But then in January 1931, something with my name on it was found in Rou Shi's pocket when he was arrested.§ Because of this, the authorities began pursuing me, and of course I had to go into hiding again. This time I had an even stronger incentive to burn all my letters before leaving home.

Because of these two incidents, I was not hopeful when I received that letter from Beijing. Fearing that I would find nothing, I nevertheless rummaged through my chests and boxes. Indeed, there was nothing, not a single letter from a friend. I did, however, come across

---

*In 1927, Chiang Kai-shek persecuted his Communist allies in a nationwide "White terror."

† The expression "melon-vine seizures" was first used in reference to the case of Jing Qing, a Ming dynasty minister who is said to have plotted the assassination of the third emperor of the Ming dynasty, Cheng Zu (r. 1403–25). When his plan was exposed, Jing Qing, his clan, and thousands of men from his district were all executed.

‡ The Freedom Alliance was established in February 1930 in Shanghai. Its stated purpose was to resist the Nationalist government's efforts to restrict freedom of the press, speech, and assembly in China.

§ Rou Shi (pen name of Zhao Pingfu; 1901–31) was a writer of fiction and a student of Lu Xun's. His best-known works include the novel *February* (*Eryue*) and the short story "A Slave-Mother" ("Wei nuli de muqin"). On February 17, 1931, he and 22 other Communist party members were executed by the Nationalist government. Rou Shi and four other authors who died with him have been canonized in Communist Chinese literary history as the Five Martyrs.

my and my wife's personal letters. These had escaped burning, not because I considered my own things so precious, but because I was pressed for time and thought they concerned no one but ourselves. I had stowed the letters in a chest, and since then they had lain in the direct line of fire for twenty or thirty days without suffering any harm.* Although a few are missing, that is probably because I was careless and misplaced them, and it should not be blamed on the hazards of war or politics.

If a person suffers no unexpected misfortunes in life, he will receive no special attention. But if he has spent time in prison or fought at the front, then even if he is the most ordinary of men, people will view him in a different light. We felt like that toward these letters. Where once we had let them sit crushed at the bottom of a chest, now that they had survived the threat of legal persecution and war unscathed, they somehow seemed special to us, even a bit endearing. During the summer evenings, when the mosquitoes kept us from writing, we used the time to organize the letters, dividing them into three sections according to where they had been written, and dubbing the whole *Letters Between Two Places*.

Which is to say, this book was of temporary interest to us, but it is unlikely it will interest others. In it you will find no life-or-death passions or elegant descriptions of the flowers and the moon. As for the language, we have not studied "The Essentials of Letter Writing" or "Epistolary Models," but have simply trusted our pens, flouting the rules of composition. Much of what we have written probably should be entered in the "Language Clinic."† As for content, we mostly talk about the unrest at school, our personal affairs, food, and the weather. Worst of all, at the time these letters were written, we lived in total blindness, hardly able to distinguish dark from light; though this matters little where we discuss private matters, it means that in conjecturing about important public affairs we couldn't escape foolishness. Looking back on them now, our confident prophecies seem like so many idle dreams. If I am forced to identify what is distinctive about this volume, then I'm afraid I can point to nothing but its ordinariness. Others would probably not bother to keep such ordinary letters. But we did, and I suppose that is a point of distinction.

What really surprises me is that any publisher is willing to print

---

*Here Lu Xun is referring to the January Twenty-eighth Incident of 1932, when Japanese military forces invaded Shanghai. Part of the fighting occurred near Lu Xun's residence.

† "Language Clinic" ("Wenzhang bingyuan") was a regular column in the Shanghai magazine *Zhong xuesheng* (Middle school student).

this book. If they want to, let them. I don't mind. But since it means bringing me face to face with readers again, I had best add a few comments here to prevent misunderstandings. First, I am a member of the League of Left-wing Writers,* and I see from recent notices about literary works that once an author turns to the left, then his old writings are elevated and even his childhood cries join the ranks of revolutionary literature. But our volume is different; it is free of revolutionary spirit. Second, I often hear people say that letters are the most sincere kind of writing, that they expose the true face of the author, but mine are not like that. No matter to whom I write, I open my letters with a few perfunctory, hypocritical comments. Moreover, in the letters collected here I often intentionally introduced a note of vagueness at critical junctures, knowing as I do that we live in a country where "local authorities" of all kinds, including post office employees and school principals, all feel free to inspect one's mail. But of course there is much that is expressed directly as well.

One more thing, I have changed several names in the letters, for a variety of reasons, some good, some bad. By which I mean, sometimes out of the fear that it will inconvenience others to have their names appear in my letters, and sometimes for selfish reasons, to avoid troubles of the "pending trial" variety.†

Thinking back over the past six or seven years, I realize that we have been beset by many difficulties. In our continuing struggles, we encountered some who helped us, some who threw stones, and some who mocked or defamed us, but we gritted our teeth and somehow survived. During those years, the stone throwers gradually sank into even deeper darkness, and two of our dearest friends, Shuyuan and Rou Shi, parted this world. This book is a memento for ourselves, an expression of gratitude to our beloved friends, and a gift to our children that they may eventually know the true story of our experiences. That is about all there is to it.

*Lu Xun was one of fifty founding members of the League of Left-wing Writers, established in Shanghai in 1930 under the covert direction of the Communist party. The league was the primary voice of radical Chinese literary opinion until its dismantling in 1936.

† On July 24, 1927, the historian Gu Jiegang sent a letter from Hangzhou to Lu Xun, who was about to leave Shanghai for Guangzhou. He accused Lu Xun of caricaturing him in his writings and said that he would go to Guangdong to "seek a legal settlement." He warned Lu Xun not to leave Guangdong and to wait for the trial to proceed.

Qu Qiubai   Superfluous Words

//// Farewell

The curtain is drawn on this farce!

My home village has a saying: "Make the old crow build a nest in a tree." This nest could never be built. It may be ludicrous that an ordinary, even silly "man of letters" assumed the position of "party leader" for a few years. This nonetheless was the case. What was accomplished during that period should not be credited to him but to the efforts of several leading comrades. His lofty words served only as ornaments and in fact had long planted the seeds of future disaster. It is time to settle this score once and for all.

Go settle the scores. You are gallantly forging ahead in the struggle. I can envy you and congratulate you, but I can no longer be with you. I don't feel that it is a pity, nor am I sorry. Although my entire life has been wasted on politics that I don't care much about, the bygones have become bygones. To look back with regret would only complicate my vexations at this moment. He who needs to be cleansed from the ranks should be cleansed, the earlier the better. There is even less need to be sentimental.

I have withdrawn from the ranks of the proletarian revolutionary vanguard, have given up political struggle, and have laid down my arms. If you—comrades in the Communist party—had discovered

This essay was the final part of a seven-part essay believed to have been written by Qu around May 17–22, 1935, shortly before his execution. Parts of it first appeared in *Shehui xinwen* (12, nos. 6–8) in 1935. The entire essay was published in *Yi jing* (nos. 25–27) in 1937. Translation by Ng Mau-sang; the editor has made substantial changes in the translation.

earlier what I am writing here, you would have expelled me from the party long ago. A weakling such as myself, perfunctory, passive, and lazy, and more seriously one who admits mistakes with empty phrases but is utterly unable to change his class consciousness and emotions. Moreover, it is fortuitous that the person is not an ordinary party member, but instead has been a member of the Politburo. How can this type of person not be expelled?

Now that I am a captive of the Nationalists, it seems superfluous even to mention these things. But what difference does it make? Free or not, I am not able to continue the struggle. Although my life will finally be terminated, I have long ended my political life. Strictly speaking, you have had the right to treat me as a type of traitor irrespective of my captivity. If I suddenly die without having the chance to let you know my most frank and truthful thoughts, you may still regard me as a Communist martyr. I remember that back in 1932 when I was rumored dead, some memorial services were held. My "accomplishments" were also cited for certain. When I heard the news in the soviet area, I shivered inside. It was too much for a traitor to pass as a martyr. Therefore, although I am now jailed, and although I could easily pretend to die impassionedly as a martyr would, I dare not do so. One cannot and should not deceive history. It is a small matter to me if I somehow attain an undeserved honor posthumously, but it is utterly wrong to mislead the revolutionary comrades on the matter of martyrdom. My life will be terminated all the same, but I certainly will not die a martyr's death.

Farewell forever, my dear comrades—this is my last time to address you as "comrades." I am no longer qualified to use the term. I want you to know that in fact I left your ranks a long time ago.

Ai! Historical misunderstandings have made this "man of letters" muddle along on the political stage for years. I am deserting the ranks not simply because I wanted to end my revolution and to end this farce, nor simply because of my illness and lethargy, but rather because I have failed to come to grips with my own gentleman's consciousness. I cannot become a proletarian fighter after all.

Farewell, my dear friends. I have grown utterly weary during the course of the past seven or eight years. So acute was this fatigue, such as at the beginning of 1930 or between August and September of 1934, that at times it was neither describable nor bearable. At the time I did not care if the universe was to be destroyed or not, or whether it was revolution or counterrevolution. I wanted only one thing—rest, rest, rest! Finally, I now have the chance to "rest forever."

I leave you these few pages—my last and truthful words. Farewell! Judgment rests in your hands, not mine. All I want is rest.

I have few friends in life, and only a handful of close ones. I have never been totally frank to you with the exception of my Zhihua.* Even to Zhihua I only dropped some hints. All along I have worn a mask. I said earlier that to tear the mask off someone's face is an exhilarating experience. This is true not only in exposing others, but also when one is exposed. It is all the more so when one lays oneself bare. Now that I have discarded the last layer of the mask, you should congratulate me. I am going to rest, forever; you should congratulate me.

I have often said that I felt the fatigue of not having slept for ten or twenty years. Now I shall have a "great" and lovely sleep forever.

Perhaps a lesson can be learned from my life: in order to temper oneself, one needs tremendous willpower, so that one can overcome all the "alienating" attitudes down to the minute "alienating" sentiments. Only in so doing can one leap from an "alienating" class and anchor one's steps in the proletarian ranks. Otherwise, it is nothing but "making an old crow build a nest in a tree." It will inevitably end up a farce.

Now, the curtain is drawn on my farce.

Who am I reluctant to leave behind? My beloved. I have stayed close to her for the past ten years. Yes, I could not have survived without a support. This was true of my political life—I was never the vanguard of struggle and have always sought an anchor. In my personal life, I also lacked the courage to struggle for survival. I do not know how to organize even the petty daily tasks in my life. All the time I was dependent on my beloved. How can I bear the thought of leaving her? I feel sorrowful because I have done her many an injustice. My cowardice has prevented me from being utterly truthful with her. How I wish that she will forever detest me, forget me, so that I will have some peace of mind.

Who else would I miss? The children thriving in this beautiful world, "my" daughter† and all the happy children. My best wishes for them.

To me, this world is still very beautiful. The new, the struggling, and the courageous are advancing. What nice flowers and fruits! What a splendid landscape! What magnificent factories and chimneys! Even the moon appears brighter than ever.

But farewell, beautiful world.

*Qu was married to Yang Zhihua in 1924.
† Yang Zhihua's daughter from a previous marriage.

A life's energy has been exhausted, leaving only a body.

If I still have a say concerning the disposal of my body, I would like to give it to the dissecting laboratory of a medical school. I know that they have a dearth of this kind of specimen for research. I have suffered from tuberculosis for many years [from 1919 onward]. I had X-rays taken as my illness took its turns. Many scars on my lungs are clearly visible on the X-ray I took in 1931, but the doctor at the time did not come to any clear diagnosis. If my lung is X-rayed again before my body is dissected in order to study it further, I am sure some discoveries will be made concerning the diagnosis of tuberculosis. But I know absolutely nothing about medicine, so what I have said may be utter nonsense.

In any case, this farce finally approaches its end. The stage has emptied, and any reminiscing is futile. It is truly a blessing that I will soon have my "great" rest. As for the body, it will not be up to me to decide.

Farewell, everything in this world. At last . . .

Forty Years: The Life of Klim Samghim by Gorky, *Rudin* by Turgenev, *Anna Karenina* by Tolstoy, "The True Story of Ah Q" by Lu Xun, "Vacillation" by Mao Dun, *The Dream of the Red Chamber* by Cao Xueqin,* all are worth reading again.

Chinese bean curd is delicious, the best in the world.

Farewell.

*A classic Chinese novel. The main character, a privileged young man in a literati family, eventually abandons his "earthly" life and leaves home to become a monk.

Wang Shiwei

Wild Lilies

//// Preface

While walking alone along the riverbank, I saw a comrade wearing a pair of old-style cotton-padded shoes. They started me thinking again about someone who used to wear shoes just like them—Comrade Li Fen, my first and dearest friend. As always happens when I think of her, my heart started pounding, and I felt the blood course more forcefully through my veins.

Li Fen entered the party in 1926, while she was a student in the preparatory course at Beijing University. In the spring of 1928 she sacrificed her life in her hometown, Baoqing in Hunan Province.* She wasn't arrested; her own uncle bound her and turned her over to the local garrison—an act that well illustrates how barbarous the representatives of old China could be. Before going to her death, she put on three sets of underwear—all that she owned—and sewed them together tightly at top and bottom. She did this because the troops in Baoqing often let hooligans defile the corpses of women party members they shot—a fact that further illustrates how dark life in the old society was, how brutal, ugly, and squalid! Since I heard of her death, my heart has burned with a fierce mixture of love and hatred. I am haunted by the image of that pure and saintly girl, dressed in three tightly sewn sets of underwear, calmly going to the martyr's death to which her own uncle had consigned her. The thought always sets my heart pounding and the blood racing through my veins. (It may seem

This essay was published in two parts in *Wenyi*, a literary supplement to *Jiefang ribao* (Yan'an) on March 13 (no. 102) and March 23 (no. 106), 1942. Translation by Marston Anderson.

*This refers to the purge of Communist sympathizers by the Nationalists.

inappropriate to tell a story like this in the tranquil atmosphere of Yan'an, where we enjoy "the caroling of Yutang Chun and the pirouettes of the golden-lotus dancers,"* but for that matter the atmosphere in Yan'an is hardly suited to the realities of contemporary events— just close your eyes for a moment and think of the sea of carnage into which, each minute, another of our dear comrades sinks.)†

For the sake of the nation, we refrain from reckoning up old scores of class hatred. We are truly public-spirited and selfless. As we struggle toward the light, we even do our best to drag the representatives of old China along with us. But in the process some of the filth and corruption of the old society rubs off on us, spreading its germs and diseases.

Scores of times I have drawn strength from that image of Comrade Li Fen, strength to live and strength to struggle. This time, reminded of her in this unexpected way, I was inspired to write several short essays, which I have given the collective title "Wild Lilies." I had two things in mind when I chose this title. First, as the most beautiful of the flowers one finds in the mountains around Yan'an, the wild lily seems an appropriate offering to that pure and saintly image I carry in my mind. Second, while it has the same layered bulb as other varieties of lilies, the wild lily lacks their sweet flavor. I have heard—though I can't say for sure if it's true—that the bitter lily carries the greater medicinal value.

February 26, 1942

I. What Is Lacking in Our Lives?

Young people in Yan'an seem to have lost their enthusiasm and even seem to be harboring feelings of uneasiness. Why is this? What is lacking in our lives? Some would answer that our food is poor and that we lack vitamins. Others would point to the ratio of men to women in Yan'an ("eighteen to one") and say that young people lack lovers. Still

---

*Yutang Chun is the protagonist of a well-known Beijing opera about a singing girl whose love for a young scholar survives a series of ordeals, including her forced marriage to a wealthy merchant. The expression "golden lotus" refers to the bound feet of dancing girls. Some readers have interpreted this passage as an oblique reference to Mao Zedong's third wife, Jiang Qing, who joined Mao in Yan'an in 1939. The individual responsible for organizing cultural events in Yan'an, however, was not Jiang Qing but the playwright and musician Jin Ziguang.

† After the Long March, the Communists set up a base area in Shaanxi centering around Yan'an in 1935. From then on, they fought off the extermination campaigns conducted by generals loyal to the Nationalist government, mobilized resistance against the Japanese, built up the party machinery, and experimented on socialist programs in the areas under their control.

others would argue that life in Yan'an is dull and monotonous and that we lack entertainment.

There is something to all of these responses. It is only natural that we desire better food, companions of the opposite sex, and some amusement in life. But surely no one would deny that the young people in Yan'an came here in a spirit of sacrifice to participate in the revolution; they did not come in pursuit of good food and a pleasant life. I therefore find it hard to believe that their lack of enthusiasm and feelings of uneasiness arise from dissatisfaction over these things.

What then is it that we lack? Perhaps the following conversation will provide some insight. During the New Year's holiday, I was returning one evening at twilight from a friend's house when I saw two young female comrades conversing in animated whispers some distance ahead of me. I quietly drew closer to listen to them.

". . . He's always accusing other people of petty-bourgeois egalitarianism, but the truth is he's a bit of an elitist. He's so preoccupied with his special privileges that he hardly seems to care if the comrades beneath him are well or ill, diseased or dying!"

"Our Comrade X is no different. They're all birds of a feather."

"It sounds fine, all this talk about class love—but dammit! they don't even show ordinary human sympathy! Most of the time they smile and try to look friendly, but it's all on the surface. If you show the slightest sign of disagreeing with them, they glare at you, put on their best senior-officer manner, and start lecturing you."

"The small-fry take their cues from the higher-ups. Our section leader grovels before his superiors, but with us he can't hide his arrogance. He doesn't even bother to look in on sick comrades, but you should have seen the fuss he made when an eagle stole one of his chickens! Now every time he sees an eagle he starts yelling and throwing stones at it—the self-centered bastard!"

They fell silent for a moment. I admired this second comrade's sharp tongue, but what she said made me feel discouraged and sad.

"It's painful to think of how many comrades have fallen ill. Actually, when you're sick, the last thing you want is a visit from someone like that. It just makes you feel worse. You can tell from their voice, their expression, from their whole attitude that they don't give a damn about you."

"I've been transferred several times in the past two years. Of the officers, section leaders, and chairmen I've worked for, far too few showed a genuine concern for the cadres."

"Yes, exactly! They love no one, and no one loves them. If they ever take up mass work, the results will be disastrous. . . ."

The two comrades continued their fervent, whispered conversation, but our paths diverged at this point and that's all I heard. No doubt what they said was one-sided and exaggerated, and perhaps the "image" that emerged from their conversation is not generally applicable, but you can't deny its value as a mirror.

What is lacking in our lives? Just look in the mirror.

II. Running into "Running into Difficulties"

On the "Young People's Page" of Issue 12 of this newspaper, I found a fascinating article entitled "Running into Difficulties." Two of the paragraphs read as follows:

A middle-aged friend of mine recently arrived from deep in the Nationalist rear. He was disturbed to find that young people in Yan'an are intolerant of the slightest setback, dissatisfied with everything, and constantly griping. "What are they fussing about!" he says. "Think of all the difficulties and abuse we run up against on the outside. . . ."

He is correct. Although life in Yan'an has its exasperating aspects and does not provide all the conveniences one might wish for, these deficiencies are nothing, mere trifles, in the eyes of those who have repeatedly encountered difficulties and abuse on the outside. But inexperienced young people, especially those of student origin, see things differently. Their families and schools have coddled them into adulthood, explaining life to them with love and warmth, and filling them with a yearning for purity and beauty. They are strangers to the ugly and harsh realities of life. Small wonder that when they encounter a little adversity they feel uneasy for the first time in their lives and start bellowing.

I don't know the identity of the author's "middle-aged friend," but I think his philosophy of resignation is not only not "correct," but actually harmful. Young people should be treasured for their purity, sensitivity, ardor, and bravery, as well as for the vitality and energy that they possess in such abundance. Young people are the first to recognize the darkness that others fail to see, the first to detect the filth that others ignore, and the first to find the courage to speak out when others are unwilling or paralyzed by fear. Because of this they seem more opinionated than their elders, but that does not mean that their opinions are mere "griping." Nor is their speech as balanced and measured as it could be, but that does not make it mere "bellowing." We should study their "griping," "bellowing," and "uneasiness" in order to discover the underlying causes of these phenomena and then proceed rationally to eradicate those causes. (Note, I said rationally! Not all young people are engaged in "ignorant rabble-rousing.") To praise Yan'an as better than the outside world, to instruct young people not to complain, to dismiss the dark aspects of Yan'an as "slight setbacks" and "trifles"—none of this will solve our problems. Yes, Yan'an is preferable to the outside world, but it can and must be made better still.

Of course, young people are often hotheaded and impetuous—a point that the author of "Running into Difficulties" takes as his theme. But if all young people were "mature before their time," what a desolate world this would be! Actually young people in Yan'an are already sufficiently mature: the two female comrades I mentioned above knew enough to confine their "griping" to whispers in the twilight. We shouldn't disparage their griping, but should use it as a mirror in which to view our own reflection!

The allegation that young people "of student origin" in Yan'an are "coddled into adulthood" by parents who "explain life to them with love and warmth" smacks of subjectivism to me. Although most of our young people are indeed "of student origin," "immature," and "inexperienced in life," the great majority of them fought a series of bitter battles before arriving in Yan'an. Their previous lives were not characterized only by "love and warmth"; one might better say that their experience of hatred and cold led them to seek love and warmth in the revolutionary camp. According to the author of "Running into Difficulties," young people in Yan'an are no better than pampered children who start whining when denied candy. As for "the ugly and harsh realities of life," our young people are hardly ignorant of them. In fact, discovering those realities in the outside world is what drove young people to seek beauty and warmth in Yan'an. Only upon discovering ugliness and harshness in Yan'an itself did they become "intolerant" and start "griping"—out of the hope that bringing this ugliness and harshness to everyone's attention would help reduce it to a minimum.

In the winter of 1938 the party conducted a large-scale review of our work, calling for "lively discussion" among comrades and for the "free expression of all opinions, correct or incorrect." I hope that we can initiate another such review to air the complaints of the young people in our lower ranks. I am certain it would have a beneficial effect on our work.

III. "Inevitability," "The Sky Won't Fall," and "Trifles"

"Our camp exists amidst the darkness of the old society, so it is inevitable that there is darkness within it too." Yes, that's "Marxism," but a one-sided kind of Marxism. The other, more important side has been forgotten by the "masters of subjectivist factionalism." What they have forgotten is this: Once we have recognized the inevitability of darkness, we must then summon a fighting Bolshevik zeal to inhibit its emergence and to limit its growth. We must exert to the utmost the power of consciousness to counter existing realities. Under present conditions, to eliminate darkness completely from our camp is impossible. But to reduce it as much as we can is not only feasible, it is necessary. But the "masters" rarely broach this matter, let alone emphasize it. They simply point out the "inevitable" and retire to their beds. But in fact, they're guilty of more than just sleeping, for they use "inevitability" as a cover for self-indulgence. In their dreams they console themselves: "Comrade, you too were born in the old society, so if there's a tiny spot of darkness on your own soul, don't be ashamed. It's inevitable." In this way, we do more than indirectly abet the darkness. We actively create it!

After the "theory" of inevitability comes a "national forms" theory called "The sky won't fall."* Yes, it's unlikely that the sky will fall. But does that mean our work and our mission can't be harmed? The masters have given little—if any—attention to this matter. But if they allow "inevitability" to take its inevitable course, then the sky—the sky of our revolutionary mission—will inevitably fall. Let us not grow complacent.

Related to this is the "trifles" theory. If you criticize someone, he admonishes you for bothering about trifles. Some masters even say, "That damn X! It's bad enough when female comrades bother about trifles, but now male comrades have taken it up too!" True, there is little likelihood that a really big problem like treason against the party or the nation will arise in Yan'an, but the small acts of individuals all make a difference, in some cases furthering the light, in other cases furthering the darkness. And "trifling" events in the lives of "great" men have a special power to stir people's hearts, kindling either feelings of devotion or feelings of dejection.

IV. Egalitarianism and the System of Ranks

I have heard that a comrade once pasted a handbill with his title on the wall of his department, whereupon his senior officer chastised him so severely that he was driven half-mad. I hope this story is fictional, but since there have been genuine cases of madness among the

*Wang is probably alluding here to the controversy about "national forms" of literature, in which party pragmatists, with whom Wang disagreed, insisted on sinicized artistic expressions.

"little devils,"* I suppose some adults may have been stricken as well. Although I feel my own nervous system may not be as strong as that of some others, I am confident that I possess sufficient life force to prevent me from going over the brink into madness, come what may. I will therefore take up where that half-mad comrade left off and address the problems of egalitarianism and the ranking system.

Communism isn't egalitarianism (nor are we at present engaged in a Communist revolution). I hardly need to write an eight-legged essay to demonstrate this fact, since no mess cook could ever imagine himself living the life of a senior officer. (I refrain from writing "kitchen operative"—although it is the form of address that both reason and conscience dictate I use when speaking with cooks in person—because of the satirical coloring it has taken on. I always say the term with as much warmth in my voice as possible—a pitiful example of warmth!) The problem of the ranking system, however, is somewhat more complicated.

Some say that we in Yan'an have no system of ranks, a view that flies in the face of reality. Others acknowledge the system's existence but justify it as rational, an opinion that merits further examination. Their arguments run roughly as follows: (1) according to the principle of "from each according to his abilities, to each according to his worth," those who bear greater responsibility should receive greater benefits; (2) the government of the tripartite rule† will soon institute a salary system, which of course will involve pay differentials; and (3) even the Soviet Union has a system of ranks.

In my opinion each of these arguments is open to debate. (1) We are still in the midst of a revolution, with its attendant turmoil and hardships. We struggle on, our bodies racked with exhaustion, and many of our comrades have sacrificed their precious health for the cause. In these circumstances it seems inappropriate to talk about "worth" and "benefits." On the contrary, those with greater responsibility should strengthen their resolve to share the suffering of the lower ranks. (This is a genuine national virtue that we should encourage.) Such an attitude would earn leaders the sincere love of the lower ranks, without which a truly enduring union is impossible. Of course, when those entrusted with heavy responsibility need special treatment for health

---

*Orphans adopted as personal assistants to the cadres.

† The Chinese Communists, in the interests of uniting the area under their control during the War of Resistance against Japan, established a system of "tripartite rule," whereby the Communist party (representing the workers and peasants), the "left-progressives" (representing the petty bourgeoisie) and the "middle elements" (representing the middle bourgeoisie and the enlightened gentry) each nominally shared one-third of the power.

reasons, it is both reasonable and necessary that they receive it. But those with medium responsibility should receive equivalent treatment. (2) The salary differentials to be established by the tripartite government should not be too great. Nonparty officials may appropriately be given favored treatment, but we party members should uphold our fine tradition of arduous struggle so that we may inspire even more people from outside the party to cooperate with us. (3) Excuse my rudeness, but I implore all you "masters" who can't speak without alluding to "ancient Greece" to hold your tongues.

I am not an egalitarian, but dividing clothes into three grades and food into five seems neither necessary nor reasonable to me—particularly with regard to clothes. (My own rank is "cadre's clothes / private kitchen," so this is not a case of sour grapes.) Our principle should always be to solve problems according to reason and need. On the one hand, sick comrades are denied even a sip of noodle soup, and young students are fed only two meals of thin gruel a day (after which the party members among them are expected to set an example by loudly proclaiming "I'm full!"); on the other hand, relatively healthy "bigwigs" receive "benefits" that they neither need nor deserve. If this condition continues, subordinates will come to look upon their superiors as an alien race; they will not only fail to love them, but will even . . . . The thought can't but make one feel "uneasy."

But perhaps jabbering on about "love" and "warmth" is a sign of "petty-bourgeois sentimentality"? I await your verdict.

March 17, 1942

Huang Qiuyun Do Not Close Your Eyes to the Sufferings of the People

//// I remember a writer made the prediction this spring that in twelve years nobody will have a worry in the world except for the person whose gifts are rejected by the one he or she loves; nobody will cry except for those who watch a moving classical drama or those who laugh too hard.*

Whether or not there will be worries and tears twelve years from now, nobody knows. Today, at any rate, our lives still possess happiness and sadness, laughter and tears. It is not always smooth sailing, where everything turns out the way we wish; but we have accomplished things in the midst of difficulties and have had victories in the midst of struggle. For this, our successes are to be treasured all the more and our victories thought more worthy of pride.

Without a doubt, the most important task of literature is to praise socialist construction and to urge people on. But many writers are content merely to praise superficially, glossing over our struggles and protracted hardships. This type of praise naturally cannot show the revolutionary spirit in our difficult struggles. Therefore, only our weaknesses are revealed, and readers are left unmoved. For example, nearly all the agricultural producers' cooperatives we see in the movies are rich and productive; the tables of every farm family are filled with meat and fish; every farm girl wears flowery new clothes and colorful scarves. Actually, this sort of scene couldn't be further from the truth, nor does it truthfully reflect the complexity of the struggles in village

This essay was written in September 1956 and published in *Renmin wenxue* (no. 9) later that year. Translation by John Balcom.

*Author's note: See "Xiang xinde gaochao qianjin" (March toward a new high tide), *Wenyi bao* 1956, no. 3.

communities or the problems and difficulties faced by the peasants.*

A writer like Nikolai Ostrovsky dared to face the hardships and sufferings of life. In his book *That's How Steel Was Tempered,*† he realistically described the people's hardships during the early years of the Russian revolution:

Every morning after drinking tea, they left for work. Their diet consisted chiefly of lentil soup and one and a half pounds of stale bread. Every day it was the same, without change.

. . . . .

Only with great effort did Pavel finally manage to pull his leg out of the mud. Because he felt a chill, he realized that the sole of one shoe had worn out and completely come off. . . . He couldn't go on that way, he would have to take leave from work—all because of his shoe. He pulled the shoe from the mud, and staring at it, he suddenly broke his oath never to swear.

These examples are not mere descriptions of the hardships of material life. Fyodor Gladkov, in his novel *Cement*, goes even further in writing about the struggle of the laboring masses against harmful tendencies within the party.

I believe this kind of writing possesses a positive function as an inspiration for the people. It is impossible for people who witness the hardships and sufferings of life or flaws and mistakes in work to lose faith in socialism. On the contrary, it is only by seeing difficulties overcome and heroism triumph over error that we can have the confidence and courage to confront severe trials. Revolution always progresses in stormy surges. The revolutionary masses will not be able to sleep sweetly in conservatories or dance on carpets for a lifetime.

For an artist, morbid pessimism is frightening and dangerous. Yet facile optimism is also damaging. Presently, in the domain of literary art, the latter ideological state is more worthy of consideration.

Only by constantly probing the depths of life can one see the sufferings of the masses. Today, in our land, famine, hunger, epidemics, and bureaucratism, as well as a number of unpleasant and unreasonable phenomena, exist. A writer with a high degree of political responsibility cannot calmly maintain silence in the face of the hardships and sufferings of the people. If a writer lacks the courage to zealously participate in solving the problems of the masses, and if a writer does not have the courage to squarely face the hardships and difficulties of life,

---

*After the land reform in the early 1950's, the Communist party started to collectivize agriculture. "The high tide of socialism," as Mao called the campaigns, occurred around 1956 and 1957. There was a great deal of resistance from independent farmers who had become relatively well off after the Liberation.

† The government selected this as a model piece of Soviet literature, and it was widely read by students.

then what kind of artist is this? A real artist must courageously take part in real life. To take part in real life means that one must affirm life as well as criticize it. Affirm those that benefit the people, and criticize those that harm them. In affirming life, one must be filled with zeal; when criticizing life one must be confident and coolheaded. These two should be inseparable.

If we write about life's hardships and pain, will we harm the socialist system we support? No. The dawn of socialism is bright and glowing, and a person with a clear mind could never mistake a patch of clouds for an entirely overcast sky. What is at question here is what attitude we must adopt and what point of view our understanding must take when we write. So long as we maintain a socialist attitude and adopt the standpoint of the proletariat in order to write about the hardships and pain in life, we would not become utterly disheartened, nor would we gloat over the misfortunes of others. Revealing life's hardships and sufferings has a curative effect: we can overcome them, we can eliminate them, and we can teach the masses how to deal with them. What is there then that cannot be accomplished?

Can the aesthetic qualities of a work of art be destroyed if we write about life's hardships and sufferings? No. Works of social realism cannot distort life, nor can they avoid or whitewash reality. Chernyshevsky, in his research on aesthetics, long ago concluded that beauty in a work of art is a result of the truthful reflection of life.* Beauty is life. Once I saw a photojournalist's picture of an autumn harvest. He complained that the farm girls were never dressed well enough, so he asked several female students to play the parts of the farm girls. To me this is whitewashing life. False beauty in a work of art can only disgust people!

It doesn't matter whether we affirm life or criticize it, we are principally concerned with reality and being close to the people. As revolutionary writers and artists, we must immerse ourselves among the masses and their blazing struggles to form one body and soul with the people, to form an alliance unto death with the people, to share their songs and tears, the sweet and the bitter. Facile optimism and indifference toward life must be changed—they must be replaced with a deep concern for the destiny of the people. The timidity of whitewashed life must be overcome and replaced with a revolutionary spirit capable of confronting reality. Considerations of individual gain and loss, advantage and disadvantage, must be done away with and replaced by a high degree of political consciousness and a sense of responsibility

*Nikolai Chernyshevsky (1828–89) was an author and journalist. He is best known for his novel *What Is to Be Done?*, the source of Lenin's title for his well-known essay.

for the undertakings of the masses. Only in this way can we reveal the inner feelings of the people and write about their loves and hates, their joys and sorrows. Only in this way can we avoid mocking or failing to praise the successes of the people and avoid closing our eyes and maintaining silence in the face of the sufferings and hardships of the people. Only in this way can we produce works that truly reflect this age of ours with pride.

Hao Ran

////

A Happy Life and the Art of Writing

Several years ago, in the postscript to a novel of mine, *The Bright Sunny Sky*, I wrote the following lines: "I, like thousands and thousands of literary workers of my country, grew up in the age of socialism. We are nurtured by the highest abundance of rainfall and sunshine— Mao Zedong thought; we grow on the richest soil—the blazing revolutionary struggle; we are tended by the most enthusiastic gardener—the nurture and assistance of the party apparatus and the broad revolutionary masses. . . ."

Now, as we commemorate the thirtieth anniversary of Chairman Mao's brilliant "Talks at the Yan'an Forum on Literature and Art," I look back on the road I have taken in my literary career. I feel all the more fortunate.

. . . . .

Chairman Mao pointed out in the Yan'an Forum: "For a long time to come, we must unconditionally and wholeheartedly go to the ranks of the workers, peasants, and soldiers, to the midst of the blazing struggle, to the only, broadest, and richest source. . . ." My personal experience has made me appreciate that this is the only route for any revolutionary literary fighter who wishes to produce writings for workers, peasants, and soldiers, writings that can serve the struggle.

But there was a period in my life when I thought I was firmly rooted in the ranks of the "workers-peasants-soldiers." I had worked as a cadre at the district and village levels* for seven or eight years and thought that I had, as the saying goes, "experienced peasant life to

---

This essay was written in January 1972 and published in the Chinese edition of *Renmin Zhongguo* in May 1972. Translation by Tam King-fai; the editor has made substantial changes in the translation.
*Sub-county-level administrative units.

the full." So, I planned to devote all my energy to writing, and to, as it were, "capitalize" on my life experiences. The works that I published in those days were well received by city readers and young people, but as for the poor and lower-middle peasants,* who carry out their struggle on the frontline of revolutionary production, my writings failed to impress them.

I wrote a novel centering on sent-down educated youths who participated in agricultural production. I was sure that I knew about this aspect of life. I had personally taken care of the living arrangements of educated youths and their work; I had mingled with them and resolved their ideological quandaries. But when I showed the piece to a village cadre, he said, "Very realistic, except that this kind of thinking is out-of-date." I was shocked by the phrase "out-of-date." Anyone could see that in response to the party's call, educated youths were heading to the countryside in large numbers. Why did the cadre consider the theme "out-of-date"? Wondering, I once again made myself get as close to people and things as possible. Only then did I realize that the attitudes of the educated youths had been fundamentally changed through education by the party. Unlike their predecessors during the days right after the Liberation, most of the educated youths were no longer disdainful of physical labor and of the laboring people. The remaining problems for them were how to better integrate themselves with the laboring people, how to quickly sink roots among the masses and be effectively tempered by labor.

Based on my new awareness and new resources, I have rewritten two stories: "Xia Qingmiao Looks for a Teacher" and "The Stout Seedling." The former is about the son of a high-ranking cadre who has volunteered for the frontline of agricultural production. With determination, persistence, and compassion, he wins the confidence of an old poor peasant who takes him in as an apprentice. The second story relates how the head of a local party organization, in much the same way as a gardener protects and nurtures young seedlings, earnestly yet demandingly helps an educated youth settle down to the life of struggle among the masses and take a step forward on the wide road of revolution. With these two stories, I finally gained the approval of the poor and lower-middle peasants.

This has allowed me to taste the sweetness that comes from "immersing oneself in life" and once again to savor the happiness of being a revolutionary literary worker. I realize that the era is advancing and the people continue to surge forward. To write, one has to continue

*Party jargon for the revolutionary classes in rural China.

to "immerse oneself in life." Otherwise, one will fall behind the revolutionary flow and cannot speak for the laboring masses of workers, peasants, and soldiers.

Chairman Mao has urged us to mingle with the workers, peasants, and soldiers and to stand firmly with them. This is an expression of how we should "for a long time to come, unconditionally and wholeheartedly" immerse ourselves in life. In a country like ours, there are plenty of chances to live in the midst of workers, peasants, and soldiers, because the party calls upon us to do so and the people welcome us. But once we get there, it is up to us to truly mix with the masses and to shift our position step by step to their side.

In 1969, I went to a big production brigade in Zhoukoudian Commune in the suburbs of Beijing to participate in labor. Before the trip, I was determined to integrate myself wholeheartedly with the poor and lower-middle peasants, to collect new materials for my writing, and to produce a work that reflected sharply the struggle of the people and that would be favored by them. On the day following my arrival, the deputy secretary of the party branch committee earnestly asked me to draft a speech for him in order to mobilize the members to devote their energies to the wheat harvest.* At the time, I was slightly displeased. First, I found it hard to get down from my high horse. I am a writer, I thought; someone who writes books should not be bothered with trivial clerical duties. Moreover, I had to collect materials for my writing during my offhours. If I were to take up these "sundry matters," it would take away too much of my "precious" time. But, the sincerity of this village cadre made it impossible for me turn him down. Reluctantly I drafted the speech for him. Just as I expected, other tasks of a similar nature began to be heaped upon me: the young people's amateur drama group wanted me to compose short skits, the village cashier wanted me to write receipts, and old grannies of some soldier families wanted me to write letters. . . . Every night, a continuous flow of people walked in and out of my room. My desk was cluttered with the "extra" duties that I could never finish, and there was no way that I could work on the materials I gathered or take notes for my writing. Surprisingly enough, I somehow got used to these chores after a few months.

On looking back, I finally realize that although it may have appeared on the surface that I had helped the commune members and cadres by performing these chores, in fact, they had given me much

---

*In the villages, most of the politically reliable peasant activists who became cadres were only semiliterate.

more. In the midst of these activities, I came to know many without consciously trying. They in turn got to know me, which drew us closer together. All these activities made it possible for me to sink roots in this unfamiliar setting, to learn invaluable things from these people, and to gather a plenitude of true-to-life materials otherwise unobtainable through meetings, interviews, and special investigations.

In my new novel, *The Bright Golden Way*, which I began last year, there are scenes and characters derived from my experiences in this way. The experience allowed me to taste the sweetness of reforming my thinking through immersing myself in life. If a writer does not reform his thinking by living close to the masses, he will not share their worries and concerns or do what is needed by them. He may appear to live with the masses, but he cannot be one with them. In that case, he might dally about in life for the longest time, but the barriers remain to block any true understanding. In the end, nothing is gained.

Only by making up his mind to join the ranks of the workers and peasants and by steadily working toward this goal can a writer become someone useful to the people and become a genuine proletarian literary fighter.

Ru Zhijuan

How I Came to Write 'Lilies on a Comforter'

//// I wrote "The Lilies on a Comforter" when the Anti-rightist Campaign was in full swing.* That was the situation the society at large found itself in; the same applied to my family. When Xiaoping was in imminent danger of being drawn in, I felt powerless to help him.† Every night after the children were asleep, I sadly recollected how we had lived during the war and our relationships with comrades. My mind was like a motion picture—there appeared the many different kinds of people I met during the war years. War never gives people the chance for a long talk, but it does produce deep friendships. It only takes the lesser part of an hour, a few minutes, or even just a fleeting glance for people to share a common destiny with the utmost sincerity.

"The Lilies" was produced in just such a time of anxieties and re-membrances—though the writing of the story and my personal anxieties were not directly related.

None of the characters or events in "The Lilies" are real, nor are they based on real people or events. The fighting in the story and the location of the battle are authentic. It was during one of the famous battles and seven victories of Suzhong, fought during the general offensive along the coast, at the time of the Mid-autumn Festival in 1946.‡ At that time I was doing war service at a first aid station at the

---

This essay was written on September 15, 1980. Translation by John Balcom from *Ru Zhijuan xiaoshuo xuan* (Selected stories of Ru Zhijuan) (Chengdu: Sichuan Renmin Chubanshe, 1983).

*The story was written in 1958; a few months earlier, Mao had started a severe purge of liberal writers and intellectuals who had criticized the Communist party.

†Ru Zhijuan's husband, Wang Xiaoping, also a writer and playwright.

‡As soon as the Japanese surrendered in 1945, the tension between the Nationalists and the Communists exploded into a full-scale civil war. Major battles were fought in north China.

frontline of the offensive. My job at the first aid station was to borrow blankets. After nightfall, as the moon rose higher and grew brighter, the first shots were heard. At first, all the casualties were new fighters, and their wounds were slight. As the fighting grew more intense, the wounded were fewer, but their wounds were more serious. Sometimes when a litter arrived, it was already too late. The litters were placed in the courtyard, where the bright moon was my light. I wiped away the dirt and gunpowder from their faces so that they would depart clean, but I never dared uncover their blankets. Even though they were pale, from their faces one could see that they were soundly sleeping young fellows. I longed to see them stand up and see their shy smiles. This type of emotion is true only when life is real. Under the enormous full moon that night, I checked their serial numbers and noted down their names and ranks. I couldn't help wondering about their families, relatives, friends, and the hopes they had when they were alive. Perhaps their slightly warm hearts continued to conceal secrets or were still troubled by worries. At such a time in such a place with such emotions and surroundings, a small notebook would have been useless. Even if I had had one, I would have been unable to put pen to paper. They were indelibly engraved on my heart, and even today they are all so clear, as if undisturbed by time.

In those tumultuous three years of the War of Liberation, when neither day nor night seemed to exist, there were too many events worthy of mention. On the chilly nights of spring in 1958, I looked back. I want to say two things not unrelated to the events in "The Lilies."

I remember it was around the time of the battle of Laiwu. I don't remember why, but one night I had to go to the frontlines with a courier. Before leaving, the courier, who acted as guide, told me we had to cross a wide expanse where the enemy often fired. He told me to be careful and that I might have to walk crouched over, but that I was not to panic. It probably would have been better had he not told me, because it only made me nervous. I made up my mind to follow him closely. If he bent over, so would I. If he walked fast, I would pick up the pace. Anyway, I didn't want female comrades to look bad in front of a soldier. As soon as we started off, however, he refused to let me walk beside him, but insisted that I keep some distance between us. I knew that by spacing ourselves out, we reduced the risks of injury or death—that is a soldier's wisdom. But on the open road with no cover and the enemy's gunfire constantly whizzing overhead, I couldn't control myself and had to hang close to him—that way I felt safe. But when he saw me draw closer, he hastened forward at a run.

As soon as he took off, I was right on his heels. Thus, under a starry sky, on barren ground, amid the roar of gunfire, the two of us became involved in an intense footrace. He and I were soon out of breath. If I grew too tired and lagged behind to the point he could no longer see me, then he turned back and looked for me. I no longer remember that courier's face, nor do I remember why I was going to the front. Oh, the sieve of memory! Sifting out the big things, leaving the small —that is why I could never be the author of an epic. There is nothing to be done about it, though. But that strange journey and that strange chase are always vivid. It's almost as if the waving grass and the panting of the courier are still before me. That's the way it was in 1958, and that is the way it is today.

There was another instance, under similar circumstances, but I can't remember which battle it preceded or followed. As I recall, Wang Suihan and I had joined a squad, and we sat around on the bunks listening to their speeches (in all likelihood a review).* Among the squad members was one who had recently been promoted to platoon leader—he was a war hero. This hero's tale has dimmed with time. All I remember is that he was very young and very shy and he spoke with embarrassment. Once when I was joking with him, he turned red, and laughing, he raised his hand just like a young Suzhou girl and said, "I'm going to hit you." Of course, he didn't hit me, but the incongruity of his girlish gesture and his heroic reputation stuck in my mind. That night I slept in a small central room on a bed made out of a plank door. Originally it had been the platoon leader's bed, but as a special favor for a female comrade, he lent it to me. The hero and Wang Suihan prepared a large bed on the floor. During the night, they put their heads together and spoke softly. Being above them, I could hear them quite clearly. While pretending to sleep, I pricked up my ears. Being curious by nature, I carefully prepared to delve into the inner world of the hero. But they never talked of anything more than mundane matters. The hero talked about his family and mentioned that he hadn't yet married and that he had no prospective match. He talked like anyone else, nothing mysterious. Feeling disappointed, I fell asleep. Although I was a bit disappointed at the time, later, when I thought it over, something good did come out of it after all—a very real impression had formed in my mind: a hero is exactly like any other person.

Although by early 1958 the Anti-rightist Campaigns were in full swing, rules and regulations governing literature were still being pro-

*The People's Liberation Army had political and cultural units to organize propaganda work. The presentation of models and heroes was common.

mulgated. Some had already come down, but none that looped around me to extract absolute compliance. After digging around a bit, and urged on by the inspiration from the past, I decided to write about a common soldier, a young courier. I felt I had known him for a long time, but all along had pushed him to the side, neglecting him. He was young, honest, and shy. He was shy because he was young. He had just begun to live, and he had not yet experienced the happiness of love. How he would act under any given circumstance, I could guess. This is what occupied my mind at that time, but I hadn't stopped to consider the main theme, the subthemes, or important events.

After I had settled on the little courier's character and special qualities, I created a female 'I' to tie the story together. In the process of writing, I developed a character from the courier's hometown to fill in impressions of the courier when he was only a common citizen. I utilized the full moon of the Mid-autumn Festival to shed some light on his childhood. At the time, it all came so simply and easily, requiring but one week to write the story.

Thinking back on it now, it was indeed fortunate that I didn't write by sticking to mere facts, but rather created a character from gut-level feelings about life, and then, based upon the needs of that character, looked back over the raw materials collected from life, altering them and synthesizing them.

From life I took the incident of the nighttime footrace with the courier. However, I abandoned the intensely charged atmosphere of a night filled with gunfire. I removed the military necessity of such action for the purpose of enhancing characterization. The journey together, in terms of developing the courier's character, was extremely important. I had to make the journey easy to contrast with the intensity of the fighting to come. Moreover, portions of the story's content could not be depicted in the midst of tense military action. Therefore, I set the story on the eve of an offensive in an interval of peace, thus assuring the 'I' and the courier a journey under completely normal circumstances. In such a way, the distance between the courier and the 'I' could be foregrounded, heightening the contradictions in his character, his youth, and his shyness with women. At the same time, I wanted to allow the 'I' to develop an emotional closeness to the courier as a comrade and as someone from the same hometown. However, their relationship was not meant to be one of love at first sight. The 'I' was to have for him a sisterly affection or, as a woman comrade, a motherly concern for his well-being. The more this kind of love had the power to convince, the more effectively the courier would move readers.

In short, it was not the seductiveness of the raw materials that gave the story its sense of reality. This was accomplished instead by breaking them up, mixing them together, and synthesizing them. Later, in accordance with the needs of the character, reality was drawn upon and selectively altered. On this point I felt very fortunate.

A second point of luck was the decision, at the very beginning, to make the courier a young soldier, an ordinary person, a young man who had just begun to live. I felt quite at ease writing about him, completely unburdened. When I wrote about the bride laughing at him and giving him a hard time, and when the 'I' made him sweat, I wrote with great spontaneity, never fearing in the slightest that his heroic image would somehow be sullied or his heroic status degraded. On the contrary, if I had written about the courier as a hero or had modeled him upon the valiant platoon leader, then no matter how warm —or even girlishly tender—I portrayed him as being, I never would have been able to rid myself of anxieties. First of all, I naturally had to consider how I was on the one hand to present his heroic deeds, stressing his tiger-like fierceness on the field of battle, while on the other hand presenting his shyness as stemming from a virtuous modesty. Perhaps a bride wouldn't dare show herself, and if she did, perhaps she wouldn't dare laugh at him. A hero can fail temporarily (such as failing to borrow a comforter), but he couldn't be mocked without ruining his image. By having the 'I' and the hero journey together, his good qualities could be revealed continuously, earning praise and possible emulation. In writing this way, after all, it remained problematic if the character could stand on his own, not to mention being a hero.*

I will say something I shouldn't: the courier in "The Lilies" does not seem such a great hero now. If we weigh his conduct as a rescue worker, he seems to be more a hero of the second degree. But I could be wrong. I am certain that the power of literature is not limited by the merits—great and small—of a character, just as the greatness of a work of literature is in no way influenced by the status of the characters.

The third point of good fortune was that during the movement to the left, I stayed put (later, I dared not to move!). The reason for this had absolutely nothing to do with wisdom on my part, but was a result of youthful naïveté. As such, I desperately wanted to write a bride into the plot. Why a bride and not a young girl or a mature woman? Now I can be quite frank: because I wanted to create a goddess in the joyous whirlpool of love to serve as a foil to the young soldier, who

*By the late 1950's, writers were increasingly required to portray socialist heroes without ambivalence or flaws.

was still inexperienced in love. Of course, I also wanted that comforter symbolic of love and purity, which is not something a young girl or a mature woman would possess.

The character of the courier developed in depth after he met the bride. Moreover, the bride he encountered was an abstract one, a very special bride under very special circumstances. If she were replaced with one who was insensitive or ill-tempered, he wouldn't have been able to borrow the comforter; if she were very sensitive and straight-forward, she would have loaned it immediately upon being asked. In either case, no conflicts could have arisen, no contradictions in char-acter, and thus no characters. The bride he ran into, however, was one who owned only one new comforter. The bride struggled silently trying to decide if she should loan the comforter. As her attitude slowly changed and she decided to lend her comforter, a certain mischie-vousness in her character was revealed. If it had not been for the critical wartime conditions, and if the comforter had not been her entire dowry, her "brother comrade" might have been made the butt of some harsh jokes. She might have offered to wash his dirty clothes while publicly ridiculing him for his dirty, patched clothing. However, since she was asked at such a critical time, she assented after wag-ing a silent struggle. When the 'I' and the courier went to her house for a second time, she had to bite her lip to keep from laughing. She thought of the nice things he had said, of the many things he had done for her, and of how she still had given him a hard time. The sec-ond time—when she loaned the comforter to him—she almost made things difficult for him again. She felt bad about it, but did not want to apologize, because it was a bit funny and it was not in keeping with her character. She appeared more controlled and kind at heart. She really thought it was funny. She suppressed her laughter, not because it was impolite, but because she was laughing mischievously and affection-ately. She laughed at the young comrade's misfortune for having run into someone like herself, untutored and unthinking. But unfortunate is unfortunate! Besides, he deserved his bad luck—who told him to come. . . .

This sequence of ideas comes to a climax when the bride grasps her comforter to cover the courier's body—an action that corresponds with her innermost feelings.* It is only at this critical and solemn mo-ment that she expresses her sorrow for, and understanding of, the young soldier. Only at that moment do the purpose of the story and the

---

*In the story, the young courier is killed. When his body is brought back, the young bride, with tears in her eyes, grasps her comforter from a helper and covers his body with it.

destinies of the characters merge and attain full completion. When a young man who had just begun to live offered everything, he attained everything: pure love and precious tears.

I sent out the story after finishing it, but it was rejected. At that time, I was not surprised that it was turned down by several editors, because it was a pastoral romance without love. I understand all of this now, but at that time things seemed much simpler. Perhaps if I had thought more about it, I might never have written "The Lilies." It's hard to say.

Once a story is written, it becomes an objective artifact. What is most important is to listen to what the critics have to say—I have merely jotted down a few random notes on the circumstances under which I wrote "The Lilies."

Li Zhun

////   I

What Did I Want to Tell My Readers?

The first volume of my novel *The Yellow River Rushes On* was completed in June 1979. I put off finishing the second volume until the spring of 1984, fully five years later. One reason is that I wrote several screenplays in between. Another is that I was ill. But there is a less apparent reason, too: I was still mulling it over. As I was excavating the family system, ethics, morality, character, wisdom, and creativity of the Chinese peasant, I discovered more than just coal in the mineshaft. There was gold, copper, iron, tin, even uranium there. So I drew out the course of my writing.

This novel is about the early years of the Second World War, when Japanese fascism invaded China and the Nationalist government breached the dikes, releasing the Yellow River in a torrent in the hope of blocking the invading Japanese army through "water in place of troops." More than forty counties in the three provinces of Henan, Jiangsu, and Anhui were inundated. It was an unprecedented calamity. More than ten million were ruined, and more than a million lost their lives.

In this novel I didn't intend to harp on the responsibility of those who brought this about. History has already rendered its just verdict on Chiang Kai-shek and Tōjō Hideki. I have written mostly about those who suffered from this tragedy—the "refugees." To some extent, then, this is a novel describing them. . . .

For several millennia, the peasants have always been bound up with

---

This postscript to the two-volume novel *The Yellow River Rushes On* (*Huang he dongliu qu*) was written in January 1984 and published with the second volume of the novel by Beijing Chubanshe in 1985. Translation by Jeffrey C. Kinkley.

their "families." Their land, their thatched huts, their farm implements, their livestock, were a unique way of life that had produced a distinctive ethics and morality. But when their fields were flooded and their families were destroyed, so that they became a horde of homeless refugees, what could they do? What changes occurred in their views on ethics and morality and, after so many of them fled to the city, in their families and interpersonal relations? My novel attempts to introduce the reader to some of those realities of life.

I've been writing fiction about the Chinese peasant for a long time. Changes in the peasants' family relations particularly interest me. In the 1950's, when I wrote "The Story of Li Shuangshuang," a Japanese critic, Ms. Matsuoka Yōko, read the story and came to Zhengzhou, Henan, just to meet me. She was very interested in what I'd written about the family lives of Chinese peasants in their thatched huts. There she'd found "the key to understanding China," she said. My answers to her questions at the time were extremely superficial. I only introduced her to some peasant manners and customs. However, her attention got me to thinking about the question of the peasant family. After the Great Cultural Revolution, I pondered the matter more deeply. The Great Cultural Revolution was another "calamity." In it our nation was covered with bruises and scars, but in the end we struggled out of it. From that it occurred to me what was at the root of our periodic times of doom. It was the magnificent vitality of the ancient Chinese people and their heavy inherited burden.

The Chinese family, I believe, is too ancient and perfect to function as the "cell" of society in an organic sense. Starting from the later Yangshao and Dahecun sites [Neolithic cultures of the North China Plain], China already has over 4,500 years of history. The Chinese word for "nation" [*guojia*] is a combination of *guo* [kingdom, state] and *jia* [family]. That is to say, the "state" is the "greater family," and the "family" is the "lesser family." The "state," in other words, is constituted of innumerable "families." One can see the rigor and meticulousness of family organization in China's domestic architecture and kinship terminology. Grandparents lived in quarters facing south. In cave dwellings, they lived in the center of the front rooms, with their children in the wings, and grandchildren in the lower summer rooms and side rooms. Family organization always gives the appearance of a "ginseng-root structure" [pyramiding up to a focal head from many branches]. Besides that, kin terminology is extremely differentiated: not only does one use special terms for one's father's elder brother, one's father's younger brother, the husband of one's father's sister, and one's mother's brother, one uses special terms for one's maternal grandfather, the husband of one's father's paternal aunt, the husband of one's maternal aunt, the husband of one's maternal cousin, plus dozens of other appellations. Another interesting thing is that Chinese peasants don't have the concept of entering "heaven" after they die, for they don't believe there is a heaven, though they do stubbornly believe that they have another "family" down in the nether world. Chinese peasants call their houses *yangzhai* [dwellings of the *yang* upper world] and their tombs *yinzhai* [dwellings of the *yin* underworld]. Graves, too, are laid out generation by generation like a ginseng root. There is not only the custom of burying husband and wife in the same grave, but of arranging marriages for deceased persons, so that relatives in the nether world will not have to be without a mate.

I have always believed that "social ethics are the basis of morality." For a long time, these deep-rooted ethical concepts have formed the Chinese peasants' moral concepts. "If you don't understand the Chinese peasant, you won't understand China." Expanding from this concept, you can say that studying the formation and changes in the Chinese peasant family is one key to understanding China.

II

In this book I have not written about extended families with four or five generations "under one roof." Instead I have described seven ordinary peasant households. I have dissected those seven ordinary cells to represent the majority of 800 million Chinese peasants. They are not seven families in some quiet village, leading pastoral lives of "working from daybreak and going to bed with the sun." This is about their lives after they became homeless wanderers. Their homes have been inundated and they are on the verge of death, yet their faith and hope of living, their capacity to withstand bitter hardship, and the strength of their willingness to work together and help each other, particularly when it is for their loved ones, their native village, and their friends, are all the more evident. This character and spirit that radiate light in all directions illuminate the essence of five thousand years of Chinese culture, and the spiritual props with which this great and ancient race of ours has survived and propagated itself.

Even as I described their outstanding moral character, I described the burden they inherited from the past—their backward and ignorant feudal consciousness. It is a spiritual straitjacket, a mesh of heavy ropes that surrounds their bodies. No doubt it is an important reason why our nation has been backwards for so long.

My reason for writing about these past lives is not of course to denounce the utter tragedy of them, nor yet to intone an elegy for the peasants who lost their lives. I want only to weigh the Chinese peasant's ethics, morality, and spirit once more in the scales of history. I want people to see the strength of their diligence and valor, of their capacity for labor and hardship, and of their spirit of mutual love and unity: to plant a faith in human survival and, from that, faith in our nation and our people. I am an optimist. I steadfastly believe that our country will get better and better—that we will leave it in better shape than it was when we entered it.

III

I first saw the nomadic life of Yellow River refugees when I was fourteen years old. In 1942 I was myself a student forced to leave home [because of the Japanese occupation]. I followed a large group of refugees who were fleeing Luoyang for Xi'an. The Longhai [Gansu-Jiangsu] Railway was a corridor of famine. Tens of thousands slowly made their way westward, pushing little carts, hefting broken hampers on shoulder poles, carrying baskets on their arms. There were pots and pans in the carts, children in the hampers, and in the baskets, roots and pieces of bark scrounged up for food.

There have been many "streams of refugees" in Chinese history, but this trek was the largest and longest. There have been many great migrations in Chinese history, too, but again, this one was the largest in number of people and area covered. Even during this life of exile, they stubbornly kept up their everyday customs and retained their moral bearing. At stops along the railway they set up mat sheds for temporary shelter. Even then they maintained the hierarchy between young and old; the merest bowl of broth would be offered to the old folk first. I once saw a peasant remorsefully slap his own face because his son had stolen someone else's carrot. I also saw a young woman sell herself for a bit of grain to feed her starving husband. She stripped off her cotton tunic in exchange for two sesame seed rolls and stuffed them into his hand as she left. It was then that I began to really know our suffering motherland and our great people.

I went to the flood districts the second time in 1949, as a credit manager for a rural bank. The peasants had returned to their homes, and I had come to distribute seeds and implements to them. Again I saw some things that were too horrible to look at. In a collapsed hut I saw the skeletons of a family of five, piled one on top of the other. They had died huddled together, in the waters of the flood.

The flood districts were already liberated, and we had announced the land reform policy, so many of the peasants had returned from afar. Hacking through brambles and thorns, they re-established their farms. The gratitude of the peasants when the right to their land was given them was enough to make one cry. They rollicked about on the newly reclaimed land, turned somersaults on it, rushed about telling the good news, reveled all night long around bonfires rather than go to bed. Many women who'd been sold away to other districts returned, too. Some had become prostitutes, and some had become concubines for landlords who lived in other parts; some had even been sold away to other provinces, as brides for poor bachelors. Every day there were tearful reunions between parted husbands and wives, mothers and daughters. The peasants' traditional views on female chastity had been destroyed. They had an unwritten rule: all the women who had been sold away to other parts were warmly welcomed back home. Regardless of what they might have been away from home, no one had the right to despise them.

One peasant had sold his wife after fleeing to Shaanxi during a famine. He had pretended she was his sister at the time. He often took his children to see this woman, whom they were told to call "auntie," and she hid steamed buns in her pockets to give to them. When she returned home after the Liberation, the children still called their own mother "auntie"; all cried inside.

During the Great Cultural Revolution, when the Gang of Four carried out their mad persecution of writers, I was named a member of a "black gang." So in 1969 I was driven to a village in the flood districts to do labor under surveillance. I lived there all of three years. At first the peasants didn't dare to talk to me, for I was there for reform under surveillance. Afterwards, realizing that I was educated, they asked me to write a "funeral oration" for an elder of the village. As usual, it recorded the life experience and all the good deeds of the deceased and was read aloud at the time of offering sacrifices to his dead spirit. It was three brothers who asked me to write that first "oration." Having lost their oldest brother, they came in white mourning clothes to my thatched hut. When they saw me, they first knelt on the ground and kowtowed (as was the custom at funerals there), then related the life of their brother through their tears.

While the family was in flight, his father and mother had been drowned by the waters of the Yellow River. He had led his three little brothers to safety in Shaanxi, worked on long-term contract as a hired hand, slaughtered cows on the side, and reared his three brothers. He never married himself, yet he got wives for his three younger brothers. Once the Nationalists pressganged the second eldest. He deserted, was recaptured, and was about to be shot. Catching up to them, the oldest brother knelt before the army officer who was to carry out the order and pleaded to be executed in his little brother's stead. The officer asked him why he was willing to exchange places. He answered that he had just found his little brother a wife. She was the only woman they had, so they were counting on the little brother to carry on the family. He himself was a bachelor, so if he died it didn't matter. Moved by this expression of ancient morality, the officer spared them both.

Because I'd written a bit of fiction, this funeral oration turned out quite well. The whole village wept to hear it, even the band of musicians. The story passed from village to village that there was one named Li who was good at writing funeral elegies. During those years I came to write several dozen of them, and by that means I came to a systematic understanding of the "family histories" of the refugees of the flood districts. *The Yellow River Rushes On,* a tale of seven peasant households in exile, is based on those "family histories."

IV

Besides writing funeral orations, I made many friends. All of them had been refugees. Their lives away from home were not all sorrow; they had a lot of romantic-sounding tales evoking their resourcefulness and humor, too. I still miss those friends as I speak of them now; among them were the men who became my characters Running Wang and Four Pens. Still today they think they've made it because they wear leather-soled shoes and dress hats like the ones cityfolk wear.

I like these stories; they all have a bit of the North China "drawl" to them. People call peasants from Henan "drawlers," and what does that signify? I understand it to mean simple, honest, and kindhearted, yet on the other hand quick-witted and cunning—apparently clumsy on the outside, but having wisdom and a sense of humor inside—stingy about little things but bold and generous when the real need comes. This must be the personality the Yellow River has given them.

This novel tells the story of half a dozen young women with special reference to their romantic lives, in which they are faithful even at the risk of death. Love is the best mirror of one's personality and character. Struggling at death's door, they hoist their lives and their loves together as banners of their existence as true human beings. The women of the flood districts in their flights traversed half a country. They cast off the shackles of feudalism through struggle. Their magnanimity is unbounded, and their ability to earn a living unencumbered. Meanwhile they retain the noble quality of seeing their spouses through good times and bad. In their own words, "people must have fellow feelings and a sense of duty."

These are the women who lived through the calamity. It is they who raised their children in the midst of the storm. And it is they who took up the axe and the plow to reclaim and replant tens of millions of *mu* of barren land and rebuild their own farms.

From their own lives of hardship they learned how to make choices: in the Huaihai campaign,* which determined the fate of China, it was these women who fed the Chinese People's Liberation Army, pushing grain to the frontlines in the very carts they'd once used to flee famine.

These epic and moving events came flooding back as memories: "The Chinese people toughed it out during that disaster; would they perish in the one created by the Gang of Four?" My answer was a resounding "No!"

Every people have their own great latent strength. That was my point in writing this novel.

*A major series of battles fought between the Communists and the Nationalists in the late 1940's.

Ah Cheng   Father

//// One evening in March 1987, I was at Xia Yang's New York apartment.* The place had been remodeled into a studio in great haste, and it looked so old that one might expect it to crumble at any moment, although in fact there was no such danger. What I did not expect, however, came through a long-distance call from the other part of the globe—my father was seriously ill. I immediately made preparations to leave for home.

My family had lived under the shadow of my father's serious illness ever since the early 1960's. In the summer, I remember, when we and our neighbors were mingling noisily in the yard, mother used to come out to hush us. We were too young to keep father's illness in our minds all the time.

Father came down with hepatitis while he was being reformed in a labor camp in Lushan. The illness went from acute to chronic, and eventually developed into the cirrhosis that was to cause his death. Just when we were prepared to face father's imminent end, the Cultural Revolution started.† Back in 1957, father had been branded a "rightist." So he was merely a "dead tiger."‡ He was "criticized and struggled against," placed beside "active" enemies at mass meetings,

---

This essay was published in *Jiushi niandai* in June 1988. Translation by Ren Xiaoping and Helen F. Siu.

*Xia Yang is a Chinese painter from Taiwan who studied in France and now lives in New York.

† The Cultural Revolution started in 1966 and officially ended in 1969.

‡ Those who had been criticized and put in the category of "enemies" before the Cultural Revolution. Although they were not the main targets of the Cultural Revolution, they did not escape. They were dragged out again for criticism, mainly for symbolic purposes.

and struggled against;* confessions, labor—all were invoked for the purpose of humiliating him symbolically. Then he was sent off to a cadre school.† In those days, whatever happened to father was taken for granted, even his certain death. But father did not die then. He actually lived to see 1979.

That was an important year to father, as was 1957. I remember one day before the New Year's, a phone call took me home to see him in the evening. Father sat by the desk, his back toward the light. He always faced the desk light when he worked and turned around when he was tired. Mother said, "A man from the Department of Organization‡ came to tell us that all cases for the rehabilitation of rightists in the country are to be cleared before New Year's. Father is on the list. What do you think of this?" The only thought I had was that the name Zhong Dianfei would no longer be preceded by adjectives.§ But I did not speak my mind because I knew this mattered very much to mother.

After 1957, mother single-handedly supported her five children, her mother, and her brother, who was a college student. It is impossible to measure, even now that I have grown up, the amount of hardship she went through. I remember that our clothes were handed down from the older to the younger brothers. The material was the most durable kind of corduroy. When we walked, it rubbed between our legs and produced scratching noises. All our clothes were home-made in the traditional style, which could be worn back and front, leaving two pale worn spots on both sides where we sat. When they could no longer be worn, grandma would tear them apart and use the rags to make soles for our shoes. Grandma always complained about the pain in her shoulder. She had to hand-stitch over twenty shoes for us every year. We raised chickens with their eggs in mind. In winter, the chicks lined up along the windowsill, picking dried paste from between the lattice and the paper, leaving the window as tattered as a temple after a storm. For people everywhere in China, those were the hard times. For a time, locust tree blossoms ceased to be only herbal

---

*A popular form of political activity during the Cultural Revolution. These struggle meetings were endorsed by the party and organized by the Red Guards and mass organizations. At these meetings "enemies" of the revolution were criticized and often physically abused.

† A re-education-through-labor program for party and government cadres as well as for intellectuals during the Cultural Revolution. It was based on a letter from Mao to Lin Piao of May 7, 1966.

‡ A major department of the party, in charge of recruitment, promotion, and other personnel matters.

§ The author's father, a well-known scholar and writer in China. After he was branded a "rightist" in 1957, his name, whenever mentioned officially, was preceded by that adjective.

medicine.* Shan Shan, my youngest sister, was weak and sick from malnutrition; Da Lu, my third younger brother, once came back with mother beaming with excitement because they had found some young sweet potato vines to feed the family; my fourth younger brother, Xin Zuo, nearly stuffed himself to death with meat at a dinner party to which he was invited—the first in our family had he died. Yes, life was harsh for everybody. But I cannot imagine how father endured life in the labor camp. Sitting in a chair, I pondered how to explain to father that I did not think much of his rehabilitation. I did not want to hurt mother's feelings. Father might also get upset because, after all, this was a matter that had altered his entire life.

That father was a "rightist" affected our lives too. My eldest brother, Li Man, could not go to senior middle school. It was because children from families such as ours were not allowed to enter college, and senior middle schools prepared students for college. Li Man was a talented student. His grades were always good. Even today, it's hard for me to imagine what kind of psychological impact this must have had on the mind of a boy only in his teens. But father insisted that he repeat the senior middle school entrance examination the following year. This, I think, was father's way of maintaining faith. In 1978 when he passed the examination and was eventually allowed to go to college from the village where he had been sent to settle,† father mentioned it only briefly in a letter. I wonder what else was on his mind when he wrote the letter by the desk light.

When I reached eighteen, father made a point of telling me: from now on, we are friends. From this I realized that I had reached adulthood. My feelings at that moment must have been similar to those of the young men in ancient China after their coming-of-age ceremonies: the feelings of self-confidence and gratitude, and a sudden surge of inner strength. So that evening I finally conveyed the words of a son from the standpoint of a friend.

This is what I said, "If I were overjoyed tonight, my past thirty years would be reduced to nothing. As a person, you have already affirmed yourself. There is no need for others to judge you. If the power of such judgment is in the hands of others, they may well support you today

---

*Locust tree blossom is a traditional ingredient of Chinese medicine. But during the famine years between 1959 and 1961, people used it as food.

† Colleges and universities were closed down for five years after the beginning of the Cultural Revolution. When most of them reopened after 1971, the university entrance examination system was replaced by the working-class recommendation system in order to emphasize the ideological background of the candidates. In 1978, with the downfall of the Gang of Four, the old examination system was restored. Li Man passed the exam that year and went to college.

and deny you tomorrow. Therefore, in my view, your rehabilitation has no real significance outside of mere technical convenience. Moreover, the political vicissitudes that have afflicted you are not without blessings. They have forced me to rely on my own efforts to acquire confidence in life, although for you these twenty years must have been brutal."

Father replied with a smile, "Now the tenure of my party membership has been confirmed as forty years. Just imagine, half of the time I wasn't in the party. Your mother has made some beef stew today. Why don't you go and see if you can buy some noodles. We're going to have beef noodles today." Mother was happy too, telling us how she couldn't have bought the beef if she hadn't asked so-and-so for help. Father then asked if she had garlic. How can we eat beef noodles without garlic!

After 1979, father started to write a great deal. His essay "Reflections on Film Literature" published in that year's *Literary Criticism* reminded many people that he was still alive. The China Film Publication House planned to put out a volume of father's essays written before 1957. So father sent me out to track down his old articles. The newspaper section and the magazine section of Beijing Library are located in two separate parts of the city. Since I had just been transferred back to Beijing from the countryside and had not yet found work, it became my full-time job to shuttle every day between east and west Beijing. Government libraries do not have an index system. I had to look through every issue and page of the newspapers. Magazines with their annual indexes were a great deal easier. For his article "The Gongs and Drums of Film," father was singled out for criticism by Mao Zedong himself. I was only eight years old at the time and did not know what to say when questioned by my teacher. So I parroted that father was a bad man. I did not use the word "enemy" because I was too young to understand what "enemy" meant. Only twenty years later was I finally able to read this article with my own eyes. I made a photocopy and took it home to father. He also had his own feelings about it. For fear of offending certain people, the publisher named the collection *The Sunken Land.** Father preferred to use the old title,

*In the early post-Mao era, although the Gang of Four had been condemned, Mao's image was still protected and his thought still held up as the only ideological guideline in China. Since Mao had personally criticized "The Gongs and Drums of Film," to use the same title would suggest opposition to Mao's thought, and Mao's associates who were still in power could find fault with it. According to Ah Cheng, his father settled on the title *Sunken Land* (*Lu chen ji*) because he wanted to indicate that a person condemned by the party disappeared from the face of the earth. Such had been his fate for the preceding twenty years.

"The Gongs and Drums of Film," but had to compromise in the end. A friend who was a seismologist would have bought the book by mistake had I not told him that it was not the kind of work of reference he thought it was.

Many people began to visit father at home. Mother reminded him to remain vigilant against certain faces. Although father understood and deplored the rapid switch from cold shoulder to glad hand, he was hospitable and offered whatever was called for. Father knew many people who did not survive. He recalled that in the 1950's he attended the premier showing of Lao She's play, *The Young Task Force.** In the midst of socializing with the guests, Lao She turned to father and lowered his voice: "Is it worth your while to come and see such a play?" Father told many stories about Zhao Dan,† but he wrote only one article about him: "Zhao Dan's Last Words." It echoed what Zhao Dan had said in his own article, "Policies Too Specifically Imposed, No Hope for Art and Literature."

My father and I used to discuss whether the professionally ignorant should lead experts.‡ I maintained the view that they should. Experts should concentrate on their profession. If they become political leaders, they would be unskilled for the task. Wouldn't that be wasteful? To quote ancient sages: "The incompetence of one makes room for many others to be competent; inactivity in one nurtures the energies of many." Father added, "It is actually the experts who are better at distorting facts and framing charges. Leaders with professional expertise can hit your vital parts, doing internal damage, while leaders ignorant of the professions can at most make a fool of themselves. For less pain and damage, the latter are indeed a much better idea."

Although I seldom offer grand theories, I use the phrase "I think" rather frequently. Father therefore told me that when doing self-criticisms in the cadre school, he was frequently caught for saying "I think": how dare he use "I think" even when he is being criticized! This is extreme bourgeois individualism! Father was very grateful to a man in the same cadre school who had been labeled a "historical counterrevolutionary."§ Seeing that father had trouble getting his self-

---

*Pen name of Shu Qingchun, a famous social novelist in China. He is regarded as the chronicler of life in Beijing just as Dickens was the chronicler of London. Most of his best works were published before 1949.

† A famous actor and writer from Shanghai respected not only for his artistry but also for his intellectual integrity.

‡ An argument of long standing in Communist China is whether intellectuals and technical workers should be supervised by nonexpert Communist cadres (the "red vs. expert" dispute). Before and during the Cultural Revolution, those who opposed this view were criticized.

§ People labeled "counterrevolutionaries" not because they actively opposed the revo-

criticism approved, he offered to revise it for him.* The product was not only approved, but also became a temporary model for other inmates. When father inquired about his tricks, this person replied, "I used to work for a Nationalist newspaper; my professional capital was the ability to write this stuff."

What a pity that the confessions and self-criticisms from all over the country had been destroyed, father thought.† It would have been a good idea to publish a selection of the best self-criticism literature. When Ba Jin‡ proposed the construction of a Cultural Revolution Museum, father said that the exhibits should include the various confessions and self-criticisms. I added the suggestion that a dictionary of Cultural Revolution terminology be published, or else future generations would find it difficult to decipher these documents. One such example was the term *jiao dai* [confession and self-criticism]. Another is *zui*, an adverb meaning "very," which was triplicated before certain nouns.§ Our descendents might think that their ancestors were, for a time, all stammerers. This could create complications for ancient anthropology, ancient medicine, and ancient semantics in future generations. My comment brought roars of laughter from father.

Father had two things which made me envious: his laughter and his nose. When I was too young to evaluate the judgment imposed upon him, his laughter convinced me that he could not be a bad man. According to physiognomy, father's nose was a sign of sure fortune and prosperity. In reality, however, his fate did not fit with what his nose suggested. I think this had to do with his involvement in films. After all, it has only been a hundred years since film was invented, too short to be embraced by physiognomy. But then, one can hardly reach such a conclusion, since the good fortunes of most film stars *do* have to do with good looks.

Every year, a film or two would run into trouble. I asked father why. He replied: "Films are the only art that can get into the central party

---

lution but because they had worked for the previous regime or had been members of the Nationalist party.

*During the Cultural Revolution, everyone who had been criticized had to write such confessions repeatedly to show repentance.

† When the Cultural Revolution ended, most victims were rehabilitated and their written confessions and self-criticisms were officially destroyed as unpleasant reminders of their persecution.

‡ Pen name of Li Feigan, one of the most highly regarded novelists in modern China. A writer in the May Fourth tradition, his trilogy *Family* (*Jia*), *Spring* (*Chun*), and *Autumn* (*Qiu*), which was published between 1931 and 1940, is one of China's modern classics. He was criticized and sent to labor in a cadre school during the Cultural Revolution.

§ For example, the standard way of saying "the great leader of China" became "the great, great, great leader of China."

headquarters at Zhongnanhai.* Access to such a place brings trouble to them." I, for one, disagreed with the theory that film scripts should be more literary. Father questioned this: "Well, how are you going to make the censors who read only classic literature understand what you want to do in the film?" I then realized that father had chosen to do something he had always known was dangerous. His nose, no matter how fortunate it appeared, could not have saved him. Mother was always angry at father because he did not bother to get proper rest. I think I understand him. Certain people simply cannot afford to rest. To them, rest means giving up, and then death approaches.

Heavy snow in New York. In America, people are not in the habit of seeing guests off at the gate. So Xia was waving farewell only at the studio door. For a moment I thought I was back in Beijing and could go straight to the hospital to see father and to joke with him. Father burst out laughing and said, "Go take a bath."

The Dream of the Red Chamber† ends with a scene of heavy snow, a scarlet cloak, and two lonely lines of footprints. What one man leaves behind is not the same as the chaotic imprints in Manhattan.

Father died on March 20. I arrived one day too late, both in theory and in practice, due to that arbitrary dateline across the Pacific.

Before the cremation, streams of visitors came and went. Some had genuinely looked forward to father's passing. This made father appear more like a soldier than the meek Chinese scholar he had actually been, who did not even have the means to take a proper bath. In the summer, he carried water out to the yard and bathed in one of the corners, surrounded by a piece of cloth. In the winter, public baths were like hospitals. One had to wait for one's number to be called before squeezing inside. Father was getting old, so I went with him lest he fainted. Soaking in the hot water, he closed his eyes tightly, painfully enjoying the luxurious comfort. I had the urge to ask him what he thought was the greatest happiness in a man's life, but I did not for fear he would blurt out his feelings. Whenever father stayed in a hotel for a conference where there were bath facilities, he would always invite friends of a similar fate to go and take a bath. Then they would sit around, their hair dripping wet, and talk about things other than bathing. Father did the same thing when he was in the hospital. The nurses were not at all surprised to see his wet-haired visitors. Ever since the

---

*The part of the Forbidden City in Beijing where Mao and other leaders lived and where the Central Party Committee has its offices.

† A classic Chinese novel, telling of the love affairs of a privileged and spoiled young man in a literati family and the vicissitudes of that large family. Tired of his life and society, the hero eventually leaves home to become a monk.

beginning of Chinese civilization, shower and bath had always been regarded as the most important things for health next to food and drink. Bathing was such a serious matter that it was supposed to have strong effects on the heart. After the Han dynasty, the Japanese imitated the bathing techniques and greatly elaborated on them. When I asked father about his impressions after he had come back from a visit to Japan, his answer was "Could take a bath any time." What else? He answered, "So we won the war."*

Although the China Film Art Research Center was responsible for arranging father's funeral, the Beijing Film Studio offered to send special staff along to help. So did film studios throughout China. Mother was deeply appreciative but declined them all. Nonetheless, Wu Tianming† managed to send people from the Xi'an Studio to help. He himself was standing outside the funeral hall, arms folded, in utter silence. People from the Shaanxi area are among those who, since ancient times, have watched many happenings in China.‡ He understood what this scholar had done in life, what he had hoped for, and what he regretted.

I went with my elder brother to collect father's ashes. The front hall of the crematorium was empty, no container in sight. It was only with the help of a worker that we finally found an iron dustpan sitting in one of the corners of the hall. We bent over to see father in grey ashes. The laughter had gone, and the nose too. Only a few droplets from his melted glasses lay frozen on the bony forehead.

"The Gongs and Drums of Film," *The Sunken Land, Essays of Inspiration,* and *The Technique of Films* were the only few offerings in front of father's portrait, books he labored from his very heart.§

*According to Ah Cheng, his father was with the People's Liberation Army during World War II and fought behind enemy lines. In 1945 he witnessed the surrender of the Japanese army. When he went to Japan and compared its postwar achievements to China's backwardness, he could not help wondering at the hollowness of the Chinese victory.

† A famous film director and head of the Xi'an Film Studio. Wu has directed a number of high-quality films in recent years and has a reputation for being extremely liberal and supportive of daring young directors.

‡ The Wei Valley and the middle Yellow River area of Shaanxi have been inhabited since Neolithic times and are considered the cradle of Chinese civilization. Xi'an and Loyang, the two major cities of the province, were famous ancient capitals. The people of Shaanxi have witnessed numerous civil wars in history and have struggled for thousands of years to harness the ferocious Yellow River.

§ According to Ah Cheng, he feels sad that due to the political circumstances, his father, an intelligent and committed person, toiled for his entire life to produce only a few works. There is a tremendous sense of waste.

Reference Matter

Glossary of Chinese Terms

The metric equivalents given below are those set by the government of the People's Republic of China. In earlier times, the values of weights and measures varied from area to area and by the item being measured. The Republican values were close to the current ones.

dan 担	A measure of weight; 100 *jin* or 50 kilograms (roughly 110 pounds)
dan 石	A dry measure for grain; a hectoliter (90 quarts)
fen 分	A measure of area; one-tenth of a *mu* or 66.6 square meters (72 square yards)
jin 斤	A measure of weight; 0.5 kilogram (1.1 pound)
kang 炕	A sleeping platform built of bricks, common throughout northern China. A firebox built into the base of the *kang* allows it to be heated.
li 里	A measure of distance; 500 meters (one-third of a mile)
li 厘	A measure of area; one-hundredth of a *mu* or 6.66 square meters (7.2 square yards)
mu 畝	A measure of area; 666 square meters (about one-sixth of an acre)
sheng 升	A measure of volume; 1 liter (roughly a quart)
yuan 元	The standard monetary unit
zhang 丈	A measure of length; 3.33 meters (11 feet)

List of Chinese Characters

The names of fictional characters are not included in the following list. The entries are alphabetized word by word.

Ah Cheng (Zhong Ah Cheng) 阿城(鍾阿城)
"Ah Q zhengzhuan" 阿Q正傳
Ai Wu (Tang Daogeng) 艾蕪 (湯道耕)
Ba Jin (Li Feigan) 巴金(李芾甘)
Bai Hua 白樺
"Baihehua" 白合花
"Ban zhuren" 班主任
Bei Dao (Zhao Zhenkai) 北島 (趙振開)
"Buyao zai renmin de jiku mianqian bishang yanjing" 不要在人民的疾苦面前閉上眼睛
Caijia Cave 蔡家窰
Cao Xueqin 曹雪芹
Chen Boda 陳伯達
Chen Cun 陳村
"Chen Huansheng shangcheng" 陳煥生上城
Chen Qingchen 陳清晨
"Chu shan" 出山
Chuangzao jikan 創造季刊
Chuangzao ribao 創造日報
Chuangzao she 創造社
Chuangzao yuekan 創造月刊
"Chui yan" 炊烟

chun 椿
Chun 春
da chuanlian 大串連
dan'gan hu 單幹戶
"Dierzhong zhongcheng" 第二種忠誠
Ding Ling 丁玲
diyi bashou 第一把手
"Diyi bu" 第一步
"Duoyu de hua" 多餘的話
Eryue 二月
Fang Lizhi 方勵之
Fang Zhi (Han Jianguo) 方之 (韓建國)
Fengtian army 奉天軍
Furong zhen 芙蓉鎮
Gan Yang 干陽
Ganxiao liuji 干校六記
Gao Xiaosheng 高曉聲
gaoliang 高粱
Gu Cheng 顧城
Gu Gong 顧工
Gu Hua 古華
Gu Jiegang 顧頡剛
"Gui qu lai" 歸去來
Guo Moruo 郭沫若
guofang wenxue 國防文學

guojia 國家
"Haizi wang" 孩子王
Han Shaogong 韓少功
hanjian 漢奸
Hao Ran (Liang Jinguang) 浩然
　（梁金廣）
He Long 賀龍
He Shang 河殤
He Weili 何偉立
"Hong gaoliang" 紅高粱
Hongshui 洪水
Hou tu 厚土
Hu Feng 胡風
Hu Shi 胡適
Huang he dongliu qu 黃河東流去
Huang Qiuyun 黃秋耘
huo Wuchang 活無常
Jia 家
Jia Pingwa 賈平凹
jian 諫
Jiang Qing 江青
"Jianji cuo le de gushi" 剪輯錯了的
　故事
jiao dai 交代
Jin Ziguang 金紫光
Jing Qing 景清
Jinguang dadao 金光大道
jinshi 進士
Jinsui Base Area 晉綏根據地
Jiushi niandai 九十年代
juren 舉人
Kang Zhuo (Mao Jichang) 康濯
　（毛季常）
kouliang tian 口糧田
Ku lian 苦戀
Lao She (Shu Qingchun) 老舍
　（舒慶春）
Li Dazhao 李大釗
Li Jiye 李霽野
Li Rui 李銳
"Li Shuangshuang xiaozhuan"
　李雙雙小傳
"Li Shunda zaowu" 李順大造屋
Li Yi (Lee Yee) 李怡
"Li Youcai banhua" 李有財板話
Li Zehou 李澤厚

Li Zhun 李准
Liangdi shu 兩地書
"Lijiazhuang de bianqian"
　李家莊的變遷
Lin Biao 林彪
Lin Gang 林岡
Liti jiaochaqiao 立體交叉橋
Liu Binyan 劉賓雁
Liu Xiaobo 劉曉波
Liu Xinwu 劉心武
Liu Zaifu 劉再復
Lu chen ji 陸沈集
Lu Wenfu 陸文夫
Lu Xun (Zhou Shuren) 魯迅
　（周樹人）
Lu Xun Yishu Xueyuan 魯迅
　藝術學院
Luo Feng 羅峰
Mangyuan 莽原
manqi 滿七
Mao Dun (Shen Yanbing) 茅盾
　（沈雁冰）
menglong shi 朦朧詩
Mo Yan 莫言
"Mouri" 某日
Naogelaoyulang 瑙格勞玉朗
neisheng waiwang 內聖外王
"Nining" 泥濘
"Niuche shang" 牛車上
"Pa man qingteng de muwu"
　爬滿青藤的木屋
"Paoxiao de Xujiatun" 咆哮的
　許家屯
"Qi wang" 棋王
Qian Zhongshu 錢鍾書
Qiu 秋
"Qiu shou" 秋收
qiusheng 秋/求生
Qu Qiubai 瞿秋白
Qu Yuan 屈原
quanwei xing 權威性
Renmin wenxue 人民文學
"Renyao zhijian" 人妖之間
Rou Shi (Zhao Pingfu) 柔石
　（趙平復）
Ru Zhijuan 茹志鵑

Yu Ying-shih 余英時
"Zai qiaoliang gongdi shang"
  在橋樑工地上
Zhang Xinxin 張辛欣
Zhang Zhidong 張之洞
Zhao Dan 趙丹
Zhao Shuli 趙樹理
Zheng Wanlong 鄭萬隆
Zheng Yi 鄭義
Zhi qu Weihu shan 智取威虎山

Zhong Dianfei 鍾惦棐
Zhong xuesheng 中學生
Zhonggu lou 鐘鼓樓
zhongjian renwu 中間人物
Zhou Libo 周立波
Zhou Yang 周揚
zui 最
"Zuzhibu xinlai de nianqing ren"
  組織部新來的年青人

Notes

Complete authors' names, titles, and publication data are given in the References Cited, pp. 335–41.

Introduction

Epigraph. *Lianhe wenxue*, 4, no. 4 (1988): 108.

1. For a concise summary of official views on the philosophical issues involved in the spiritual pollution dispute, see Liang Liyi 1984. Liang's article is an analysis of Hu Qiaomu's essay "On Humanitarianism and Alienation," which was published in *Renmin ribao*, Jan. 27, 1984. See also the summary written by Li Si (1983).

2. See the debates in the Hong Kong literary journal *Renditions* in the 1980's and in the collection of essays edited by Bi Hua (1983). Xie Mian, an editor of the poetry journal *Shikan*, speaks on behalf of the younger experimental poets. He and Xu Jingya, a sympathetic critic, argue that the attempts at self-expression represent a reaction against the party's past distortions of poetic sensitivities.

3. See the introduction in Tay 1988, which outlines the major issues in the controversy. Liu Xiaobo's criticism of the new-style writers is noteworthy. See also the analyses of the fiction of Bei Dao (pen name of Zhao Zhenkai) by Bonnie McDougall (1984) and of the debates centering on Wang Meng's experiments with the stream-of-consciousness technique by William Tay (1984).

4. Critical realism as a genre of writing was popularized in China during the 1920's, when Russian influence was strong. Lu Xun, for example, introduced many pieces of Russian literature to Chinese intellectual circles (Lee 1987a). The early Chinese leftists adopted the theories of the Hungarian György Lukács and attempted to reflect in their work the totality of an epoch and to present the human predicament through dramatic plots. However, the Stalinist era brought a shift toward a more formalistic socialist realism. The Chinese Communists selected the most "advanced" pieces as models, and Maoists pushed the Stalinist line further (Ng 1988). The critical and the humanist strains in art were thus severely suppressed.

5. Liu Binyan joined the party in his youth. In 1957, he was labeled a

"rightist" because he portrayed the dark side of the party. After his rehabilitation in 1979, he intensified his efforts to expose the corruption of power. His "People or Monsters" ("Renyao zhijian") and "A Second Kind of Loyalty" ("Dierzhong zhongcheng") are both well known. In 1985, he was elected to the executive committee of the Chinese Writers Association by a popular vote. He was expelled from the party in 1987 together with the playwright Wu Zuguang, the philosopher Wang Ruoshui, and the physicist Fang Lizhi. All are outspoken critics of the party. Liu has lived in the United States since 1988 and has joined the exiled leaders of the pro-democracy movement. For a summary of his views, see Liu Binyan 1988 and an interview of him by Li Yi (1988c), the editor-in-chief of the Hong Kong intellectual journal *Jiushi niandai*.

6. See the interviews of Tu Wei-Ming by Xue Yong, a reporter in Beijing (Tu 1985), and by Li Yi (1989c), which focuses on the May Fourth movement. Tu is interested in the recent efforts at "cultural reflection" in China. The issues surrounding "tradition" are reflected in the debate triggered by the television series *He shang*; see Sanlian Shudian 1989. See also the discussion among Li Zehou, Liu Shuxian, and Li Yi (Li Yi 1988b).

7. See Li Zehou and Liu 1988; Ren 1988, which quotes Liu Xinwu; and Liu Xinwu 1988.

8. Among his more famous pieces are the short story "Leader of the Class" ("Ban zhuren"), the novella *Overpass* (*Liti jiaochaqiao*), and the novel *Bell and Drum Towers* (*Zhonggu lou*). He was an editor of *Renmin wenxue* (People's literature).

9. The March and April 1989 issues of *Jiushi niandai* contained the text of the open letter and several reports and analyses of the letter-signing campaign; see Li Yi 1989a, b; and Qi 1989a, b.

10. Liu Binyan divides the young writers into two groups. Bei Dao and Han Shaogong are among those whose works are still engaged in a dialogue with political reality and are therefore acceptable. He dislikes those who explore their inner emotions to the exclusion of social concerns. See Liu Binyan and Chen 1988.

11. See Li Yi 1989a, b; and Qi 1989a, b.

12. A growing pool of their writings has been identified as the literature of the sent-down educated youths. See the special section devoted to their works in *Lianhe wenxue* 3, no. 12 (1987): 82–147.

13. See three articles by Xie Mian (1983a, b, c) and the one by Xu (1983). On the generational divisions of modern Chinese intellectuals since the May Fourth period, see Schwarcz and Li 1983–84.

14. The "literature of the wounded" and the "exposure literature" were the first waves of literature to emerge after Mao's death in 1976 to reveal the horrors of the Maoist period. See Siu and Stern 1983 and Link 1983. See Kinkley 1985 and Duke 1985 for later developments.

15. I refer to Lu Xun's classic 1918 short story, "The Diary of a Madman." Through the eyes of a paranoid, he described the traditional ethics that formed the habits of the heart and that killed human feelings and critical self-reflection.

16. For a description of Gu Cheng's poems by his father, Gu Gong, see Siu and Stern 1983: 9–15. The translations of the excerpts here are from Siu 1983: 1–7, 11–13.

17. An art show in Beijing in 1989 confirmed the worst fears of politically concerned artists. Some young artists, calling themselves the Xingdong pai (Action school) deliberately attracted attention to their art by "unconventional ways." Two of them obtained a gun from the home of a close family friend, a high military official, and shot at a painting in the exhibition hall. Whatever the "artistic" value of their expression, their reliance on their families' power and privilege was distasteful to those artists who have tried to use unconventional art forms to express their opposition to political orthodoxy. See Ya 1989.

18. Ah Cheng 1988: 12.

19. Quotations from Schwarcz 1986: 13.

20. Lee 1985: xiii, 31.

21. This term comes from Wang Ruoshui 1985, which was written for Chinese youth.

22. Ah Cheng 1985*b*: 92. For other advocates of "roots" literature, see Zheng 1985; Han 1985; the interview of Han Shaogong in Lin Weiping 1986; and Shi Shuqing 1989.

23. For different aspects of how modern Chinese intellectuals relate to the state, see Yue and Wakeman 1985; Kinkley 1985; Duke 1985; and Goldman et al. 1987, particularly the article by Rudolf Wagner.

24. Cheng 1987; Mote 1971: 5; Chang Kwang-chih 1983.

25. Mote 1971: v.

26. See Balazs 1964; Chang Chung-li 1955; Chang Kwang-chih 1983; and Ho 1962.

27. For comparative purposes, see Goody 1986 on writing and the organization of society.

28. Birch 1977: x–xi.

29. See Liang 1949: 19. This is not to deny the legalistic elements in the Chinese polity and their ancient roots in the first dynasty, the Qin, which, according to Mote (1971: 114), "expressly denied all humanistic values, and [was] quite implacable in its scorn for venerated tradition."

30. Qu Yuan, a poet and official of the third century B.C., represents loyal opposition and honor even in banishment. He drowned himself in protest, an act remembered in the popular culture in connection with the Dragon Boat Festival, when rice cakes wrapped in leaves are thrown into rivers supposedly to feed the fish so that they will not disturb his body. There are many other such examples. Tao Yuanming, a poet and official of the fourth century A.D., resigned from office and became a hermit. His chrysanthemums became a symbol of a gentleman's retreat.

31. Yu Yingshi (1978) has analyzed the interconnections among Confucian scholarship, the rise of the large lineages from which the scholars emerged, and dynastic fortunes. He argues that the scholars also shared artistic tastes based on Daoism that were not necessarily related to the pursuits of officials. These self-conscious, anti-official identities were forcefully expressed during the Wei-Jin period (third century A.D.) when many scholars engaged in metaphysical studies and refused to acknowledge the Confucian order in social and political life. This trend of thought was a genuine component of the scholarly culture, Yu argues, and scholars in the later periods resorted to its symbols of scholarly retreat when the political arena became too treacherous. *The Scholars* (*Rulin waishi*), an eighteenth-century social satire on scholars and

their attempts to come to terms with the growing disparity between their aspirations and the political constraints imposed by the late imperial state, reveals the powerful ideological forces to which intellectuals felt compelled to attach themselves (Ropp 1981).

32. Schwarcz 1986.

33. Spence 1981: xiv–xv.

34. See Tu 1985, 1987; Lee 1987*b*, 1989; Schwarcz 1986: 8; and Li Yi 1989*c*. For the interactions of the traditional assumptions of modern Chinese intellectuals and political power, see Goldman 1967, 1981; and Goldman et al. 1987.

35. For a detailed analysis of this tension, see Li Zehou 1987; and Liu Zaifu and Lin 1988. See Chow 1960 on the May Fourth Movement and its implications. See also Goldman 1977 on the literature of the May Fourth period.

36. Yu 1983. Some intellectual self-examination was achieved at the beginning of the May Fourth period, as shown in the earlier works of Lu Xun and Hu Shi. However, the period was short lived. From the late 1920's on, even Lu Xun was somewhat drawn into the political whirlpool.

37. See Li Zehou 1987; Liu Zaifu and Lin 1988; and Gan 1989*a, b* on the unfinished process of cultural reflection.

38. Their eagerness for Western technology did not entail a willingness to embrace Western cultural values. As advocated by Zhang Zhidong in the late nineteenth century, the goal was to use Western means while retaining the Chinese essence.

39. See Alitto 1979 on the maneuvers of these military bosses.

40. This division is epitomized by two literary clubs, the Wenxue Yanjiuhui (Literary research society) and the Chuangzao She (Creation society). According to C. T. Hsia (1979), the first one used *Xiaoshuo yuebao* as its mouthpiece, and the other published a series of journals, *Chuangzao jikan, Chuangzao ribao, Hongshui,* and *Chuangzao yuekan,* to counter the realism of the first. From the late 1920's on, writers in the Chuangzao She increasingly combined romanticism with revolutionary fervor to promote the Communist cause. A representative figure is Guo Moruo.

41. For recent evaluations of Qu, see Wang Shiqing 1984 and the biographical accounts by Chen Tiejian (1986) and Pickowicz (1975).

42. See Meisner 1969 and Johnson 1962.

43. Although Mao was most concerned with class, his tactics justified a united front for national salvation in the 1930's and 1940's. For studies of the rural economy in the Republican era, see Myers 1970; Alitto 1979; Perry 1980; Philip Huang 1985; Duara 1988; and Faure 1989. For studies of how the Communists attempted to mobilize the peasants, see Johnson 1962; Hinton 1966; Selden 1971; Pepper 1978; Thaxton 1983; Chen Yung-fa 1986; and Mao 1990.

44. See the writings of Qu Qiubai and Hu Feng on Marxist literary criticism and on relations with the Chinese populace.

45. See Ding Yi 1955; Ding Wang 1978; C. T. Hsia 1979; and Lee 1987*a*. See also the articles by Huters and by Holms in Lee 1985. This view should be distinguished from Qu Qiubai's opinions in the early 1930's concerning excess "Europeanization" in leftist literature. Qu's concern was along class lines. He was afraid that the bourgeois, urban, elitist assumptions of many writers prevented them from speaking a language the peasant masses could appreci-

ate. See Pickowicz 1975. Hu Feng, a Marxist literary critic, staunchly opposed sinicization. He and Lu Xun were friends, and his views brought him into opposition to Mao Zedong in the 1940's and 1950's.

46. C. T. Hsia 1971: 533. Russian literature with a moral thrust and a populist sense of compassion for the peasants was influential in the formation of this attitude. See Ng 1988, and Pickowicz 1975. Also, many of those thinking in Marxist terms, such as Wang Shiwei and Hu Feng, were later persecuted as Trotskyists and revisionists by a party heavily influenced by Stalinists.

47. For a critical evaluation of the Yan'an Forum and the subsequent twenty years, see Tsi-an Hsia 1963. See also Dai 1988 and Selden 1971 on the rectification movement in Yan'an. For a survey of the literary debates during the Yan'an period, see Liu Zengjie et al. 1983.

48. Tsi-an Hsia 1963: 232.

49. Gregor Benton (1982), who translated Wang's essay "Wild Lilies," said that Wang spoke more from the heart than from the mind. For his ordeal, see Benton 1982: 168–86; Dai 1988; C. T. Hsia 1979; and Cheek 1984.

50. See Dai 1988; Ma 1975; and Cheek 1984 on the incident. Dai asserts that the incident was intimately tied to the sinification of Marxism under Mao.

51. Dai 1988: 23.

52. Dai Qing (1988) suggests the order came from Marshal He Long, who was given control of the base area at the time and who obviously did not feel bound by legal procedure. Many intellectuals considered these military leaders semi-bandits. He Long, for his part, had little patience with intellectuals.

53. Hu Feng became friends with Lu Xun during Lu's last years. In 1935 party pragmatists sent four representatives from the League of Left-wing Writers to warn Lu Xun against the friendship, accusing Hu of being an "internal spy." The act infuriated Lu Xun, who nicknamed them the "four fellows" (*si tiao hanzi*) and refused to cooperate (C. T. Hsia 1979: 312).

54. See Ding Shu 1987; and Ba Jin 1986: 150.

55. See Ba Jin 1981*a*.

56. Schwarcz 1983.

57. Ba Jin 1982: 69.

58. Two notable examples of loyal opposition are Wang Ruoshui 1989 and Wang Ruowang 1989; both men are prominent Marxist philosophers and literary critics.

59. An autobiographical short story by Shi Tiesheng, "My Distant Qingping Bay" ("Wode yaoyuan de Qingping wan"), describes a common bond between an old peasant and an educated youth paralyzed by disease. Due to its length, I could not incorporate it in the volume.

60. See Chen Cun 1985: 64. See also Zeng 1985 on the works of Zhang Xinxin, and Ding Fan and Xu 1986 in defense of the "roots literature." In a recent letter (personal communication), Han Shaogong said that he no longer wrote this kind of literature.

61. A student leader (*New York Times*, June 3, 1989) commented that his one regret was that the students had been unable to link up with intellectuals, writers, and journalists.

62. This idea was suggested to me by Ng Mau-sang. See also Schwarcz 1986 on Zhang Shenfu's feelings of superfluousness.

63. See Hobsbawm and Ranger 1983 for the concept of the invention of

tradition. See Liu Na 1986. Liu distinguishes traditional literature, which functioned as social mediation, from modern literature, which has been used as an active tool to promote national salvation and social reform.

64. See Lee 1986; and Ji 1986.

65. In a dialogue with Liu Binyan, Leo Lee (1986) summarizes the complexity of the issues involved. He shares Liu's sentiments, but objects to Liu's appeal to social conscience to prevent artistic explorations that have not been allowed in the past four decades. Lee hopes that after a period of chasing after art or cultural roots, the young writers will acquire enough vision to link an abstract exploration of cultural roots with immediate issues in social and political life. See also Shi Shuqing 1989 for interviews with Liu and other writers.

66. My intentions in exploring this cultural critique seem best summarized by Marcus and Fischer (1986: 114): "The philosophical critique is most securely grounded in the sociology of knowledge, a questioning of the relation between the content of beliefs and ideas, and the social position of their carriers or advocates. The effect of this style of cultural critique is demystification; it detects interests behind and within cultural meanings expressed in discourse; it reveals forms of domination and power; and thus, it is often posed as the critique of ideology."

67. Ba Jin 1988: 212–15.

68. After 1949, there were works on workers and soldiers, but a large number of writers were sent to the countryside to "experience" peasant life and to write about how the peasants were "embracing" a revolution conducted in their name.

69. Schwarcz 1983.

70. Bai Hua, a middle-aged writer in the army, wrote *Unrequited Love* (*Ku lian*) in 1980 and became the target of official wrath in 1981. For an interview with him seven years later, see Li Yi 1988a.

71. C. T. Hsia 1979; Tsi-an Hsia 1968.

72. Lee 1987a: 39.

73. For similar political problems faced by East European writers, see the works of Milan Kundera, Josef Skvorecky, and Czeslaw Milosz.

74. See Williams 1958, 1977, 1979, and 1980 for theoretical statements on culture and political economy, and on Marxism and literature. See the works of the new historicists (e.g., Stephen Greenblatt) on how literary voices are encoded by their political-historical environments. Although one may conclude that voices of self-assertion are inevitably shaped by social codes and political agendas within a historical context, the Chinese texts appeared to engender themselves. See also Stallybrass and White 1986 for a summary of Mikhail Bakhtin and revisions of his work in relation to cultural hegemony and subversive voices in literature and cultural performances.

Introduction to Part I

1. During the war, he did not join the Communists in Yan'an. He never became a party member. See the memorial essay by the leading scholar of his work in China, Yue Daiyun (1981). For biographical information on the authors discussed in this volume, I have relied on *Zhongguo wenxuejia cidian* (Dictionary of Chinese authors), 2 vols., comp. Beijing Yuyan Xueyuan (Hong

Kong: Wenhua Ziliao Gongyingshe). I have also consulted *Who's Who in Communist China*, 2 vols., comp. Union Research Institute (Hong Kong, 1969); Ding Wang 1978; and C. T. Hsia 1979. In cases of discrepancies, I have followed the *Zhongguo wenxuejia cidian*. For the younger writers, I have secured information from their publications or from personal communications.

2. C. T. Hsia 1979: 301–2.

3. See *Zhongguo wenxuejia cidian* (1979).

4. For Xiao Hong's life and work, see *Lianhe wenxue* 33 (1987) and *Zhongguo wenxuejia cidian* (1979). I have drawn on Howard Goldblatt's (1976, 1982, 1985) analysis of her work. For recent Chinese evaluations of her work, see Xiao 1984 and Xing et al. 1981.

5. See Huang Manjun 1980 and Wang Xiaoming 1982 for his explorations in realism in that period.

6. See C. T. Hsia 1979; Jin 1983; and the introduction to Ai 1978 for more details of his life and work.

7. In a 1989 letter to me, he said that he wrote the story in a Nationalist jail in 1931. The story was published in 1933.

Introduction to Part II

1. The revolutionary value of his work was confirmed by the leading writers Mao Dun, Guo Moruo, and Zhou Yang. The stories were also popular on the stage in the Communist base areas. For a recent Chinese evaluation of this work, see Dong 1986. For a collection of his works, see Fudan Daxue, Zhongwen Xi 1981. The Shanxi group of writers is known in literary circles as the Rustic School (Shanyaodan pai; literally, the Potato School).

2. Much of this biography is taken from *Zhongguo wenxuejia cidian* (1979). For an evaluation of his work, see Ding Wang 1978, and for a summary of his work, see Li Kailing and Liao 1984.

3. Ye 1981a: 13.

4. For a 1963 critique of this story by a literary critic who accused Fang Zhi of maintaining "traditional morality" in his use of words and in character portrayal, see Zhao 1963. See also Ye 1981a, b; and Ba Jin 1981a.

5. Hao is a prolific writer, and his career lasted beyond the Maoist era. As late as 1981, a collection of his short stories was published.

6. Among the four writers in this part, Hao Ran was probably an exception. He became famous when his work was popularized by Maoist radicals from the 1960's on (Fan 1965).

7. Other well-known cases were Liu Binyan, who was condemned for his story "At the Bridge Site" ("Zai qiaoliang gongdi shang"), and Wang Meng, for his "The Young Man Who Has Just Joined the Organization Department" ("Zuzhibu xinlai de nianqing ren").

Introduction to Part III

1. The peasants who congregated in Beijing soon after the fall of the Gang of Four in 1976 were an important topic in post-Mao poetry and fiction.

2. See the memorial of Fang Zhi written by Ye Zhicheng (1981a); see also Ba Jin 1981a.

3. After the Democracy Wall movement in 1978–79, unofficial publications

mushroomed. Both the style and the content of established writers' works were liberalized. Bai Hua was a writer in the army when he wrote the play *Unrequited Love* (*Ku lian*). He was singled out and severely criticized, together with a host of dissidents.

4. For an evaluation of Gao Xiaosheng and the "Lu Xun whirlwind," see Shi Hanren 1984. See also Decker 1987 on Gao's satire and the preface by Yin Qi in Gao 1987. Among his best-known short stories are "Li Shunda Builds a House" ("Li Shunda zaowu") and "Chen Huansheng Goes to Town" ("Chen Huansheng shangcheng").

5. In this aspect of his work, he belongs to the camp of the Xun gen pai.

6. Since then, she has written other essays and novels reflecting on the ambivalent relationship between intellectuals and the state. A recent one is Yang 1988.

7. Young writers associated with the "roots literature" include Zheng Yi, Zheng Wanlong (who focuses on the mountains of Heilongjiang), He Weili, Mo Yan (whose story "Red Sorghum" ["Hong gaoliang"] takes place in the loess hills of China's northwest), Ah Cheng, and Jia Pingwa. See *Lianhe wenxue* 3, no. 9 (1987): 136–81, for a discussion of these writers.

8. See Wang Chan 1985a, b. These two essays are comments on Ah Cheng's "King of Chess," which focuses on hunger.

Introduction to Part IV

1. See Benton 1982: 170.

2. See Song 1985: 123. Huang was purged in 1964 and stopped writing for fourteen years. For his selected works, see Huang Qiuyun 1986.

3. The story, "Lilies on a Comforter," was translated and published in Hsu and Ting 1980. Ru is a very polished, middle-aged writer. In 1979, she published a famous piece, "A Badly Edited Story" ("Jianji cuo le de gushi"), which depicts the long history of socialist transformation through the eyes of an honest old peasant.

4. See Zhu 1980.

References Cited

Ah Cheng. 1985a. *Ah Cheng xiaoshuo xuan*. Hong Kong: Tuqi.
———. 1985b. "Wenhua zhiyue zhu renlei." *Pinglun congkan*, no. 10: 90–92.
———. 1988. "Fuqin." *Jiushi niandai*, June, pp. 12–14.
———. 1989. "Chui yan." *Jiushi niandai*, July, pp. 11–12.
Ai Wu. 1978 [1959]. *Ai Wu duanpian xiaoshuo xuan*. Beijing: Renmin Wenxue Chubanshe.
Alitto, Guy. 1979. "Rural Elites in Transition: China's Cultural Crisis and the Problem of Legitimacy." In Susan Mann, ed., *Select Papers from the Center for Far Eastern Studies*. Chicago: University of Chicago: Center for Far Eastern Studies, pp. 218–75.
Ba Jin. 1979. *Suixiang lu*. Hong Kong: Joint Publishing. Reprinted in Ba Jin 1988.
———. 1981a. "Dao Fang Zhi tongzhi." In Ba Jin 1981b, pp. 9–12.
———. 1981b. *Tansuo ji*. Hong Kong: Joint Publishing. Reprinted in Ba Jin 1988.
———. 1982. *Zhenhua ji*. Hong Kong: Joint Publishing. Reprinted in Ba Jin 1988.
———. 1984. *Bingzhong ji*. Hong Kong: Joint Publishing. Reprinted in Ba Jin 1988.
———. 1986. *Wuti ji*. Hong Kong: Joint Publishing. Reprinted in Ba Jin 1988.
———. 1988. *Ba Jin suixiang lu*. Hong Kong: Joint Publishing.
Balazs, Etienne. 1964. *Chinese Civilization and Bureaucracy*. New Haven: Yale University Press.
Bei Dao. 1988. "Wuti." *Lianhe wenxue* 4, no. 4: 108.
Benton, Gregor, ed. 1982. *Wild Lilies, Poisonous Weeds*. London: Pluto Press.
Bi Hua, ed. 1983. *Jueqi de shiqun*. Hong Kong: Dangdai Wenxue Yanjiu She.
Birch, Cyril. 1977. "Foreword." In Andrew Plaks, ed., *Chinese Narrative*. Princeton: Princeton University Press.
Chang Chung-li. 1955. *The Chinese Gentry*. Seattle: University of Washington Press.
Chang Kwang-chih. 1983. *Art, Myth, and Ritual: The Path to Political Authority in Ancient China*. Cambridge, Mass.: Harvard University Press.
Cheek, Timothy. 1984. "The Fading of Wild Lilies: 'Yan'an Talk' in the First CCP Rectification Movement." *Australian Journal of Chinese Affairs* 11 (Jan.).

Chen Cun. 1985. "Guanyu 'Xiao baozhuang' de duihua." *Shanghai wenxue* 9. Reprinted in *Pinglun congkan* 1985, no. 12: 63–66.

Chen Tiejian. 1986. *Qu Qiubai zhuan.* Shanghai: Shanghai Renmin Chubanshe.

Chen, Yung-fa. 1986. *Making Revolution: The Communist Movement in Eastern and Central China.* Berkeley: University of California Press.

Cheng, Te-k'un [Zheng Dekun]. 1987. *Zhonghua minzu wenhua shiliao.* Hong Kong: Joint Publishing.

Chow, Tse-tsung. 1960. *The May Fourth Movement: Intellectual Revolution in Modern China.* Cambridge, Mass.: Harvard University Press.

Dai Qing. 1988. "Wang Shiwei yu 'Ye baihehua.'" *Wenhui yuekan*, no. 5: 23–41.

Decker, Margaret. 1987. "The Vicissitudes of Satire in Contemporary Chinese Fiction: Gao Xiaosheng." Ph.D. dissertation, Stanford University.

Ding Fan and Xu Zhaohuai. 1986. "Xin shiqi xiangtu xiaoshuo de dishan yanjin." *Wenxua pinglun*, no. 5: 11–18.

Ding Shu. 1987. "Zhenfan, sufan ji Hu Feng an." *Jiushi niandai*, Sept., pp. 109–13.

Ding Wang. 1978. *Zhongguo sanshi niandai zuojia pingjie.* Hong Kong: Ming Bao Yuekan.

Ding Yi. 1955. *Zhongguo xiandai wenxue shilue.* Beijing: Beijing Zuojia Chubanshe. Reprinted—Hong Kong: Wenhua Ziliao Gongyingshe, 1978.

Dong Dazhong. 1986. "Zhao Shuli yanjiu shuping." *Zhongguo xiandai wenxue yanjiu congkan*, no. 1: 178–90.

Duara, Prasenjit. 1988. *Culture, Power, and the State: Rural North China, 1900–1942.* Stanford: Stanford University Press.

Duke, Michael. 1985. *Blooming and Contending: Chinese Literature in the Post-Mao Era.* Bloomington: Indiana University Press.

Fan Zhilin. 1965. "Shi tan *Yanyang tian* de sixiang yishu tese." *Wenxue pinglun*, no. 4: 16–23.

Faure, David. 1989. *The Rural Economy of Preliberation China: Jiangsu and Guangdong, 1870 to 1937.* Hong Kong: Oxford University Press.

Fudan Daxue. Zhongwen Xi, ed. 1981. *Zhao Shuli zhuanji.* Fuzhou: Fujian Renmin Chubanshe.

Gan Yang. 1989a. "Ziyou de linian: 'Wusi' chuantong zhi queshi mian—wei 'wusi' qishi zhounian er zuo." In Lin Yusheng et al. 1989.

———. ed. 1989b. *Zhongguo dangdai wenhua yishi.* Hong Kong: Joint Publishing.

Gao Xiaosheng. 1987. *Gao Xiaosheng daibian zuo.*

Goldblatt, Howard. 1976. *Hsiao Hung* [Xiao Hong]. Boston: Twayne.

———. 1985. *Xiao Hong pingzhuan.* Harbin: Beifang Wenyi Chubanshe.

———, trans. 1982. *Selected Stories of Xiao Hong.* Beijing: Panda.

Goldman, Merle. 1967. *Literary Dissent in Communist China.* Cambridge, Mass.: Harvard University Press.

———. 1981. *Chinese Intellectuals: Advice and Dissent.* Cambridge, Mass.: Harvard University Press.

———, ed. 1977. *Modern Chinese Literature in the May Fourth Era.* Cambridge, Mass.: Harvard University Press.

Goldman, Merle, with Timothy Cheek and Carol Hamrin, eds. 1987. *Chinese Intellectuals and the State: In Search of a New Relationship.* Cambridge, Mass.: Harvard University Press.

Goody, Jack. 1986. *The Logic of Writing and the Organization of Society*. Cambridge, Eng.: Cambridge University Press.

Han Shaogong. 1985. "Wenxue de gen." *Zuojia*, no. 4. Reprinted in *Pinglun congkan* 1985, no. 5/6: 94–97.

Hao Ran. 1981. *Hao Ran duanpian xiaoshuo xuan*. Shijiazhuang: Hebei Renmin Chubanshe.

Hinton, William. 1966. *Fanshen: A Documentary of Revolution in a Chinese Village*. New York: Monthly Review Press.

Ho, Ping-ti. 1962. *The Ladder of Success in Imperial China*. New York: Columbia University Press.

Hobsbawm, Eric, and Terrence Ranger, eds. 1983. *The Invention of Tradition*. Cambridge, Eng.: Cambridge University Press.

Hsia, C. T. 1971. *A History of Modern Chinese Fiction*. Rev. 2nd ed. New Haven: Yale University Press [1st ed., 1961].

———. 1979. *Zhongguo xiandai xiaoshuo shi*. Translation by Joseph Lau et al. of C. T. Hsia 1971. Taipei: Zhuanji Wenxue Chubanshe.

Hsia, Tsi-an. 1963. "Twenty Years After the Yenan Forum." In Cyril Birch, ed., *Chinese Communist Literature*. New York: Praeger, pp. 226–53.

———. 1968. *The Gate of Darkness: Studies in the Leftist Literary Movement in China*. Seattle: University of Washington Press.

Hsu, Kai-yu, and Ting Wang, eds. 1980. *Literature of the People's Republic of China*. Bloomington: Indiana University Press.

Huang Manjun. 1980. "Sha Ting 'zuolian' shiqi dui xianshi zhuyi de tansuo." *Zhongguo xiandai wenxue yanjiu*, no. 3: 100–21.

Huang, Philip. 1985. *The Peasant Economy and Social Change in North China*. Stanford: Stanford University Press.

Huang Qiuyun. 1986. *Huang Qiuyun zixuan ji*. Guangzhou: Huacheng Chubanshe.

Ji Hongzhen. 1986. "Duozhong wenhua sixiang de chongtu." *Zhongguo shehui kexue*, no. 4. Reprinted in *Pinglun congkan* 1986, no. 11: 30–45, 51.

Jia Pingwa. 1986. *Jia Pingwa ji*. Fuzhou: Haixie Wenyi Chubanshe.

Jin Kui. 1983. *Sha Ting yanjiu zhuanji*. Hangzhou: Zhejiang Wenyi Chubanshe.

Johnson, Chalmers. 1962. *Peasant Nationalism and Communist Power: The Emergence of Revolutionary China, 1937–1945*. Stanford: Stanford University Press.

Kinkley, Jeffrey, ed. 1985. *After Mao: Chinese Literature and Society, 1978–1981*. Cambridge, Mass.: Harvard University Press.

Lee, Leo [Li Oufan]. 1986. "Cong liangge wenxue huiyi kan Zhongguo wenxue de fansi." *Jiushi niandai*, Dec., pp. 78–81.

———. 1987a. *Voices from the Iron House: A Study of Lu Xun*. Bloomington: Indiana University Press.

———. 1987b. "Zhongguo xiandai wenxue zhong de xiandai zhuyi." *Jiushi niandai*, Sept., pp. 96–99.

———. 1989. "Modernity and Its Discontents: The Cultural Agenda of the May Fourth Movement." Paper given at the Four Anniversaries China Conference, Annapolis, Md., Sept. 1989.

———, ed. 1985. *Lu Xun and His Legacy*. Berkeley: University of California Press.

Li Kailing and Liao Chaohui, eds. 1984. *Kang Zhuo yanjiu ziliao*. Changsha: Hunan Renmin Chubanshe.

Li Rui. 1988. *Hou tu: Leiliangshan yinxiang.* Taipei: Hongfan Shudian.

Li Si. 1983. "'Jingsheng wuran' yanlun zonghui." *Wenyi qingkuang*, no. 91 (Dec. 21). Reprinted in *Qishi niandai*, Mar. 1984, pp. 42–51.

Li Yi [Lee Yee]. 1988a. "Bai Hua hai zhimi buwu de kulian zuguo ma?" *Jiushi niandai*, Jan., pp. 84–92.

———. 1988b. "Ting Li Zehou, Liu Shuxian tan *He shang*." *Jiushi niandai*, Dec., pp. 88–91.

———. 1988c. "Zai fang Liu Binyan." *Jiushi niandai*, May, pp. 16–30.

———. 1989a. "Qianming yundong yiyue lai de fazhan." *Jiushi niandai*, Apr., pp. 16–20.

———. 1989b. "Wo yu Wei Jingsheng you gongtong de lishi: Fangwen sanshisan ren gongkaixin faqiren Bei Dao." *Jiushi niandai*, Mar., pp. 22–23.

———. 1989c. "Wusi de kunjing yu jintian de tupo." *Jiushi niandai*, Mar., pp. 68–75.

Li Zehou. 1987. *Zhongguo xiandai sixiangshi lun.* Beijing: Dongfang.

Li Zehou and Liu Zaifu. 1988. "Wenxue yu yishu de qingsi." *Renmin ribao* (overseas ed.), Apr. 14, p. 4.

Liang Liyi. 1984. "Zhonggong zhongyang wei rendao zhuyi he yihua wenti dingdiao." *Qishi niandai*, Mar., pp. 40–41.

Liang Shuming. 1949. *Zhongguo wenhua yaoyi.* Reprinted—Taibei: Zhengzhong Shuju, n.d.

Lianhe wenxue 3, no. 12 (1988): 82–147 [special section on literature by educated youths sent down to the countryside].

Lin Weiping. 1986. "Wenxue he ren'ge." *Shanghai wenxue*, no. 11: 68–76.

Lin Yusheng et al., eds. 1989. *Wusi: Duoyuan de fansi.* Hong Kong: Joint Publishing.

Link, Perry. 1983. *Stubborn Weeds: Popular and Controversial Chinese Literature After the Cultural Revolution.* Bloomington: Indiana University Press.

Liu Binyan. 1985. "Dierzhong zhongcheng." *Fazhi wenxue*, no. 6. Reprinted in *Jiushi niandai*, Oct. 1985, pp. 94–109.

———. 1988. *Liu Binyan yanlunji.* Hong Kong: Xiang Jiang Chuban.

Liu Binyan and Chen Yingzhen. 1988. Dialogue. *Huaqiao ribao* (New York), Aug. 12, p. 28.

Liu Na. 1986. "Zai yixianxiang zhong xingjin de xinshiqi wenxue." *Wenxue pinglun*, no. 5: 16–20.

Liu Xinwu. 1988. "Zhongguo zuojia yu dangdai shijie." *Renmin ribao* (overseas ed.), Mar. 11, p. 4.

Liu Zaifu and Lin Gang. 1988. *Chuantong yu Zhongguo ren.* Hong Kong: Joint Publishing.

Liu Zengjie et al., eds. 1983. *Kang Ri zhanzheng shiqi Yan'an ji ge kang Ri minzhu genjudi wenxue yundong ziliao.* Taiyuan: Shanxi Renmin Chubanshe.

Lu Xun. 1933. *Liangdi shu.* Shanghai: Qingguang shuju.

Ma Li. 1975. "Wang Shiwei shijian de yanjiu." Postgraduate thesis, Guoli Zhengzhi Daxue, Dongya Yanjiusuo, Taipei.

Mao Zedong. 1990 [1930]. *Report from Xunwu* [*Xunwu diaocha*]. Ed. and trans., and with an introduction, by Roger R. Thompson. Stanford: Stanford University Press.

Marcus, George, and Michael Fischer. 1986. *Anthropology and Cultural Critique.* Chicago: University of Chicago Press.

McDougall, Bonnie. 1984. "Zhao Zhenkai's Fiction: A Study in Cultural Alienation." *Modern Chinese Literature* 1, no. 1 (Sept.): 103–30.

Meisner, Maurice. 1969. *Li Ta-chao and the Origins of Chinese Marxism.* Cambridge, Mass.: Harvard University Press.

Mote, Frederick. 1971. *Intellectual Foundations of China.* New York: Knopf.

Mu Fu. 1984. "Zhonggong zhiguo de sanci dacuobai." *Jiushi niandai*, Oct., pp. 41–48.

Myers, Ramon. 1970. *The Chinese Peasant Economy: Agricultural Development in Hopei and Shantung, 1890–1949.* Cambridge, Mass.: Harvard University Press.

Ng Mau-sang. 1988. *The Russian Hero in Modern Chinese Fiction.* Hong Kong: Chinese University Press.

Pepper, Suzanne. 1978. *Civil War in China: The Political Struggle, 1945–1949.* Berkeley: University of California Press.

Perry, Elizabeth. 1980. *Rebels and Revolutionaries in North China, 1845–1945.* Stanford: Stanford University Press.

Pickowicz, Paul. 1975. *Marxist Literary Thought in China: The Influence of Ch'ü Ch'iu-pai.* Berkeley: University of California Press.

Qi Xin. 1989a. "Sishier ren gongkai xin xiaoxi." *Jiushi niandai*, Apr., pp. 21–22.

———. 1989b. "Zhongguo zhishijie de tupoxing xingdong." *Jiushi niandai*, Mar., pp. 20–21.

Ren Wen. 1988. "Yao youdian 'shiming gan.'" *Renmin ribao* (overseas ed.), May 20, p. 2.

Ropp, Paul. 1981. *Dissent in Early Modern China.* Ann Arbor: University of Michigan Press.

Sanlian Shudian. 1989. *Longnian de beichuang.* Hong Kong: Joint Publishing.

Schwarcz, Vera. 1983. "Reflections on the Intellectual Climate of China." In Ronald Morse, ed., *The Limits of Reform in China.* Boulder, Colo.: Westview, pp. 121–37.

———. 1986. *The Chinese Enlightenment: Intellectuals and the Legacy of the May Fourth Movement of 1919.* Berkeley: University of California Press.

Schwarcz, Vera, and Li Zehou. 1983–84. "Six Generations of Modern Chinese Intellectuals." *Chinese Studies in History* 17, no. 2 (Winter): 42–56.

Selden, Mark. 1971. *The Yenan Way in Revolutionary China.* Cambridge, Mass.: Harvard University Press.

Shi Hanren. 1984. "Gao Xiaosheng he Lu Xun feng." *Wenxue pinglun*, no. 4: 37–46.

Shi Shuqing. 1989. *Wentan de fansi yu qianzhan.* Hong Kong: Ming Bao Chubanshe.

Siu, Helen. 1983. "Mao's Harvest: Voices from China's New Generation." *China Update*, Mar., pp. 1–7, 11–13.

Siu, Helen, and Zelda Stern, eds. 1983. *Mao's Harvest: Voices from China's New Generation.* New York: Oxford University Press.

Song Suiliang. 1985. "Xuelei wenzhang zhanshi xin: Huang Qiuyun lun." *Dangdai zuojia pinglun* 2. Reprinted in *Pinglun congkan* 1985, no. 5/6: 121–28.

Spence, Jonathan. 1981. *The Gate of Heavenly Peace.* New York: Viking.

Stallybrass, Peter, and Allon White. 1986. *The Politics and Poetics of Transgression.* Ithaca, N.Y.: Cornell University Press.

Tay, William. 1984. "Wang Meng, Stream of Consciousness, and the Controversy over Modernism." *Modern Chinese Literature* 1, no. 1 (Sept.): 7–24.

———. 1988. *Bayue jiaoyang.* Taipei: Hongfan Shudian.

Thaxton, Ralph. 1983. *China Turned Rightside Up: Revolutionary Legitimacy in the Peasant World.* New Haven: Yale University Press.

Tu, Wei-Ming [Du Weiming]. 1985. "Chuantong wenhua yu Zhongguo xianshi." *Jiushi niandai,* Nov., pp. 56–68.

———. 1987. "Dui chuantong jinxing fansi." *Dangdai* 5, no. 1: 16–23.

Wang Chan. 1985a. "Ji'e er bugan shenlun de linghun." *Huaqiao ribao* (New York), Dec. 17.

———. 1985b. "Siceng xiangshi yan guilai." *Huaqiao ribao* (New York), Dec. 21.

Wang Ruoshui. 1985. "Zhihui de tongku." *Qingnian luntan,* no. 2. Reprinted in Wang Ruoshui 1989: 313–18.

———. 1989. *Zhihui de tongku.* Hong Kong: Joint Publishing.

Wang Ruowang. 1989. *Tiandi you zhengqi.* Hong Kong: Baixing Wenhua Shiye.

Wang Shiqing. 1984. "Guanyu Qu Qiubai de pingjia wenti." In Beijing Shifan Daxue, Zhongwen Xi, Xiandai Wenxue Jiaoyanshi, ed., *Xiandai wenxue jiangyan ji.* Beijing: Beijing Shifan Daxue Chubanshe, pp. 162–76.

Wang Xiaoming. 1982. "Lun Sha Ting de xiaoshuo chuangzuo." *Zhongguo xiandai wenxue yanjiu,* no. 4: 247–71.

Williams, Raymond. 1958. *Culture and Society.* London: Verso.

———. 1977. *Marxism and Literature.* London: Verso.

———. 1979. *Politics and Letters.* London: Verso.

———. 1980. *Problems in Materialism and Culture.* London: Verso.

Xiao Feng. 1984. "Xiao Hong yanjiu." In Beijing Shifan Daxue, Zhongwen Xi, Xiandai Wenxue Jiaoyanshi, ed., *Xiandai wenxue jiangyan ji.* Beijing: Beijing Shifan Daxue Chubanshe, pp. 215–31.

Xie Mian. 1983a. "Zai xinde jueqi mianqian." In Bi Hua 1983: 83–85.

———. 1983b. "Shiqu le pingjing zhihou." In Bi Hua 1983: 89–92.

———. 1983c. "Tongwang chengshu de daolu." In Bi Hua 1983: 130–36.

Xing Fujun, Lu Wencai, and Leng Shufen. 1981. "Xiao Hong chuangzuo chulun." *Zhongguo xiandai wenxue yanjiu,* no. 3: 215–33.

Xu Jingya. 1983. "Jueqi de shiqun." In Bi Hua 1983: 97–129.

Ya Lan. 1989. "Qiangsheng xiang hou: Xiandai yishu zhan de fengbo." *Jiushi niandai,* Apr., pp. 50–52.

Yang Jiang. 1981. "Ganxiao liuji." *Guangjiao jing,* no. 103 (Apr.). English trans. by Howard Goldblatt: "Six Chapters of My Life 'Downunder,'" *Renditions,* no. 16 (Autumn 1981): 9–43; republished as a book: Hong Kong: Chinese University Press of Hong Kong; Seattle: University of Washington Press, 1983, 1984.

———. 1988. *Xizao.* Hong Kong: Joint Publishing.

Ye Zhicheng. 1981a. Foreword: "Quzhe de daolu." In Jiangsu Renmin Chubanshe, ed., *Fang Zhi zuopin xuan.* Nanjing: Jiangsu Renmin Chubanshe, pp. 1–26.

———. 1981b. "Yi Fang Zhi." In Jiangsu Renmin Chubanshe, ed., *Fang Zhi zuopin xuan.* Nanjing: Jiangsu Renmin Chubanshe, pp. 418–27.

Yu Yingshi. 1978. *Zhongguo zhishi jieceng shilun (gudai pian).* Taipei: Lianjing Chuban Shiye.

———. 1983. *Cong jiazhi xitong kan Zhongguo wenhua de xiandai yiyi.* Taibei Shi Bao Wenhua Chuban Shiye.

Yue Daiyun. 1979. "Mao Dun zaoqi sixiang yanjiu." *Zhongguo xiandai wenxue yanjiu congkan*, no. 1: 134–58.

———. 1981. "Mao Dun de xianshi zhuyi lilun de yishu chuangxin." *Zhongguo xiandai wenxue yanjiu congkan*, no. 4: 39–60.

Yue Daiyun and Carolyn Wakeman. 1985. *To the Storm: The Odyssey of a Revolutionary Chinese Woman*. Berkeley: University of California Press.

Zhao Tian. 1963. "Cong 'Chu shan' de pinglun tanqi." *Wenxue pinglun*, no. 1: 9–17.

Zeng Zhennan. 1985. "Qihang! Cong zuihou de tingbodi: Du Zhang Xinxin de jinzuo suixiang." *Wenyi bao*, no. 4. Reprinted in *Pinglun congkan 1985*, no. 7: 23–26.

Zheng Wanlong. 1985. "Wode gen." *Shanghai wenxue*, no. 5. Reprinted in *Pinglun congkan 1985*, no. 10: 88–89, 92.

Zhu Bing. 1980. "*Huang he dongliu qu* de minzuhua tese." *Wenxue pinglun*, no. 5: 93–101.

Library of Congress Cataloging-in-Publication Data

Furrows: peasants, intellectuals, and the state : stories and
histories from modern China / compiled and edited, with an
introduction by Helen F. Siu.
    p.   cm.
Includes bibliographical references.
ISBN 0-8047-1805-9 (cl)   ISBN 0-8047-1838-5 (pbk)
    1. Short stories, Chinese.   2. Chinese fiction—20th century.
3. Peasantry—China—Fiction.   4. Authors, Chinese—20th century—Political and social
views.   I. Siu, Helen F.
PL2653.F87   1990   89-49254
895.1'3010805—dc20   CIP

  ∞   This book is printed on acid-free paper.